—JANET—
HOLMES
à COURT

JANET
HOLMES
à COURT

PATRICIA EDGAR

HarperCollinsPublishers

HarperCollins*Publishers*

First published in Australia in 1999
by HarperCollins*Publishers* Pty Limited
ACN 009 913 517
A member of the HarperCollins*Publishers* (Australia) Pty Limited Group
http://www.harpercollins.com.au

HarperCollins*Publishers*
25 Ryde Road, Pymble, Sydney NSW 2073, Australia
31 View Road, Glenfield, Auckland 10, New Zealand
77–85 Fulham Palace Road, London W6 8JB, United Kingdom
Hazelton Lanes, 55 Avenue Road, Suite 2900, Toronto, Ontario, M5R 3L2
and 1995 Markham Road, Scarborough, Ontario M1B 5M8, Canada
10 East 53rd Street, New York NY 10032, USA

The National Library of Australia Cataloguing-in-Publication data:

Edgar, Patricia, 1937– .
Janet Holmes à Court.
Includes index.
ISBN 0 7322 5715 8.
1. Holmes à Court, Janet, 1943– . 2. Holmes à Court
family. 3. Women executives – Australia – Biography.
4. Businesswomen – Australia. Biography. I. Title
338.092

Cover photograph: Austral International
Index by Russell Brooks
Printed in Australia by Griffin Press Pty Ltd, Adelaide on 79gsm Bulky Paperback

9 8 7 6 5 4 3 2 1   02 01 00 99

Our thanks go to those who have given us permission to reproduce copyright material
and photographs in this book. Every effort has been made to contact copyright holders,
and the publisher welcomes communication from any copyright holder from whom
permission was inadvertently not gained.

CONTENTS

To Don, Susan and Lesley.

*'The unexamined life is not
worth living.'*
SOCRATES

ACKNOWLEDGMENTS

In this work of nine years duration I have had the assistance of a great many people. My two major supporters, advisers and helpers over this long period have been my husband Don, and my colleague and friend of twenty-four years, Glenda Wilson. I owe them much more than my words can express. I took this book on as a hobby, an interest, and it became very much more than that. Balancing my work, my family, and my 'interest' could not have been possible without Don's abiding support. He was my sounding board, my editor before my editor; he has helped me harness the reams of information, transcripts, files and clippings that I had amassed, not always as methodically as I should have. He kept my spirits up when I felt overwhelmed and listened as I wrote and talked my way relentlessly through the material. Glenda typed interviews, organised my files and helped me research and coordinate the material I needed from the vast Heytesbury archive of clippings, correspondence and material I had collected. She also typed the many drafts of my messy longhand that led to the final manuscript. Thank you also Liz Coote for your role in these tasks.

I want to thank the Holmes à Court family – Peter, Catherine, Simon and Paul – for their cooperation, and Darrel Jarvis (who, over time, spent several days with me talking through his experiences with Heytesbury and the Holmes à Court family) for his frank account.

Bern Ranford, Janet's mother, and Ethnée Holmes à Court, Robert's mother, spent many hours reliving their lives and those of their children – in Ethnée's case inspiring her own memoirs. I thank them both.

All of the following people assisted with interviews, information, leads, anecdotes and references: Roderick Anderson, Bob Baker, Stephen Barton, Katherine Bialo, Nicholas Blain, Charles Bright, Wim Burggraaf, Nica Burns, His Excellency The Hon Sir Francis Burt AC KCMG QD, John Byrne, Kevin Campbell, Belinda Carrigan, Roz Chalmers, Betty Churcher, Sir Michael Clapham, Sue and David Conners, Joan Cooley, Geoff Cornish, Tania Cowen, Josephine Cumming, Keith Drew, Rebecca Earney, Jon Elbery, Barry Farmer, Alan R Foyster, Caroline and Alan Gelb, Paul Graham, Dr Stephen Grenville, David Gwynne, Barbara and Dallas Hamilton, George Hanlon, Peter Holmes à Court (cousin), Will Holmes à Court, Dr Rex Hughes, Lord William and Lady Sue Huntingdon, Richard Johnston, Steve Johnston, Tony Jones, David Karpin, Patricia Kershaw, Dale Kessell, Cameron Mackintosh, Alec Mairs, Pat J Martin, John Murdoch, Geoffrey Miller QC, John McIlwraith, Brian McKay, Michael Owen, Frank Parker, Karl Paganin, Val Pitman, John Ranford, John Reynolds, Andrew Ross, Dr Bill Ryan, Ray Schoer, Mick Sheehy, Noel Sheridan, Roger Sleight, John Studdy, Chris Tangney, Theo Tangney, Peter Thompson, Loretta Tomasi, Tim Threadgold, Geoff Warn, Sandy White, Ian Wildy, Derek Williams, Peter Wood, Robin Wright, Phillipa Young. I express my appreciation to you all.

My thanks to Angelo Loukakis, Robin Freeman and Carolyn Leslie of HarperCollins for your friendly and efficient contribution to this process of converting the manuscript into a finished product.

And Janet, my friend, we have shared so much together. Thank you for trusting me with your life, your story. It has been an extraordinary experience, I think, for both of us.

INTRODUCTION

This is a book written by one friend about another. The idea of writing it evolved over time. It was one of those situations where a direction is taken and, before you know it, you are somewhere you didn't expect to be.

Janet and I had become close friends working together over eight years on the Australian Children's Television Foundation (ACTF). I enjoyed Robert's company and was intrigued by his intellect and unique style. Although I had not spent long periods of time with him, I had dealt with him as an investor in the ACTF's first production 'Winners' – an anthology of children's television programs – and as chairman of the Robert Holmes à Court Foundation, of which I was a trustee. I had stayed with Janet and Robert in their homes, observed them together, seen Robert relaxed and debated with him on the topics he set for dinner conversation. While I did not know him as well as those who worked with him daily, I knew several sides of the man and I knew him better than most people who, as I discovered, knew only the side Robert wanted them to see.

I had met Janet in December 1982 in Perth. Syd Donovan, whom I'd known since my days on the Australian Broadcasting Control Board in the mid-seventies and who was, in 1982, an employee at TVW7, a Perth television station which Robert had acquired, had taken me to Janet's home in Osborne Parade for lunch. I had no real stake in the meeting, but was interested to meet Janet. While Robert was becoming well known through the media, Janet's profile was still low. As we approached the house, Syd expressed some nervousness about Robert's possible presence in the house and the fact that Robert was ill with something as yet unknown. His words and manner made me feel we were entering the world of some mysterious figure in a Brontë novel. Janet, on the other hand, was lovely, hospitable, charming, down to earth, lively and seemingly most interested in whatever it was we were talking about. She served a simple, informal lunch and the mysterious figure who was apparently upstairs didn't materialise. I wondered what he was doing, as there was no sound from him and Janet didn't refer to him. Very likely he was asleep. Syd seemed well satisfied with the lunch and I'd enjoyed meeting Janet.

Some months after the lunch, Sir James Cruthers (who represented Western Australia on the board of the Australian Children's Television Foundation) phoned me to say that he would be resigning to go to New York to run Rupert Murdoch's television operations. He thought Syd Donovan would make an ideal replacement for his position. I had other ideas. I wanted Janet Holmes à Court.

I was dependent upon Sir James to put Janet's name forward to RJ Pearce, the Western Australia Minister for Education who had the responsibility of appointing people to the board. He disliked Robert Holmes à Court because of his experiences when Robert acquired TVW7. As well, he had a good opinion of Syd Donovan, who had formerly been his employee. So I decided to make a direct approach.

I learned Janet was staying at the Wentworth Hotel in Sydney. We had not spoken since our first meeting. I phoned her in her room and I asked whether she would like to join the board of the Australian Children's Television Foundation. Her reply was an immediate and enthusiastic 'I'd love to'. I had told Janet when we first met about the objectives of the ACTF, which were to develop high-quality programs for children and to promote their wider use in the community, to produce viewing highlights that children could identify with and be challenged by amid the sea of crud generated by commercial television. Janet had little time for television and monitored her own children's viewing. She related to the objectives of the cause and wanted to be part of it.

When I phoned Sir James to tell him what I had done, he gave me some advice I never forgot. He said Janet was a lovely woman, but if I ever let 'that man' Robert near the ACTF I would regret it. The dislike was evident in his words. He had little choice but to recommend Janet for the position to the Minister and Janet and I began a long-term working relationship.

In my capacity as director of the ACTF, I found that Janet gave me commitment, complete support, interest and she had huge enthusiasm for the work of the Foundation. She came to her first board meeting on 1 December 1983 and was elected chairman on 18 September 1986, a position she has held ever since, being re-elected each year by fellow board members. She still represents Western Australia, having been appointed by successive ministers for three-year terms.

No chief executive could be blessed with a better chairman. No door is closed to Janet Holmes à Court and no phone call goes unreturned. Together we have lobbied politicians in all states to support the ACTF. Janet has a natural talent for lobbying. No matter whom we wanted to see, they would all make time for her. As the ACTF's catalogue grew, the programs spoke volumes to the children of the politicians more effectively than even we could and Janet sent the programs far and wide, even eventually setting up a library of tapes within each Heytesbury enterprise for the employees to borrow.

While Janet chaired the board, the ACTF owed its start in production to Robert himself. The first major series developed by the ACTF was 'Winners' – an anthology of eight hour-long films written by top writers and directed by Australia's leading directors. It was budgeted at $3.8 million. The ACTF needed a distributor for its prospectus to ensure the financing of the project. Robert owned ITC Entertainment Pty Ltd, based in the UK, as well as SAS10 Adelaide and TVW7 Perth. I thought having his name associated with 'Winners' would mean the much-needed dollars would walk through the door. Janet had only been on the board a few months (a period of time encompassing two meetings) and I was nervous about asking if she would put the suggestion to Robert. It was clear that she was uncomfortable as well and I sensed this would not be a straightforward matter. She agreed to find the best opportunity to raise the financing of 'Winners' with Robert. But it was some time before she told me Robert had agreed to see me. I was to meet the mysterious man who had been upstairs.

Anticipating the meeting was an experience in itself. Robert would come to Melbourne, where I was living, and he would see me sometime in the next few days, I was told. No one knew when the call would come, but I should be prepared to come promptly. When Robert was ready, that was the time. There may not be another opportunity if this one were missed. I could not leave the phone. What a nerve-racking process it was. The days went by, extending over a weekend, but weekends meant nothing to Robert.

Eventually the call came on 16 March 1984. He would see me in twenty minutes, his secretary, Val Pitman, told me. Graham Morris, the lawyer for the ACTF, and I hurtled towards Collins Street and the twenty-first floor of Collins Tower, where the Bell Group office was located. When we were ushered into the great man's presence, I offered my hand and babbled on about the fuchsias in the pot in the corner, without realising at the time they were artificial, as we walked to a couch. Robert stopped, looked long and hard at the fuchsias, then long and hard at me, then said with a slight curl to the lip, 'I don't do the flowers'. I spoke no more. I'd heard about the silent spells in meetings with the famous man and I was prepared for them. We sat down and no one spoke for an eternity. I wasn't about to make further comment on the office furnishings, so I waited. Eventually his quiet voice said, 'It's a very nice project'. My relief was profound.

Throughout the following two hours Robert sat and chatted as though he had all the time in the world. He told anecdotes interspersed with questions, each one a probing test aimed at revealing my competence, my character, my intelligence, my style. Midway through the meeting I realised my body was rigid from head to toe and I began to try to release the tension by consciously relaxing my body bit by bit. But the outcome was critical to the future of the ACTF and it was not at all clear how the meeting would end. Robert was charming, interesting, with an outward calm. In fact, he was fascinating but I could see the potential in him to be terrifying. During the many interviews I conducted for this book, people spoke of such meetings with Robert and it was evident many of those people were completely unnerved by him.

Robert did decide to underwrite 'Winners' when he was satisfied that I seemed to know what I was doing. He liked the concept; quality was something he was always attracted to. I am also convinced that he agreed to help finance 'Winners' for Janet, to help the organisation she was representing get a start within a difficult industry. However, as it turned out Robert's name was not sufficient to attract all the necessary investment, so a further meeting was arranged to see if he would underwrite the series. He did not hesitate and on 25 June 1984, five days before the end of the financial year, Robert wrote to me saying:

The Bell Group is very committed to this project and I believe it is important that the Foundation and all the talent it has assembled have an opportunity to show what can be done in this field in Australia.

For these reasons the Bell Group will commit to underwrite the balance of the funds required [$1.8 million], at no fee, to ensure that the project proceeds.

By 30 June 1984, the shortfall was $748,000, which Robert invested, without demur, through SAS10.

Altogether Robert made a generous and timely investment in the ACTF's future at Janet's behest. 'Winners' set the ACTF on its feet and established its reputation for quality children's productions.

After Robert died and Janet took over Heytesbury, my research instincts drove my discussions with Janet. She was in an extraordinary situation. Robert had been a unique man who had made a permanent impact on Australian business and the nature of the financial institutions and share trading. He had established, and left behind, a diverse family empire which Janet decided – without question – to run. The unfolding events had to be documented.

Before I established the ACTF I had spent my working life as an academic, a researcher and a writer and I missed these elements in my life. I saw the recording and researching of Robert and Janet's lives as a very interesting hobby – a very long-term project that eventually could lead to my writing a book. Janet and I spent very little time discussing the project. Her view was that someone was going to write a book and she would rather I did it than anyone else. There was also the need to move quickly to interview both Bern Ranford, Janet's mother, and Ethnée Holmes à Court, Robert's mother, as they were in their eighties and we did not want to lose their stories. So I began work, allocating a weekend here and there to the project.

Janet facilitated my contact with those I wanted to interview. She phoned those I wanted to speak to to let them know she supported the project. She made suggestions about whom I should approach, but each interview opened up other leads.

She gave me open access to all Robert's files and archives, which were predominantly press clippings. He collected avidly but he did not keep diaries, write letters (except to those he had to) or keep notes, and minutes of meetings were very concise. The information he needed was in his head so there were meagre records of Robert's thoughts, his business dealings, no emotional or angry correspondence – little that gave away his inner feelings.

As time went on and my research and interviews on different continents opened up, my interest and main focus became Janet.

That raised some difficult issues for me. It was not a simple matter to write about someone whose life was still in progress, and in certain respects where I was an active participant. I had some soul-searching moments and nearly abandoned the project. Although this biography was being written with the cooperation of the subject, I could not be simply a mouthpiece for Janet – nor did she want me to be. I had to write without fear or favour. At the same time, there are the bonds of friendship and the intimacies that friends divulge to one another. A clear line had to be drawn between the material I gleaned from interviews with Janet and others, and personal matters I was privy to that no other researcher would know. Eventually I worked out a process that I was comfortable with. I interviewed Janet over many hours (between fifty and sixty) and those interviews are my primary source materials. In my interviews with others where they have independently volunteered and verified information, I have used it.

There is a significant difference in writing a biography about a living person and one who is dead. People are generally unwilling to be critical on the record of those who are living and in positions of power. But in some cases where I expected to find bitterness, for example in those dismissed by Heytesbury, I found people were generous towards Janet and the Holmes à Court family.

I would have gone on with my hobby for some years more were it not for the intervention of one tenacious publisher, Angelo Loukakis. He attended an art exhibition Janet opened and after she spoke he asked her would she agree to have a book written about her. Janet was vague in response and said that someone was writing a book but she couldn't remember who. Angelo persisted with his enquiries and eventually tracked me down. At first I avoided his calls but finally spoke with him. His call came at a time when two other publishers were sniffing around about doing a book on Janet. I had to face up to deciding whether I was going to publish this book or not. Up to this point I had written only about Janet's and Robert's mothers' lives but had accumulated a mass of information and completed a very large number of interviews.

Still wrestling with the problems of writing about someone who had become a very close friend, and always an avid reader of biographies, I now delved into reading about the discipline itself. What type of book was I trying to write?

Was it a critical biography, was it a history, was it a social biography? How much right did I have to interpret Janet's life? Could I be objective? Must the reader have a complete story to explain a life and personality? Can we ever know the reality of a life? We can certainly never know the biographical subject's inner life no matter how thorough the research. I tormented myself for some months and subjected Angelo to my misgivings. He was patient, supportive, encouraging and kept advising me to get on with it. My anxieties were normal for a biographer.

In the end he won and I resolved my dilemma about writing about a friend. Firstly, my objective was to tell a story as accurately as I could about the lives of two extraordinary people. The process would take time, given that writing the book was my very part-time activity outside my full-time work. I didn't mind the time, for I was fascinated by Robert and Janet. Their story and its researching were stimulating subject matter. The task would have been unbearable had that not been so. Secondly, I have a great affection for Janet so I am sympathetic to all she has been through. That was an important factor because I could not have spent years writing a book about someone I did not like. Thirdly, Janet has made a success of her life and her work and I find that admirable for I believe individuals can make a significant difference to their world and we have an obligation to try to do that.

Given those pre-conditions, the questions that intrigued me that I wanted to pursue were: how could an intelligent, talented woman in a feminist age play the role she did as 'the good wife' for her famous husband? How did Janet reconcile her socialist upbringing and values with the ownership of such wealth? How could someone with so little direct experience of business take over a business empire and make it a success? What were the qualities Janet had that allowed her to master such diverse roles? These are the questions that have guided my story and my shaping of the mass of data I had assembled.

Had this book been completed during any other year since Robert's death the story would have differed from this one. Circumstances have varied year by year for Heytesbury and Janet Holmes à Court and she has evolved year by year. She will continue to do so. But in undertaking a process such as this, eventually you reach a point where the critical mass of information reveals regular and consistent patterns of behaviour, only the anecdotes vary.

I don't believe in objective biography. I could not write about Janet's life as separate from my own feelings and prejudices. There is little meaning in facts. Meaning comes from the relationship of facts and the different interpretation all those involved bring to those 'facts'. I have tried to write about that meaning.

In essence, this is what Stephen Oates calls a 'pure biography'[1], as opposed to a critical study or a scholarly chronicle though, like all biographies, there are elements of all three forms present in this work. I make no pretence that it is totally detached or scholarly and I had no wish to impose some sort of psychoanalytical theory on Janet's story. It is not my voice as author that matters; rather, I have tried to let my subject have the whole stage, to give some sense of a life unfolding. No biographer can explain everything about another person's life, whether living or dead, but it is my hope that in outlining the details of Janet's life and her life with Robert Holmes à Court, the reader will get some sense of the story as it evolved, some sense that in this complex, technical age, the individual does count, people do shape their own lives and those of others around them as much as they may be a product of their time and circumstances.

Though the research has been painstaking and I have come to understand Janet intimately through mapping her life experiences, I do not feel compelled to expose the titillating details of her sexual or private life in the Kitty Kelly biographical style. I certainly have gained, and I hope the reader will too, a greater empathy for her life with its challenges and contradictions.

Janet Holmes à Court is a woman of substance, intelligence and wit; she is not perfect, not always self-insightful, but full of a zest for life and a desire to make a mark on the Australian landscape, to strike a blow for the common good.

Janet's life is a fascinating one and I have been consumed by it. I have appreciated Janet's confidence in me. I hope I have been able to provide Janet with some insights into her life which has been packed to overflowing with activity, challenge and achievement, none of which shows any sign of abating.

AN END AND A BEGINNING

It was Saturday 1 September 1990. Robert Holmes à Court had spent a quiet day at his Heytesbury horse stud at Keysbrook, in the shadow of the Darling Ranges about three-quarters of an hour's drive south of Perth. The property is one of the finest in the country, a focus for the family that Robert and Janet had created together during their married life, a place where they had spent many happy weekends and where Janet had planted thousands of trees and flowering shrubs. A day such as this, spent relaxing, reading, talking, observing, was a rare occurrence in the life of Robert Holmes à Court. This was a man who had built a reputation for himself as a champion of entrepreneurs, with a unique approach to the art of business. An enigma who had been much feared and little understood. A man who lived to work.

Robert Holmes à Court first tasted the excitement of business takeovers in Western Australia at the height of the Poseidon boom in the early seventies when he acquired a 22% interest in WA Albany Worsted Woollen Mills for the sum of $75,000. Using this company as his takeover vehicle, by 1973 he had acquired 82% of Bell Brothers

Holdings. Bell became his flagship for a further series of takeover bids which steadily increased his assets base. He began with the London-based Emu Wine Group in 1975; moved on to the Perth building supply company HL Brisbane and Wunderlich (now Bristile Ltd); the Western Coalmining Company; and then also in 1975 unsuccessfully bid for Greenbushes, a tin and zinc mine.[1] In 1979, and still relatively unknown outside Western Australia, he bid for control of Ansett Transport Industries. Although he failed to gain control, his consolation prize was $11 million capital profit. He moved on to target Elders Smith Goldsbrough Mort in 1981, and accumulated strategic stakes and subsequent profitable sellouts in TNT, the Herald and Weekly Times and Rolls Royce. He acquired Associated Communications, Britain's leading film and entertainment group, in 1982, then in late 1983, with what was regarded by the establishment as a cheeky, preposterous move, he announced a takeover bid for BHP, the Big Australian. By February 1984, Robert was being taken very seriously by the Australian business establishment.

Had it not been for the October 1987 stock market crash, Robert may well have realised his ambition to control and chair BHP, Australia's largest and most famous company. Instead, understanding the implications of the crash long before his peers, he restructured the Bell Group and made a remarkable recovery from what seemed to be an impossibly exposed financial position. In what is considered by some to be his greatest coup, he sold out of the Bell Group and consolidated his interests in his private company, Heytesbury Holdings. The sale of Bell's BHP shareholding reaped $2.3 billion, 40% of which was owned by the family. Bond Corporation and the Western Australian Government, through the State Government Insurance Commission (SGIC), each purchased a 19.9% parcel of Bell shares from Robert, the maximum number allowed by law without having to seek the permission of the public shareholders – a deal which one commentator has described as 'tawdry'.

The eighties had been a wild ride across the range for the financial cowboys from the West, but all that was over at the start of the new decade, and several of them were about to have their day in court. The Western Australian Government had set up a Royal

Commission to inquire into the activities of 'WA Inc', as Premier Burke's Labor Government's partnership with the Western Australian business sector had come to be known.

On Saturday 1 September 1990, Robert had been reading a report on WA Inc by Malcolm McCusker QC, the contents of which pleased him. He commented to Janet that there was nothing in the report to worry about. But at that moment Janet was more concerned about Robert, who did not look after himself, smoked incessantly, exercised rarely and ate what pleased him. As he looked such a dreadful colour, she encouraged him to go for a walk with her outside in the sun. They spoke about Fairfax and the best use of Robert's junk bonds in that company. Attempting to motivate Robert, Janet suggested they should fly to Sydney and buy Fairfax. But Robert's response was less than enthusiastic, saying that they wouldn't do that because, 'Firstly, we'd have to go and live in Sydney, and you'd hate it; secondly, I'd have to go to the office every day, and I'd hate it; and thirdly, the journalists would have to be pulled into line, and they would hate it'.

This was symptomatic of a recent change in Robert. The usual aggression was gone, he was tired and staff close to him were finding there did not seem to be the same edge to their activities as there used to be. In the UK, for instance, the research had been completed for a move on Dalgety's PLC but Robert was stalling. He had been unusually reflective and interested in others around him. The previous week, Robert had even asked Val Pitman, his secretary of twenty-four years, about her investments – something he had never previously done – and was pleased to know she had invested wisely.

That first weekend in September, Robert and Janet's oldest son, Peter, was home from Oxford and at the Stud with his friends Tom Warner and Ben Patrick. Their daughter Catherine, who rarely went to the Stud, was also there for the Friday and Saturday evening. She was anxious to speak with her father about a trip she wanted to make to Europe and was looking to get his approval. Simon, who was studying law at the University of Western Australia, had opted to stay at home in Peppermint Grove, Perth, and Paul, the youngest son, was at school at Geelong Grammar in Victoria. It had been an unusually sociable Saturday evening meal with Tom and Ben there, and Peter would later recall the evening as one of the happiest they had spent as a family. Although obviously tired, his father was in excellent spirits.

Robert's good mood suggested to Catherine that it was timely to speak to her father about her travel plans, so she stayed up until after Janet had gone to bed. They had what she would recall as a memorable and satisfactory conversation, one that she was pleased she had been able to have. Catherine and Robert were often in conflict. He did not like the way she dressed, or some of the friends with whom she kept company; nor had he been happy with her academic performance. But this particular evening Robert had told Catherine, 'You'll be all right'.

Robert retired for the night, but in the early hours of Sunday morning – Father's Day – he was disturbed by what he thought was indigestion. He got up and Janet made him a cup of tea. They sat together on the side of the bed, then Robert rose from the bed and walked around. He sat down once more and began to sweat. Janet moved to the bathroom to get him a towel to wipe his face and in those moments Robert suffered a fatal heart attack.

Janet screamed and called for Peter and Catherine. She rang the vet who lived on the Stud. Together they tried to revive Robert. The ambulance from Jarrahdale arrived eventually and the ambulance officers continued the attempt to restart Robert's heart. 'Was he on any medication?', they asked. 'No', replied Janet who, throughout their married life, had complied with Robert's secretive approach to his diabetes. 'He's an insulin-dependent diabetic', said Catherine, the only one of the four children to have previously guessed her father's condition. Despite all efforts, Robert did not respond.

Janet sped down the road, at times reaching 150 kilometres an hour, following the ambulance to the Armadale hospital. There she was told what she had already sensed. 'Mrs Holmes à Court, there is absolutely nothing we can do. Your husband is dead.' She was distraught. Robert could have afforded the best medical care in the world but she knew it was much too late. 'What would the family do?', she thought. The master of the deal, the most cultured of the predators, the greatest chess master we are ever likely to see in the share markets was gone at the age of fifty-three.

On the Sunday morning, 2 September, Hartley Mitchell, Paul's housemaster at Geelong Grammar came to Paul's room to wake him. He told him to get up and get dressed. Paul, who was the prefect for the day, thought he must be late for duty and that the headmaster was mad at him. When he was told of his father's death he was shocked. He did not know Robert well, but he had a son's love for his father and valued highly the few close conversations they had had. But he calmly packed his bag and rode with his housemaster in a taxi to the airport to travel in a chartered jet with Angela Nordlinger to Perth for the funeral.

Angela, a partner with the legal firm Corrs Chambers Westgarth, was a friend of Janet's and was to help her with the organisation of the funeral. She intercepted the many phone calls over the next few days, including those from insistent members of the press who demanded Janet should speak to them. While they wanted to know if Janet was up to the task that lay ahead – namely, the management of one of Australia's largest business empires – Janet was preoccupied with more immediate concerns – the death of the man she had served and loved. She placed a notice in the obituary columns of Tuesday's *West Australian* which was also to be included in the record for Robert's memorial service. It read:

My darling Robert,

Thank you for 24 fantastic years and four wonderful children.
You had such courage, wit, style, compassion and integrity.
I am so honoured that you chose to share half your life with me.
Goodbye to my best friend.

Janet.

All senior Heytesbury employees were notified of Robert's untimely death and they flew from the US, the UK and from around Australia to Perth. The news had a devastating effect on staff. Most people in Heytesbury knew one another and worked as a team for their high-profile boss. Several of the staff were young and they viewed him like a father; they were all Robert's chosen people. Robert did not believe in contractual job security and there were many employees worried about their future when the news of his death became known. As staff had not been aware that Robert was unwell, his heart attack was completely unexpected. Robert *was* Heytesbury, a company whose hierarchy comprised only the one person, and he made all the decisions. Each of them worked for Robert, no one else.

Many members of Heytesbury travelling to Perth saw no future for the company. Jon Elbery, Heytesbury Group general manager, described the first day after Robert's death: 'When I walked back into the office [on Monday] at 9.00 am, there was confusion, a lack of understanding ... There was a feeling of "Do we now just turn off the lights and put all the money in the bank?"'.[2] Jon was to learn very quickly it would be business as usual.

Mark Burrows, the head of Baring Brothers, Burrows & Co Limited, a merchant banker who had been employed by Robert to give advice from time to time, had flown to Perth for the funeral and to offer his advisory services to Janet. He considered there would be troubled times for Heytesbury. He believed that the banks were going to be very concerned about the future of Heytesbury, a company with considerable debt and now without its major asset, Robert Holmes à Court. He was of the view that none of the managers in the company had the experience to give Janet the advice she would require, and, further, that the banks knew the managers were not the decision-makers. The bankers, bruised from the experience of the eighties, were beginning to close in on the corporate beneficiaries of their profligate lending practices. Mark Burrows seemed to think Heytesbury could not now keep them at bay. Only Robert gave the bankers confidence. For her part, Janet rejected his offer.

Robert was cremated at a private ceremony on the Wednesday morning, attended only by the family and senior members of Heytesbury. Before the ceremony, Janet had gone with her family to the funeral parlour and had addressed Robert. In moving and inspiring terms, she spoke at length about the responsibilities Robert had left behind, and gave thanks to Robert for her four wonderful children. She saw Peter, Catherine, Simon and Paul as his gift to her.

Robert's coffin was almost completely covered with the most beautiful red roses. The private crematorium service was brief. The Holmes à Courts were not a religious family. Peter was chosen to speak for the family. A tall, handsome young man with a thick growth of hair, Peter had cultivated mannerisms that were uncannily like his father's. At the hospital, he had said to Barry Farmer, Robert's manager at the Stud, 'This is heavy shit'. He was clearly overwhelmed by the burden he thought his father's death would likely place on him, as the oldest son. For the memorial service, Peter quoted from John F. Kennedy's book *Profiles of Courage*, choosing the following words:

> *And when at some future date the high court of history sits in judgement on each of us, recording whether in our brief span of service we fulfilled our responsibilities, our success or failure will be measured by the answers to four questions:*
> *First, were we truly men of courage . . .*
> *Second, were we truly men of judgement . . .*
> *Third, were we truly men of integrity . . .*
> *and finally, were we truly men of dedication?*[3]

He saw his father as epitomising those qualities. He spoke extremely well, in a way that could only contribute to the myth, the stature and the enigma of his father. Afterwards, Janet and the children moved among the grief-stricken and stunned employees and spoke to all of them. Janet and her four children remained composed.

The family returned to the house at Peppermint Grove in preparation for the public memorial service to be held later that day at the University of Western Australia. Janet entered Winthrop Hall with Peter by her side, followed by Catherine and Simon, behind whom came Paul and Ethnée Holmes à Court, Robert's mother.

They walked the full length of the hall before a thousand people. At the service three men gave orations: Jon Elbery, who spoke with affection and admiration of Robert the chairman; Sir Ronald Wilson AC, KBE, CMG, who spoke of Robert the citizen; and Charles Bright, director of Potter Warburg Ltd, a long-time telephone confidant and friend, who spoke of Robert the man.

The flowers, sent from all over the world and now lining the sides of the hall, were spectacular. Extravagant, extraordinary floral arrangements had also begun to fill the house. It was said that Perth ran out of flowers that day. In an ironic touch, one of the biggest wreaths in Winthrop Hall came from the man once responsible for bugging Robert's telephone, on behalf of an old business rival.

After the memorial service, tea, soft drinks and food were served in the gardens of the University. Janet stood with her sons and daughter while a thousand people lined up to speak to them and express their condolences. Janet did not want the crowd diverted and instead spoke personally with every single person who came by her. She was dignified, gracious and put others at ease.

Janet had been known around Perth business and social circles as the devoted wife of Robert Holmes à Court. Throughout their married life Robert had come first in her consideration, certainly before herself and even before her children. She had stated publicly many times that she loved Robert, that he was her superior, that her task was to serve him. She was fiercely loyal. No man in Robert's position with Robert's agenda could have made a better choice of partner. Janet was vital, attractive and had exceptional social skills. People warmed quickly to her and her immense charm facilitated Robert's life and business significantly. She had recently told me, 'Robert is 95 percent of my life'. Now he was gone.

The general manager of Heytesbury Pastoral, Darrel Jarvis, held back from the crowd. As someone who was not of the inner circle and who did not feel part of Heytesbury, he wasn't sure that he was invited to the after-service drinks. He had not shared a comfortable relationship with Robert and did not know Janet well. Certain he would soon be out of a job, he approached Janet shyly and tentatively at the end of the long queue. But she greeted him warmly and said, 'Darrel, I need you'. Darrel, an emotional man, was deeply touched. In that moment his attitude to Heytesbury changed. Darrel worked best when he felt needed and Janet had struck just the right chord with him.

That evening Janet turned her thoughts to the company. She had addressed the staff in the office the day before the funeral, reassuring them that she had a vision for the future. There was never any doubt in her mind that she would run the company, but such a possibility had not occurred to Heytesbury staff. They were later to be astonished by her plans, as would sections of the media. To them, Janet was simply not a candidate for managing the affairs of a diverse financial empire, especially not one which might be in trouble.

Janet had been Robert's helpmate, the wife who took and placed his phone calls (often in the middle of the night), who served his tea, who was always there when needed. She laid out his clothes and did his packing. She would not leave the house or go to bed unless Robert released her to do so. She would not eat without him. She accompanied him on all his travels. She organised the meals when staff came to dinner. Perth society gossiped about the relationship. Those who had known her in her earlier life were intensely curious that Janet, the vivacious, outgoing young woman who had it all at university, the one most likely to succeed, had given up everything to look after Robert.

'Robert and I', she said, 'have a relationship where we both work extremely hard at what he is doing. Any money he earns he would feel was partly earned by me'.[4]

No one knew to what extent Janet was involved in Robert's business affairs, whether he valued her views or even discussed business matters with her. Staff certainly knew Janet as the friendly, vivacious, gracious hostess, the sociable partner in the family. They knew her passionate defence of causes – children's television, Aboriginal people, the environment, the arts; they were aware as well of her left-wing leanings, but they knew little of her strength, resilience, versatility, intelligence and determination.

A part of Janet's life had ended. Her character and strength were about to be tested in a new arena. How would the woman who had played the supporting role to Robert Holmes à Court measure up in her own right as a leader in the tough commercial world? Would the liberal principles she espoused hold up when they came in conflict with the bottom line and the profit imperative on behalf of shareholders?

The key to Janet's personality and character and to the way she would operate as the richest businesswoman in Australia lay in the way she was formed and the values she was taught in her childhood by radical and unusual parents.

JANET'S EARLY YEARS

Janet Ranford was born in Perth, Western Australia, on 29 November 1943. The birth was 'very quick and pretty violent' according to Bern, her mother, who was glad to have it over and done with. Bern had been only three weeks pregnant with Janet when she was hospitalised with hyperemesis (excessive vomiting), and for eight of the nine months could not hold down any food. She was too weak to walk and could only crawl to get around the house. She could not lie down properly, so would sleep standing up in a corner propped up against the wall with a rug around her, or on her knees leaning over the front of a lounge. 'It really was terrible and I was skinny as a rake', she said.

Yet Janet was born eight-and-a-half pounds, a strapping, very healthy baby. Her mother recalls looking out and seeing an egret in the tree outside the window of St David's Private Hospital at Mount Lawley and thinking, 'It was just as though the stork was bringing my baby. She was so active before she was born, she nearly kicked me to death. She was a beautiful baby, the best thing'. Many years later, Bern gave Robert a snapshot of Janet as an infant. Of the small girl sitting up alert in her pram with a little bonnet on her curls, which were sticking out at the front and the back, she said, 'Now doesn't that look like a girl who's going somewhere!'.

Bern spent a fortnight in hospital, in the days where new mothers were not even allowed to sit up. She then went up to the hills to Sawyer's Valley, twenty-three miles east of Perth, to live with her mother, Violet. World War II was in full swing and Fred Ranford, Janet's father, was away at Nungarin in a small signaller's unit, only able to visit his new daughter when on leave from the army. For her first two-and-a-half years, Janet lived with her mother and grandmother on the orchard at Sawyer's Valley along with Reenie Lee (Bern's sister-in-law) and her daughter Judith, who was two years older than Janet. Like many other women during the war years, Bern relied on her family for support, and Janet spent her early years in the company of women left to make their own lives while the men were at war.

When Fred returned from the war, he and Bern acquired a half-acre of land at Greenmount, fourteen miles from Perth, where they built the new family home. It was a bare block, away from the people Janet knew and in unfamiliar surroundings. She was only two-and-a-half years old and very disturbed by the move. Bern had left her with her grandmother Violet Lee for a couple of days while she moved into Greenmount to unpack the china and the crystal. When Grandma Lee brought her to the new Greenmount house, Janet cried all day. She was inconsolable. But on the evening of that first day she walked out the back door onto the verandah and suddenly stopped crying. She came running inside calling, 'Mummy, Mummy, the stars are here. Why didn't you tell me the stars are here?'. The stars were the one familiar thing to a little girl feeling lost in new surroundings on a bare block without a single tree. From then on, she settled in and felt secure.

As a child Janet loved nothing more than playing with her dolls; she was always busy with them. When her younger brother John came along she mothered him, too. Bern says that her daughter had strength of character and a sense of responsibility from a very early age. She was three-and-a-half when John was born, and Bern was so pleased that she now had both a girl and a boy – a complete family.

John was placid and cuddly, with a mop of fair curls. He was developing well until, at eight months, he developed infantile eczema from an allergy to cow's milk. The doctor said it would probably last until he was six, but Bern was not prepared to accept this diagnosis. John was uncomfortable and in pain, so she searched until she eventually found a dietitian/naturopath called Madame Myra Louise. In three weeks, with Madame Myra's advice and the help of soy bean milk and carrot and celery juices, the eczema was under control. Janet remembers the kitchen was like a laboratory, with the table covered in mashed carrot and strainers, mashers and beaters everywhere. Bern learned a lot about diet from Madame Myra and the family's diet was wholesome. Her parents grew their own vegetables and the family ate lots of fruit. Janet still eats salad and fruit daily.

There was no triple-antigen in those days and John contracted a serious attack of whooping cough. Janet got a milder dose but John was extremely ill and soon after, at two-and-a-half, he had an epileptic seizure in the front garden where he was helping Fred with the watering. It was a Sunday morning and Bern and Janet were in the house. Bern was cooking, wearing slippers and a house-dress. Both parents were very upset, but Janet didn't panic. While Fred got out the car, Janet went inside to Bern's wardrobe and selected a pair of shoes and a going-out dress because she knew that her mother never went anywhere in slippers and a house-dress. She was five-and-a-half and she knew what to do. Fred was so upset, he ran over John's trike near the front gate and destroyed it. Janet sat in the back of the car and didn't say a word as they drove all the way to the doctor's. She was no trouble and quite in control in the situation.

John's fits continued for some time, becoming nocturnal events. As Janet and John shared a room, she would call out to her mother that John was 'being sick'. Bern always admired the way Janet handled the situation. John remembers: 'Janet was maternal. She would grab a wet cloth and wipe my face. She's always been a pretty loving person'. John's illness was a family preoccupation and Janet would sit at the table watching as John would get up from his seat, sit on his mum's lap and have a cuddle at the end of a meal. According to Bern, there was no hint of jealousy from Janet, who also remembers special times with her mother. She recalls a dress her mother wore, a white dress with red spots, when they went on a picnic over the road and sat on a rock. 'This was a special time for me. Probably it was a sandwich in a bag, but it was a special occasion.'

Janet's affinity with the Australian landscape was nurtured in this raw suburban environment. The property bordered John Forrest National Park. Janet and John would explore it endlessly, building cubbies in the bush, catching tadpoles in the creek. They would perform 'fantastic engineering feats' building dams across the creek and strengthening the walls with bamboo and incorporating outlets with corks. They would climb around a huge rock they called 'Elephant Rock', but they did not pick the wildflowers – that was taboo. They were allowed to build small, safe fires under a tree at the back of the half-acre lot where they lived, to cook small potatoes or damper and make toast.

Their Greenmount block was long and narrow. The house sat back from the road, with a trellis on the side of the back wall which divided the house from the orchard, newly planted by Fred and tended with loving care by Bern. The fruit trees included oranges, apples and a cumquat tree. Jan (as her family called her) and John used to play tricks on people who had never eaten cumquats, pretending they tasted sweet and offering them to the unsuspecting to watch their response. Along the back fence was a chookyard, which had a beautiful bougainvillea growing wild over it. Next to that was a big lemon-scented gum, near which they used to light their fires and cook their dampers. The ground was rough gravel and clay, so shoes wore out quickly. Jan wore shoes, but John didn't.

One of Janet's earliest memories is of going to the railway station with her father to pick up a box of trees which had been sent from a nursery 60–70 miles south of Perth. They walked to the station, a long walk as she remembers it. She can still see:

a flat wooden box with a vertical piece of timber nailed to each end. A rod across the top made a support for the hessian which protected the trees as well as a handle. They came on the train and we went to the station to pick them up. It was so exciting. I can remember the box more than anything else and walking back up the hill with it.

Like all children, Janet and John squabbled at times and Bern, being a pacifist, could not bear it. She had what she considered an infallible method of dealing with their fights. She would mark a line from each side of the house to the fence. One of the children would be sent to the front of the block, the other to the back, and they were not allowed to cross the line. In no time at all Bern would see them creep up to the line and stand close to it but dare not cross over it. When Bern gave permission, they would fall into each other's arms hugging and forgiving, quarrels forgotten.

About her early years, Janet remembers mostly that her mother was always working, because she was the practical person in the family:

In winter my mother would dig drains to stop the house being washed away by the runoff from the house next door. My father didn't really have a sense or an understanding that if there was a slope on the block and water was rushing down every winter, perhaps the house might float away one day. My father wasn't interested in material things at all. He wouldn't have noticed that the guttering needed repainting or other maintenance. It was always Mum who did those things. They're the things my father should have done. But he wasn't interested and she always did the job that was required. She was always working.

Bern was indeed just like her mother Violet in that respect. And if Bern and Grandma Violet were always working, Janet was always helping. Bern came from tough pioneering stock. Violet's parents (Blenkhorns and Bardons from Yorkshire) had four children and had emigrated from Bradford to the colonies, arriving in Brisbane in 1894. Violet was nine years old and went to school in Gympie, where her father Richard Bardon readily found work as a wheelwright in the days of horses and carriages. Though she left school early, Violet returned to teach the younger children, and her love of reading was passed on to Bern and, later, from Bern to Janet.

Violet was engaged to George Lee by age twenty, but this match was temporarily thwarted by her parents' decision to move to Perth around 1905 in search of better opportunities. George's family had also emigrated to escape from the poverty in Bridport, England, but his father, John Bartlett Lee, died soon after arrival and George, aged fifteen, had to support the family.

Despite a happy marriage, Violet pined for her family back in Western Australia and, after nine years, she persuaded George to move. It was 1918; he had volunteered for the army but could not go to war because of his age. They settled on a ten-acre orchard at Sawyer's Valley, a small railway stop town that was struggling. George and Grandfather Bardon built a house, living in an old humpy while they did so. Violet and the children stayed with the rest of the family in Mount Lawley. The orchard was hardly a paying proposition, so George supplemented his income as a butcher and Violet made jams and sauces to sell at the markets. As Bern puts it:

All of my family, aunts, uncles, cousins, Dad, Mum and my brothers, were hard workers. That was our life. We had a cow, some pigs and a horse, vegetables my father grew, milk, cream and butter, and my brother kept bees. But money was short and orchards didn't pay. You could send beautiful fruit to market and get nothing back except a bill for the commission for the wholesalers.

It was doubtless that this tough upbringing fostered Bern's strength and determination. Bern's mother's endless sewing, bottling, making do with little; her father's devotion to duty and the family; the injustice of working hard for little gain and the vagaries of the market system; the love of reading and discussing ideas engendered by Violet in her children; and Bern's loneliness as the only girl in the family, wandering alone round the orchard, the packing sheds, exploring the surrounding bushland and the old convict-built road from Perth to York – all gave Bern an insight unusual for a girl of her times. She was to become a thinker and an activist, and she retains a radical perspective to this day.

Bern's passionate nature has carried over into Janet's approach to good causes and to life itself. Janet Holmes à Court's own values, personality and attitudes to life are easier to understand in the context of her parents' lives and the sort of home they provided their daughter.

Bern has a vivid memory of when her own political ideas were first formed. One of Violet's cousins was married to a man called Decke. He was taken prisoner in Germany and persecuted because, despite his German name, he had been fighting with the allies. He returned from the war very disturbed, with a metal plate in his head, and Bern, after seeing him in church one Sunday in Fremantle, resolved she must campaign against war and killing. She became an ardent pacifist, a founding member in Australia of the Women's International League for Peace and Freedom (WILPF), a member of the Australian Communist Party for a time, and a strong defender all her life of the rights of the Aboriginal people.

Janet's grandparents kept a full house and led full lives, despite the hard times. Assistant teachers from the school lived with them; Violet and George were secretary and president of the school's Parents and Citizens Association; and Violet encouraged her children to join in the adult discussions at the dinner table.

It was the strong women of the family who stand out in Janet's memories of her childhood. Grandma Lee; Grandma Louisa Bardon (with whom Bern stayed in Perth once she started at Perth Girls' School in 1926 – 'a dumpy little lady, very gentle but very strong'); cousin Jean who was clever and outwardly confident; Bern herself who vowed in her teens, because she was overshadowed by her cousins in sewing, schooling and sports: 'I will be as good and as clever as they are; in fact, I'll be better one day'. Janet grew up surrounded by women who did not assume the mantle of dependent housewife and servant to a dominant male. The men themselves did not expect it, and their marriages were equal partnerships and full of love. In this respect, Janet's partnership with Robert Holmes à Court was to be an anomaly.

Bern left school lacking in confidence and found work as a trainee hairdresser, work she hated but was good at and which paid pretty well at fifteen shillings per week. For her twenty-first birthday, her father gave her the money for a five-week cruise to Fiji. The next year, 1936, he died of cancer, leaving Violet aged only fifty-two.

Both mother and daughter were devastated by George's death, and life became harder. During World War II, Bern's brothers went into service and Violet held onto the orchard in case they wanted to take it over on their return. They didn't, so Violet eventually built a small house for herself in Mundaring which Janet remembers as 'a doll's house'. She also remembers her grandmother's sharp wit, the dictionary under her pillow, her cryptic crosswords and the salt and bicarbonate of soda she put in her beans. No additives were allowed by Bern at home. Janet loved her grandmother and enjoyed her company and the special things they would sometimes do together. One morning at Greenmount, when Janet was five, Grandma Lee and Janet got up at the crack of dawn to pick passionfruit. They put them in bags and took them on the train to the Metropolitan Market and sold them. They then went to Boans store (now Myers) and bought enough material with the money to make two matching dresses, one for Grandma Lee and one for Janet. 'It was pink voile printed with tiny rabbits like a Laura Ashley print. It was a huge adventure to do that. A huge adventure.'

Janet's father, Fred Ranford, had an even longer Australian pioneer background. His great-grandfather, Benjamin Bristow Ranford, had set sail from Bermondsey, England, in 1848, to join his oldest brother in Adelaide. As a successful tanner, Benjamin was soon enticed to Perth to buy the Padbury Tannery; there he met and married Sarah Ann Summerland in 1853. Sarah had been born in Fremantle in 1832, only three years after the disastrous Swan River Scheme.[1]

Sarah had six sons and four daughters. Henry Samuel Ranford, the eldest son and Fred's grandfather, travelled as a surveyor with John Forrest and became government surveyor of a large area in the south-west of Western Australia. He married Jane Eliza Jewell whose architect father, Richard Roach Jewell, designed the Perth Town Hall, the Treasury Building, the Pensioners' Barracks, Wesley Church and the Deanery and Cloisters, all well-known landmarks of Perth. Their son, Henry Andrew Ranford was born in 1886, married Rosina (Ivy) Fraser and ran the government stores. But he died in 1934, aged forty-eight, when his son Fred was only eighteen.

So both of Janet's parents, Bern and Fred, had lost their fathers before they met each other. Janet's grandmothers lived longer lives, Violet very active and hard-working, Ivy a sickly woman, coddled by her family and, as Bern says, 'as narrow as the Puritans. Unforgiving of human frailty. She was kind in some ways, but never forgave me for not being a church-goer. She embarrassed Fred very much at times'. John Ranford describes this grandmother as 'very Victorian, very straightlaced and, without exception, humourless. Jan and I didn't have a great relationship with Dad's mother. You had to be careful. Dad had to be careful'. This severe woman had sold up the family possessions, even Fred's cricket bat and crystal set, when her son went to war, convinced he would never come back, so Fred had to struggle to support her on his return. He had matriculated on a scholarship from Modern School, but could not go on to study maths or science. Instead he applied his talents to a job doing calculations on an irrigation scheme at Harvey, south of Perth. At school, Fred had loathed the discipline and what he considered to be 'the silly nonsense' of cadets, which was compulsory for all boys; he developed an anti-war stance from an early age.

Fred and Bern met during the war. In 1942, as a change from hairdressing, Bern joined the newly-formed Australian Women's Army Service. Following a recruits' course, about thirty women were sent to Northam Army Camp about sixty miles from Perth and with twenty other young women they were the first girls in Australia to be living under canvas. There was no special training, so they were expected to do what they could with the talents they had. Bern was assigned to Canteen No. 9 and that was where she met Fred Ranford.

There were 9,000 men in Northam Camp waiting to be sent overseas, or wherever the army decided, and out of that 9,000 men Bern chose Fred. For Bern:

It was not a hard choice. As soon as I saw Fred I knew he was the one. Fred was refined and well-mannered, unlike many who were quite uncouth and threw money at you for a packet of cigarettes. Fred was always so polite when he asked for his packet of Capstans, always saying 'please' and 'thank you'. There are people who stand out, and he was one of them.

Bern saw her late husband as, 'Unselfish, undemanding, intelligent. Loving but not overtly demonstrative. We suited, complemented one another'. And after she was 'manpowered' out of the army to help her mother work the orchard, Bern and Fred's brief three-month courtship led them to marry in October 1942. They had a four-day honeymoon, which Bern describes as 'a desperate affair' because they didn't know if, or when, Fred would be drafted out for overseas duty. This was typical of wartime marriages when couples were no longer prepared to wait until the proper time to marry and grasped instead at a few short days or months of happiness, just in case.

Janet was born on 29 November 1943. Soon after the birth, Fred was transferred to Balcombe in Victoria and from there to Darwin, where he stayed until the end of the war. It was then that Bern and Janet lived with Bern's mother Violet, Reenie Lee and her little daughter Judith in Sawyer's Valley. Uncle George was in the air force. Bern remembers clearly the horrifying news that triggered the end of the war, the nuclear bombing of Japan. The slaughter and the devastation appalled her, but the end of the war also meant that a few months later, in 1946, Fred came home.

The sort of home and family life Bern and Fred built together was unusual for the times. It was at once the normal, outer suburban, backyard existence of most post-war families, and yet also a world of radicalism, cultural pursuits and pariah politics. Janet is a creature of this dichotomy, growing up thoroughly imbued with the submissiveness and domestic focus of women in that age of familism, but absorbing at the same time the knowledge that women as well as men were supposed to think and act on their beliefs, and that the system often stank of corruption and injustice.

Bern and Fred were kindred spirits, idealists united against oppression and the horrors of war. Fred had spent time with several intelligent servicemen at Nungarin during 1943 and their discussions of social issues convinced Fred that socialism was potentially an answer to the world's manifest economic problems.

As individuals, Bern and Fred were completely compatible and complemented each other. Fred and Bern also shared the same philosophical values. Bern says, 'We wanted better things for the people of this world. We wanted peace and justice. We wanted for everyone opportunities for personal growth, education, a well-balanced life, art and culture. We wanted an end to the slaughter'. Bern's political views today are unchanged:

I believe in peace and freedom. I believe in a good deal, that people who work should be amply paid for what they do, a fair go, a fair day's pay for a fair day's work, and I believe in work. I came from a working-class family. I'm on the side of the workers. And so was Fred really. His mother would never have admitted it, but his father would have.

They did what they could within their own lives to further their ideals. It was the people Fred met in the army who influenced his thinking, not his family. His father had been a Labor voter but he had died young. His puritanical mother supported the United Australia Party (UAP), and did not approve of Fred voting Labor, which he did all his life. After Bern married Fred, he helped her crystallise all the concerns she had carried but never been able to express. With Fred, Bern became a committed and dedicated supporter of radical causes. They joined the World Peace Council and Bern joined the Modern Women's Club.

Much of Janet's childhood was spent with adults and, in the years before she went to school, she was a regular attender, and helper, at the Modern Women's Club. The club met at lunch time on Fridays in a basement on the corner of King Street and St George's Terrace. Janet would enjoy setting the tables. She was not aware of other children being there, only adults. The Modern Women's Club had a small dais where people could stand and speak. It had a curtain made of hessian-coloured cloth featuring bare-breasted Aboriginal women running across it; Janet remembers the image clearly. There were film nights at the club where Chinese and Russian films were shown. She remembers a Russian version of *Don Quixote* with a supporting film about beavers which, as a girl from the bush who built dams in the creek, stayed in her mind.

The Modern Women's Club folded after one of the members managed to get hold of 'the J paper', a classified, secret document that had a bearing on the Petrov Affair. They had a reading of the paper, which Bern considered a foolish thing to do. Shortly after, she was proven correct, as the landlord told them they would have to get out when their lease expired.

Of her parents' attitude to Prime Minister Menzies, Janet says, 'Our family thought he was just disgusting. We were as biased one way as other people were biased another'. Fred and Bern couldn't stand Menzies. Bern says, 'He was a liar for one thing, and I can't stand a liar'. She recalls when the Exmouth Communications Base was first mooted, the Women's International League wrote to Menzies protesting that the radio signal to be used at Exmouth was not a civilian signal. Menzies wrote back saying, 'The base has no military significance whatsoever.'[2] History proved otherwise.

Among the Ranfords' friends were Katharine Susannah Prichard, a neighbour in Greenmount and a well-known writer and Communist, and Irene Greenwood, a great Western Australian feminist. The leafy hills of outer suburbia in that era hid more than docile housewives, and the group discussions were lively, if the meetings sometimes furtive. These were the years of the Cold War, fear of 'reds under the bed', the time of Menzies's unsuccessful attempt to outlaw the Communist Party, McCarthyism in the United States and the Petrov Affair, which kept Dr Evatt's Australian Labor Party out of office.

Janet when she read, read 'good books'. She was not allowed to read comics because comics weren't considered good enough to spend time on. Katharine Susannah Prichard once bought Janet a book from Russia titled *Diary of a School Teacher*, by Vigdorova. Inscribed 'For Janet from Katharine', this was a book which Janet devoured. She also had books about the lives of composers (and still has two of these, on Chopin and Brahms). When she had her tonsils out, she was given *Til Eulenspiegel*, German stories about Til, a naughty elf, and *The Folk Tales of the Channel Islands*. She particularly liked books about real people, a less common preference for young children. Janet says, 'I wouldn't say I was an avid reader, but I was a reader, and I suspect that most of the people I went to school with weren't'.

Janet was often at Katharine Susannah Prichard's house. She was allowed to walk through her garden to take a shortcut home. Katharine had a grandchild, Karen, who would come to stay, and Janet would be invited over to play with Karen. They would have a 'wonderful, creative, artistic time with poster paints and paper'. She can't remember a single conversation that ever took place there but she remembers the ambience – the smell of Katharine's kitchen, the rock cakes, the sherry, the antique telephone. There was a courtyard where there was always a tray of lemons for guests to take, so the whole place smelt of lemons.

The atmosphere 'seemed bohemian to me. I don't think she had much money but she looked elegant, very Bloomsbury, I have an image of her in brown velvet'. If Katharine wanted a lift to Perth in the morning she would drape a white towel over the front gate and Janet's father would stop and pick her up. Bern believes that 'Fred got a lot of ideas from Katharine'. Janet was aware that Katharine 'was a unique person' and 'probably in the back of my mind thought it odd that we knew her, but couldn't speak of her outside because she was a communist'.

Fred and Bern were also interested in the plight of Aborigines. They attended adult education classes to become better informed on the subject and from 1955-69 Bern was a delegate from WILPF to the Western Australian Aboriginal Advancement Council. She found this representation a great experience. She worked with Aboriginal people to raise funds for an Aboriginal Social Centre, which was eventually established near Perth. She gave her support until the Aboriginal members of the Advancement Council wanted to take over the management of the venture themselves, 'which was as it should be', she believed. In the meantime, Bern helped at a kindergarten in an Aboriginal settlement near Perth.

In 1963, Bern and Fred became foundation members of the Western Australian Epilepsy Association. Fred was president for many years and Bern has remained a member – still helping every Wednesday – their interest prompted by their son John's epilepsy. From the beginning of their marriage they were members of one committee or another. Fred 'always got on well with people. He was respected, a sensible man. He always thought before he spoke and could be relied upon to make good decisions. He had, also, a great wit and sense of humour'. In comparing herself with Fred, Bern believed that very often she spoke before she stopped to think.

Bern joined WILPF in 1953, and is still a member. The primary objectives of the League are the 'achievement of total and universal disarmament, the abolition of violence or other means of coercion for the settlement of all conflicts'. The League sees as its ultimate goal 'the establishment of an international economic order founded on meeting the needs of all peoples and not on profit and privilege'.

This was a radically different household from that of Janet's childhood friends. Bern and Fred would go on peace marches and attend silent vigils carrying banners. They collected thousands of signatures for a petition aimed at banning the atomic bomb. They were accused of being communists but were not worried by such accusations. Fred used to go to meetings in Midland. Bern recalls, 'They were called "progressive" meetings, but they were actually Communist Party meetings and I think he learned a lot from them; we both did, but in the end found that it just didn't suit'. Bern was uncomfortable with the rigid Party line. She thought you should have a right to express a different opinion. This self-proclaimed conformist did not like conforming, so Bern left the meetings first and Fred followed, saying, 'No, you're right, it's not for us'. But Fred was committed to the principle, 'From each according to his ability, to each according to his need'. They believed they had to keep trying to improve social conditions.

Janet's hometown life was not, however, entirely untypical. Living in a bush suburban area, community life was very active and centred around family pursuits. Janet's father was a very good sportsman and played cricket until age forty-five, when he took up golf. The family used to go to the Greenmount/Swan View Matting Association matches. Bern says:

> They were friendly country events where the women and kids would sit in the tin shed and watch the game. There was lots of chatter, laughs and cheering – the very best sporting atmosphere. The copper was boiled to make hot water for the tea. The grape-growing Yugoslav people from around the Swan River Valley would play. They were fine people and great workers.

Fred's working career was stable. He stayed with the AMP throughout his working life, moving through the different departments. At one time he ran a unit for sales representatives. But he and his friend Ken Mahoney were both held back by their political views. One of Janet's current friends told her that when he went to work at AMP at the age of sixteen he was told, 'Don't mix with those two blokes over there, Ranford and Mahoney, they're communists'. Janet once encountered this same attitude at Modern School. She can remember the very strange feeling she had when one of her schoolfriends said, 'Oh, my parents don't like me being with you, because your parents are communists'.

So Janet was the daughter of industrious, hard-working, intellectual people with a strong interest in left-wing politics who were committed to achieving social goals. They had a love of the environment. Their mealtime conversations concerned the political events and social issues of the time. There were many books in the home and literature was valued. The music Janet heard was exclusively classical; she never heard the pops. The family had a little record player, and Bern and Fred loved the music of Beethoven, Brahms, Mozart, Schubert and the glorious voices of Elizabeth Schwartzkoff and Jussi Björling. Janet did not know there was any music other than classical music until she went to Modern School.

Through her childhood and teenage years Janet learnt to live in two radically different worlds. She absorbed the values of her very serious-minded politically radical, culturally highbrow family, but she was a very sociable girl and enjoyed the frivolous fun in the more ordinary households of her friends. She did not speak of her family life to her friends; she knew her life would be considered odd and that others would not accept her parents' views. Janet learnt from that necessary deception how to mask her true feelings, how to move comfortably from one world to another. She became an adept performer who could conceal her true feelings, or elements of her feelings, when she wanted or had to, and she learned to enjoy a wide range of diverse experiences unavailable to most people her age. While her background and family values were unusual, the fact that she could adapt, and fit in, to all the environments she encountered made her even more unusual. She was not limited or restrained by her home environment – she was enriched by it.

The Ranford household was a happy, if serious, household. Fred and Bern were not only husband and wife, they were the best of friends. And their friends were people like themselves, who were kind to one another and respected children. The men and women had views in common. Though the women still did most of the domestic work, in these families they were viewed as equals and were sometimes celebrities in their own right. Living in Greenmount was like living in a village. Bern says, 'It was simple, and very innocent. We had a ball'.

Along with the Mahoneys their closest friends were the Robertsons. Bill Robertson, who had four children, founded the architecture school in Perth. The Mahoneys had three daughters and the two families spent a good deal of time together at the beach where they lived. Ken was Fred's best man at his wedding and Janet was born on his birthday. Don Wilson, a doctor, was another family friend. Janet does not remember a lot about the wives of these men when she was young. She remembers the men very clearly, and especially the fact that they did not treat her like a child, but like a 'real person'. She enjoyed their company.

Janet's recollections of her childhood are patchy, but warm. Her circle of friends widened through attending Greenmount Primary School. With Shirley Newman and Dale Hunter she would climb up Big Hill, play around the waterfalls and go to visit an old Italian man called Joe. He lived in a stone cottage that was tucked away in the bush and which he'd built himself. It was unlikely that he owned the land and he was probably a squatter. Janet and her friends would sit and talk to him and eat Milk Arrowroot biscuits. 'It was something parents probably wouldn't let their children do today, but it was all very safe then.'

Dale Hunter was Janet's special friend. She lived about half-way between Janet's home and the school on a large area of land which had been a guest house and golf course. There were a couple of Dale's aunts who had houses on the land as well. Dale's mother worked, so Janet and Dale used to have the run of the house. It was very hot in the summertime and they would fill up an old tin bath, run soap around the edge and slide around in the water. They would mix up concoctions of Nestles milk and Weetbix and put the plate by the bath, sit in it and sing various silly and funny songs they invented.

For outdoor fun Janet and Dale used to ride their bikes up and down the hills. They would peddle like mad down the hill, shouting 'Get your poos up', so then they could get as far up the next steep hill as they could. Dale says, 'It sounds silly, but it was such fun', and Janet loved fun. Their favourite snack was a mixture of condensed milk and coconut. Coming from a household where wholemeal bread and essential wholesome food was the regular diet, condensed milk and coconut was a luxury for Janet. Dale's family also ate white bread with lots of butter, while at home Janet ate margarine. Dale's mother was a milliner and 'Dale's fancy dress costumes had to be seen to be believed. Mine were absolutely fantastic too, but they were different. Mum made exquisite clothes out of remnants of material. She was very clever'. But the contrast left its mark and, in a way she didn't understand, Janet felt somehow different from her friends.

Janet attended Greenmount Primary, a three-teacher school with about eighty children. The main building with two classrooms was brick and the third classroom was a temporary demountable. Grades one and two were together, grades three and four were together and grades five, six and seven were together. Janet's first teacher was Mrs Howell and Janet suspects that she did not approve of her parents' left-wing politics:

> Mrs Howell was more affectionate towards Dale, who was always in the pretty clothes and looked attractive. I felt I should have been getting the attention because I was more clever. I can remember as a six-year-old asking to go to the toilet and being told, 'No you can't go to the toilet now', and wetting my pants on the floor and having to wipe it up.

In third and fourth year, her teacher was Mrs McNamara, who seemed to like the fact that Janet was intelligent. 'She was a teacher who wanted kids to learn; it didn't matter who had the prettiest dresses on, and I think she did a lot for me'. Team sports were big at this school. While Janet was strong in her academic work and always full of energy, she was not much good at ball games. Her brother John says Janet couldn't see the ball because she was long-sighted. If she played tennis, she'd miss eight times out of ten because she lost focus on the ball and then picked it up too late. Dale recalls:

> You'd be throwing the softball to try to get someone out and there would be Jan doing a quick handspring or handstand in the middle of the games. She couldn't just stand and wait for the ball. She was very hyperactive and full of life.

At the same time as Janet's education in cultural matters and political thinking was developing at home, she had a growing awareness of the double life she was leading between home and school. Janet recalls, 'The food we ate was different, the books we had in the house, the music we listened to, the clothes I had, every single aspect of our life was different from most of the people who were around me'. While the others were eating cake and biscuits from Mills and Wares, Janet would be eating wholemeal biscuits spread with cream cheese and mixed fruit. Janet's clothes were practical. Her mother would spend hours getting 'the right sort of shoes because they had to be good for your feet. Where other people had pretty shoes, I had sensible shoes'.

When she was five, Janet started music lessons with Mrs Dixon, the local piano teacher. The piano came from Grandma Ranford, the only thing she had kept when her son Fred went into the army. The piano lessons became an exciting part of Janet's week and she came to enjoy playing music. Fred and Bern were also ABC subscription holders and the family went to concerts and to the ballet. Janet loved these outings.

Among Janet's cherished memories of her father is one which dates to when she was nine years old. Bern met her after school and took her to the bus stop – an ugly memorial to Katharine Susannah Prichard's first husband Hugo Throssell – and there Janet changed into a mustard-coloured dress with little white spots with a white collar and cuffs. She travelled the fourteen miles to Perth by bus, by herself, to meet Fred who took her to dinner at a restaurant called The Golden Wattle and then to see *The Mikado*. It was a significant event for Janet, a special adventure with her dad.

But none of Janet's friends at school knew about these activities:

None of them were surrounded by music at home; they weren't great readers like Mum and Dad were, they weren't political. In fact there'd been a conscious decision on my parents' part not to talk politics with those people because they would have been on a different wavelength. There were some normal things in our lives like the local cricket club and the Saturday afternoon matches. Afterwards the families would go to the hotel but we'd always be the first to leave. They didn't join in with the majority of the local community. Although they were leaders in the P and C, they had an independence of spirit. I suppose a lot of our friends were not the local people; they were friends through politics. A big part of my childhood was spent with members of the far, far left who were friends of my parents.

The paranoia about communism in Australia at that time was quite intense and included a war on suspect books. Janet recalls one dramatic event when they had a warning phone call from a friend, Alec Jolly, to say the security police had been to his home and that they'd had to hide their books. Fred's response was to go to his old Ford Prefect, rip the back seat out and put all the books on political thought or theory behind it. Janet describes that experience as:

> pretty traumatic stuff. You didn't go off to school next day to tell the kids what happened . . . You don't suddenly wake up one morning and think, I'm different from everybody else, but subconsciously I knew we were different.

She knew too that neither of her grandmothers approved of Bern's and Fred's political interests. On hot summer nights in Greenmount, when the beds would be dragged out on the verandah, Janet would lie in bed listening to Violet and Ivy talking in the sitting room about her parents' friends and saying:

> it was 'a shame about the politics'. They were both very conservative people and although they were as poor as church mice, they had a superior attitude, believing that the workers of the world voted Labor and to vote Labor was not nice.

Before Fred died, Janet asked him how he had come to join the communist movement. Fred responded that after going through the Great Depression, he and his friends thought that there must be a better way. They did not believe it was right for a country like Australia to have the massive unemployment it did, with the consequent unhappiness in the community and they thought communism could be the answer. They were very bored during the war and read a lot of books. As Janet puts it:

> My father was a thinker and a rebel. I know he must have been a rebel at school because when I first went to Modern School, after about three weeks, I was sent to the headmistress for laughing in class. She asked if any of my relatives had ever been to the school. I

said, 'Yes, my father'. My friend who was with me, who had been giggling too, said, 'Yes, my aunt'. We gave their names and the headmistress disappeared for a while. When she returned she said, 'Well, the Lockhart record in this school is okay, but I'm not in the least surprised at your behaviour, Janet, because the Ranford record for behaviour in this school is appalling'. My father was furious when I told him.

In Janet's final three years of primary school, she was taught by Tom Harvey, an interesting character, a devoted teacher, and a man who enjoyed a drink. He had taught a number of pupils in Greenmount who had won scholarships to Modern School, which was rather unusual given the small pool of talent he had to work with. Tom could do wonderful chalk drawings of spider orchids and wildflowers. Although no one in Greenmount talked about the environment, the children were surrounded by, and grew up learning to appreciate, the natural world. Tom Harvey saw in Janet another opportunity for a student of his to win a scholarship. He had help from Janet's father who wanted her to go to Modern School, as he had, having won a scholarship in 1927.

Janet does not believe that she would have made it without her father:

He really prepared me for the scholarship exams: he did the whole maths course with me, he went through the English books with me and he taught me when I got home from school. He tested me. Tom Harvey gave me a good general education. We got a good grounding in reading, writing and arithmetic, we did folk dancing, had fancy dress balls and performed spectacular costumed concerts – but it was Dad who did the coaching.

He clearly had good material to work with. Janet had an affinity with maths, which had been evident throughout primary school. This must have run in the family as Janet remembers her father sitting well into the night doing trigonometry problems just for fun. 'He loved it.'

Perth Modern School was a government high school established in 1911 for academically gifted girls and boys and entry was by scholarship. Some very famous Australians received their education at Perth Modern School, including former Prime Minister Bob Hawke, Nugget Coombes, Ian Temby QC, Attorney-General Daryl Williams and Geoffrey Miller QC. It was co-educational from the start, taking in one hundred students each year, with equal numbers of boys and girls. It was an exclusive group. Entry was at the end of primary school, at age eleven or twelve. Janet was young for her intake, being born in late November. The scholarship exams were held at Midland High School, which was an adventure in itself for Janet, coming from a small town community school in Greenmount. At Modern School there were four classes, 1A, 1B, 1C, 1D, with around twenty-five children in each class. Janet received what was called an 'entrance' in the second round of offers. Some pupils did not take up the scholarship if their families opted to send them to a private school, so the second offers resulted. There was family jubilation when Janet was able to go to Mod.

Janet's father was not a very demonstrative person and she suggests she 'was probably a bit scared of him'. She has a clear memory of walking down an arcade in Midland through shops to an apartment where his great friend Don Wilson, the doctor, lived. As they walked, he squeezed her hand and said, 'Do you know what that means? That means I love you'. Janet was about seven years old and she was moved by this sudden and uncharacteristic display of emotion and affection. On the day of her scholarship success his emotions were clear and his pleasure evident.

On the first day of high school the classes were divided and seats were allocated alphabetically. The boys were segregated in 1A and 1B and Janet Ranford was in 1D, sitting next to Joan Rapley. Very few people knew anyone else, as scholarship students came from all over the state. Joan Rapley was 'the blonde bombshell of [our] time', recalls Janet. She was vivacious and nearly drove the teachers mad. She was very intelligent and the male teachers in particular couldn't handle her. In her final year of history, Joan was ejected and had to sit in the hall teaching herself. She went to the headmaster and asked for a copy of the curriculum, taught herself and finished up with the exhibition (first place in the State) in history.

Joan and Janet soon became friends. Despite the occasional naughty stunt, such as dropping the odd penny into nitric acid during chemistry lab, the two were hard-working achievers who imposed their own discipline on their work routines. But they were also too high-spirited for the teachers to select them as models for the other girls and they were not selected by the teachers as prefects.

When I wrote to the school to see what record they had of Janet, the response from Elizabeth Green, Perth Modern School Historical and Museum Committee, read:

> *Little is known of Janet Holmes à Court during her time at Perth Modern School. I have been through the school magazine,* The Sphinx, *for the years 1956–60 but can find nothing of relevance. She passed the Junior Certificate in 1958 and the Leaving in 1960. She returned to teach at the School in 1965 and 1966.*

Nonetheless, Janet and Joan were among the elite of their year, and were certainly remembered by their peers. Joan remained a friend to Janet through school and into first year at university. They were both interested in maths, chemistry and science more than the arts subjects and they were partners in the laboratory. Janet and Joan were part of a group of friends which included Bronwyn Dennis, Frances Meadows, Pam Burgess, Margaret Thackrah, Cally Walker and Sue Osborne, but Janet's special friend, the one to whom she was closest and with whom she spent most time, was Sandy Stock. They enjoyed being with one another, had a similar sense of humour and similar interests.

Janet lived twenty miles away from school but sometimes Sandy would stay for the weekend, or Janet would spend time with Sandy and her parents at their beach house. Both girls enjoyed the other's family. Sandy:

> *used to love [Janet's] mum and dad. Mrs Ranford was always on the side of the underdog and fostering people who were less well off than*

others. I didn't ever see any of those people. I just gained that impression from being with her. Apart from being a really lovely and a warm, gorgeous lady – and she still is – she used to grow gourds and I was fascinated by them. I'd never seen a gourd.

Something else Sandy noticed was that Janet's room was 'very spartan. She had a chrome bed head and I can't remember any coloured quilt or anything on the bed'.

Janet was equally fascinated by what she found at Sandy's house. She was astonished the first time she visited to see all the different frilly, lacy nighties and shortie pyjamas Sandy possessed, which were bought at somewhere like Sussan. Janet's were made by her mother and trimmed with broderie anglaise. Where Janet might have owned two, Sandy would have several. It was the era of the stiff petticoat but 'my mother would not let me have stiff petticoats with skirts sticking out. They were not for people like me. They were "common"'.

The teenage years, when being like your friends is of fundamental importance, were the years when Janet most noticed the difference she felt and the schizophrenic lifestyle she led. Sandy remembers Janet looked 'a little bit old fashioned, not that she was. She had beautiful russet hair hanging in a long plait down her back, but she wasn't traditionally pretty'.

Sandy's father managed a small monumental masonry business. Janet was attracted to the family because it was so different from her own. Sandy's parents' beach house was one of eleven asbestos shacks that had been used by the army during the war. The family had acquired a lease and used to go there occasionally for weekends or for the holidays. The end of the road was some distance away, so everything had to be carried to the house. There were three basic rooms, the parents' bedroom, a big room with a stove, a large table and a bath tub, and another room subdivided by an asbestos screen, with the boys on one side and the girls on the other. If you wanted a bath you went for a swim or filled the tub. They would play cards and games together. Instead of playing Scrabble (which Janet's family played at home), they played Cheats. She remembers her days with Sandy as a wonderfully free time. They both had an adventurous spirit and Sandy says 'a deepness in our conversation, a feeling about other people; we were conscious of how other people might feel about things'.

Janet was always serious about her work. She never complained about the distance she had to travel, but between school, travel, music and homework, Janet was very fully occupied. She did well. From day one at Modern School the emphasis was not on passing exams but aiming for exhibitions. In Janet's final year, twenty-two of the exhibitions in the State went to Modern School. Janet got three distinctions, in Maths A, Maths B and Chemistry. She didn't consider herself outstanding at Modern School. 'I just worked extremely hard.'

From Bern's perspective, Janet studied well and always worked hard. She loved exams and got excited about them. Bern recalls:

You could always tell when there was an exam coming on. We had an angled passageway and on one side of the wall there was a linen press. Before an exam you'd find her standing on her hands with her feet up against the linen press doors. She's the only person I've ever known to get excited about exams. She must have felt very confident. She was a happy, vital person always. But she was also very patient. Like my mother, she was patient.

Janet, also like her grandmother and her mother, was very creative. She had learnt craft, sewing and knitting from both and she would sit for hours patiently knitting with the finest needles, making tiny doll's clothes, inventing the styles. Her aunts had been employed as seamstresses and made exquisite lingerie. The petticoat that her grandmother wore under her wedding dress was museum quality – hand pin-tucked. Janet had a collection of beautiful handmade 'wonderful things I'd made at school'. One night Bern and Fred were having a party and Janet was told to go to bed:

I was so furious that I fetched my beautiful sewing and gave pieces to all the women at the party. I don't know quite what motivated me. I remember waking up the next morning and thinking, 'I've lost all my work'.

When other girls from Mod came to stay at Janet's for the weekend, Bern says, 'they were bored stupid and thought there was nothing to do'. They wanted to go to the pictures. Initially, Janet couldn't believe they were bored by Greenmount. But she was acquiring a taste for a different life and, while still enjoying both worlds, as the years went by she began to spend more time whenever she could with other families.

Janet changed music teacher to Gertrude Carey, who accepted Janet because she was a Modern School girl. 'Modern School girls are taught how to learn', she said. Janet studied with her for about six years. She describes her teacher as:

> *positively Victorian in her attitude. She spoke beautifully and quietly. Music lessons started with afternoon tea: shortbread biscuits and a cup of tea from a silver teapot. You were really being groomed.*

Janet must have had some talent as a pianist, for when she finished Modern School, Gertrude Carey wanted to take her to England to a better teacher to develop her playing. Janet never considered that this was an option. She just said, 'I can't do this. I must get a degree and earn some money'. Hard work and self-discipline were the ways she had learnt.

Sandy remembers how thoughtful Janet was about social issues. On one occasion, they were asked to write an essay describing their home. Whereas Sandy wrote about how her bedroom might be decorated, Janet wrote about her feelings about home – how secure and nurturing it was. Sandy was struck by the difference and thought Janet 'caring and thoughtful, humorous, witty and intelligent. Well-liked by people but not a leader. She didn't show any interest in debating or performing'.

Around age fifteen, the girls at Mod began to take a more systematic interest in boys. They loved to sit on the lawn and look across at the creatures who occupied a separate part of the schoolyard. They would go to the school shop at lunch time – the one place where you could meet boys – and Janet looked forward to the weekend visits to

Sandy's house where there were more boys around. In their early years at Mod, Janet was unsophisticated and there were no boys in her life, though she had the normal curiosity of a young adolescent girl. Along with cooking classes, where they were taught to cook things like lamb fricassee in white sauce, and in starched white aprons serve teachers their lunch, all students were required to attend religious instruction. The most popular minister was Reverend Dowding who, Joan Rapley says, was particularly:

> *interested in the stories of the Bible and in who begat who. Although he preached hellfire and brimstone, it was the beginnings of sex education and the girls would giggle and get very excited. We [Joan and Janet] would go into Reverend Dowding's class and soon there would be girls coming from all directions until the teachers would appear to ask what we were all doing there and why the other ministers were being deserted.*

From age fifteen says Janet 'We had stacks of boys and reasonably serious relationships. It was all very healthy and wholesome and good fun'. There was pretty heavy petting but no real sex. 'A cuddle was very exciting in that era.' As Sandy says, 'We were terrified we might get pregnant if we tried anything else'.

When Janet successfully completed Modern School at the end of 1960 and was to go to university, Bern and Fred decided to move to Claremont, ten minutes away from the university and one hundred yards away from the Teachers' Training College where Janet had to attend twice a year because she had accepted a teaching bursary. This was the only way her parents could afford to send her, and for a woman in the sixties teaching was considered to be a most desirable profession. This bursary bonded Janet to the Education Department to teach for three years at the end of her degree, but it gave her a modest income. As she lived at home she could keep herself quite comfortably as a student.

Janet had begun making some of her own clothes now, using Vogue patterns; so adept did she become that she would sometimes come home from university to lay out a pattern and material on the floor, cut into it and go out the door wearing the new dress that evening. The sewing skills her mother had taught her were now paying off and with the needle under her control she could dress with much more flair – the emphasis was now on style, not practicality.

She felt fortunate to be able to carry on her friendship with Joan Rapley at university. Joan would pick Janet up in the morning in a little Morris Minor and they would travel to university together. They studied the same subjects and were prac partners in first year physics. As two lively, attractive girls, they had fun with 'a really delightful physics demonstrator', Peter, who helped them with their experiments. The honours students tutored the first year prac students and they enjoyed having a couple of girls in the physics class. Peter took Janet out for a time. Then, at the end of first year, Joan decided she wouldn't continue with university, leaving Janet as one of only a few girls studying science. She remembers going to the Physics Department to see who would be her partner for prac that year and seeing an ashen-faced Grant Patterson saying, 'I've got Ranford for my partner'. He knew, Janet said, that she 'was going to be useless'.

The love of Janet's life in her first year was a young man called Don. They met at a twenty-first birthday party. It was one of those looks across a crowded room: they fell for each other instantly. He was older. Don and his twin brother worked in their father's printing business. At the weekend the boys played hockey and there would be a family dinner on Sunday evenings, which Janet enjoyed. The brothers were very social and there seemed to be an endless string of parties and balls to attend. She describes the relationship with Don as a 'fun, wild time'. They danced very well together, gave jiving exhibitions and would perform, singing songs. It was a new and exciting time for Janet.

She says, 'My parents would have been appalled if they'd seen me in action. It can give the wrong impression'. A girl in Janet's class at school spread the rumour that 'Janet slept around'. It meant young men were disappointed when, having taken Janet out, they found they were going to have an unsatisfying end to their evening. The general pattern was that 'boys came to our houses, picked us up, we went out and then we would have an hour of groping'.

The romance with Don extended into Janet's second year but then started to come unstuck. Don used to pick Janet up from the chemistry lab where she had to put in many hours of work each week. He couldn't understand why it wasn't possible for Janet to go out every night. It wasn't easy for Janet to maintain a relationship with someone who was free each day after he finished work, while she had to study. In the end, Don terminated the relationship and Janet was shattered. It was the only time in her life when a male friend told her that he was not interested in her any more. It took her a long time to recover. Janet didn't want to see or speak to Don again; in fact, she didn't see Don for some twenty-five years after the break up.

The next young man who mattered to Janet was also older by six or seven years. Jim was a mature student who moved in an older group and Janet became 'besotted' with him. She says he had 'a wonderful little shed' at the back of his parents' house with a veranda and creepers growing on it. They used to spend a lot of time together in the shed. Fred and Bern did not approve of Jim or the relationship and Janet believes 'it lasted much longer than it should have done, because they couldn't stand him'.

Janet doesn't recall how this relationship ended, but it wasn't traumatic. Jim went back to the woman he'd been dating before Janet and they eventually married, while Janet continued her social whirl going to classes, sitting around with friends sipping coffee for hours or drinking in the university pub.

John Byrne who, according to Janet, 'was wild and a very good mate', was one of the group. John was a kindred spirit for Janet socially and politically – they were both on Guild Council. John, who was studying law, was elected to the Guild in 1963. He says, 'We were so bloody poor at university. I remember Janet and I going around and collecting Coke bottles from the Ref [the Refectory] so that we could get enough to go down to the pub and get a jug of beer because we'd both spent our studentship. And she'd love going down the pub and having a beer'.

John asked Janet to stand for Currie Hall as the entrant in the Miss University Quest. He says:

We had a lot of fun doing that. We did the Prosh – the university fundraising parade Prosh. Prosh was drunk speak for procession through the city streets. I remember us getting our photos on the front page of the Daily News *for some demonstration; still got the photos. Janet loved social life. She was going out with different people to dances, balls, functions. She had a lot of intellectual interests and progressive ideas. On Guild Council for instance.* Honi Soit *at the University of Sydney was waging an anti-censorship campaign and Martin Sharpe was prosecuted – the famous prosecution for the 'Gas Lash' cartoon. He was defended by Edward St John and they sought money from other universities to help fight the case. I moved, and Janet seconded, a motion on Guild Council that we make a substantial donation and that got on the wick of the person who became Senator Peter Durack, who was the Member of the Legislative Assembly (Liberal) for Perth, Western Australia. (He represented the University Senate on Guild Council.) We had some quite bitter battles with him and I remember Janet backing me up in some of my attacks on him. So she had progressive ideas then. The legend about her was that her grandmother and her mother had been involved in the founding of the Prisoner's Aid Society and they were doing things that ladies didn't do in those days. They were supposed to drink gin and play cards and dye their hair blue. As young people we used to go to her parents' place and it was always a nice place to go because the people were interesting.*

This was in the conservative 1960s when many of the accepted conventions and institutions were being challenged. Janet was opposed to the Vietnam War. She was politically liberal and politically involved. She and John were radicals on a conservative Guild. John said:

The university was very conservative. It had a flannel blazer atmosphere and the Liberal Club was much stronger than the Labor Club. The Law School was full of Freeths, Hassells, Haslucks and Chaneys, numerous sons and daughters of Liberal Ministers. But the Guild had a lot more power and freedom than similar university organisations in other States in that it had the financial control of student services, including the refectory, so the Guild was administering a large budget.

John and Janet were more brother and sister than boyfriend and girlfriend, and John would often accompany or double-date with Jim and Janet.

Janet had also acquired some other friends after Joan's departure from university. There were two other girls doing science subjects. One was Louis Evans whom Janet had met in zoology class. The other was Leanne Banfield, who was six feet tall in her socks. She and Janet made a striking pair on campus. Leanne was 'elegant, beautiful and a very nice person'. She was from Dalkeith, the Perth equivalent of Toorak in Melbourne, or Vaucluse in Sydney. She was beautifully spoken, beautifully dressed and very intelligent. Leanne was a calming influence on Janet and showed her a different way of behaving. Indeed, of Leanne it could be said she behaved the way that, later, Robert wanted Janet to behave.

Then there was Tim, who had been around the group since first year. Janet had known Tim for quite a time before she became involved with him. Sandy describes Tim as having been 'gorgeous, a real softie. He was a slightly gawky sort of bespectacled professor-type, but lovable'. Janet loved his voice, his family, his life. 'He was incredibly intelligent, very very funny, passionate about music and books', and he loved Janet dearly. Janet had to choose, ultimately, between Tim and Robert.

When Janet reflects on her time at high school and university, her dominant memories are not about her own home where she sometimes felt uncomfortable for her friends.

I loved going to Don's house, to Tim's. I loved going to Sandy's or to Joan's because there was laughter and more fun. My parents were so concerned about the world's problems, which were all too serious. There was fun, but it was snatched. It was more common for me to be at other people's houses than for other people to be at my house. My father was stern and I think he frightened a lot of my friends. I had friends stay with me and he would impose his ideas about food and what they should eat. It was clear that he expected them to eat what was put in front of them.

The things that were important to Janet as a student were not what went on in the lecture theatres. Academic work seemed extraneous to what was happening in the Science Union and the Guild – the Student Union. Janet got involved in both, very early on in university life, as John Byrne attests. At the end of her first year, in 1962, Janet was asked if she would be interested in standing for Guild Council. The Council had twelve members, nine men and three women. Janet stood for Guild and was elected and that consumed the rest of her university life. In Janet's campaign speech to be elected to Guild Council, she said that councils had been dominated by lawyers and it was about time science and engineering students were heard. She said she 'had the desires of these students at heart'. Being one of few women in both faculties at the time, this made good copy and resulted in many jokes, told mainly by the lawyers. She stood also for the Science Union Council, on which she served for several years. At the end of her first year the entire committee, except for Janet, failed their exams or left university, so she was left as president, secretary and treasurer of the Union. She ran the Science Exhibition which the Union organised to alert students in high schools to the opportunities that could open up in science education. Her extra-curricular activities were the main event in those years.

In second year, Janet failed physics and was required to do a supplementary exam. In third year she failed her major subject. She doesn't know how she eventually passed the year, as she spent minimum time in the laboratory. She says:

I've often thought they probably gave me my degree to get rid of me because I used to have fires all the time and break equipment. I was expensive. I just wasn't that interested. I was in the wrong place. When I was at Mod the place to be was in the group of friends that I had. At university the place to be was on the Guild, as part of the governing body of the institution, knowing what was going on, making a difference and creating a bit of change.

Janet's parents were generally supportive and proud of her achievements; if concerned that the Guild took up so much of her time, they never said so. In fact her mother is to this day proud that Janet was for a period the Guild's acting president, the first woman to hold that position. As regular committee members themselves, and with radical political values, Bern and Fred approved of the student Guild's stand on Cuba and Vietnam and the messages of solidarity that were sent off by the Guild to the students in these countries. And Janet's views on these issues had undoubtedly been influenced by her parents.

They were, however, sometimes concerned that too much time was spent with boys and not enough time studying. Bern says the boys 'flocked like flies'. She even became involved in dealing with them, including one East Fremantle footballer who was so infatuated with Janet he would phone every Sunday. Finally she spoke with him and said, 'You'll just have to leave my daughter alone'. Despite her inattention to her studies, Janet did graduate in organic chemistry.

Janet's home life had played its part in developing her serious side, her political and cultural values, her sympathy for the downtrodden, her love of art and music and imbued her with a strong work ethic. Her university life had meanwhile expanded the gregarious, fun-loving social side of her nature and had in particular exposed her to the company of men, many of whom either sought her friendship or admired her from afar, only confessing their admiration much later in life.

Janet's love of people led to the development of her formidable social skills. These may have been cultivated by a very strong motivation to be a part of a lifestyle she did not live at home because of the serious committed thinking of her parents. Whatever the basis, both sides of Janet's personality merged into a unique blend – she was a political activist who was the social belle of the university, a prominent figure who would not go unnoticed by a man who valued quality in all things. A mysterious new presence, an enigmatic loner by the name of Michael Robert Hamilton Holmes à Court was about to enter Janet's exciting life.

WHO WAS
ROBERT HOLMES à COURT?

Robert was an enigma at the University of Western Australia. Already older and more mature than most other students, he held aloof from the social life of the Law School and the University. Though he kept his promise to Professor Braybrooke, who had agreed to admit him to a late academic start on condition that he would work hard to catch up, Robert thought swatting was a waste of time when there was money to be made by applying his talents to more promising enterprises. He wasn't interested in going to the pub or going to parties and balls; he had already worked that out of his system in Cape Town, South Africa.

But he was interested in debating and in cars; horses also were of particular interest, allowing him to enhance his income through betting at the racetrack. The word around Law School was that Robert was a serious punter. He founded the University's Flying Club and through some financial wheelings and dealings managed to get the club an aeroplane. He drove a trendy car and would park it illegally wherever he pleased, including outside the Vice Chancellor's office. Such behaviour was looked upon by his fellow students with some awe; conformity to authority and deference to one's elders were strong mores in the early sixties. Here was a man who was at once bold and resolute, reserved and charming; and he cultivated an air of mystery by never speaking of his family or his past. No one knew exactly where he had come from or what he had done during the intervening years between leaving school in South Africa and arriving in Perth in 1962 at the age of twenty-five.

Janet first encountered Robert over the telephone. His soft, cultivated voice impressed her. She invited Robert to attend a student Guild Council meeting. When Robert walked in and saw Janet, he said to himself, 'I must remember to marry that girl one day'. Though it was hardly a whirlwind romance, and an engagement did not immediately follow, sparks of destiny were struck in their first few encounters.

Janet was intrigued. She liked this tall, exciting, mystery man; he was different from her other male friends.

The two were brought together through the activities of Guild Council. Robert stood for election as the Western Australian representative for the National Union of Australian University Students (NUAUS). In those years, NUAUS was a radical organisation but Robert was not a person who fought for radical causes in the Guild environment – unlike Janet who was Vice President and active in every radical cause. John Byrne, Janet's great drinking partner and later Robert's partner in legal practice, did not consider Robert to be a significant figure in Guild Council – and it never occurred to him that social, gregarious Janet would find the anti-social Robert remotely interesting.

Despite their apparent dissimilarity, Janet and Robert clicked and became good friends. For a long time they both continued to go out with other people. Janet occasionally made recommendations about the girls Robert might like. Janet was meanwhile closely involved with Peter. While she saw him, Robert was squiring a former Miss University. Then came a Guild Council summer camp at Point Peron where Robert and Janet were leaders. While Miss University was there somewhere, Janet managed to scheme and organise events so that Robert was the one who took her home.

Janet has a recollection of Robert ringing her. 'He'd been planning to take so and so to the races, but she was sick.' He said, 'You can come along, so long as you don't wear a hat'. They went to the races and Robert won £60. He took Janet to pick up Chris Tangney, his landlady, to spend all the winnings on dinner. Janet was very impressed by Robert's thoughtful treatment of his landlady. She thought Robert 'very nice', but there was no romantic involvement. Janet was simply someone who was available on a Saturday afternoon.

The next year they ran another camp together and the relationship began to develop. Janet's overriding impression of Robert was that he was different from everybody else she'd known in her life.

He didn't appear to be slightly interested in the things that all my other friends were interested in, like going to the pub. I can't remember Robert ever coming with John Byrne and me to the hotel. He was older than all of us. He was self-contained, private, had a better car than everybody else on campus. He wore a suit and when he wasn't wearing a suit, he was wearing a smart jacket and trousers. He never had a pair of jeans in his life. He smoked, was a bit aloof from the rest of the campus. He had a sense of humour; he was good fun to be with. Not in the way that I had fun with anyone else — going to parties, moving en masse — it wasn't that sort of thing. He was not a social person. We would go at the weekends for a day drive up to Mullaloo or Wanneroo, fifty miles up the coast, in Robert's old Volkswagon and go crayfishing. He'd dive down and catch a couple of crayfish. Or we'd drive round looking at real estate for hours.

If they were going to be late home, Janet would always have to ring Chris Tangney to let her know Robert would be late. He was always considerate of his landlady and would let her know his whereabouts, because she would get a bit huffy if Robert was taking Janet out to dinner instead of eating in.

That year, Janet and Robert went together to a NUAUS conference in Melbourne. To her surprise and excitement, Robert bought a Karmann Ghia there for £650 and they drove back across the Nullarbor. While Robert slept, Janet drove. They enjoyed the time together and the adventure of the long journey. Appreciation of fine cars was to become part of their life.

Janet remembers only rarely going to a party with Robert during their student years. 'I invited him to my twenty-first birthday party and he came for maybe ten minutes, had a sausage roll and left, but he sent me beautiful flowers, the best flowers I'd ever received, with a card saying, "You're a big girl now".' They were to marry eighteen months later, but not before some considerable emotional turbulence.

Ethnée Holmes à Court, Robert's mother, arrived in Australia in January 1965. She had been through a traumatic time. Charles Trevor, her third husband, had been attacked by a swarm of bees while boating with some friends on the Chobe River and died in hospital a few weeks later. Ethnée sold her interests at Chobe and decided to visit Robert in Australia.

Robert particularly wanted Ethnée to meet Chris Tangney, who was worried that Robert was going to move into a flat with Ethnée. She had no need to concern herself, as Ethnée had never ironed, cooked, cleaned or washed a car. She would not take over the motherly role with Robert, a role she had never played.

The story of Robert's background and family life emerged only gradually as Janet got to know Robert and his mother better. Indeed, Ethnée's life epitomises the aura of mystery Robert deliberately cultivated. She is, herself, not averse to a little myth-building as her memory of husbands and events pulls in and out of focus. Just as Janet's early life had been filled with strong women who lived long, Robert grew up knowing little of his father or other men; his was a strong mother very involved in her own affairs.

Michael Robert Hamilton Holmes à Court's life had the makings for a novel of mystery and romance, even had he not played on the unknown to enhance his own mystique. He had arrived in Perth in May, 1962, already mature and sophisticated in his ways. His was a late entry into Law School, having decided that studying forestry in New Zealand was not his metier. He had already tried his hand at running a restaurant in Cape Town, which failed, then had for a short time run successfully his mother's kitchen and hotel staff at the Chobe Game Resort. He had made money out of punting on the horses wherever he went, and had played the sharemarket with his uncle in South Africa.

His childhood had been both lonely and unusual, though not entirely unhappy. His mother, Ethnée Celia Jones, is listed in Burke's Peerage and Baronetage by the name of Cumming, but that is the name she took by deed poll to please her stepfather before she married Peter Holmes à Court. She was a baby of World War I, born in Somerset East, Cape Province, South Africa, on 15 October 1915. Her father had been a philanderer; her mother, Florence Oates, never wished to discuss him, and so, for Ethnée, 'He didn't exist'. Florence's parents had been early settlers in Grahamstown in 1820, and Florence travelled away from home as a maternity nurse, leaving Ethnée in the care of her grandmother Celia Hill and grandfather, the Reverend William Oates. Her own lonely childhood and learned independence helps explain some of Robert's own drive, his aloofness and his willingness to try his hand at anything that might make money.

The image of Robert Holmes à Court as the self-made millionaire genius, turning humble beginnings into wealth, does not fit well with the facts. Though Ethnée's own origins were fairly humble, her mother's subsequent marriage to Harry Cumming gave her a taste of the good life. She had servants to do all the menial chores, and access later to inherited money, which put Robert and his brother Simon through expensive private schools and made it possible for her to indulge Robert's whims in both study and business ventures.

'Old Man' Cumming was a pioneer of Rhodesian colonialism. He was the first in the country to grow tobacco, the first to grow cotton, the first to export blackcat oranges. He introduced asphalt strip roads to Rhodesia after seeing them in New Zealand and settled on 13,000 acres of land near Fort Rixon, calling it Altyre after his native Scotland, and later renaming it Christmas Gift Farm. He was, perhaps, an early model of entrepreneurial inventiveness for Robert who, while he did not know him, came to regard him as his real grandfather.

Ethnée herself was always one to see a good business chance, and she was not averse to hard work once she put her mind to it. She spent much of her childhood with horses, which she loved. Her angry resistance to her mother's marrying Harry Cumming and moving to Christmas Gift Farm soon gave way to delight when he gave her one of the farm horses.

Old Man Cumming may have been an eccentric who came to bed in bedsheets soaked in milk and built a new house with a sundeck just so he could sunbake nude, but he knew his women, and Ethnée adored having her own room, a kitten, a puppy, a vervet monkey, a donkey and various exotic birds in her private menagerie.

As a child at Christmas Gift Farm, Ethnée was also allowed to drive the car, her short body propped up on three cushions so she could see the road. She learnt carpentry and made a little cart for her dog to pull. She wore shorts, cut her hair like a boy's, rode a boy's bicycle and played boys' games. In fact, Ethnée wished she was a boy.

Ethnée was a rebel, spoiled by this idyllic life and impatient with the world of ordinary women. When she was introduced to Janet, at first under the impression that Janet was Robert's secretary, only to find out the relationship was more intimate, she disapproved and felt Janet was not good enough for her son.

At eighteen, Ethnée was sent to an exclusive and expensive art school near Johannesburg. She showed some talent with drawing and crafts, but her real interest still lay with horses. Her cross-country riding instructor recognised her ability and she began showing hacks at the shows for money, where she earned enough to buy her own horse. In typical fashion, Ethnée used to prepare her horse Barbara for jumping by riding down mine dumps. The dumps were large and extremely steep, but they were ideal to muscle up the horses. It was vital to come down a slope in a straight line in 'Man from Snowy River' style and this required great concentration. One day when she had negotiated the dump successfully, she looked up to see two men with her instructor at the foot of the slope. She had made a great impression. The instructor introduced Ethnée to Peter Holmes à Court and his brother Anthony. They rode back to the stables together and Ethnée was offered a ride back to the city.

Peter Holmes à Court, according to Ethnée, was 'very, very, very English and very shy'. He was the youngest of three children, eight years younger than his nearest sibling, and therefore brought up as an only child. The family came from Devon and lived near the sea. As a youngster, Peter frequently sailed alone. His father was the Honourable Henry Worsley Holmes à Court and his mother the Honourable Evelyn Spencer Holmes à Court – a very distant cousin to the late Diana, Princess of Wales and descendents of the first Baron of Heytesbury. These links with the British peerage were very important to Ethnée and Robert, who both made much of the Heytesbury name, which is listed in Debretts Peerage and Baronetage, the first baronet for Heytesbury going back to 1795.[1]

Peter had joined the navy as a young cadet and had travelled extensively, including to Sydney, Australia, where his uncle had worked with Dorman Long as an engineer on the Sydney Harbour Bridge. Peter had also visited Anthony, his engineer brother, in Johannesburg and had fallen in love with Africa. His mother Evelyn came out with him and bought him a position in the firm of Ferguson and Mallack, where Peter started a new career with the Stock Exchange.

After their meeting at the mine dump, Peter and Ethnée began to go out regularly together. They had a mutual interest in horses. He was tall, very good-looking and Ethnée thought 'a really nice, interesting person'. She describes Peter as having 'a great sense of humour but, rather like Robert, a very dry sense of humour which people didn't always understand'. Like Robert too, a lot of people felt they never really knew Peter. At New Year, Peter drove up to Christmas Gift Farm and asked for Ethnée's hand in marriage. She was twenty, Peter twenty-three, and the Old Man considered them both 'much too young'. But Ethnée prevailed and the engagement was agreed to and announced on 23 January 1936, with the Old Man insisting they 'should be engaged for at least two years'.

After eight months, Ethnée had worn down family resistance and it was agreed that she could marry Peter. The wedding would have been a splendid affair, but shy Peter insisted on a quiet wedding (held early in the morning so no one from the Stock Exchange would come) at St Martin's in the Veld in Johannesburg on Friday 2 October 1936. Ethnée's family and several relatives came down from Rhodesia and only close friends attended. The wedding cake was in the form of three tiers of horse shoes.

On 27 July 1937, nine months and three weeks after the wedding, Robert arrived. Ethnée, in typical fashion, had continued to ride and to go over small jumps until a few weeks before Robert was born. The birth went as smoothly as the pregnancy and Ethnée did not even see the labour ward or the doctor. In what was to be an uncommon occurrence for Robert later in life, he arrived speedily. Ethnée watched the birth and saw the sister hold her screaming, red-faced son by his feet. Ethnée thought, 'What a long boy, he is going to be tall like his dad'. They called the baby Michael Robert Hamilton Holmes à Court. Michael was the name they liked and the baby was called by this name for the first nine months of his life. Robert was for Harry Robert Cumming and also Anthony, Peter's brother, who was Robert Anthony Pearce. The Hamilton was for Robert's godfather, Hamilton Ching, an English friend of the Holmes à Court family.

Someone must have had an intimation of greatness in Ethnée's son, judging by the level of detail recorded about his first year of life. Most of this was written down by his grandmother; Ethnée still has the document, which she values for the detail, and proudly shows to people. The notes record that Robert was born a healthy 8 lb 9 oz. He measured 20 inches. He had his first outing on his ninth day. He was breastfed on a strict, three-hourly regime for the first month, and four-hourly from then on. Robert had trouble with his bowels and the doctor ordered a ten-day course of milk-sugar powders and his bowels responded regularly after that. He had his first teaspoon of diluted tomato juice at four months and cut his first tooth on 26 March 1938. Every cold, tooth, his hours of sleep, the clothes he wore, his daily routine, when he began to notice his surroundings, are all logged.

At six weeks he smiled from his cot. He was attracted to the family pets and liked to touch the horses. At eight weeks he knew his parents, followed them with his eyes and took delight in being held. At four months he was given his first toy, a rubber cockerel which squeaked. At nine months he stood, at ten months he walked around furniture, and on 11 August 1938 he took his first steps from dada to mother. At ten months he spoke his first words, 'baba', 'dada' and 'bow wow'. At eleven months he said 'Oh damn!'. Such detail of his infancy stands in stark contrast to its marked absence about Robert, the adult, a man who kept no diaries, wrote few letters or personal papers and avoided people other than those he needed to do business with.

Robert was baptised in the Church of St Martin's in the Veld on 15 August 1937. It was at 10.45 a.m. on a Sunday, and he wore his first short frock. Seventeen friends were present and Michael Robert Hamilton was christened with water from the River Nile. When Robert was nine months old, Peter came home from the Stock Exchange saying, 'We can't have him called Michael any more. They're all having sons and they're all calling them Michael'. So Michael became Robert, although Robert retained the M in his signature and signed MRH Holmes à Court all his life. Peter was like that, Ethnée said. 'If he set his mind on something, nothing would change it. Just like Robert.'

Robert started riding at the age of two when Ethnée took him on the leading rein; and Simon, Robert's younger brother, first sat on a horse at the age of six months. Both boys became proficient riders. They were country boys, so they made their fun on the farm and, like Ethnée when young, played with the animals. They attended the birthday parties of the other children in the district and fancy dress parties were special events. Ethnée remembers two notable parties. Once she arrived on the doorstep with her two boys all dressed up, holding their presents, but they would not part with them. Ethnée was very embarrassed, but Robert instructed Simon, 'You hang onto that present'. Ethnée had to extract the presents and take the boys home. She said of Robert, 'He used to do some naughty things and then some delightful things. He was a born leader. He would organise games and hold the floor as a very small boy. He'd dig his toes in at times – he would really dig his toes in. That's another side of his nature. It showed up very early'. On another occasion at a party for Baden Powell's grandson, Robert had a fist fight with the host on the verandah and the boys had to be separated. Ethnée says, 'He really disrupted the party'.

Shortly after moving into their new home, they were having morning tea on the verandah. Ethnée was reclining on a swing seat listening to the radio. It was 3 September 1939, and war was declared. Ethnée and Peter had a new business (the Gwelo newsagency), a new home, baby Robert, and another baby on the way. Simon Roger arrived early on 26 October 1939.

Peter, because of his years in the navy, was in the Royal Naval Reserve, so it was inevitable that he would be called up. The cable arrived in May 1941. Ethnée was twenty-five when Peter left and she and the boys (by then aged two and four) would not see Peter again for nearly four years. When the manageress Peter had appointed also enlisted, Ethnée had to take over the newsagency. She was 'surrounded by files and papers of which [I] knew absolutely nothing'. The war, with its disruption of paper supplies and depletion of the population, made business increasingly difficult and within a few months the Gwelo newsagency changed hands, with a considerable loss to the Holmes à Courts. Ethnée had had her first experience of business failure.

In late 1941 Ethnée joined the Air Force at Thornhill Air Station outside Gwelo. Robert and Simon were cared for by Ethnée's mother and by the servants, and Ethnée did not have a lot of time to spend with the children. Peter was concerned, and suggested in his letters that she resign from the Air Force to spend more time with the boys and be free if he got the opportunity to take leave. He was worried that living with Ethnée's parents would spoil the boys. But, as Ethnée said, it was the nanny who did most of the caring for the children in places like Rhodesia, not the grandparents or the parents. She had grown up with a working mother absent for long periods of time, was cared for by her aunt, grandparents and nanny and saw nothing unusual in her own children having the same experience.

When he was older, Robert spoke very little of his childhood. But he did recall the war and living with his grandparents. The only written documentation about Robert's childhood beyond the log of Robert's first year is a list of anecdotes about Robert as a five-year-old, written by Ethnée's mother and dated February 1942. They include, 'Simon and Robert were having a quarrel. Robert said to Simon, "Stop that you M'sasa bugger"'. (The M'sasa is one of the beautiful indigenous trees of Rhodesia.) Another story reads, 'Robert and his Geggie [the boys' name for their grandmother] were not on good terms at the moment. Robert said angrily, "I do not like you any more. I wish a bee would come and…" Then, catching a look in his grandmother's eye that suggested she was in no mood to stand any nonsense, he modified the end of the sentence to "…make honey for us"'. He was a lateral thinker, even then. A third note records thoughts of his absent father. 'Robert was at the station the other day watching a train come in. He said how nice it would be if his daddy could arrive unexpectedly. On being asked what he would do in that case he said, "I should make such a music that the Germans would hear it, then they would not make war any more"'.

Undoubtedly the little boy missed his daddy. But no leave eventuated; instead news came through on radio and in newspapers that Peter's ship, the *HMAS Delhi*, had been badly bombed in the Mediterranean. The survivors were eventually taken to England where Peter remained until June 1944 when the navy decided to send him to a shore job in Simonstad, Cape Town, South Africa. The family was then reunited after more than three years.

The following year, from June 1944 to August 1945, was to be the only year that Ethnée, Peter, Robert and Simon were to spend together as a family in happy times, marred only by Peter's nightmares and headaches, the residual effects of the bombing. In retrospect, family life in the usual sense of time spent together, shared understanding and mutual support was not to be a feature of the Holmes à Courts' experience. Soon after VE day in August 1945, Peter was informed that he would be sent back to Rhodesia to be demobbed. It was time to think seriously about the future, Peter's work and the boys' schooling. Peter's career options were diminished. There was no job at the Stock Exchange and no newspaper agency to return to. Ethnée, on the other hand, had grown in confidence and experience during the war years. Her independent spirit and her experience with horses were to stand her in good stead. Ethnée, as the years ahead would show, was undaunted[2] by setbacks and tragedy.

Neither Janet nor her children knew much of this sequence of Robert's life until I began piecing it together. Robert did not dwell on the past except for a few anecdotes that took on the status of myths, and in later years the family had visited South Africa briefly. But for a man who grew up to be Australia's first billionaire, exposed to relentless media speculation, his life story from childhood on is remarkably patchy. It is a story, however, that explains partly at least some of his personal traits, his particular cast of mind, the solitary style, his resistance to emotional involvement, as well as the drive for power and material possessions which he shared with many successful entrepreneurs.

Robert's was no ordinary story; with a mother such as Ethnée, and early years lived in the context of a seething South African race problem, his life could never have been humdrum. Janet, and her peers at university, sensed this difference in Robert, sensed his brilliance, his aloofness and cultivated reserve, and they were drawn to him as a curiosity. For Janet the attraction was overwhelming.

But Janet was not the simple Perth girl, strangely drawn into a marriage with this odd genius of a man. She had grown up within an actively political family, surrounded by strong women who knew their own minds. She was strangely physically attracted to Robert and he was her ticket to excitement. She had a sense that, despite her good looks and obvious popularity, there was much more to life than she had yet experienced, or that her life had equipped her for. She understood this potential and she wanted to be part of his future. From the beginning she pushed him to succeed and go on to bigger and better things. She loved the challenge he represented. Robert warned her that she would not have him long, knowing his own family history of early deaths from the complications of diabetes, including his father and his paternal grandfather. But Janet was not deterred. She was someone who lived for and made the most of the moment and she would look after Robert – nothing was inevitable, she thought.

Robert the enigma, Robert the loner, Robert the survivor, and Robert the go-getter had few male role models to follow. He was too young to remember the lifestyle of Christmas Gift Farm and the strong will of Old Man Cumming, but he knew the history of the Rhodesian entrepreneur and Ethnée's mother had made sure her daughter was well looked after. Until the year spent as a family together in Cape Town, Robert and Simon were reared by women in the absence of men. There was no grandfather for the boys on Ethnée's side and Old Man Cumming had died in 1941 when Robert was three-and-a-half. Peter's father had died in 1924 aged fifty-three, before Peter was married, and other relatives and friends lived far away in England.

During the year in Cape Town with their father, the boys attended Lioncrest Kindergarten, travelling there each morning by bus. Peter was adamant that the boys should be independent, so they travelled on their own. Robert handled the finances and paid the bus fare. Simon finished half an hour earlier than Robert, and used to wait for him so they could travel together. One day when he couldn't be bothered waiting, Simon arrived home early; a kind passenger had paid his penny fare. Robert kept the saved penny – he already knew the value of money.

Ethnée and Peter wanted the boys to have the best schooling available and they were determined to put the money together for their boys to attend Cordwalles Preparatory School and then the elite senior school, Michaelhouse. The school was considered one of the best in South Africa and boarding school would continue to develop the independence that Peter thought essential and that Ethnée took for granted in herself.

Cordwalles was situated on fifty-two acres on the Town Hill, a location some hundred metres above Pietermaritzburg near Durban in Natal, South Africa, and 1,600 kilometres from home in Salisbury (now Harare), Rhodesia (where Peter and Ethnée had returned to live after leaving Cape Town). Substantially built of brick with tiled roofs, the buildings were grouped around two courtyards connected by verandahs and covered ways. They consisted of dormitory and classroom blocks, a sick bay, gymnasium, art room, carpenter's shop, libraries, changing rooms and lavatories. There was a large open-air swimming bath and a rifle range. Morning and evening prayers were held daily in a brick chapel at the north end of the large courtyard. The domestic management of the school was under the personal direction of the headmaster's wife, who was also responsible for the health and general welfare of the boys.

Boys were normally admitted at age eight. The school year consisted of four terms or quarters beginning in January. The curriculum was on similar lines to that followed in English preparatory schools and full preparation was given for cadetships in the Royal Navy. The school demanded a high standard of scholarship and in its information package parents were told that 'under no circumstances will any form of cramming be countenanced'. Rugby, football and cricket were the school games. There were two first-class hard tennis courts and coaching was available. Swimming was taught by a qualified instructor. Every boy was put through a carefully thought-out course of physical training under the personal supervision of the headmaster. Much attention was also given to 'the proper employment of leisure'; clubs and societies run by the boys and sponsored by staff included music, crafts, play acting, debating, stamp collecting and nature study. All boys were taught singing and music appreciation.

Parents could visit only on half-holiday afternoons or school match days and leave was given at the discretion of the headmaster. Ethnée travelled with Robert to deliver him to Cordwalles, changing trains at Johannesburg. She took Robert to the school, gave him some comics and a bag of sweets, kissed him goodbye and took the train back that night. Ethnée never forgot standing there under an archway with Robert, with not another soul around. Robert did not forget that experience either. He later told Janet he felt completely alone. He thought to himself at that time, 'I'm on my own'. When he read

Bryce Courtenay's novel *The Power of One*, he related closely to the main character's loneliness and school experience. Janet believes this feeling of isolation and the need to be independent and rely on no one stayed with Robert, and was a motivating factor all his life.

During his schooling, from the age of eight until sixteen, Robert returned home only twice a year. Robert's parents were too far away to visit often. He was later to answer a journalist who asked who had brought him up that he had brought himself up.[3] The experience of bringing themselves up was to be repeated by Janet's and Robert's own children. It is not, in itself, an explanation of Robert's solitude and single-mindedness but, combined with his mother's determination to run her own business, the later separation of his parents, and the affluence and white supremacist attitudes of his forbears, it provides a window into how his mind developed and his own private search for a place in the sun. No one could be trusted except yourself, and if you did not achieve, and look after yourself, no one else would.

While Robert was away at school, Ethnée established a successful riding school. When Peter left her for Hilde Hunt, a neighbour, Ethnée's business, together with her inheritance from her mother, meant she was able to maintain a comfortable position. She remarried, this time to a journalist, Ian McKenzie, whom she had known during the war. The boys were not pleased about the marriage and Ethnée herself soon realised he was not what she wanted in life. Peter married Hilde in 1952, living with her until his death in 1966. After the marriage the boys rarely saw him and doubtless they were hurt badly by their father's rejection. They were also uncomfortable with their new stepfather.

The boys were now attending Michaelhouse, the secondary Diocesan College at Balgowan in the coastal province of Natal, high in the foothills of Drakensberg and isolated from town life. It was a large Anglican school in the mould of British public schools: elite, rigid, hierarchical and harsh in its methods of breaking in the boys to the traditions of their class. The school was situated in a rugged environment 1,300 metres above sea level, and on Sundays the boys were free to hike in the mountains and woods, swim in the rivers and picnic around the waterfalls. The school had around 135 acres containing buildings, playing fields, gardens and agricultural lands, including a large vegetable garden.

Around 330 boys attended this exclusive school; there was a broad curriculum, physical instruction under a fully qualified instructor from a British Army School, and a school diet based on the instructions and advice of the British Medical Association. Robert learned boxing and a range of other sports. The boys were encouraged to develop their natural interests and hobbies through membership of school societies including literary, debating, natural history, photographic and dramatic societies. All boys were required to be members of the Cadet Corps and to attend chapel daily. In this formal but rich environment, Robert Holmes à Court forged his own way.

He had developed an interest in photography, joined the photographic society, and soon found another way to make money. He would take photographs of the various sporting teams, attending even the most minor events, and then sell the photographs to the boys. He was the accredited photographer at the school dance, although he was too young to attend in a social capacity. By 1953, Robert ran the photographic society and wrote the short report in the *St Michael's Chronicle* about the society.

Robert also persuaded Ethnée to allow him to have a horse called Razzle Dazzle at school, and he gave riding lessons for which he charged the students. He joined the debating team and took part in all sports including boxing, but did best at swimming and athletics.

Robert later talked to Janet about Michaelhouse and about the great fun they had on the trains. At school it was a completely male environment, but on the train travelling back to school after the holidays, there would be a carriage of girls going to a girls' school. They all stayed overnight in Johannesburg and their parents would give the boys money for this purpose. Simon, always very careful with money, discovered it was possible to sleep for nothing on the roof of the hotel. Robert, on the other hand, would occasionally book himself a suite and invite people to dinner. One day after such a stopover, friends and parents were on the platform waving goodbye as the whistle blew – but when the engine puffed off, the carriages remained stationary. They had been uncoupled from the engine. There were hoots of laughter, many from the hero himself, Robert, who was always highly amused at his own telling of this story.

Simon and Robert were close as brothers, sticking by one another at school and sharing many interests. But where Robert was reserved, Simon was rather adventurous. He once smuggled a suitcase full of snakes onto the train. Another holiday he got off the train to spend time on his own in the bush. Home was not what it used to be.

One source for journalists in the eighties who attempted to make sense of Robert's background was Ronald Brooks, the Tatham housemaster who knew both Robert and Simon. He confirmed Robert's reserve and his charm, his money-making ventures (he ended one term with a profit of R60) and his patchy school record.[4] Robert showed an aptitude for science and maths, even winning the maths prize one year, but attaining erratic results. He matriculated at seventeen, a year younger than most of the boys, with a 'good' second-class pass and no idea of what he wanted to do. It was once reported that Robert said he had obtained first-class honours in the preceding mock matriculation exams and didn't bother to work after that.

The headmaster at Michaelhouse was keen that Robert should return to school for a further year to repeat sixth year, as he was too young to go to Oxford as planned; given his results, he believed the extra year would be beneficial. Robert did return and began to specialise in many extra-curricular activities that year. He was commissioned in the Cadet Corps as a lieutenant, he played a lot of sport, he led the debating team and he was a prefect. A former student at Michaelhouse said Robert never threw his weight around as a prefect; he relied on persuasion, a style he later developed to a fine art in the business world. He was very easy-going. If he caught anyone misbehaving he would glare and leave it at that.[5]

Robert also knew how to get around the rules. When Robert died, Michaelhouse Old Boys' Club published an obituary which referred to Robert and his car and read in part:

Those of us who knew him as a boy at Michaelhouse searched in our memories for early indications of exceptional potentiality in him. There was one particular instance of that bravado which, in later years, caused boardrooms around the world to fear him; it was when he came by road from Salisbury and arrived at school for the start of his Sixth Form year driving an MG sports car, with another boy as passenger. He pointed out to the Rector that he had broken no rules; he had a driving licence; it was school holiday time; he would not drive the car during the term, but he asked permission to leave it at Michaelhouse until the next holidays began.

The Rector was flabbergasted and nonplussed. Robert's sportscar remained at the school during each term that year, cleaned and polished regularly by his fag . . .

In early 1956, after completing his final year at Michaelhouse, Robert went to Whitestone School for boys in Bulawayo, where he taught for six months and coached swimming and boxing – boxing was to remain a lifelong interest. Robert was considering studying forestry and agriculture at this time and Mr Fisher, one of the masters at the Whitestone School who came from New Zealand, told Robert not to go to Oxford. 'What do you think you will learn about forestry there?', he said. 'You must go to New Zealand – that's the place for forestry.'

Robert had another reason for wanting to leave Rhodesia at that time. He did not want to do national service. So he decided to go to New Zealand. He suggested to Ethnée that she finance him with R2,000, that he would earn money during the vacations and come home with a diploma. She agreed. So Robert went to Durban and sailed on the *Oxford* to Port Pirie in South Australia.

From Port Pirie, Robert travelled to Melbourne and for a short time took a job in an insurance office. He went to the 1956 Olympic Games. He visited Tasmania and phoned his relatives in Sydney. Dr Alan Holmes à Court, who had a daughter and a son, Peter, who was a little older than Robert, invited Robert to stay over the Christmas vacation. Alan was a distinguished medical practitioner, and the family welcomed Robert. His wife believed Robert picked up a tea towel during that visit for the first and last time in his life.

Robert was by no means your typical young man, given that in those days money was scarce and only the rich could indulge their children in this way. He enjoyed Christmas with his relatives. His cousin Peter was then studying at university and Robert wrote to Ethnée telling her what a great time he'd had and that he was determined to graduate and do well, live in comfort and have at least one luxury car. These were the first signs of any career plan on his part.

Robert later told Janet that he felt more at home in Australia when he stepped off the boat and onto Australian soil than he ever had in South Africa. From that time he believed that he would come back to live in Australia one day. Meanwhile he went on to Auckland, New Zealand, where he took a room with Mrs Deveral, the first of Robert's landladies, who were all very fond of him and would spoil him thoroughly. Having always had servants when not at school, Robert had never cooked and Mrs Deveral attempted to teach him basic cooking. She gave up after Robert tried cooking peas which boiled all over the floor. He apparently drilled a hole in the floor to drain the water rather than wipe it up.

Ethnée, meanwhile, had bought a farm further out in the country and her business continued to develop. She married her third husband Charles Trevor in 1956, but she was never sure of Robert's and Simon's feelings about that marriage. In fact, the boys had long ago learned to live independent lives. Nevertheless, Robert's independence relied on his mother providing a source of funds. But as the riding school was doing very well, money was not an issue for Ethnée.

After a year at Auckland University doing science subjects, Robert went to Massey College in Palmerston North, which was renowned for its agriculture and forestry degree. It was 1958. Robert found another landlady, Mrs Murphy, to spoil him, although she must have noticed his spending enough to write to Ethnée at one time suggesting that she shouldn't send Robert any more money.

Robert joined the flying club and learned to fly. He joined the Debating Society and travelled around New Zealand in a debating team with two lawyers. Everyone else who was studying was too busy to travel, but not Robert. The lawyers, who were impressed by

Robert's advocacy skills, suggested to him that he should be doing law. Robert thought this was not a bad idea as he found he was not fully committed to forestry.

Robert turned twenty-one in July 1958 while at Massey College. Ethnée rang to wish him happy birthday. When he called her reverse charges to wish her happy birthday in October, he said that he wanted to come back to Rhodesia because he'd now decided he wanted to be a lawyer. He also wanted money so that he could return via the Panama Canal and England. Robert had been due some money when he turned twenty-one from a legacy left to him by an uncle of Ethnée's, so he used this as part payment for his voyage on the *Southern Cross* via Panama to London. There he met his godfather, Hamilton Ching, for the first time. Ching gave him a silver mug for his twenty-first. Robert also met his Aunt Marjorie, who was also his godmother. Several Holmes à Courts were brought together to meet Robert and for the first time he got to know something of his father's earlier life and his establishment background. Robert liked England and enjoyed his stay. He was interested in the family and in being a Holmes à Court, with an aristocratic history. It was important to him. He retained a strong interest in the family history all his life and always responded courteously to letters from people with family connections, however remote and however demanding.

Robert flew home for Christmas in 1958 for a family reunion after two years away. At the same time as Robert decided to study law, his brother Simon decided to become a game ranger. Robert chose Cape Town University to read law, but before he did he visited the doctor as he had been feeling very tired. He had first noticed his fatigue when skiing in New Zealand that year. Ethnée was sitting with Robert when the doctor came in and said, 'I've got bad news for you my boy. You've got diabetes, but if you look after yourself it mightn't be too bad'. The doctor advised Robert to see a specialist in Cape Town.

Soon after Robert arrived in Cape Town, he was hospitalised with glandular fever. When he left hospital, he stayed with Dr Paul Oates, Ethnée's uncle, and Paul started Robert on insulin. He also encouraged Robert to take an interest in the stock market and Paul, his wife Joyce and Robert dabbled with shares and made some money.

Whether it was the illness or old habits, Robert gave up attending lectures at a very early stage in the year. Instead, he became very active on the social scene. At twenty-one, and older than most of his fellow students who had just left school, Robert stood out from the crowd. He was tall and good-looking, well-travelled and charming. He wore embroidered waistcoats. His tough schooling and years on his own had made him very independent. Altogether the girls found him very appealing and he began to enjoy life in Cape Town.

Robert met an old friend at university who had been at Michaelhouse, Robin Hamilton, and they decided to establish a restaurant. It opened in December 1959. They gave it a nautical theme, with a ship's lamp and other seaside accoutrements as decorations and called it La Corvette. Robert and Robin would dive at Half Bay for crayfish for the menu. One day they were caught by the police for bringing up undersized crays so Robert presented the policeman with the biggest of the catch and that was the end of the matter. Ethnée guaranteed the restaurant, without Charles Trevor's knowledge – he had been insistent that Ethnée had paid out enough for Robert's adventures. The restaurant did eventually go bust. The two years spent in Cape Town had added up to a good time for Robert as well as being his first experience of a failed business enterprise.

Charles Trevor was a civil engineer. At a cocktail party in Cape Town, Ethnée heard the High Commissioner mention the idea of private enterprise developing a camping site on the Chobe River and later a hotel for the Game Park. Ethnée, always one to seize an opportunity, pricked up her ears and asked, 'Where is the Chobe River? Is there permanent water?'. The Chobe River flowed into the Zambezi River, at a point where four countries met. There were trees and game in abundance. The area was untouched, with no roads, just sand tracks. Ethnée suggested to the High Commissioner that she and Charles might be the 'private enterprise' he was looking for.

She and Charles drove to Victoria Falls, chartered an aircraft and flew over the area. They were enchanted by what they saw and made an immediate decision to develop Chobe.

Robert's view was that Ethnée and Charles were mad. 'You can't go and live among wildlife on 6,000 square miles and start something in the bush', he told Ethnée. Her response was, 'You'll be surprised what I can do'. And Robert was surprised. Ethnée sent Robert the money to come home after the two years in Cape Town, but he spent the money on a farewell party. He hitchhiked instead from Cape Town with his corgi Bridget Bardog, the Africans picking him up because they were sympathetic to the poor little dog. He travelled part way by bus and finally via a goods train in the guard's van and arrived in Livingstone in Northern Rhodesia, sixty miles away from where Ethnée and Charles were establishing the park. He phoned to be collected and Ethnée and Charles drove across two countries to pick him up. The only way onto the Chobe site was by pontoon. Robert stood on the pontoon looking at the Chobe River for the first time and said, 'This is fabulous, absolutely fabulous'.

Robert settled in his own rondavel and stayed until September 1961, working in the newly-built portion of the hotel. It was his job to manage the kitchens. The guests had been arriving from the time Ethnée and Charles arrived, camping before facilities were built. Late in the evening, when guests were around, they would often sit in the kitchen, where Robert would make omelettes. He loved to toss them and the guests would clap. 'He was a great show-off at times', said Ethnée. As the building progressed, they would dance on a little verandah by the bar and Robert was very popular with the guests. 'The married women loved him, the single women loved him, he was a great asset.' They would enjoy a few glasses of wine at night and one evening a guest dared Robert to swim across the Chobe River, which was full of crocodiles, hippos and sometimes elephants crossing. It was foolish and dangerous but Robert took the dare and survived unscathed.

Robert wanted to take over the hotel and run it but Ethnée told him that was not on. So Robert decided he would move on. Robert left Chobe on 2 October 1961, then took a job working in Bulawayo at the Law Courts to gather some money to return to Australia.

Supposedly, he had been studying law by correspondence from London while in Chobe. He did not want to go back to Cape Town and he saw no value in studying Roman Dutch law. He believed there was no future in Africa. Riots were breaking out and Robert said, 'There will be more riots. They will always riot'. Since Robert had enjoyed his time in Australia and New Zealand, he decided to return. The restless spirit had not yet found the path to follow.

Robert flew from South Africa to Perth in May 1962. He did not have much money and for that reason he decided to stay in Western Australia rather than travelling further to the eastern states. The university year had started in March, but Robert persuaded Professor Braybrooke to admit him after he sat some tests. He asked for a scholarship as well, which he didn't get.

He found yet another landlady, Chris Tangney, who also became devoted to Robert. He moved into her very modest house, with a toilet out the back, and a very modest room where he lived for five years. Robert required full board. Chris looked after all his meals and his clothes. She knew of his diabetes and would collect his insulin from the chemist. Robert took care of himself comparatively well in those days with regard to exercise, but he was addicted to Coca-Cola and nicotine.

Robert never clarified his past, and journalists, until the day he died, spoke of 'the missing years' as though there was something that needed to be hidden. There was not. Robert's life had been fairly aimless from an academic and career point of view, with stops and starts and not much commitment evident. Little is known of his involvement with particular women, although there was one in Cape Town to whom Ethnée believes Robert was very close. He had acquired exotic interests in flying, polo, the stock exchange and vintage cars. He had travelled widely and been given freedom to follow whatever direction he wished, largely because his mother was always preoccupied with her own life adventures and could afford to supplement his income. Robert brought himself up just as Ethnée had done. She was a survivor and an African pioneer. Mentally and physically she was tough and she remains so to this day.

Robert had developed his own style. He was independent, aloof, very much a loner. Although up to this point unfocused, he had from boyhood been very interested in money-making schemes of all kinds. Rules could be circumvented with a little thought and imagination. He was to become a remarkable entrepreneur and the first Australian billionaire. Janet Ranford was to become his partner and his support in the extraordinary future he carved for both of them.

FAMILY AND EMPIRE

Janet was vivacious, witty, charming, the desired partner of several eligible young men around town. Initially, she worked hard at her tertiary studies, but she was also enjoying university life, and Guild Council and social events took precedence over study. Clearly, she was looking for something more than a quiet married existence. Yet she was a woman of her time, not particularly feminist, despite her parents' political radicalism. In fact, the political Left had never been any more concerned with women's rights than the conservative Right. Bern was involved in women's groups but they focused on peace and politics – not female liberation.

Janet may well have imbibed much of the spirit of female independence from contacts such as Katharine Susannah Prichard, but Janet's parents, Fred and Bern, were very happily married and the era of post-war familism was still in full swing. Marriage was to be the lot of almost every woman of Janet's era, whether they were looking for something else or not. Few women pursued a career and if they did it was expected they would give up their job as soon as they had children.

This was the mid-sixties, and Western Australia was a conservative state. Despite her years as a campus radical on the Guild and her exposure to radical feminist women through her mother's political activities, Janet had no feminist attitudes of the Germaine Greer variety.

Michael Robert Hamilton Holmes à Court came into Janet's carefree life at the University of Western Australia. Robert was an older, mature, experienced, independent, suave, charming, sophisticated young man with a quiet, softly-spoken, English-styled voice and gentle manner. He was always vague about his background and cultivated an air of mystery about his exotic past, which wasn't difficult to do given his career and travels up to this point. Most of the other students Janet encountered had never been outside the state.

By the time Robert's mother Ethnée arrived on the Perth scene, Janet and Robert had developed a good friendship, a budding romance, but there had been no talk of marriage.

Janet was extremely helpful to Ethnée when she arrived. She went with her to choose a fridge, a TV set, an iron and ironing board. Ethnée had no idea what it meant to set up house without her African servants. It was Janet who gave Ethnée her first ironing lesson and showed her how to use a broom. She even made Ethnée some curtains. Cooking did not come easily for Ethnée, and dinner with Robert was a grilled steak and a bottle of wine. Ethnée was lonely and missed Africa. But Robert would bring his girlfriends to the flat and, Ethnée says, she met many of them during the eight months she stayed. Robert 'was going out every night of the week with somebody different'. Ethnée also says that Janet and her family were very good to her. 'Frequently on a Sunday I would catch a bus, another new experience, and go and spend a day with Janet's parents. They often took me for drives to show me the countryside and wildflowers. I appreciated this very much.' But Janet felt Ethnée did not regard her as good enough for her son.

Having graduated and completed her Diploma of Education Janet began teaching in 1965 at Perth Modern School, the school where she had completed her own secondary school education. Janet thinks she was 'a pretty hopeless teacher, not with the fifth year students who wanted to learn and had an exam at the end of the year, but with the fourteen-year-old boys. I had had no experience and I had no idea how to control them'. Her remedy for dealing with the five boys who gave her trouble because they disrupted the class so much, was to order them outside. They spent most of the year outside the classroom, while she taught the others. She managed to get most of the students successfully through their Leaving chemistry exam and, as usual, she enjoyed the camaraderie with the other staff. Years later, she met two of the demons as handsome, grown men at a Save the Children Fundraiser and when they asked if she remembered them she said, 'I'll never forget you, you little bastards'.

During this year of teaching at Modern School, Janet became more seriously involved with Robert. She used to meet him at the beach after school. Although Robert smoked incessantly, drank gallons of sweet Coca-Cola and loved junk food, at that time he did do regular exercise. Janet had fallen in love with Robert and she was to become obsessed with him. Robert had had servants, landladies and women to wait on him hand and foot. As Janet says:

Chris Tangney waited on him and I fell right into the same trap. Nine times out of ten when we went out, I would drive him home, drive myself home in his car and then deliver his car back to him in the morning. And I'd often get up and clean it before I took it back! I was so obsessed, thinking subconsciously that this was the way to get this man. I fell into the trap of being his slave very early on in our relationship. He completely took my actions for granted. When I look back now, I think 'Why the hell did I drive him home?'. All the other boys in my life used to take me home. I've always been mad about driving and he had nice cars. Maybe that's why. Why did I clean his car? Maybe I didn't like to see the car dirty. It's not entirely a one-way thing. I felt I was a slave but I got enormous pleasure out of trying to please him. He was, if you like, the man most likely to succeed at university and it was a great buzz to be with him.

Although everything about Janet exuded self-assurance, she was anxious about her own self-worth and her belief about Ethnée's attitude to her did not help. She became determined to captivate the man she considered the most eligible one she knew.

Despite her passion for Robert, there were still other men in Janet's life. Tim, in particular, was to provide her with a very difficult choice, for Janet was very involved not only with him but also with his family. She was a regular visitor at his home and he at hers. He loved her and wanted to marry her. Tim was the preferred choice of Janet's parents. His family lived in a modest house which his mother had redecorated very cleverly with little money. They were a very creative family. His aunt was a theatre critic and his grandfather was the music critic for the *West Australian*. Tim had a sister who was Janet's age who was a friend. They all lived an interesting life, which Janet enjoyed, and they all adored her. Tim would go to her house and sit down with her parents, listen to music and talk about books. He was close enough to them that he and Janet, as a joke, once tried to clip the Ranford front hedge into the message, 'Fred is a lazy old bugger', because Fred wouldn't clip the hedge.

This was not Robert's style. Tim was part of a warm family relationship of the kind Robert had never experienced. He did not like to visit, so Bern and Fred were very apprehensive about Robert. They could see, Bern said:

> that Robert would be wealthy. We knew he didn't have much money then, but we knew where he was going. I always felt money can spoil people and I didn't want [Janet] spoiled. We had nothing against him really, except that he was very determined to marry her and I thought if he's as determined as all that he might not be easy to live with. All these things go through your head and I said to Fred, 'If she marries him, she'll never win another argument'. Fred didn't feel as strongly as I did. Nothing against Robert, except I thought there might be domination.

Janet, however, did not believe that Robert was ever going to get married. She thought he was a confirmed bachelor who was playing with her affection. He took her one day to look at an engagement ring in a shop and Janet told Robert, 'I think it's most unfair for someone who is never going to marry to take someone to look at engagement rings'. She did not know that he went back and bought the ring the next day and then put it away.

She thought Tim was a fantastic friend and boyfriend and a great person to be with. She had fun with him and he really wanted to marry her. But once again Janet felt she was leading a double life, for while she loved Tim, Robert had this extra element of attraction. When she came to the conclusion that he would not marry her, Janet broke off the relationship with Robert. If it was a tactic, it was the most effective approach Janet could have employed – Robert always needed and wanted to win. He then began to display more determination and emotion than she had seen or believed him capable of. He became very upset and started taking out girl after girl, to wreak his revenge, but he told Janet if she changed her mind to let him know.

Janet went to live in Tim's house to get away from Robert, but she was obsessed and could not give him up or forget him. She was a romantic and felt, 'like Fleur in *The Forsythe Saga*. That if I married Tim, there would always be someone else to whom I was attracted out there'. Robert was the fatal attraction and no one else could stand a chance.

Janet finally decided she would marry Robert and, in March 1966, accepted the engagement ring he had secretly bought. She broke Tim's heart. Robert went to see Bern and Fred because he knew they were not happy about the engagement. Bern recalls, 'we had a long talk and we were all reconciled ... we accepted one another. Well, you have to when the time comes, and that's it'. Robert reported simply, 'We got on very well'.

They discussed how many children they would have. Robert thought twelve was a good number and Janet said she'd be 'happy to have the first six'. Janet looked forward to having children. That was what she wanted most, to be a wife and mother. Although she was teaching at the time, she had no interest in a career. She never considered any other option.

Some of her friends were astonished by the announcement of the engagement, not really knowing the ache for adventure that lay behind Janet's vivacious exterior and her overwhelming physical attraction for Robert. In retrospect, the uniqueness of Janet's early life had prepared her to make a choice like marrying Robert. Other women might have been frightened of a life with such an unusual man, but she knew what she wanted. Robert, too, was looking for someone out of the ordinary, someone who would facilitate the ambitious plans he had in mind. And in keeping with his methodical and careful approach to securing his interests, Robert put a lot of thought into the act of choosing Janet Ranford as his life partner. Two unusual people had found one another and the world was to look on in astonishment as they built their life together.

Janet was unaffected by the views of others. Her school friend Sandy thought Robert was 'wet. I wondered what on earth she was doing marrying Robert. I didn't find him interesting or attractive at all'. John Byrne was amazed. He said:

I never got the impression Janet wanted to marry anyone at that time and [Robert] never struck me as a person who would interest Janet . . . I just didn't think that the two of them were the same sort of people.

Although Janet was a demonstrative person Bern describes her daughter's relationship with Robert as:

not a demonstrative courtship from an onlooker's point of view. I don't think I ever saw him put his arm around her or anything like that, which a lot of courting couples will do in other people's company.

Their personal life together was to be a very private matter.

By the time the engagement was announced, Janet had returned to Modern School to teach for a second year. The wedding was organised very quickly as they both thought it would be a waste of time to have a long engagement. As Janet was teaching, the school holidays presented the opportunity so the date was set for 18 May 1966. Janet and Robert thought they'd like about twenty people for strawberries, cream and champagne, but then learnt that weddings were not organised by brides or grooms. There were people on lists who could not be excluded, so it became a much bigger wedding than either of them really wanted. Janet had four bridesmaids – Sandy Stock from high school, Dale Hunter from Greenmount Primary School, Louis Evans and Sandra Brown from university days. Robert had four groomsmen – Graham Scott, Bob Pullan, Bruce Duckham and Eric Heenan.

At such short notice, the main wedding reception locations were booked, so they settled on the Highway Hotel, half a mile from Janet's parents' home. Their choice to marry them was Father Mark Haynes, a member of the Society of the Sacred Mission, who was not attached to a church. Janet was an atheist and Robert was not religious, but it didn't occur to them not to marry in a church. The first church they approached, Christ Church, knocked them back. Through another friend, Nick Blain, they approached his father, the Reverend Barney Blain, who was the Anglican Rector of St Lawrence Church, Dalkeith, and who knew Father Haynes. Reverend Blain agreed they could be married in his church with him performing a minor role.

On the morning of the wedding, Chris Tangney took a cup of tea in to Robert to wake him up and he said to her, 'You know, I don't think I've had my dinner suit cleaned'. So Chris took it to the dry cleaners and got them to clean it immediately. There was mud all round the cuffs. If Chris hadn't been able to get the cleaners to do the job she would have done it herself. It was nothing more than she was always willing to do for her adored Robert.

The wedding was a great day. Robert had decided that he would hire vintage cars for the bridal party, something that was to become fashionable, but was not common at that time. The wedding party spent so much time driving around in them between the wedding and the reception that the guests were kept waiting. The speeches were exceptional. Roger Chongwe, an African law student friend of Robert's from Zambia, proposed Ethnée's toast. He knew something of Harry Cumming, Ethnée's colourful stepfather. Professor Braybrooke proposed the toast to Janet and Robert, and Ken Mahoney, Fred and Bern's great friend, proposed the toast to them. Robert spoke eloquently. Between getting engaged and the wedding, Robert and Janet had bought a house in Darlington, a picturesque old stone house built in the 1890s – one of the original houses in Darlington – which needed a lot of work. They gave each of the groomsmen engraved paint brushes with an invitation to come and help fix up the house.

Ethnée, who had earlier returned to South Africa, came out especially for Robert's graduation and the wedding. Janet still felt that Ethnée didn't think she was good enough for Robert. She says:

I think that Ethnée would have liked Robert to have married some member of the establishment in Perth, someone who lived in Peppermint Grove and didn't have parents who were like mine ... It's quite interesting, because Ethnée thought I wasn't good enough for Robert and my mother probably thought he was too good for me. They both probably felt the same way. That is, not entirely happy about the marriage.

Janet and Robert went straight from the wedding to the airport, flew to Sydney, stayed at the Australia Hotel, and next morning flew to Norfolk Island. They moved out of the hotel the travel agent had booked them into because it did not serve green vegetables, one of Janet's passions. They did some shopping and Janet bought Robert the watch he was still wearing when he died. Robert seized a business opportunity and investigated the idea of registering an office, as Norfolk Island was a tax haven. Meanwhile, as they were close to New Zealand, they decided to fly to Auckland, rent a car and drive to Wellington. Robert showed Janet his old haunts and introduced her to Mrs Deveral, Robert's landlady from his student days there, 'who was beside herself with excitement to see Robert'.

The drive to Wellington Airport was hair-raising as they were late. Robert pulled up in front of the terminal, left the hire car at the door and was accosted by an official who told him he couldn't do that. Robert replied, 'Just watch me', produced his Rhodesian driver's licence – after four years in Australia still the only one he had – and then proceeded to miss the plane. So Janet and Robert had to retrieve the car and return to the same motel where there had been an argument about their payment.

Back in Perth, Janet and Robert moved into a small, transportable weekend cottage belonging to a friend of Ethnée's while they renovated their Darlington house. Janet had discovered on her honeymoon that Robert's dirty clothes would just lie on the floor until she picked them up. She can remember thinking, 'This is my responsibility now. Chris Tangney is not here to pick them up. I'll have to do it'.

Janet was not prepared for the strain of doing it all – teaching, driving to school, cooking, washing, with no sharing of the workload at all. The laundry was downstairs from the bedroom and, one day, she asked Robert if he would mind throwing his clothes down the stairs to the laundry rather than leaving them on the floor. Robert's response was to throw all the clothes from his wardrobe, including his freshly ironed shirts, down the stairs onto the floor where they stayed for a few days until Janet picked them up. That was a shock, and a lesson, for her. She did not try again to get Robert's cooperation in household tasks. While Janet's mother had always done all the work around the house both inside and out, Fred made a cup of tea for Bern every morning of their married life until his death. Robert made Janet a cup of tea only once, one morning in a Sydney hotel. When he brought it into the bedroom, Janet thanked him profusely and he replied, 'I made it for myself. I forgot you were here'. She never knew if that was Robert's sense of humour at work.

Janet, all her married life, had difficulty in getting out of the house on time for her commitments, as Robert would leave late and did not want her going until he was ready. Robert was late for everything. Time did not matter to him and Janet was always in a rush after getting his breakfast and laying his clothes out, driving at high speed to get to school on time.

When Janet arrived back at school after her honeymoon, she discovered she'd lost the chemistry class she believed she would have as the most senior chemistry teacher in the school. Instead, she had been assigned to the lower classes, teaching art and geography. The headmaster thought she might get pregnant and leave. Janet asked if he had ever heard of the pill. But he was unconvinced.

At 9.30 a.m. Janet went to the Education Department's head office to ask for a copy of the regulations pertaining to married teachers so she could take them to her lawyer, not mentioning the lawyer was Robert. She was asked to sit down and, after explaining the situation, she was moved immediately to Governor Stirling Senior High School only five or six miles from where she now lived in Darlington. By 11.00 a.m. her new principal was asking, 'And what would you like to teach?'. She was given two senior classes of mainly boys to teach, and had a great year.

The problems experienced at Mod were not in evidence at Governor Stirling. Janet loved teaching there and, in the two classes she taught, only one boy failed the year. She made friends with the boys, went golfing with them, and one night even stood in for the regular projectionist to screen *Psycho*. She was so terrified, the boys had to take her home and deliver her to Robert. She wouldn't shower behind a shower curtain for a long time after that.

At weekends Janet and Robert worked on the Darlington house together, including wallpapering, surviving an activity that often leads to marital disharmony. They sometimes had dinner with friends and, when he found an interested partner, Robert would bring out the chess set. Janet didn't play chess. The strategy involved didn't suit her way of thinking and Robert would, of course win, but they frequently played Scrabble where they were more evenly matched. It was a game they would play throughout their married life, particularly on their plane when travelling the many miles they did together. Janet was very upset when she found after Robert's death that the pad with all their Scrabble scores had been tossed out in a clean-up. The pad was a record of the many times she had beaten Robert at Scrabble. She says, 'There were two things I could do better than Robert – play Scrabble and chop wood'.

Life in Darlington was like life in a small village community. It was a well-treed bush environment and housed many artists. Robert didn't relate to the people very much. He used to say he was the only person who didn't wear a smock. Janet, however, enjoyed the community. While Robert worked, she coached two students at night in maths and joined the Darlington Players, acting in two plays and playing the piano in one. In one play, Janet was to play a young girl. The older players told her she should remove her wedding ring to play the part, but Janet did not want to take it off. In the end she covered it with a bandaid so that it could not be seen. She never removed her wedding band from the time it was placed on her finger until after Robert died.

Meantime, Robert was busy and would arrive home late at night. He had begun his articles at the beginning of 1966 with the law firm of Keall, Stables & Brinsden. It didn't take long before Robert fell out with his principal. He refused to accept his pay packet and sent it back unopened. He considered that if £12 was all the firm could give him, their needs must be greater than his, so they could keep it. A story went that Robert used to send other people to the Titles Office to do his searches for him. Peter Brinsden suggested to Robert that he should go down to the Titles Office because one day the boy behind the desk might be the Registrar of Titles and he might need his help. Robert's attitude was that if he wanted help from the Registrar of Titles he would phone him – he didn't need to get to know him as a boy and follow him through. Articled clerks normally knew their place and did what they were told, but the firm never knew where Robert was. They thought it outrageous when he took off for his honeymoon and stayed away as long as he liked.

It has proved very difficult to establish the facts regarding Robert's income during his early married life. From Janet's point of view Robert's money was his business. She was prepared though to put her teaching salary into the pot. It was Robert, however, who paid for the honeymoon and the house. Before long they had bought a couple of farms and acquired their first painting, so they were clearly not the ordinary, struggling, newly married couple of the sixties. Robert also bought himself a secondhand Mercedes Benz, which irritated one of the law firm partners because Robert's Mercedes was not only bigger but newer than his. Robert took a keen interest in the horses, real estate and taxation matters, and he always studied the finance pages of the paper. He did work hard, but he wasn't interested in his articles. His principal once commented that Robert was getting more mail than he was. The reason for this was that he was receiving volumes of information on the Stock Exchange. The mining and share boom was just beginning and Robert was a serious student of the financial trends.

Robert decided to transfer his articles to a firm elsewhere in the building, where he believed he would learn more. He became an articled clerk to Geoff Hammond of GG Hammond and Company. Geoff Hammond was highly regarded. He was a jovial family man with three children, a good tennis player who loved life, loved the law and loved Robert. The families spent time together, and bought a farm together as part of a syndicate at Jurien Bay where they would go crayfishing. They had about 7,000 acres of land that circled the town. It was not good farming land, but very good real estate. The sheep they ran often ended up as crayfish bait.

Geoff Hammond was extremely generous and accommodating. He admired spunk and agreed that Robert could serve out his articles running a separate branch of Hammond and Company in a nearby office at Pamos House, 249 Adelaide Terrace. Geoff knew Robert wanted a practice of his own and that he would not stay with him, so he assisted in this de facto arrangement, which continued until the day Robert was admitted to the bar. GG Hammond's branch office stationery was returned that day; MRH Holmes à Court and Co stationery was put on the table, and Robert's practice started officially. Ethnée had returned, this time to make her home in Australia, and she came into the firm as a bookkeeper.

It was a generous act by Geoff Hammond and an audacious one by Robert. The law was so stuffy, it was unheard of to start a new firm. As John Byrne said, 'It just didn't happen. The people who started new firms were the people who weren't good enough to be taken into the big conservative firms'. But Robert was ambitious; he didn't wish to work for anybody else and this arrangement allowed him to get off to a flying start. He employed a secretary, Val Pitman, who was to remain as Robert's secretary until he died.

Val described Robert at that time as 'boyish, gangly, quiet', but eager to enthuse her about his plans. She wanted to work part-time because she had two young children. Robert guaranteed that she would have time for her family, a commitment from which he never deviated for the twenty-five years they worked together. She started work at 9.30 a.m. after she sent the children off to school. She was also given the freedom required to attend to them, if needed, during the working day. This was a very enlightened work–family attitude in its day, one Robert did not apply to his employees in later years. Robert never imposed on Val Pitman the way he did on others, particularly Janet.

Janet was able to give up teaching at the end of 1967, after Robert negotiated a release from her teaching bond. It took some to-ing and fro-ing, and legal argument, but in the end the cost of Janet's release was very small. She subsequently went to work with Robert. From then on, until his death, he was the main focus of her life.

The first day Janet began working with Robert, she was sent to the Titles Office. She didn't have the faintest idea what she was doing, but she found herself taken under the wing of Paddy McFadgen, who was the Titles Office clerk for another law firm in Perth. Paddy worked with a cigarette hanging from the corner of her mouth and visited the TAB regularly. She found Janet looking completely nonplussed, introduced her to the people she needed to know and taught her how to register titles. They related well and soon Paddy joined Robert's firm, sharing an office in the annex next to the toilet. The practice was growing and taking over every possible space on the second floor of Pamos House.

MRH Holmes à Court and Co was the first new law practice in Perth in years and the old establishment law firms hated it. A comment came back to Robert that 'every profession has its cross to bear and we have Holmes à Court'. In fact, the practice was successful and earned a reputation for getting things done. Robert would dictate, Val would type, Janet would take documents to the Companies Office; working together like this they would form a new company in days while other firms took months. Robert was called before the Barrister's Board to explain why his charges were so low. His answer was that he was actually earning more than the Chief Justice and he asked if they thought as a young lawyer in his first year through his articles, should he be earning more? He was a thorn in the legal profession's side.

Western Australia had a very strong mining and agricultural base and the boom was under way, but there were few country law practices. Esperance, on the south coast of Western Australia, was one of the boom towns. Tens of thousands of acres were opening up, agents were bringing in trainloads of machinery, money was coming in from America for land development and there was no lawyer. John Byrne, Janet's friend from university days, saw the potential for a branch office there and drew this to Robert's attention.

Robert set up an office in Esperance which he and Janet would visit once a month. They would leave after work on Thursday with Janet most often at the wheel for the 720-kilometre, part-unsealed drive, arriving around midnight. Their offices consisted of two rooms in an old house. For three days, Robert took half-hour appointments. On Sunday evening they would leave for Darlington. Janet would then stoke up their slow combustion stove for hot water. A local accountant would set up appointments but the word soon spread that there was a lawyer in town. Sometimes there would be people waiting for them when they arrived on Thursday evening, 'My husband's coming in tomorrow to get a divorce. Don't act for him, act for me', or, 'My partner's going to sue me. Don't make an appointment with him, act for me'. It was a great experience for a young lawyer. Janet says:

We formalised adoptions that had never been formalised. We formed partnerships for people who'd been in partnership for twenty years but had never had it documented. We did wills. I'm sure I'm a witness on half the wills in Esperance. We took on a murder case. Robert defended a young man who was arrested for using obscene language because he'd told the local policeman 'You give me the shits', and Robert had him acquitted.

Monday mornings, Robert would dictate all the Esperance follow-up work and Val Pitman would pound the keys typing up every agreement and then have them bound. The next month Janet and Robert would return. While Robert saw new clients, Janet would make them cups of tea and deliver the wills and witness the signatures. Janet remembers those days as 'a time of immense excitement, just extraordinary fun'. Robert used to joke that the only client he had in Esperance who didn't pay was the one Janet brought to him. He was a prisoner Janet found gardening outside the courthouse. Janet suggested he should see her husband as he might be able to get him his release. He did.

The MRH Holmes à Court practice built up quickly, both in Perth and in Esperance. As the work expanded, Robert had discussions with Nicholas Hasluck, the son of the former Governor General, and with John Byrne about coming into partnership with him. Nick, who had previously debated with Robert at university, joined the firm first. Robert's timing was always good – Nick at that time was bored and struggling to make ends meet.

He was to alternate with Robert at Esperance. When they went south together the first time, he found that Robert had been cited by the magistrate for contempt of court and refused leave to appear. Robert had been provocative and amusing but arrogant; he was, as Janet says, 'the young smartarse lawyer with an old magistrate who couldn't cope with his manner, couldn't understand it'. John Byrne said, 'Nick saved Robert's bacon, he could well have been disbarred'. Nick made an effective apology on behalf of the firm, which was accepted, and the court proceeded.

Nick says of those days:

> Rob was no more experienced than me but, by virtue of his boldness and native ingenuity, he had much to teach me ... Rob was a law unto himself. I tried to keep regular hours but he never felt so constrained. He arrived at the office shortly before midday and worked through until late at night, seldom leaving his desk, gaining energy as the hours went by, smoking incessantly. He was constantly ingenious, on his own behalf, and on behalf of his clients. He wasn't altruistic but he loved outfoxing his opponents, especially government departments.[1]

Robert's first office move for reasons of space was to 168 Adelaide Terrace. Janet took charge of the decoration and made some more curtains. Byrne agreed to join as a partner to run the Esperance office. The idea of being a partner in a country practice appealed to him. He says, 'I was hungry to make money. I had nothing; the only thing I had was my law degree'. He'd won a Commonwealth scholarship to get through university and, after completing his articles, had an overdraft. He thought Robert, Nick and he:

made a good trio ... Rob had quite rapidly built up a client base on his own, Nick was very bright and I was a conveyancer. Rob was interested in tax matters and company law and Nick was the common lawyer.

The plan was that, after Esperance, they would expand into Albany and Geraldton. John visited Esperance with Nick. There was a mountain of work to be done. He went down to Esperance for six months to sort it out. It was a long six months; he went in March 1969 and stayed until May 1985. The Esperance business became, he said, 'a real little cash cow. Robert was always ringing me asking, "How much money's in the general account?" and I'd say, "$5,000" or "$3,000", and he'd say, "Send it all up"'. Byrne operated the branch practice with its own trust account and came back to Perth once a month to have the accounts done, and to catch up.

Although they worked as partners, they did little together socially. Robert focused on business. In John's words:

I don't know anything Robert did except think about business. He was always very interested in the intricacies of the company world. He once presented me with a book about merchant banking. No one knew what merchant banking was in Western Australia in the late sixties. But he knew what it was. He would ask, 'Why don't we start a trustee company?' He was very much a lateral thinker ... and also a punter.

Robert had also set up a branch practice in Norfolk Island, where the firm was doing around 25% of the registration of all companies formed in Western Australia. The nickel boom had been replaced by the land boom and clients were registering their businesses in Norfolk Island to avoid paying tax. Tom Bannerman came in to run the Norfolk Island practice and handle the company registrations.

Janet and Robert travelled to London and Moscow and, in their absence, it became apparent much work had been left undone. Nick Hasluck asked John Byrne to come to Perth to help him sort out the mess. John drove up overnight and walked into the office to find 'this little real estate chappie with his big blue Jaguar in the car park asking for all his companies'. John opened the file and found a piece of paper with a date and the figure 'one million dollars' in Robert's small neat writing. That was the total file. John said, 'Robert was a hopeless solicitor because he just wasn't clerical enough'. Then Nick and John found that few of the files contained any details. Between them, they sorted out the work.

Although Robert's style was unsettling, according to John, they were all well paid. Robert may not have had clerical skills, but he was strong on ideas. They may not have known what he was up to and their financial position was ambiguous, but the new letterhead bore the name 'MRH Holmes à Court and Co' with Robert's name and those of Nicholas Hasluck and John Byrne, indicating they were partners. They were all signatories to the general accounts. John says he is:

> not sure whether we ever signed the business name registration form. I really can't remember that. But I said to [Robert], 'Look, we're holding ourselves out as partners — are we partners?'. 'Yes', Robert said, although I never ever saw a set of partnership accounts and I don't know whether we made any money or not.

John opened the newspaper one morning towards the end of 1969 and read that a solicitor, MRH Holmes à Court, had made an offer to purchase WA Woollen Mills at Albany for $75,000. John and Nick were concerned and spoke to each other. The cheque had been written on the general account without Robert having told them and they did not know what their position was. They considered they were probably responsible jointly for the overdraft. As the press were saying that the deal would fail and the deposit would be irrecoverable, Nick and John feared they would have to pay back money they simply did not have.

This incident led to the breakup of the partnership. Robert explained that he planned to take over the mill on the basis that they would both get shares, but the venture was too unnerving for the young lawyers. John took over the practice in Esperance with a 'quite generous arrangement' and Nick went back to work for the firm Keall, Stables and Brinsden where Robert and John had both worked as articled clerks. Nick says, 'The parting was civilised, but not entirely cordial'.[2]

The ex-partners often talked about what would have happened if they had stayed. John says, 'We might have been mega-millionaires. Either that, or in jail, or dead'. John has missed Janet over the years. 'She is the sort of person that I would have liked to remain in close contact with all my life, as I have with other people from those university days. What did Robert Frost say? "Two paths, I took the one less travelled". So there you go'.

Robert never practised law again. The advocacy game was not sufficiently stimulating or rewarding for his talents. He walked out of the practice and never looked back. He worked from home until he set up his next office.

It was January 1970 when Robert gained control of the Western Australian Worsted and Woollen Mills Limited (WA Woollen). This was his first successful takeover and it gave Robert the vehicle he was seeking to develop his entrepreneurial activities. Blanket manufacturing was not a business Robert wanted to run; it was the opportunity this struggling company gave to list on the Stock Exchange that he was after.

In the late sixties, nickel fever was so widespread in Western Australia that WA Woollen moved to acquire four groups of mineral claims in the Pilbara area. WA Woollen had suffered trading losses in each of the six years to 1969. The company desperately needed new equipment but had no funds for capital investment. With its Pilbara applications, WA Woollen was able to make a new issue of shares.

Through his law practice, Robert had been meeting a host of would-be entrepreneurs with the desire to take advantage of the nickel boom and get rich quick. Through Robert they got fast, efficient, inexpensive legal service. One of his first clients was Denis Watson who became a partner (along with Geoffrey Hammond and other friends) in the syndicate Robert formed to invest in a wheat farm at Eneabba, 280 kilometres north of Perth. The vehicle for the venture was the Wongaburra Pastoral Co Pty Ltd, formed on 28 February 1967. It was Robert's first directorship and he described himself as a law graduate. Robert held 10,000 $1 shares, paid at 50 cents each. Robert had grand plans for the property, despite its barrenness and the low bushel yields from the first crop. It had an excellent scenic location and Robert saw the real estate improving in value, but the venture never took off and Robert moved on.

Watson and Robert again decided to venture together. Watson held about $100,000 in property investments in a company named Stanford Securities Pty Ltd and he was looking for a broken-down company to use for backdoor listing Stanford. Robert's assets then were unknown, even to Watson, but Robert didn't seem to think money would be a problem. WA Woollen had a very good cash flow and Robert was very persuasive with his bank manager. In two days he bought 150,000 shares in WA Woollen, 21% of the ordinary shares. Watson and Robert found the company in even worse condition than expected. Robert hadn't even seen the mill before purchase and on his first visit, when he picked up some blankets, he said to the manager who offered them at cost, 'No, I've seen your accounts and I think I had better pay retail'.[3]

The Western Australian Minister for Industrial Development, Charles (later Sir Charles) Court, anticipated that Robert's takeover of the mill was motivated by a desire to use the ailing company as a backdoor for the public listing of mineral prospects, so he called Robert in to see him and threatened to appoint a receiver if this were the case. Robert asked for time to present a proposal. The company owed the Western Australian Government more than $330,000, with no hope of repayment, and the situation for the mill was disastrous. Robert proposed to Court that the Government write off its loans but continue to provide financial subsidy. In return Robert promised a $500,000 modernisation program. It was an audacious proposal but Court agreed; he had little option. The mill was the biggest employer in an isolated country town; a receiver could only keep the mill open with government funding, so politically it was a sensible solution. In Robert's terms it was 'the correct decision', 'a sensible commercial arrangement', phrases he would employ often in his future deals. Robert had placed himself in a position of tactical advantage. He had taken over a company someone else wanted to defend. So Robert and his partners were relieved of a financial disaster and the Minister had a way of helping the people of Albany.

Robert earned the initial $500,000 needed to invest in new machinery by trading in the stock market. Over time this amount was increased to a $5 million investment. The mill got its face-lift, a new manager in Jim Morrison, a retired Scot who was experienced in mill manufacturing and who stayed until he died in 1985. Robert and partners got their backdoor listing through WA Woollen. By July 1970 Watson and Robert controlled nearly 800,000 shares in WA Woollen out of an issued capital of nearly $2 million, the new machinery had been found in Belgium and the acquisition of mining titles was under way. On 2 October, the company contracted to buy eighteen claims at Mount Clifford from a company controlled by a Perth solicitor, Jim Mazza. The offer for the claims drove WA Woollen shares to $2.50. Using the excitement generated through the claims, WA Woollen placed new shares which raised $1.5 million. Robert now had cash to modernise the mill and to conduct a series of further takeovers. The share placements were made before the option on the claims was exercised. It soon became apparent, however, that Mount Clifford was not going to be a nickel mine and WA Woollen shares retreated to $1.00 by December. The Mazza Syndicate never got its money, or its shares.

In May 1971 Robert, through WA Woollen, advised the Perth Stock Exchange that the company's legal advice indicated the vendor did not have certain title because the claim was not properly pegged and they were entitled to treat the contract as void. The Mazza Syndicate sued WA Woollen, but in the end did not proceed with the claim. Robert got his money with no outlay and paid for the claims, which again inflated his share price. Robert had demonstrated he could move quickly.

Robert began to travel east to meet the money managers and found that in the entrepreneurial world it was common for women to be provided to businessmen – to make their stay more appealing, to relieve the boredom. He would tell Janet of these opportunities, but he never took part. Extra-marital affairs were of no interest to Robert and sex debts he saw as foolish obligations.

Robert was soon involved in another venture in which he gained business experience but was not quite so successful. He bought control of Westate Electrical Industries in September 1970 and in December, Westate took over the Pilbara plumbing business of Gavin Dewar and Co Pty Ltd. In this company, as in future business operations, he gave the managing director free rein, but kept a very close eye on all capital expenditure items and on the salaries paid to executives. In this case, Robert decided the market did not warrant modernisation.

Robert would later say that 'he drifted into commerce'. He claimed that he had no plan, that he had not intended to leave legal practice. Events determined his future. What he enjoyed, he said, was the opportunity to provide business solutions, as he had with WA Woollen. He told Trevor Sykes:[4]

I have an enormous belief in the power of logic and the right decision. I don't try to persuade people to accept my view of something. I agonise over the problem until I have a solution and I am then trying to sell something I believe in that is backed by logic.

By the early seventies, Robert had begun enjoying his new entrepreneurial life and was certainly not missing his law practice. In any event, he had so much at stake in WA Woollen that he had plenty to occupy him. And Janet was enjoying the support role that would become her full-time job.

MARRIED TO THE MASTER

It took Robert just fifteen years to become Australia's richest man. In building his empire, he relied heavily on Janet for her support and enthusiasm. Together, they were a stunningly successful team, totally unalike yet united in purpose; unequal yet indispensable to one another. Their relationship was of endless fascination to the media and the wider public because of the enigma it posed. How could someone so charming be married to someone so cold and remote? How could Janet share such wealth and not be spoiled? How could a woman from such a background reconcile her political values with the role of being married to the richest man in Australia? In turn how did he accommodate those values? How did an intelligent woman of the seventies and eighties find satisfaction in subjugating herself so completely to her husband? What role did Janet play in the building of the Holmes à Court empire?

While Robert planned takeovers Janet carried babies. Janet conceived Peter, their oldest, on one of the many trips to the legal practice in Esperance. Unlike her mother's own experience carrying her, Janet had a very healthy pregnancy, continuing to work until the day before the birth, when she top-dressed the lawn. Her body, she says:

> *thought it was the best thing that ever happened to it. Mine was, to quote Steinbeck, 'a retort perfect for the distillation of children'. I got more wolf-whistles when I was pregnant with Peter than I ever got at any other time in my life. I felt fantastic. I think I had wanted to be a mother for a long time. My mother told me that when I first started to menstruate I was so excited, because it meant that I could then have a baby. I became pregnant very easily and I was as fit as a fiddle and incredibly excited about the whole thing.*

Janet went to Ronald Giles, a gynaecologist friend of her father's who had rooms in Midland, and gave birth at Swan District Hospital on 11 November 1968. The baby was induced because, Janet says, 'I'm a huge sook and wanted it to be as painless as possible'. She went into hospital in the evening and was induced at 8.00 a.m., going into labour a few hours later. Robert was with Janet for most of the day. About 6.00 p.m. Robert went back to Darlington to have dinner with their friends, June and Harvey Phillips and their children, and Peter was born while Robert was away. June told Janet that 'when the call came through Robert absolutely glowed and was out the door without even saying goodbye he was so excited'.

When Robert arrived at the hospital Janet described him as being 'beside himself'. She was feeling fine after the birth, so she took him down to the nursery to point out Peter through the window. They named him after Robert's father. In celebration, Robert bought Janet a pair of antique diamond earrings. It was a very happy time. Dale Kessell (nee Hunter), Janet's friend from Greenmount, remembers Robert phoning to tell her Janet was in hospital, and of his excitement.

Janet's life then changed dramatically. She had a mothercraft nurse who helped her in the house for a few weeks after Peter was born. The nurse was a mature person who knew all the rules and regulations governing the role of a mothercraft nurse; therefore she didn't do anything but look after the baby. Robert would tell Janet,

'You're spending half your life looking after her, waiting on her, cooking her meals'. It would have suited Janet much better to employ a cook and look after the baby. But Janet had always done everything herself; she had no experience of handling staff. True to her upbringing, she could never sit while someone else worked.

Most of the time Janet was on the move. She would put Peter in the pusher and walk along Darlington Road, across the old railway line, down the hill, across a little creek and up to June and Harvey's place. Harvey loved babies and would change Peter's nappy. Their school-age daughter used to babysit at times. Other days Janet would:

wash and bathe Peter, put him in the bassinet and spend the day with Mum or with one of my friends in town, and then make sure I was home in time to cook Robert's dinner.

She spent very little time in the house; she wasn't a homemaker at that stage. 'I wasn't interested in buying things and arranging them to make it look homely.' Having a baby did not seem to take up much time and Janet was finding it difficult to handle the fact that she was no longer working. She used to joke with her friends that Peter must have thought for the first two years of his life that the sky was cream vinyl, because that was what he saw on the roof of her car.

Within three months of Peter's birth, Janet was pregnant for the second time. Once again it was a healthy pregnancy. Three months into her pregnancy, Robert wanted to go overseas to a legal conference in London and to visit Moscow. Janet would not think of leaving Peter behind and Robert considered the decision to take the baby to be totally hers. She took the advice of a friend and instead of taking a pusher, took a 'papoose' to carry Peter on her back. The theory was that rucksacks were fashionable and fathers would feel more comfortable with them than a pusher, but the result was 'an absolute nightmare'. Janet says:

I should have known that Robert would no more wear the papoose than fly over the moon, but I didn't and so I had to carry Peter round Moscow while being pregnant. I missed out on so many things because I just couldn't cope. It was incredibly hot. I didn't go to the Kremlin because it was just too much of an effort. Robert's attitude was: 'You wanted to bring the baby, you look after the baby'. So that was pretty tough going for me. But I was happy. I just willingly did those things.

Janet could have taken someone with her to help look after Peter, but it did not occur to her to do that. It was *her* job. When they arrived in London things were easier because they stayed in a flat and she had help with Peter there.

Robert wanted to move from Darlington, a suburb he had never identified with so they moved to Osborne Parade in Cottesloe, a few weeks before Catherine was born on 24 November 1969. Once again Robert was 'over the moon'. A few hours after Catherine was born, Robert returned to the hospital with Peter and gave Janet the key to a new Mercedes. She left the hospital in her nightie and went for 'a burn around the block' in her gift. She now had a baby girl, a one-year-old son, and a new house to organise for Robert.

Robert was focused on plans for his public company and takeover activities and Janet's role was primarily to service his needs, to facilitate his work and to ensure there were no distractions. He had Val Pitman in the office fulfilling that role and Janet at home. Both women knew their place. Janet was rarely seen at the office. Val Pitman said she learnt quickly that Robert would not be pushed, not by anybody, and that if she wanted to work for him she had to do it his way. She was the buffer in the office, fielding his calls and all manner of contacts. Val, like Robert, was a very private person, very discreet and very loyal and she accommodated Robert's idiosyncrasies. She thought her relationship with Janet was strained from the beginning. She also thought Robert crushed Janet, that he treated her very badly. Janet was so exuberant and Robert wanted to tone her down. She heard Robert being very harsh and humiliating to Janet at times, while Janet would take what Robert said and not respond.

Robert could not have chosen a better partner as part of his team and he undoubtedly knew that. While Val Pitman doesn't know how Janet endured what she did, she admires Janet's style, her tenacity and social skills and recognises how much Robert needed those skills.

Janet's mother argues that Robert:

> would have had a much harder row to hoe without Janet. She looked after him through it all, cared for him, cared about him. Most women wouldn't have been able to. It would have had to be someone very special to look after Robert.

Janet saw Robert as special. When she was doing the mundane tasks, making the tea, answering the phone, she felt she was serving a very useful purpose. She thought, 'this is a most amazing man and he doesn't need to make cups of tea, so I'll make them and be his handmaiden and lay out the clothes'. Robert was:

> so focused on what he was doing that I [Janet] felt important in the scheme of things. If he said we've got to catch a plane in an hour, there was only one person who was going to pack the bags and make sure everything went smoothly ... Everything had to be organised like clockwork to get him where he was going ... it was my role ... Val obeyed his every whim and anticipated his every move. So he had her in the office and me at home. We just smoothed the path for him wherever he went, so he never had to think about anything as mundane as 'What am I going to wear tomorrow?', or 'Which tie will I choose?', or 'Will my shoes be polished?', because it was done by me. I thought that was valuable and maybe it was, I don't know.

Janet always deferred to Robert. She would knock on his door before she entered at the office. He never said 'thank you' for anything she did, for his endless cups of tea or for the appetising trays of food she would prepare hoping to entice him to eat in a more healthy manner.

In 1983, Janet told the *National Times*:

I am sufficiently unliberated to believe that Robert comes first and I rarely ever leave the house until he has. I think if he is here, he needs me here. Robert does an enormous amount of thinking and planning and the sort of process he goes through would be entirely disrupted if he had to answer telephones. If he had to turn into a telephonist, he would not be able to achieve what he has achieved. Making cups of tea and looking after his physical wellbeing as well as keeping the place quiet and calm is all part of allowing him to get on with what he does best.[1]

Janet maintained this view throughout her marriage. In 1990 (following Robert's death) Sheryle Bagwell wrote:

The more gregarious and affable of the two, Janet was never apologetic about her total devotion and loyalty to husband and family. Her love and admiration for Robert, indeed her awe of him, were characteristics often mentioned by her friends. 'I know I have worked hard', Janet said once, 'but not as hard as he has. It would be extremely presumptuous to say that, because his brain is a million times better than mine'.[2]

Robert didn't like family visits, so Janet's relationship with her own family changed. They were rarely part of an extended family unit. Janet can count on both hands the number of occasions in their whole married life that Robert saw her parents. As they did not go together to Fred and Bern's house, Janet would visit alone, grabbing time when she could. Nor were they, nor did they want to be, part of a social group. Janet had allowed herself to be convinced by Robert that parties were a waste of time and, as long as she saw friends during the day, she did not miss such social activities. They were a self-contained couple and would become more and more so as the years progressed.

Today, Janet finds it difficult to believe that she had what she describes as 'so little self-esteem'. She says:

I was so obsessive in my will to please Robert. I suppose I thought that if I didn't put up with it I might lose him and that would be dreadful. At no stage did I ever want to lose him ... But I can't understand why I didn't pay someone else to do some of the things I did or why I didn't put my foot down and say 'No, I'm not going to do that'.

Janet's gregarious nature did not change. While she was prepared to devote herself to Robert in a one-on-one relationship when he so required, she did have other outlets for her social needs. A great source of stimulation and company for her came through the infants' playgroup she started soon after moving to Osborne Parade. She set up the playgroup in a big area above the garage. She and her friend Liza Newby, who had just returned from Oxford, saw a need in this old suburb into which young families were moving and where there were no facilities for children. Janet and Liza began the playgroup for their friends, with the original intention that mothers would come with their children. The mothers could talk while the children played, and then go home. When it was Janet's turn to supervise, she would devise interesting activities for the preschool children. She 'had people washing out paint pots in my laundry. It was a fun thing to do. It was lovely to have the space used'.

But Janet and Liza soon found several of the mothers didn't want to be involved in the organisation of the group, and would instead just dump their kids and run. So the playgroup moved into a more formal phase where there was a charge of $3 for a morning's care. The money went to pay a trained child care worker to run the group and for paint, toys and equipment. The playgroup remained, although never certified, at the Osborne Parade venue for twenty-five years. A trust account was set up to handle the playgroup's finances and Robert signed the cheques. He was very happy to house the playgroup and when he left for work there would often be a couple of little girls who would stand up and give him a kiss as he went down the drive.

Even after Janet and Robert moved to Peppermint Grove in 1983, the Osborne Parade house was retained and rented out for another twelve years because Janet didn't want to close the playgroup. They always ensured there were sympathetic tenants living in the house who tolerated the playgroup.

In the early seventies, Simon Holmes à Court, Robert's brother, came to visit and stayed about nine months. He had sailed his yacht *Maggie May* from Southhampton to the Galapagos Islands, then to the Seychelles, filming his voyages, before finally coming to Perth to put the film together. Simon was incredibly shy. He was always a loner and in Africa would go off for long periods of time travelling into the game reserves. Robert was secretly quite proud of him and his achievements and Janet believes he really liked him. 'As young people they had had fun together', but they hadn't had much to do with one another for a long time.

Robert wanted Simon, his only brother and only regular companion from his childhood and youth, to stay in Australia; he felt that if Simon went north and looked at the land and the lifestyle there he might like the country and settle. Robert thought there was no future in Africa for any white person, so he was disappointed when Simon decided to go back to Africa after completing his film. On learning later of his brother's disappearance, he became very concerned. Robert financed the search until its tragic outcome. Simon's truck was not found for two years; his remains were discovered much later some distance away. When Robert was told of the discovery of Simon's remains he retired to his office and Val Pitman served him a cup of tea. Robert said little but he had lost the only member of his family of origin to whom he was close.

Robert meanwhile was launching WA Woollen on a string of successful and unsuccessful bids for small Western Australian companies, using both Stanford and Westate as vehicles. This culminated in the takeover of Bell Bros to form the Bell Group in 1973. Robert had for some time been studying the transport and contracting business, which had been decimated by the slump in the mining industry. The thoroughness of his financial planning was to become his hallmark. Citibank lent him the money and after three bids, and a bitter fight with the Bell Bros family, Robert succeeded in the takeover. The bid cost WA Woollen $9.6 million but it immediately recouped $3.5 million by the sale of Stanford to Bell Bros.

Dennis Watson, Robert's partner in Stanford, had retired to become a fibreglass manufacturer in Sydney. For his part, Robert was on his way to becoming the master of the takeover, one of the most feared sharemarket traders the world has seen. To those who would later claim he never built anything productive and was just a wheeler, dealer and greenmailer, Robert Holmes à Court's early business ventures give the lie – he went on to work the mill and run the business. He didn't just trade shares. The Albany woollen mill became the most modern woollen mill in Australia, importing wool from New Zealand, turning it into carpet yarn and sending it back more cheaply than New Zealand mills could manufacture carpet yarn. And Robert remained attached to WA Woollen, which became a small but consistently profitable contributor to the Bell Group. Janet and Robert also became very involved with the town of Albany, spending time with Jim Morrison and his wife, and later buying the local newspaper and radio station.

Robert set up a board of four directors, with himself as both chairman and CEO. He retained Phillip Hardcastle and Frank Downing QC, a highly respected Perth director, who were on the Bell Bros board. He sacked the other directors and invited John Murdoch, a chartered accountant for forty years, who had retired in 1973 as managing partner in the Western Australia firm Arthur Young & Co. John had been chairman of a public quarrying company, Swan Quarries Ltd, which had previously been taken over by Bell Bros. He had also been a director of Trans Australian Airlines (TAA) from 1957–70 and was an experienced director of public and private companies. Robert phoned him out of the blue and asked him to join the Bell board. He knew nothing of Robert other than what he had read in the newspapers, but Robert had done his homework and John remained a member of the Bell board well beyond the statutory age for the retirement of directors. He shared this status with Frank Downing, who was also elected each year at Robert's request by the shareholders until

Robert sold his shares in Bell to Alan Bond and the SGIC in 1988. John and Robert developed a solid working relationship. John found Robert:

hard to assess on first meeting, a quiet, unassuming man who discussed business only, nothing personal. A man of very few words who put down little on paper; it was all in his head. He had a wonderful brain. He was an honest man. He wouldn't do anything over the board table unless it had the confirmation of the directors. He had a QC and a chartered accountant on the board and never made a decision without our approval.

For four years Robert personally managed Bell Bros from Guildford in Perth. He arrived early in the morning and left late every night. Not a single contract – transport, earthmoving, whatever – was entered into without Robert doing the negotiation, the costing and the signing. He was the hands-on manager. The reason, Robert said, was very simple:

We had shareholders' funds of $1 million; we paid $1.8 million for the company which the year before had been capitalised at $50 million. It had lost $3 million the year before. We took it over and it needed every minute of my attention, and it got that.[3]

Robert also did all his own industrial relations. Roger Sleight, who was the senior unionist with the Transport Workers Union (TWU), dealt with Robert extensively from 1974 throughout the rest of the seventies. His first impression was that Robert was the wrong type for transport – that he wouldn't survive. 'He seemed too simple.' He asked the secretary of the union, Robert Cowes, 'Does this bloke know anything about transport?'. To Roger, 'Robert was the epitome of the aristocrat. He walked, talked, acted and behaved like an aristocrat', but 'he also had the common touch. There was nothing in any way snobbish about Robert. He always treated everybody fairly and straight'. Roger never felt uncomfortable in Robert's presence. He found he had infinite patience. The shop steward had a serious stutter and Roger recalls waiting in the boardroom where the shop steward tried to talk to Robert. 'You could hear the moths on the windows but [from Robert] there was never a flicker, not the slightest flicker of impatience.'

Robert and Roger developed a mutual respect for one another over the years. During an owner-driver dispute in 1977, Roger organised the blocking of the Bell Bros entry gate. It was a cold, rainy day, he was stopping traffic, people were arguing and getting to the edge of violence. The police were there and there was general chaos. Robert's office sat high in the freight terminal building facing the gate and Robert sent a police sergeant to ask Roger to see him in his office where he told him, 'I want you to know there's nothing personal in this. I understand that you do what you have to do and I'm up here doing what I have to do'. Roger responded, 'I'd rather be up here looking down on it'. But he admired the way Robert analysed every situation. He was used to the anger strikes could engender from managers, but with Robert:

if he felt any anger he would have to be the best actor you've ever seen. It was a game. Life was a game, and Rob had a certain way of playing it. He didn't believe you made good decisions when you were angry.

Robert would explain he could only pay what the market would carry.

Although Roger perceived him as 'a very hard man,' he really liked him.

He always said what he meant and he meant what he said. On the telephone you'd think he'd gone to make a sandwich because he took so long to answer. I believe that was because he was making sure that he said what he meant to say.

Roger says he spent a lot of time drinking with Robert. But whereas he learnt a lot about every other man or woman he drank beer with over a period of time, with Robert:

I may as well have drunk coffee because he would never tell you any more than he wanted to tell you, whether he was drinking coffee or beer. Robert had a pretty good suit of armour.

But he did learn one evening that Robert aspired to buy back the family home – the Heytesbury mansion in the UK. Family, heritage and empire were now driving Robert's ambitions.

After one particularly sticky dispute, Robert rang Roger and said Bell was going on strike. It was a strike against John Holland Construction, which one day was to be Janet's company. Robert had his workers down tools because John Holland Construction would not abide by its contract with Bell. Roger backed Robert and Bell Bros before the Western Australian Industrial Relations Commission and would not allow anyone else to complete the contract. The TWU, the Metal Workers and Federation of Engine Drivers were all behind Robert in that dispute. When the matter was resolved, Roger and Robert were going to the Palace Hotel for a drink and Robert realised (as usual) he didn't have any money in his pocket. He was a very wealthy man by then, but everyone in the office was offering him money to buy a drink.

Bell Bros did not occupy Robert so much that he could not keep a very close eye on the stock market. Before he moved east to take on Ansett, Robert had moved on Emu Wines, Griffin Coal and Greenbushes Tin.

Between 1974 and 1979 Robert retired 'unsuccessfully' from several takeover bids, with profits of up to $1 million each time. Robert had been dubbed 'the place-getter'.[4] Robert denied that these were cases of greenmail. He would each time judge the price too high, or the profit irresistible, and then would sell. John Murdoch said that Robert would 'get things moving without confirmation of the Bell directors straight away. But when he saw things coming to fruition he would discuss them with his co-directors'. The board was very comfortable with this method of operation. John Murdoch said he didn't think other chairmen or chief executives would make the decisions Robert made, but Robert 'had the right as chief executive and with success all the time, how could you stop a man doing it in his position?'. So Robert did his share trading and reported to the board as he went along and they were content, as their Bell shares grew in value. He had to be doing something right, even if his methods were unorthodox.

The seventies were, Robert would say later to Janet and others, 'the best times, the exciting times'. He said to Roger Sleight, 'Money doesn't make happiness', to which Roger replied, 'Rob, don't give me one of those old chestnuts'. And Robert said, 'I know a lot of people who have a lot of money and it hasn't bought them happiness', and Roger replied, 'I know a lot of people without any money and it hasn't brought them any happiness not having it'. To Robert, money was the scoreboard to see how well he was doing. Roger believes that climbing the mountain was what Robert got his kick out of, not so much enjoying the top when he got there.

In 1979, Robert was about to climb the highest mountain. He had honed his financial planning skills and his negotiating tactics. He had developed a unique approach to stalking his prey, but his strategy was consistent. He studied the company over a long period of time. He employed financial analysts to provide him with data. He listened to views, then always made a decision for himself.

Yet for a man so sure of himself, in many ways he was remarkably reserved and uncomfortable in company. He liked one-to-one conversations where he could be in control, but he knew if he was to achieve what he had in mind, he needed to engage socially with his employees, directors and with his targets. He could have found no one more skilled for this role than Janet. She loved people and whether she liked particular individuals or not, they would never know. Janet ran Robert's social events. There was always a Christmas party at the house, with everyone invited. Robert would greet the guests, but instead of mingling would remain on the edge of the crowd. On one occasion Roger Sleight asked Janet why Robert didn't mix in and she said, 'Robert's like that; he just likes looking into a goldfish bowl'.

Robert's growing business and income had by now enabled him and Janet to acquire some very serious leisure interests such as art, vintage cars and horses. These collectibles were to become the outward trappings of their success. In particular, the stud farm south of Perth began to play a significant role in family life. It was a project that grew over the years and involved the whole family. The farm was a major focus of the children's lives and their happiest childhood memories involve Keysbrook.

In 1971 Robert and Janet began the development of the 300-hectare Heytesbury Stud at Keysbrook, sixty-five kilometres south-west of Perth. Robert's plans as usual were grand – to develop the best stud in the Southern Hemisphere and to breed super horses, among them the next Phar Lap. For the next twenty years this property was Robert's hobby and his main source of relaxation. It was where the family gathered and, ultimately, where Robert died.

Ethnée had instilled in Robert a love of horses and had taught him to ride well as a child. At university Robert was a regular race-goer and soon after he and Janet were married they acquired two horses at the yearling sales and gradually began to race them. The Keysbrook farm was originally purchased because Janet and Robert needed somewhere to keep their horses. As became the practice with Holmes à Court real estate, Janet did the searching and found the Keysbrook property. This then became the focus for their family weekends as they planned and implemented the development of the model stud. Janet played a significant role in the design of the farm and the planting of tens of thousands of trees at Keysbrook.

Most weekends the family would drive down to stay, initially in a caravan. Ethnée went to live in one of the small houses they built there, delighted to be back among her beloved horses. The Holmes à Courts built a series of small houses over the years which would be passed on to staff as the property expanded. Janet personally decorated, furnished and made curtains for each one of them.

At the Stud was an old house which was occupied during the week by young stablehands, who would go home to their parents over the weekend. As this house was where the Holmes à Courts would stay on weekends, Janet would arrive with Peter and Catherine to clean up before Robert appeared around midnight from his office at Bell Bros. The farm boys always left a mess that attracted rats, so she would put a rug on the floor, a playpen on top and sit the kids in there until she had removed the mess. Janet didn't employ staff for these sorts of tasks:

> because I wasn't in the habit of having other people do things for me I suppose. But it was quite mad and it was quite exhausting . . . I think sometimes that I was running so fast I didn't stop still to think about what I should do about this situation. I thought that this was what I was expected to do.

When Robert arrived, there would be discussions about fence lines and where the next trees would be planted. Janet was Robert's calculator. They would do endless calculations on Robert's cigar boxes, figuring out how many horses there would be in ten years if they started with five mares and how many mares they needed to ensure one horse would race every week. Such were their dreams.

Robert had also developed views about breeding from established bloodlines and was convinced that although Western Australia had no national record in racing, the climate and the right pastures could produce outstanding horses. Robert was to prove his theories were correct.

Robert slipped quietly into the racing industry in Western Australia, a dignified, well-dressed racegoer with a style quite unlike that of most in the close-knit racing circle. He began to produce the occasional winner. He met and got to know Barry Farmer, the *West Australian*'s racing writer, through interviews conducted at the races. Robert would give Barry what the latter regarded as 'terrific stories'.[5]

At that time Barry had a radio program about racing pedigrees. He thought he had a good knowledge of thoroughbred bloodlines, but was stunned by Robert's knowledge and felt he couldn't begin to match him on the subject. Robert's retentive memory made him a master in bloodlines as it did in the movement of stocks and shares. He did not spend much time poring over racing magazines, but breeding was his forte. He was as bold and lateral in his stallion acquisitions as he was in his share acquisitions. The planning was always long term.

Robert was obsessive about the quality of his pastures. He stressed the need to eradicate weeds, keep the pastures clean, promote better pasture growth and not overstock the paddocks. He would walk with Janet through the paddocks pointing out there was too much of this or that and demonstrating that while he had appeared to pay no attention during his classes at Massey University, he had absorbed significant agricultural knowledge. Robert could almost certainly have been a good farmer or a stud master; he knew the land, he rode and he handled horses particularly well.

When Robert died, Tommy Smith, a leading Sydney racehorse trainer, stated Robert had the best eye for a horse of anyone he'd ever met. Progeny from Heytesbury won over $20 million in prize money and claimed close to 200 Group and Listed events. Heytesbury won Western Australian Breeder of the Year on six occasions, as well as Sire of the Year on seven occasions and three Broodmare of the Year awards.[6] Robert's unorthodox breeding of his Melbourne Cup winner Black Knight demonstrated the lateral thinking which he applied to his horses as well as to his companies.

Robert bought Brenta, a mare he admired, for $600 in 1971. Brenta, a winner of two races over short distances, was bred in Victoria. She had seven foals for six winners including Black Knight, the 1984 Melbourne Cup winner. The sire was Silver Knight, the 1971 Melbourne Cup winner. Silver Knight, a New Zealand horse, was bred at Trelawney, a stud Robert later acquired, and one which had a remarkable record. When Robert was looking for a stallion in 1972 he approached some equine brokers to assemble some options. He liked none of them. One of the brokers, Bill Quinn, heard of the availability of Silver Knight but the asking price was $65,000 which he thought would be too high for his client. Nonetheless he phoned Robert, who responded with one of his shorter pauses and said he would take the horse 'subject to veterinary examination'. It was an audacious decision and certainly no one in Western Australia had ever paid such a sum for a horse before. His objective with the stallion was to inject some staying blood into his lush Heytesbury

Stud. Robert had great faith in Silver Knight and bred him to some high-quality mares, but it was the sprinter Brenta, a winner at Seymour – a small race in a small town – which mothered the Melbourne Cup winner Black Knight, who in turn made history as the son of a previous cup winner Silver Knight and the first Western Australian bred horse to win the cup. At the time the race was run Robert was asleep in London, not even bothering to wake to listen. Janet was at Flemington with Peter, where she led the horse in from the track, received the Cup, and made a commendable speech, which was televised thus giving many viewers their first impression of Janet Holmes à Court.

While weekends focused on the farm Janet would fit in daytime activities with her friends during the week. She formed a very strong friendship with Sue Conners, whom she had met through St Hilda's Kindergarten, which Peter attended. With sons the same age, Janet and Sue found they shared much in common and enjoyed one another's company. They had domestic interests with the garden, the house and a mutual interest in art. Sue's husband David was a mining engineer and got on well with Robert. Sue and David were invited to visit the Keysbrook farm and would take walks or ride horses and play backgammon. They enjoyed listening to Robert's stories and hearing his views. Sue liked Robert and Robert liked Sue who, among other things, was an avid gambler.

Sue Conners recalls helping with the massive tree planting program and riding horses, with Ethnée leading them around the property. Sue and Janet were, in contrast to Ethnée, nervous riders. Through Sue, Janet later met Maggie Venerys, whose son was in Peter's class at school. The three women were good friends and Robert decided he would lease them a horse. The traditional arrangement in Australia when you lease a horse is that the person who owns the horse receives a third of the winnings. The lessees pay the training fees and receive two-thirds of the winnings. Janet, Sue and Maggie did a deal with Robert whereby they would pay half the training fees and get half the winnings. They named the horse, appropriately, Partly Ours and, as Sue couldn't follow the race through binoculars, chose silks in a shocking pink with a lilac

Maltese Cross. They were the first to run a horse with pink racing colours in Western Australia, agreeing that, for a syndicate with three women, pink was the most appropriate colour.

On race days Janet and her friends would do the housework and drive to various country racetracks in time to lay their bets before the race, watch it, jump in the car and arrive back home to meet the kids. Janet didn't bet, but had as much fun as the others anyway. The horse ran in country races and after the race they would have a beer with Vernon Brockman, the trainer. They chose him as trainer because he was handsome and fun to be with.

Partly Ours was a hopeless horse and won only one race from many starts. Robert convinced them to get rid of him and gave them another which they named Brazen Beauty, which did better and even won a few races. They then leased a third named Haulpet. They never paid Robert anything nor did they receive any money in return. The attraction was in the excitement, in having their names and their own racing colours out there.

Janet's friends enjoyed her company, her warmth and consideration, her capacity to have fun, and her skill and creativity. But they were amazed by the way she looked after Robert. Sue Conners said Janet:

> was the perfect wife for him. She could have perhaps done a lot more for herself in those early years, but she found pleasure in supporting him. Without her he would have found it very hard. She is the classic good woman behind her good man.

And Robert was not an easy man to live with.

Every weekend the family would leave the farm with Robert in a bad mood because Ethnée would come each night for a meal. It became a source of great irritation to Robert, who finally insisted she was not to be fed, so Janet would have to apologise. When they were leaving, Ethnée would cling to the side of the car to talk and delay them until Robert would mutter to Janet, who was driving, 'Go, go!'. He would not say anything to Ethnée; it was left to Janet, but it would put him in a foul mood every Sunday night, and Janet did not enjoy the trip back to Perth. Robert would walk inside the house to go about his business, while Janet would be left to get four tired children into bed. Then she would ensure that all the washing was in the machine and serve Robert's dinner. She was completely caught up in the role of supermum.

Janet's life with Robert at this stage was something of a roller-coaster ride. There was a new adventure and a new venture at every turn. As Robert's business activities expanded, he needed and expected Janet to be with him more of the time. The children were left at home more often, with a babysitter/housekeeper, and gradually each one was sent off to boarding school. Janet's domestic focus shifted more and more towards her public role as Robert Holmes à Court's wife. She began travelling everywhere with him, making his appointments, dialling his overseas phone calls, fielding the media inquiries so he would be disturbed as little as possible, ensuring that meals, clothes, every little detail of their lives went as smoothly as possible. Janet had become very good at organisation; she was indefatigable and energetic, amazingly cheerful in the face of what seemed to others to be subservience to Robert and even indifference on his part. In fact, Robert and Janet were partners in this exciting enterprise and Janet enjoyed her life, admitting in later years that she was always pushing Robert on to bigger and better things. As well, her own profile as a dedicated worker for various public causes was on the rise, and Australia looked on in bemused admiration at this odd couple – the enigmatic, somewhat terrifying and aloof Robert, and the attractive and vivacious Janet. They were the stuff of myth-building in those halcyon years of economic boom. He was much more interesting than the ebullient Alan Bond, she much more fascinating than the dowdy or preening wives of some other business magnates.

Robert had been eyeing Sir Reginald Ansett's seriously troubled air and road transport empire. He was not the only one. Sir Reginald was in his seventies and looking for a successor. Having taken write-offs from the losses of a disastrous finance subsidiary, Associated Securities Ltd (ASL), Ansett's vulnerability was apparent not only to Rupert Murdoch and Sir Peter Abeles, chairman of Thomas Nationwide Transport (TNT), Australia's biggest freight carrier, but to Robert as well. Aviation had always appealed to him, even before he started the University of Western Australia's Flying Club, and Robert was seriously interested in taking over Ansett.

Despite the apparently casual nature of his actions, Robert's acquisition of shares had always been systematic and strategic, not just aimed at making money, and the move on Ansett was no exception. In 1978, Robert acquired 5% of Ansett. On reaching this level, his first target was Sir Peter Abeles, whose TNT company held 13% of the Ansett shares and an agreement with Ansett not to purchase more.

In typical Robert Holmes à Court fashion, Robert had divulged his plans for Ansett to Janet at the Perth Airport. They were on their way to Sydney and Robert said, 'I've just thought of a company we could buy'. 'What's that?', asked Janet. 'Ansett', replied Robert. He wanted to phone his office, so Janet dialled from a public phone and Robert issued instructions about the buying of shares.

Between April and November 1979, Janet and Robert lived for much of the time in Melbourne, in a suite in the Southern Cross Hotel with an adjoining office. It was a flat where the parents of the hotel owner had lived. There Robert focused all his intellect on the battle for Ansett.

Having acquired an option on Abeles's shares, Robert made himself known to Sir Reginald Ansett and declared his intention to acquire 20% of the company. Robert admired the tough old individualist who had built his airline from nothing, and Ansett, who had fallen out with his sons and had no successor, was impressed with Robert's intelligence and charm. Sir Reginald agreed Robert could acquire 20% if he would limit his voting rights. Robert declined and the negotiations broke down, beginning a prolonged game of strategy.

Ansett was a big and famous Australian company and the media were taking a great interest in the gentleman from the west, so boldly making a bid with his relatively small Bell Bros company. It

Bernice Lee on Scarborough Beach, who was later to marry
Fred Ranford, around 1934.

The wedding of Ethnée and Peter Holmes à Court
Johannesburg, 2 October 1936.

Baby Michael Robert Hamilton
Holmes à Court.

Robert as a one-year-old
toddler.

Robert celebrates his third birthday with younger brother, Simon.

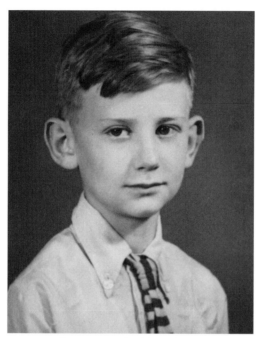

Robert at Cordwalles school.

The young Janet Ranford.

Janet and her brother, John.

University Ball, 1965.

Janet and Robert at her
Graduation Ball.

Robert, with Ethnée, at his
graduation in 1966.

Janet and Robert's wedding day, May 1966.

Janet's father Fred, Janet, Bern, Robert and Ethnée.

With sixteen-week-old baby Peter.

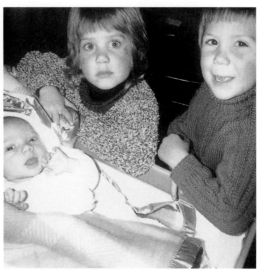

Peter and Catherine.   Catherine, Peter and baby Simon.

Horsing around with Dad.   While Robert planned takeovers,
                                   Janet took care of the children.

It took Robert just fifteen years to become Australia's richest man.

Delighted owners, viewing Tom Roberts' *Settler's Camp* at the *Golden Summers* exhibition.

After winning effective control of Ansett, October 1979.

Robert meeting
the Queen
Mother.

Vernon Brockman, Janet, Sue Connors, Maggie Venerys and
jockey Mark Sestich on race day.

The business world saw Robert and Janet as an indomitable partnership.

Janet and Peter holding the 1984 Melbourne Cup, won by Black Knight.

Robert on Black Knight.

Janet, Peter and Robert at the 1985 Melbourne Cup.

At the National Gallery, Canberra, during the 1986 BHP takeover.

The Holmes à Court family at Middlebury College
in 1987, where Peter was a student.

Paul Keating and Robert touring BHP Wollongong on the day of the
stock market crash, October 1987.

Robert on the day of the stock market crash, October 1987.

was a unique challenge and the press were very excited. Journalists camped outside their suite for days, making it difficult for Robert and Janet to get in and out. One afternoon, Janet received a phone call from a journalist saying, 'You won't believe this Mrs Holmes à Court, but we were just going down to get something to eat and we're all stuck in the lift'. Janet joked, 'Oh how sad', then she and Robert went down in the other lift to go out for a walk and a meal. Janet became friendly with the journalists and gave an interview one night. When asked what Robert's attitude to female pilots would be, she said she didn't think he would be even slightly concerned. They had flown from Moscow to New Delhi on Aeroflot quite happily with an all-female crew. The next day when Janet's views were printed, Sir Reginald rang Robert to tell him to keep 'his bloody wife away from the press'. He was livid because he was, at the time, fighting a public campaign to keep Deborah Wardley, the first female commercial pilot, from flying one of his planes. 'I've seen those Russian women pilots', he said. 'They've got balls.'

One evening Janet and Robert received a call from the front desk saying 'a friend of yours called Alan Bond is here. We are overbooked and the only room available is the one in your flat. Will it be all right if he stays there?'. The Holmes à Courts didn't really know Alan Bond. Janet said, 'Yes, it will be fine, as long as he doesn't have any strange women in his room at night'.

Robert arrived at the point of being Sir Reginald's chosen one. He held 14% of Ansett stock and refused two offers for his stake at profits of many millions, but he told Sir Reginald on 18 October that he would sell if an arrangement could not be reached. Sir Reginald challenged Robert to commit to running the company. Robert agreed and Sir Reginald approved Bell buying 20%, with no restrictions on voting rights.

Robert phoned the two other major shareholders, Rupert Murdoch and Sir Peter Abeles, and they met at Cavan, Murdoch's property, to discuss Robert's plan to distribute the shares at an agreed price. He said he had Sir Reginald's approval, but he would go away if they wished to buy his shares. It was Robert's classic option, an escape hatch for all. From the meeting, Murdoch rang Sir Reginald to confirm his offer to Robert, without divulging the meeting was taking place. Janet recalls the look on their faces when it was revealed she had Sir Reginald's phone number, while neither Murdoch nor Abeles did.

At a meeting the following day, Sir Reginald told the media, 'The only fellow who has always done the right thing in the whole business is Robert Holmes à Court. I will gradually hand over to him'.[7] Robert was invited to work from the Ansett building in Swanston Street. But a month later the agreement came unstuck. Sir Reginald changed his mind. He learnt of the clandestine meeting at Cavan and felt betrayed. More importantly, the main problem for Ansett's directors was that Holmes à Court was not at this stage big enough to buy the shares in Ansett without Ansett buying Bell, as had occurred with the WA Woollen takeover. This time, the deal was vigorously opposed. Janet says Robert was 'absolutely furious' when he learnt of Sir Reginald's change of heart. He felt he had been doublecrossed, but he phoned Murdoch to say simply, 'There's been a slight change of plan. You are now the purchaser and I am the vendor'.

The day all this happened was Janet's thirty-sixth birthday, 29 November 1979. She went to the hairdresser, where they offered her champagne to celebrate. She returned to the Southern Cross in a very happy state and joked that she'd been drinking champagne because she always drank champagne on her birthday. No one had remembered, least of all Robert. From then on, Bert Reuter, Robert's right-hand man, always sent her flowers on her birthday.

The next day Janet and Robert were on the way home to Perth, Robert $11 million wealthier as a result of the sale and with a good deal more experience in the strategy of dealing with aging chairmen.

The four children were at home with a babysitter throughout this period and they were putting together scrap books on Robert, who was in the paper day after day. They were so proud of him and were devastated when he ultimately sold out of the Ansett deal. The next year Peter and Catherine, disappointed in their father's failure to succeed in taking over Ansett, went to school in Melbourne. Peter did not want to return to Christchurch (his Perth school) after the humiliation he felt.

The Bell shareholders weren't disappointed by Robert's failure to take over Ansett; in fact they gave Robert a standing ovation at the annual general meeting. After that sort of profit, they had no intention of withdrawing their support. Over the next twelve months, Robert built strategic stakes in TNT, the Herald and Weekly Times, TVW Enterprises, Quarry Industries, Swan Brewery, and the pastoral group Elder Smith Goldsbrough Mort. Bell share placements were keenly taken up by institutional investors and by late 1980, Robert had more than $100 million in cash, plus credit lines for the same value.

Robert upset the business establishment because his targets were established companies which were considered invulnerable. The efforts of the managers to muster powerful friends to defend these bids led later to inquiries and sometimes jail sentences. Though labelled a greenmailer, Robert always insisted his takeovers were genuine. He would not, however, buy at any price. He would place an appropriate value on a company's shares and he would not exceed that limit. At the point that price was reached, he then became a seller.

Nor did his tactics follow the accepted formula, where a raider would buy around 20% of a company in secret, then declare himself and make a formal takeover bid. Robert would secretly buy 5%, announce himself and his intentions, usually by a leak to a selected journalist, in order to flush out any other potential bidders, and then place himself in a better position to price his bid. If then there was an eager competitor, he could sell at a profit; if not, he could make his takeover play without being locked into a bidding war. It was always a win-win situation for Robert.

By June 1980, Robert had spent $25 million acquiring 10% of TNT and had established a good relationship with Sir Peter Abeles. Abeles said publicly that Robert never bought a share in TNT without asking him first. Later that year, the two men jointly paid $8 million to buy 22% of the Belgian shipping company, ABC Containerline. Each new venture enabled Robert to gain insights into new industries, learning as he went.

Travel became a larger part of the Holmes à Courts' life. First to the farm regularly, and then to the east coast, with occasional trips overseas. Robert enjoyed his children, but he did not have much time to give. Peter says he never saw his father in the morning – he had either gone, or was away, or asleep. Peter recalls that at night, he and Catherine would be in bed and hear the car come up the drive. The wrought iron door latch would click and resonate through the house and they would rush to play with and see Dad. He remembers Dad's homecoming as a happy family time. Robert would roll up the newspaper and smack it on his hand saying, 'Up, up, up to bed. Up to bed', and they'd reluctantly go to bed. Peter's memory is of a mother who did absolutely everything for them as children (which he took for granted), and a father who was away quite a lot of the time, 'but when we were together, being a very happy family'.

Catherine had a downstairs bedroom and used to get up and down from her bed interrupting Janet and Robert's evening meal, saying she was hungry and thirsty or she had a stomach ache or a headache (which she didn't). Most nights Robert would come in and sit on her bed and talk to her and say goodnight. While she did not see a lot of him, she has memories of her dad as a real friend. He would say to her, 'How's my best mate?', and while he may have said that to all the kids, it made Catherine feel special. She didn't like to hear the conversations down the hall and not be part of them, so she'd go out with any excuse. Her memory of her mother was that she was always there, taking her and Peter to school, picking them up and feeding them as they came through the door. Snacks were celery and carrots; there was no sweet cordial or Coca-Cola. As Janet's mother had fed her healthy food all her childhood, Janet was determined to feed her children the same way.

The children don't remember ever having stories read to them. Robert would talk to them, but not read. Janet helped with the homework and very occasionally Robert would play cricket or ball with them at the weekend. The busier Robert became, the less time there was for the children and he saw less of Simon and Paul than he did of Peter and Catherine. It was difficult to travel with four children, so Simon and Paul would often stay behind with grandparents or babysitters. Janet remembers Robert being quite excited about taking Peter and Catherine on their first trip to Melbourne. Robert took a suite in the Hotel Windsor. It was an old-style hotel and he thought they would enjoy that. Catherine was very young and she spent much of the time playing with the linen hand towels in the bathroom, using them as tablecloths and putting them around the room. On another occasion, Simon and Paul stayed home with a nurse while Peter and Catherine went to London.

But all four children were taken to Disneyworld when Robert went to Florida to buy the stallion Pago Pago[8] for his breeding strategy at the Stud. Robert suggested they take his nephew, Will Holmes à Court and his wife Jane with them to help with the children. Janet remembers it as a nightmare trip. Their plane was a day late in leaving Perth, throwing the entire trip out, leaving Janet to spend 'almost the whole trip on the phone in America, holding on, listening to music' to alter bookings.

Janet was the travelling secretary, packer, chauffeur, luggage organiser. She booked into the hotels and she carried the bags. Robert carried nothing. Robert did not expect to organise himself and Janet had not yet acquired the skills, nor the confidence, to delegate to others, so she endured a difficult and uncomfortable time, despite Robert's wealth.

Will and Jane viewed the trip as a great opportunity and they were thrilled to accept Robert's invitation to look after the children. Will and Jane flew to Perth and spent a week there before departing initially for the UK. There they became the nannies, taking the children around London while Robert and Janet did their own thing. Robert surprised Will because he seemed to be oblivious to the effects of jetlag. His advice was to just keep on going until they got back into the cycle, an approach which didn't work for Will and Jane, who became very tired. During the week they visited Heytesbury, the family seat. Then they flew to Washington DC.

Robert did not like the hotel and insisted they move. Janet had no option but to pack up everything, arrange another hotel, and move the lot yet again. Much of the time they sat around waiting for Robert to decide what he wanted to do, or else waiting for room service. It would be one o'clock in the morning and they would still be waiting for room service. There seemed to be no direction to Robert's plans. Everyone became tired and frustrated, including Robert. But he kept changing his mind; he worked himself into a state of extreme frustration, Will observed:

> by exceedingly poor planning. Janet just wanted to do what Robert wanted to do, but nothing seemed to work out smoothly ... Robert always seemed to run his life this way, waiting. It might have been he was thinking things through, but the world waited while he waited and it was a very frustrating process for people around, just waiting because Robert was running the show ... Things would have to happen without him thinking he was being pushed into spots, because he wanted to control the situation, but it just got out of hand. Instead of saying, 'Let's have dinner at eight', time would drift by until late and then he would say, 'Yes, we should have dinner. Let's look up room service', and room service would take hours with everyone exhausted and Robert getting irritable.

Will thought Robert's judgement was affected by the travel stress and that eating irregular meals contributed to the problem.

No one except Janet knew of Robert's diabetes. It was a well-guarded secret, kept even from his children until his death, though Catherine had guessed and kept it to herself. Janet would dispose of his needles and no concessions were made for his illness, certainly not a proper eating habit. Amazingly, Robert found ways of managing the disruption travel caused to his system and the irregular eating patterns his meetings and endless telephone calls necessitated. He could out-sit and out-pause everyone. He could sit through a seventeen-hour meeting, as he did on one occasion, and then come home to phone the other side of the world to mull over strategy or to decide his share trading for the day. He might then sleep for an hour and go into the office again. Janet says, 'His stamina was extraordinary'. The bowl of sweet biscuits would be nearby and blocks of chocolate were always in his bedroom drawer.

It seems highly likely that such a routine and such management of the sugar levels in his system would produce extreme tiredness and irritability and that this, without knowing of Robert's illness, was what Will and Jane witnessed. In due course Robert announced he'd had enough and was leaving on the first flight. Then Will and Jane suggested they take the four kids on to Disneyworld and meet Robert and Janet later in Orlando after they had completed their business. Will remembers Janet had tears in her eyes as they left with the children. When they arrived the next day, Robert settled in and began to enjoy himself. Will recalls, 'He loved to sit around the pool and just chat. He enjoyed playing video games. He just liked to socialise with the family or with close confidants. He could have sat there all night, but I wasn't used to keeping those sort of hours, nor the jetlag and travel stress'. Although very tired at the time, Will and Jane remember the experience fondly as it consolidated their relationship with Janet and the children in a way which allowed them to play a closer role later on when they were needed.

Janet learnt over time, and from some difficult experiences, to be more proactive in organising Robert. He always ran the show but, with experience, she was able to anticipate, adapt and have contingency plans. She provided the environment where Robert could do what he wanted. She oiled the wheels all the time. Her interests were his interests. They were 'both very busy doing what Robert wanted to do'. As Janet learnt to do her job more effectively, Robert depended on her more and more. They were a very good team, but an unequal partnership. She was subservient and malleable, Robert's best friend and someone with unique social skills who provided Robert with a human face.

The price she paid for what she received from this unusual relationship was that she was unable to be a mother to her children in the way she would have wished. But that was a choice she made knowingly. Janet believed:

if you were performing your role as a mother properly, your children would grow up to be beautifully independent individuals, you'd push them out of the nest and then you'd be left with your husband. If you attached yourself to your children and neglected your husband then when your children went, you'd be on your own, so I felt I had to put Robert first. So I did unashamedly at the time.

That decision led to the development of four very independent and strong-minded young adults who would have their say, when the time came, about the future of Heytesbury.

In early 1981, Elders Goldsbrough Mort was vulnerable, facing a slump because of a major drought. A *Business Review Weekly* story in February revealed the Bell Group owned 7% of the shares. The alarmed company board, shaken out of its complacency, reacted quickly and defensively. They would not speak with Robert, instead approaching the South Australian Government to enact legislation to prohibit shareholdings of more than 10%. Robert announced a $120 million takeover bid for half the company on 19 March 1981. He personally visited Acting Premier Roger Goldsworthy and Attorney General Trevor Griffin to reassure them, as he would do with Prime Minister Bob Hawke and Treasurer Paul Keating during his later BHP bid.

He told them that Elders Goldsbrough Mort would retain its separate identity; he would not disturb its traditional business; it would continue to provide a broad-based service to South Australia; and employment opportunities in the State would be maintained or enhanced.[9] The Acting Premier's response was to decide in favour of Robert. His charm and reassurance won the day. There was no legislation to stop his bid.

Elders Goldsbrough Mort gathered in its friends, but the company was never to be the same. Returning from the meeting with the Acting Premier, Robert received a message via his pilot that the friends were buying. He decided then the situation was disadvantageous to Bell and sold out at a profit of $16.5 million, but only after he was assured the buyer was known to, and approved by,

Elders Goldsbrough Mort. A furore developed over the buyout, with accusations that the friends had acted in concert. Robert's profit was not taxed because he sold the company that had acquired the shares, Petroleum Distributors, rather than the shares themselves – a tax loophole he had exploited earlier and which the Federal Government immediately moved to outlaw. Robert was eventually forced by the South Australian Government to proceed with his takeover offer even though he had sold out.

Robert was out of Elders Goldsbrough Mort before John Elliott came on the scene, but their later encounters were spawned by the circumstances Robert created for his Elders bid. In 1982, Robert bought shares in Carlton and United Breweries (CUB), which held 50% of Elders IXL. Elliott bought out Robert and concluded, wrongly as he would discover later, that Robert would sell under pressure. A year later, Robert moved on Elders (which included CUB), again with the same result. He was also building up a stake in the Herald and Weekly Times group but was finding the going tough so he turned his attention to the UK where he was unknown; there he demonstrated that greenmail was not his mission. He sought and won control of the British entertainment group, Associated Communications Corporation (ACC). The takeover allowed Robert to apply all the skills he had acquired to date. It transformed his activities and expanded his base for the future.

Robert enjoyed London. He took his aristocratic heritage very seriously as evidenced by his thoughts of buying the Heytesbury home, an eighteenth-century mansion with Elizabethan origins. The seventeen bedroom house, which belonged to the Holmes à Court family from 1743–1926, had been bought in 1933 by Siegfried Sassoon, the famous poet of World War I. In 1978, Robert visited Sassoon's son George, who had inherited the house and allowed it to become run down. Robert did not make an offer on the house.

Robert's first foray into the UK in the early seventies with Emu Wines yielded a good profit when the takeover did not proceed. In 1980, he put in a bid for the *The Times*, perhaps to annoy Rupert

Murdoch, and in 1981 he bought a small stake in Britain's Rugby Portland Cement. His next UK stake was an acquisition of 4% of Rolls Royce, from which he audaciously bid for 25% of the company, the highest level a foreigner could control. Robert admired Rolls Royce cars and by 1986 had seven of them in his collection, but the move was probably designed more to boost his image than for its business potential.

Once again, he gave a purring assurance to fellow shareholders that 'he was not seeking to control Rolls Royce – it would maintain its existing traditions', but his bid was rejected and Robert was rebuked by the City of London Takeover panel for not seeking its approval before making his offer. Robert pleaded ignorance and retreated. ACC was a different matter.

It is thought that Robert began his foray into ACC as an investment into a company whose shares were undervalued as a result of some disastrous film investments, and that originally he did not intend to take control.[10] ACC had a chain of cinemas, a chain of London theatres, Northern Songs (a music publishing company, which included The Beatles' song book), commercial property valued at £90 million, a travel and leisure division and a half interest in a television franchise. The initial share buy was only 2% of the capital in non-voting shares.

Lord Lew Grade, the 75-year-old chairman of ACC, fancied himself as a movie mogul in the tradition of Samuel Goldwyn or Louis B Mayer – autocratic heads of Hollywood studios who decided the fate of stars and movies and gambled many millions on their creative judgements of scripts and directors. Grade had built a highly successful company, but in the seventies had overseen a number of failed movies. These included the disaster film *Raise the Titanic*, where the budget had blown out from $US8 million to $US42 million. Grade was a former tapdancer, a genuine showman who loved the film industry, but he was not a good businessman. The company and the senior executives, who all drove Rolls Royces, enjoyed the liberties their ACC credit cards gave them. The remuneration packages and the terms of deals negotiated by Grade didn't go to the board.

Robert made himself known to Grade at a meeting set up by Lord Windlesham whom Robert had met in Perth. As he had done in past company takeovers, Robert revealed during that meeting that he had bought about a million shares. He was informed that he had bought at good value. As the year progressed, Robert cultivated a father-son relationship with Grade (the age difference was thirty-one years), who was himself facing a personal crisis with his disintegrating empire, and who confided in Robert. Robert stroked the older man's ego and Grade thought him a charming young man. Robert continued to buy ACC shares and, realising the company had very serious problems, took a keen interest in finding out as much as he could about the way the company was run. Grade and his wife Kathie took to Robert and Janet and wined and dined them, finding them very pleasant company. Grade said:

Robert would come in to see me at the office regularly and sit with me while I conducted various business negotiations. He appeared to be fascinated with the way I operated and just by being in the same room, he was, he said, learning so much about the entertainment industry . . . As we spent more and more time in each other's company . . . I grew to like him immensely.[11]

By September, at the time of the annual general meeting, Robert held 30% of ACC's non-voting shares. A revolt was brewing among the hundred shareholders present and Grade's bluster did not go down well. Robert knew he had to prise Grade's voting shares out of him and he set about, with Janet's help, strengthening the bond between them through social engagements. Grade arranged dinner and a private screening for Janet and Robert of the recently completed film *On Golden Pond*, which they thoroughly enjoyed. Robert, Janet, Grade and his wife travelled together to the US to see the ACC US operation and, at Grade's instigation, went to Las Vegas. There were flowers and fruit in the opulent suite. Wherever they went they were given fabulous attention, the best seats in the house and no bills to pay because they were the guests of the ACC chairman. According to Janet, wherever they went, money seemed to jump out of the slot machines at them as well.

Robert and Janet enjoyed meeting Sammy Davis Jnr who was starring in a show at that time. They went backstage to meet him and Robert asked him to visit Perth for TVW7's 1982 Telethon. Robert enjoyed Sammy's kind of music and was a real fan.

Grade, who was now without a finance director as the result of a dispute, increasingly came to see Robert as his saviour. By December, when Robert held 57% of the non-voting shares, Grade invited him to join the board. He agreed to sell 2.2% of his own voting shares, after which Robert and Janet returned to London for Christmas with their family and Robert attended his first board meeting. There he found the depth of the problems he had invested in. He was horrified. There were loans outstanding of £50 million and no money to pay the interest. The company was on the verge of insolvency. Robert called in his Perth staff to go through the books. Bert Reuter arrived and stayed eighteen months.

Grade entertained the Holmes à Courts over the Christmas season and on 3 January 1982 Robert travelled with Grade to the US to see the New York operation, staying at the ACC apartment in Manhattan. Grade said he took Robert into his confidence. He figured that with Robert around, all his troubles could be solved. Robert reasoned that, with Grade out of the way, he could sort out the company. Martin Starger in the New York office was the highest paid ACC executive and Robert was horrified to learn the level of his remuneration. According to Falk and Prince:[12]

Holmes à Court played his trump card on the way back to London by telling Grade he'd support him, pay him and give him a generous contract but as the company was bankrupt, it was only fair that he had the main say in the way the company was run, for which he needed Grade's votes. He further suggested to Grade that it might be his duty as a director to investigate the relationship the old man had with Starger.

So on 6 January 1982, Grade gave Robert his word that he would sell him his voting shares in ACC. Robert made his bid for the company, beginning one of the most complex power struggles the London courts had seen. (The legality – and the process – of the takeover was examined by the courts.) This time, taking a profit was not Robert's plan; he intended to be the sole shareholder in ACC. Wednesday 13 January 1982 was one of the longest working days Robert had put in. As the *Business Review Weekly* reported, it didn't begin well because the news came from Australia that Paint the Stars, the two-year-old colt Robert had bought for a record $825,000, had finished last in his debut at Flemington Racecourse.[13] Paint the Stars was suffering from shinsplints and proved to be one of Robert's biggest disappointments in racing. But the day was ultimately to yield its reward. In a meeting that began before lunch, Robert gave the ACC board until midnight to accept his bid. Just before midnight Gerald Ronson, a character more like Alan Bond than Robert, arrived with a higher bid. The meeting continued until 4.00 a.m., when Robert's offer was accepted. Ronson went to court alleging a 'cosy deal' and the appeal was upheld. Robert launched another separate bid and took control in late April. The company taking over ACC was not Bell, but TVW Enterprises.

Robert considered that as the offer of a contract to Grade had been made through the Bell Group, now that TVW had control they were not obliged to honour the agreement. He announced to the press that he did not consider himself bound by any former contracts the company had made. Grade walked out of the company he had built on 17 June 1982, with his pension. Over the period of a year Robert had gone from being in Grade's eyes 'that Australian', to 'my great friend Robert', to 'that man'. Grade regarded Robert as a major miscalculation in his life. Heads began to roll at ACC, from the tea-lady on up. At board level, Robert asked for the resignation of all directors, then reinstated the three men appointed by the London Takeover Board to remain to help him sort out the mess. They included Sir Michael Clapham. Robert quipped, 'I've fired two lords and three knights and I'm now going to appoint some men of stature'.

Robert sold ATV Music, PRT Video, the Airport Park Hotel and Jet Save. He managed to find only five of an alleged sixteen

Rolls Royces, using one for himself when in London. The film division found itself facing very different criteria from the ACC under Grade. Alan Pakula, the director of *Sophie's Choice*, who was paid a million dollars to write and direct the film, had to put up half the completion guarantee money if the film went over budget, a tactic that worked because the film came in under budget. Grade, meanwhile, did not get his screen credit on *Sophie's Choice*, which became a great critical success. Robert said he had no knowledge of the decision to remove the credit and that *Sophie's Choice* only went ahead through his own good graces. Jim Henson was forced to modify his aspirations with the post-production and distribution of *Dark Crystal*, which bombed at the box office.

A little more than a year after he took over ACC, Robert gave an interview to *Australian Business*.[14] ACC, Robert said, would be the strongest performer in the Bell Group in the financial year. His holding company was worth $44 million in 1981 and its last stated profits were $7 million. In the 1981–82 financial year, ACC made a $60.1 million loss; the next year Robert was anticipating a healthy profit. The film division was back in the black, the theatres in the West End of London were enjoying their best season ever and, with prime income-producing property, Robert was quite confident he had not paid too much for ACC as suggested by his critics. 'Grade was on the show side of show business; he [Robert] was on the business side.' At the previous annual meeting of Bell shareholders he was able to tell those who had invested $16,000 in Bell ten years earlier that they had an investment on that day worth $1 million. Robert had no ten-year plan; he said his only strategy for the Bell Group was to enhance its existing business. He made a prophetic statement: 'I really don't know where the company will be in ten years' time. It might even find a better manager than myself'.[15] By 1993, Janet was managing a very different company in Heytesbury.

Janet always went to shareholders' meetings. Robert being as shy and retiring as he was, Janet stood by him, organised cups of tea and introduced him around. She comments:

Quite seriously, Bell Group shareholders' meetings were like church services where everyone went to pay homage to Robert. Robert just loved it. He played to the gallery. He was a good actor in those situations and he loved the applause. My father would nudge me and say 'They're clapping for money'.

Few shares in Australia would have been as successful for their investors as Bell Group. After the ACC takeover, the initial $16,000 investment in Bell was worth $2.3 million and Robert had 400 shareholders attending his 1983 meeting, more than attended BHP's annual meeting. By 1985, the $16,000 was worth $8 million, assuming all share issues were taken up and dividends reinvested.

Sir Michael Clapham remained on Robert's ACC board until after Robert's death. There too, Robert had directors much older than himself. Deputy Chairman of ICI until retirement at sixty-two, Deputy Chairman of Lloyd's Bank, President of the Confederation of British Industry, Sir Michael was an experienced and cultured man, who said of Robert:

I don't think I ever got to know him really well. I couldn't understand quite how his mind worked. I couldn't understand why he wanted directors whose opinion he had never sought before taking action, only after it . . . Why employ dogs and bark for yourself? But he was supremely confident in his own judgement and he didn't really want other people's advice. It was not the way I'd been used to being treated as a director. I'd always belonged to a rather collegial board. In ICI we took decisions as a body. It was not that way on the ACC board or the Bell board or the Heytesbury board later on. The decisions were the chairman's. The board was there to comment and help, but not to take the major decision.

Only once did Sir Michael disagree with Robert's handling of matters – over the ACC pension fund. Robert wanted to close down the fund, which had a handsome surplus, and start a new one. He was convinced he could have used the cash better. Sir Michael wrote, 'Dear Robert, Your project for the pension fund is one that as a Trustee of the fund I couldn't recommend and as a director I would not support'. Robert left the money where it was. It was a misuse of a company pension fund that brought down Robert Maxwell, the British tycoon who died mysteriously at sea.

To the various letters Sir Michael wrote to Robert, he received an answer in writing to just one, all other responses were by phone. There is very little documentation of Bell business dealings. Board minutes meticulously recorded decisions, but not the reasons why decisions were taken.

Robert's philosophy regarding boards was that boards should never initiate anything; they should only approve or disapprove of propositions put up to them by management. The board's role was to be reflective, to provide checks and balances on what management could do. The board shouldn't modify a proposition, but ask management to come back with a different proposition.

At one level, Robert was careful about every dollar he expended, from establishing a share price he would not exceed when engaged in a takeover, to setting the level of remuneration of his executives and directors (which was never generous), even to approving personally all items of capital expenditure over $1,000. He would have invoices in the same pile from several dollars to several millions of dollars. Professional consultants usually had problems extracting fair payment without a debate.

On the other hand, when he had a personal fascination with an area, he was willing to lose a lot of money to gain experience and understanding or else to achieve a goal. He then applied the same approach as he did to his studs and horses – spend extravagantly to get it right. He liked to be regarded as someone who did not waste money. When accused of paying too much for ACC shares, he was pleased to prove his critics wrong. But with both the newspaper business and with BHP, he spent money with far less caution than he did with all other business dealings.

The newspaper business fascinated him. He began in 1973 by acquiring a 49% controlling interest in the ailing *Albany Advertiser* for $77,000, in the town where he first went into business. Robert said the price was double the newspaper's worth. One day Bert Reuter phoned Robert saying, 'I've got some good news and some bad news. The *Albany Advertiser*'s had a fire and there's a lot of damage'. 'Oh yes', Robert said, 'and now what's the bad news?'. He immediately saw the chance to rebuild and put in new equipment; the apparent disaster could be turned into a benefit.

Within three years he had overhauled the newspaper, introducing new technology and turning the company into a profit centre. Control of the country paper brought with it the Albany radio station 6VA and another country newspaper, the *Great Southern Herald* in Katanning. In 1979, Robert began buying shares in broadcaster TVW Enterprises, which had controlling interests in TVW7 Perth, SAS10 Adelaide, two radio stations and some cinemas.[16]

But it was the profitable Perth newspaper the *West Australian* that Robert had in his sights. Late in 1979, he approached the chairman of the Herald and Weekly Times Group, Sir Keith Macpherson, who informed Robert in no uncertain terms that any sale would be over his dead body. Robert responded, 'For a moment I thought you were going to say it was not for sale at any price'.

Robert therefore decided to launch a competitor to the *West Australian*. With the head of TVW Enterprises, Sir James Cruthers (a former journalist), he discussed launching an alternative, but they fell out. They both had strong wills and big egos. Sir James had built TVW7 and, although he didn't have a very big shareholding, he regarded it as his baby. He was an experienced newspaper man and Robert was a Johnny-come-lately. There was much potential for conflict between them.

Robert spent hours discussing his philosophy and learning about the newspaper business with journalists he knew and with contacts who understood the press. He got to know journalists well because he did believe in talking to them and educating them about his business plans. It was not a short-term aim to feed disinformation to suit his purpose; it was to build up a relationship of trust. So journalists always got through to Robert or had their calls answered.

Two journalists he cultivated through the seventies were John McIlwraith, the Western Australian correspondent for the *Financial*

Review, a journalist with Canberra Press Gallery experience; and Alec Mairs who was the finance editor of the *West Australian* from 1971–78. Robert got to know both men well after they took an interest in his takeover of WA Woollen. With them he built up an understanding about when he was speaking off the record and when he could be quoted. They respected his confidences and indulged his penchant for gossip, which journalists thrive on. Over time, they would speak of his business philosophy and eventually his attitudes to newspapers. When Alec left the *West Australian* to go into business on his own as an accountant, Robert offered him a job, which he declined, but he did agree to work as a consultant on individual projects. They spent countless hours over cups of tea and on the phone chatting about newspapers. Then one day Robert announced to Alec he wanted to start a newspaper in Perth from scratch. John Reynolds, whom he had met as executive officer of the Joondalup Development Corporation which Robert chaired, moved to Bell and worked for Robert in the personnel area. Both Alec and John developed an understanding of Robert, admired him and got along with him; they found him an extremely difficult man to work for, but struggled hard at understanding him and achieving what he wanted.

John Reynolds, with Alec Mairs as consultant, was given the job of setting up the newspaper. The first meeting was on a trestle table on the first floor of the AMP Building, in very inauspicious surroundings. The paper was first called the *Perth Advertiser*, but Robert liked the name *Western Mail*, which had a history and a strength to it. They brought together people from inside and outside the Bell Group to produce the first edition of a weekend paper which would ultimately challenge the *West Australian*, a paper grown complacent in its monopoly of the market and through its management by the Herald and Weekly Times group based in Melbourne. The morale at WA Newspapers was low, so a plan for a new paper captured the local journalists' attention and attracted some of the top journalists to the *Western Mail*.

The first edition, launched to much fanfare on 8 November 1980, was a disappointment, but under Robert's leadership John Reynolds's team (which was joined by Tim Treadgold and Simon Hadfield) improved the masthead and the appearance of the paper and added additional sections to the paper. Barry Farmer, who had been a journalist for the *West Australian* for twenty-one years had become the racing writer, the prime sporting job of that paper. Robert wanted him on the team. The potential excitement was too much for Barry and he agreed to join him. Then Barry discovered he may not only be working for the paper; there were the studs and the racehorses and, if things worked out, he could be involved in Robert's racing affairs. So Barry joined the *Western Mail* for the same money he had been earning at the *West Australian*, despite the drop in status.

Robert also made a general and informal approach to John McIlwraith to come and work for him, to which he replied, 'I'd rather be your Boswell than your slave', inferring he preferred to write from the outside of Robert's organisation. John says:

He used to collect people. He'd sometimes pursue a well-known journalist or television executive but once he'd collected them, he'd lose interest and actually became quite critical of them sometimes. He was fascinated by journalists with reputations, and he was fascinated by Hollywood and film stars for a while.

Robert's interest in and association with Sammy Davis Jnr confirmed this revealing characteristic. Davis had accepted Robert's invitation to the TVW7 Telethon and they became friends.

Working on a weekly paper was a different proposition from working on a daily. The team was keen, they worked hard for long hours and they were severely under-resourced given their objective. But progress was made, even if at substantial financial loss to the Bell Group. Robert kept a watchful eye. One Saturday afternoon, he came to the AMP Building with a heap of cheques drawn on the newspaper and tore them all up in front of the executives, throwing them around the room like confetti. They sat with their mouths open, wondering what was going to happen next. It was Robert's way of saying that they were not looking closely enough at expenditure. But he could see beyond the immediate position, and the end-play could be many moves away. He wanted to take over the *West*

Australian. There were many paths to that objective and one of them was to begin by starting another newspaper, a hazardous approach with few models for success.

The Australian media speculated about Holmes à Court as a potential new rival to Rupert Murdoch or Kerry Packer, an image Robert did not discourage because it helped build up the perception of power. However, Robert was not of their ilk. Alec Mairs describes Robert as 'probably the most non-interventionist proprietor you could ever wish for'. He would never ring up and direct Alec to do anything to do with the general running of the paper. He would ring with a suggestion, always interesting and well based in logic, then leave Alec to recognise the value of the suggestion. However, he did consider the editorial page to be his space. As Alec puts it:

> *He would often ring on a Saturday. I'd usually get the dreaded phone call at home to review what was in the paper and he'd say, 'I don't like that story; it was too shallow; we didn't flesh it out enough', or 'That was a great front page', 'That was strong'. He took a great interest in the editorial, which was always faxed to him for comment. No editorial would go to press without Robert's approval. He wanted to learn everything he could about a newspaper, then expand.*

Having begun buying shares in TVW in 1979, Robert continued to buy, grappling with Alan Bond in the market. By July 1981, he had 22% of the company which he would later merge with the *Western Mail*. But Robert's resolve to take over the bigger target of the Herald and Weekly Times did not lessen. Each time he visited Melbourne, he would request a meeting with Sir Keith Macpherson, but it was always declined. Robert chose his 1981 shareholders' meeting to announce his takeover offer for a total of 50% of the shares of the Herald and Weekly Times. A reporter from the *Age* turned to his colleagues. 'Jesus', he said. The word carried through the room.[17]

In an interview with the *Bulletin*, Robert said that the media, transport and resources were the three main interests for his company; that he found the role of entrepreneur 'deeply satisfying'; that his talent was 'to put together the ingredients'. 'They've criticised me on the grounds that I haven't had any experience in running a newspaper. I don't want to run a newspaper. I'll get the best man in the world, Sir Larry Lamb, to run the newspapers. I have other work to do'.[18]

This time round the offer for the Herald and Weekly Times did not succeed but the *Western Mail* began to collect a following. On Rupert Murdoch's advice, Robert went on to appoint Sir Larry Lamb, a seasoned Fleet Street journalist, as editor of the *Western Mail*.[19] Sir Larry had increased circulation to 150,000 by 1983, using the attraction of high-prized bingo games. In 1984, Robert developed the idea of offering free classified advertising. He also agreed to pay a dollar to charity for every copy of the newspaper sold on the first weekend of the promotion. 283,000 copies of the paper with eighty pages of free advertising were printed, ostensibly as part of TVW7's charity Telethon, at an estimated cost to the *Western Mail* of $500,000. The *Western Mail*, which came out on Friday evening and put out updated editions on Saturday, aimed to break new ground in Australian publishing by publishing continual edition updates between Friday evening and Sunday morning. The paper claimed a circulation of 160,000 while the *West Australian* sold 238,000 copies and the *Sunday Times* sold 252,000. The *Western Mail* had $20 million worth of printing equipment which allowed full colour throughout the paper. They proposed to run a 270-pager with a sixty-page full-colour magazine insert.[20]

Every idea and response was thrown at the *Western Mail*, including advertising on the Bell Group's radio station. It was a very aggressive campaign and as rival papers joined the advertising war, money continued to flow out of the Bell Group to subsidise the *Western Mail*, at the rate of $12 million a year over its six-year life.[21] It was the only loss in the business that Robert tolerated.

Robert held high ideals for the media, which he expounded on in the Graham Perkin memorial address he gave to the Melbourne Press Club in November 1985. He spoke of the editor's and the proprietor's duty to maintain the integrity of the press and to comment on government and the business world. He described journalism as one of the great professions in the world and separated print from television in its importance in preserving Australian culture, 'seeing the world through Australian eyes'.[22] If Robert was not then a media mogul – he controlled ACC in the UK, TVW7, SAS10, radio stations in Perth and Adelaide, two Western Australian country stations, thirteen cinemas and nine drive-ins in 1986 – he planned to be. He kept the heat up on the Herald and Weekly Times, on Fairfax and on Packer's Consolidated Press Holdings through the stock market, all the time informing journalists of his views with not-for-attribution quotes and information.

Although selective about which journalists he would speak to, he cultivated various senior financial journalists to whom he would speak for hours, including Terry McCrann (*The Age*), Brian Frith (*The Australian*), Robert Gottliebsen (*Business Review Weekly*) and John McIlwraith (*Financial Review*). The time he invested on the phone yielded very favourable coverage for Robert, as he well knew it would. He leaked information, gossiped about his competitors, floated ideas, gave off-the-record briefings at such length that journalists, anxious to get on with writing their stories, sometimes couldn't close a conversation and get off the phone. Robert chose their company rather than the company of his business peers. Certainly they had a use, and other businessmen were his competitors, but he genuinely preferred their conversation. Most of them admired Robert and felt privileged to have his ear. He played games with them as well as engaging them in occasional battles. He would rebuke them for their errors. He sent a calculator to Terry McCrann, the *Age*'s business editor in 1982, when he disagreed with Terry's interpretation of the Bell Group's accounts and followed that with the calculator's instruction book when he still didn't get them right in Robert's view.

Although Robert spoke of the public interest outweighing a businessman's discomfort when debate and analysis are public, he did not appreciate an article by Terry McCrann in the *Age* that the Bell Group was doing badly when a Bell share issue was undersubscribed by 95% (this on the day Robert was to address potential investors at a luncheon). He sued Terry personally, not the publisher. When the *Australian*'s business editor Trevor Sykes described Australia's richest man as 'miserly and parsimonious', Robert phoned him reverse charge, but these were minor hiccups in generally congenial relationships. When Peter Smark questioned Robert about the writ he served on Terry, Robert said, 'That was quite friendly. It was my duty to do that. It's what he deserved. He has no sense of humour: I tell him that when he's working for me, it will all be ironed out'. 'When you're running the world?', quipped Peter. 'Yes', said Robert with a laugh.[23] Robert's files contain the draft manuscripts of several attempts by different writers to write a profile or an article about him. He would cooperate, then withdraw support, to the frustration of the writer and sometimes fury of the editor who had to find a substitute story at the last minute.

Late in 1986, the move the Australian media world was expecting and Robert was waiting for finally took place. Rupert Murdoch, on 3 December, bid $1.8 billion for the Herald and Weekly Times to claim what he considered his birthright. On 24 December, Robert made a $1.95 billion bid in a classic Christmas Eve raid. On 1 January 1987, he improved his offer to $2.025 billion. On 4 January, Fairfax bid $910 million for the Herald and Weekly Times affiliate, Queensland Press Ltd, linked to Robert's offer for the parent company. On 9 January, Murdoch's News Group upped its offer to $2.3 billion, topping Robert's and Fairfax's with a $1.05 billion offer for the Queensland affiliate as well.[24]

On 15 January, after Murdoch was forced by the Australian Broadcasting Authority to give up his controlling position in the Australian company because of his American citizenship, Murdoch and Robert agreed on a Herald and Weekly Times carve-up. While Fairfax made a subsequent larger bid, it was rejected by the Herald and Weekly Times board and Murdoch's restructure passed the legal test. Robert had extracted an agreement from Murdoch that he would pay $200 million for West Australian Newspapers and $260 million for HSV7, with the proviso that in the event of the sale of HSV7 to anyone else, the monies paid above $260 million would be subtracted from the price paid for West Australian Newspapers. When HSV7 later went to Fairfax for $320 million and the Herald and Weekly Times rural papers for $40 million, Robert had $100 million slashed off the price of the *West Australian*. The Bell Group had an asset in the *West Australian*, which was a newspaper monopoly in Perth and made a net profit of $10 million in 1987.[25] The long wait had at last paid off. Robert felt vindicated.

On 20 January, Alan Bond announced he had taken over Kerry Packer's radio and television interests for $1.055 billion. He was trumping his arch rival from the West, or so he thought.[26] Australian television would never be the same. The massive debt altered the nature of production. Robert's tactics in the West had reduced the value of the *West Australian* and the venture with the *Western Mail* had paid off. He now set his sights on Fairfax and the *Financial Review*. His down-market venture with the *Western Mail* was not to his taste. It had served its purpose; now he could focus on a quality paper which suited his business interests. He also had in his sights the *Times on Sunday* and New Zealand's *National Business Review*.

Meanwhile, Warwick Fairfax announced his bid for the family company on 30 August 1987. Robert and Packer both wanted the *Financial Review*. The price was close to $300 million. On another of Robert's negotiating marathons, conducted on a return flight to Perth with Laurie Connell, Robert got the assets he wanted – the *Australian Financial Review* and the *Times on Sunday*, the *National Business Review* and the Macquarie Network for $475 million. The *Financial Review* was making tax profits of around $14 million, while the *Times on Sunday* was losing money and Macquarie was earning $2 million. Altogether it was a very good buy.[27]

Janet had been closely involved in all of this activity, though always in the apparently peripheral role of dutiful wife. It was an exciting and heady time. Here they were, from small-time Perth, now in control of the biggest media group in the UK, bidding for huge stakes against the major players in Australia's business and political life. Ansett Transport was one thing; control of major newspapers was another. Life with Robert was always exciting.

THE GOOD WIFE

The children had been marginalised in the whirl of their father's takeovers; Janet had decided by now that Robert had to be her main focus and the children would grow, in any event, into independent adults leading their own lives. Robert argued that the children should be sent to boarding school for their secondary schooling. Their mother did not want her kids to go to boarding school, but she did not express that opinion very loudly. She knew it was a *fait accompli;* they would be going. The choice of school was partly precipitated by Robert's move on Ansett and the fact that they would be living in Melbourne much of that year (1979). The choice for Peter was Geelong Grammar, while Catherine would go to Glamorgan for a year before joining Peter at Geelong. Simon and Paul would remain in Perth with carers while Janet and Robert came and went. Janet felt guilty about the children but also felt some relief in that she thought school would bring some stability to Peter and Catherine's lives. Being left at home, with their parents coming and going, increasingly meant that the children would be without structure and discipline.

Robert simply believed in boarding school as a part of life. He thought it character building, that it toughened you up. It had certainly toughened up the little seven-year-old who went to Cordwalles School in Natal. Robert didn't believe Peter was tough enough and thought it would be a good experience for him. Janet was sad about sending Peter and Catherine off at the ages of eleven and ten. She recalled:

The poor little girl was sent off without knowing a soul. Pete was sent off without knowing a soul — traumatic experience, awful. They seem to have survived it, but the fun I've had with these kids, the huge pleasure I've had from them in the moments I snatch with them now, make me really resent the time I didn't spend with them when they were growing up. On the other hand, I wouldn't have been able to spend that time because I was on the road with Robert a lot of the time . . . it couldn't have worked. We had plenty of people to look after them, but four teenagers in a house with a babysitter while their parents are away — you just can't do it.

Val Pitman believes that Robert forced Janet to send the children away to school so that she could give him total attention and the kids would not get in the way. Robert was attentive to his children when they phoned him; he always took their calls, always interrupted what he was doing. If he could not speak immediately he would get back to them, but Val Pitman did not believe he was passionate about his children.

Peter and Catherine went to boarding school when Simon was eight and Paul was seven, so the four children were separated early in life and did not grow up with close family bonds. Peter and Catherine, although close in age, were not close in spirit. Simon and Paul, on the other hand, developed a strong bond. They recall a succession of babysitters, including Mrs Gray, who ran the playgroup at Osborne Parade for a time. She was the closest they came to having a nanny. She would help with their homework and helped them with their artistic endeavours — painting and music. She lived in the house that backed onto 6 Osborne Parade, which Janet and Robert had also purchased.

Simon was the most practical child in the family. He liked to play with Lego blocks and his Meccano set. Although he has only a reconstructed memory of the incident, as a toddler he once pushed a car key into a power point and received a severe electric shock. His finger was partly cooked and he required skin grafts. Throughout the ordeal he did not cry or complain. He was stoic, while Janet felt guilty. He had a cast on his hand for some time, with which he used to hit his brothers and sister. He scored some more stitches in his head when he tripped over a wheelbarrow. He liked to build things and remembers tying the whole house up with string and being amazed to discover that if he tied string to the knob of his door and closed it, he could open another door downstairs.

Simon says he and his little brother Paul were both 'big pyromaniacs. We lit everything'. Simon would get boxes of matches, take the heads off, then light them all at once. He lit fires in the backyard, would put a hose on the barbecue gas cylinder, light it and create a flame thrower; with the little camp gas-bottles they would put a hole in the top, light it and get a huge jet of flame.

Once, down at the farm, he lit a fire using a magnifying glass. It was mid-summer. The long dry grass caught and burned out an acre. He felt mortified and dreaded the lecture that would follow, but he got off lightly. It was treated as an accident. Simon doesn't know if he was unsupervised or the fire antics were condoned. His father enjoyed playing with Simon's chemicals and one time together they filled old cigar containers with gunpowder (not tightly packed), put them in the planters at home with a long wick, lit them and watched. Simon says:

Dad got boyish and played with us. When I got the steam engine, that brought out the boyish side in him and I don't think Mum thought that was too dangerous, but I don't think she was too impressed with the gunpowder in the plant pots because it would leave sulphurous residue behind and stink.

The pyromania came to an end when a few friends were playing with a small burning jar of mineral turpentine and one boy kicked the can onto another boy, whose clothes caught on fire. They had to break into the house to put him under a cold shower and after that Simon lost interest.

The boys didn't have carpentry tools at home – no hammer or screwdriver and no father knocking something together for them to play with. Every year at school there was a go-cart race and Simon really wanted to enter. He would trail after Jimmy Diggins, the odd-jobs man at Bell Bros. Simon worked for $3 an hour, handing Jimmy things he needed and running his errands. He was able to play on the heavy machinery and enjoyed that, and Jimmy helped Simon build 'the go-cart to beat all go-carts'. It had a full steering wheel, some pedals and a bonnet you could lift up to service the steering wheel. It was spray-painted with the Bell logo and a number on the side. Simon was really proud of it. But when it came time to take it to school, he felt really embarrassed:

> because everyone else had fruit boxes that they'd knocked together with their fathers and in a way my father had helped me knock mine together but in a very indirect way . . . he gave me the run of the Bell Group odd-jobs man and his resources.

On the first corner, Simon took it too wide and crashed. It was sad; the go-cart was very special.

A new stage of life had begun for Janet. She had, with Robert's encouragement, begun to expand her community activities. Robert had no time to spare for such interests but it helped and softened his cold, reserved image to have a wife who was actively involved in the arts, education and welfare. He recognised this and was supportive, providing Janet always remembered he was the number one priority. For Janet there was no pretence. She was involved for her own needs, not Robert's; these areas were fields of genuine and passionate interest to her and although her life was packed with activity she took on more and more committee work over the eighties.

In 1983 Janet and Robert moved to a larger house in Peppermint Grove. They had the luxury of being able to buy whatever they wanted and, indulging their interests and tastes, they bought art, cars, wine and objects of quality. And Robert had high ambitions for his horses. From the early days of their marriage he and Janet had started to buy selectively and build their knowledge of their collectibles. These were their hobbies, but they were very serious about them and only the best would do.

The building of their collections was something they could do together, an interest that could be shared. Acquiring art at auctions, generally by phone, was a particularly exciting experience for Janet, who immersed herself in the expansion of the Robert Holmes à Court Collection. The cars, while ostensibly of interest to Robert, were used very little during his lifetime; the Vasse Felix Winery was something Robert bought on a whim at Janet's urging, while the horses remained his great love. As Robert pondered his breeding strategies, Janet helped create the environment of the Stud where, as the children grew older, they could come to relax more easily than they did elsewhere.

Robert Holmes à Court, who had become a household name in Western Australia, was becoming a household name nationally. But little was really known about the character and background of this enigmatic man from the west and even less about his wife and their relationship, until the *National Times* published a profile on Janet Holmes à Court and Eileen Bond, comparing their lifestyles and the different ways the women coped with marriage to two of Australia's wealthiest and most aggressive businessmen.[1]

The article put on public record Janet's total devotion to Robert – 'I think he is just charming, I think he is superb. I love him' – as well as her belief in his 'brilliance of mind' and her role in nurturing that brilliance. The Perth gossip circuit wagged their tongues. John Byrne said, 'When I saw that awful bloody article about her in the *National Times*, I thought, "You've lost it. Why are you saying things like that? Why are you not yourself?"'.

Janet didn't simply mouth the words for the media; she loved and believed in Robert so completely that she was the classic 'good wife'. Despite her natural ebullience, she learnt to control her behaviour for Robert's social and, ultimately, business benefit. When he wanted her to speak, she could turn the words on like a tap; when he wanted to speak, she knew how to take a back seat. She learnt how to dress for success and mastered the art of packing to look smart always when she travelled. She never forgot she was there in a support role helping Robert further his plans by ensuring his comfort and that of his guests, supplying a ready patter of charming conversation when she sensed it appropriate. Yet Janet never complained because in her mind Robert was worthy of such attention and devotion and she found other outlets for her own interests and personality. The remarkable thing is that Janet Ranford did not become spoiled by the luxurious life she led. She was indulged and she enjoyed it, but she never forgot her roots.

While Janet was depicted in the media as simply the subservient home maker and wife, she was actively pursuing a variety of activities – some with Robert, but mostly outside the family. These involved the arts, health, children and education – all interests instilled in Janet by her socialist parents. All involved the welfare of others and often involved a cause. These were areas of genuine need, areas which were people-intensive and where her natural enthusiasm, charm and people skills meant she would excel. Generally, she found her way onto committees or boards outside the mainstream. She became associated with causes, visionary ideas and alternatives that needed passionate supporters, not fellow travellers; where you ran the risk of getting your fingers burnt, of failing, but where success was sweeter because of the amount of work needed to achieve it. The people behind these causes were Janet's kind of people and many of them became firm friends. They were people who worked for social change and concerned themselves with social injustice. They helped appease Janet's political conscience while she lived her dual life – supporting her causes at the same time as she was supporting her multi-millionaire husband's business pursuits.

Peter and Catherine were at school in Geelong when Janet's volunteer work began. Simon and Paul were growing up in the hands of loyal carers and she made sure she was available for all the key childhood moments and events that her role as mother required. While her pre-eminent place remained by Robert's side, increasingly she wanted some meaningful and independent life of her own that reflected her personal values and beliefs and released her from her domestic and secretarial role. While Robert encouraged Janet to take her place in the wider world, he did tend to refer to her, when at meetings, as being 'with her ladies'. He didn't need community causes. He had a single cause – to work his way to the peak of the business world in Australia.

One of the first causes Janet agreed to join was the fight to prevent the closing of the Claremont School of Art by the Western Australian Government. The School was a unique, small, single-purpose art school existing on the fringes of the TAFE system. The arts always sat uncomfortably with TAFE's industrial imperatives for training. At the best of times, art schools struggle to maintain a profile and compete for funding – and this art school was seen as expendable when the WA Government needed to save money in 1981. A lecturer, Tony Jones, helped lead a movement to turn around the government's attitude. Tony Jones had supposedly been doing too much by organising weekend workshops and bringing in artists such as John Firth-Smith. The government accused the board, of which Tony and Janet were members, of putting 'too much enrichment' into practice. Tony was accused of having too many easels in the room, and of making a mess of the place. He wanted artists-in-residence and art prizes; he wanted to stimulate artistic excellence.

Together with an accountant friend, Bob Poolman, who suggested they enlist the support of credible people who could speak on behalf of the School, Tony Jones planned the Claremont School of Art Foundation. Janet readily gave her name to the cause and joined the board. The government's attitude was turned around and the School was saved. Tony found in Janet the same qualities that have endeared her to everyone she works with – warmth, care, commitment and passionate support. Tony says, 'Most people won't run with you. They'll come on board when it's all changed and you've made it round the corner and then say, "What a great idea it is", but not Janet. She bobs up everywhere'. She attended meetings, got involved in the proposals, contributed financially and housed visiting artists in a flat she and Robert owned in Peppermint Grove. Tony says he always saw Janet 'as a friend who could be approached for advice or support, and even invoking the name of Janet was helpful in earning support'.

Janet remained involved with the arts community, where she met an artist, Brian McKay, with whom she developed a close bond. He had been working in the UK for ten years, and had been radicalised by the experience. He first met Janet when he won an art prize of $1,000 for his work. Janet was one of the judges. On the night of the prize-giving, he was struck by the presence of a good-looking woman who was gathering people around her and he asked, 'Who is that dishy woman who's so prominent in here?'. It was, of course, Janet. They were introduced and he found her to be 'one of those people that you just like immediately – she was so vivacious and so sparkly, so positive and warm'. Brian was a friend of Tony Jones, and was also involved in the fight to save the Claremont School of Arts. Brian's ambition was to develop a place in Perth where ideas could be discussed, where alternative arts activity could take place, where views could be exchanged between dancers, sculptors, filmmakers and choreographers; where they could examine the processes of art rather than the practice. Instead of working alone in a studio, this venue would enable artists and performers to share experiences and interact with the experiences of others. Brian went to see Ron Davies, the Minister for the Arts, proposing an Institute of Contemporary Art for Perth (PICA). The Minister was receptive and told him to come back with an accountant and a business person to help form and administer a trust. Brian phoned Janet, who was immediately attracted by such a progressive concept, and she agreed to be a member of the trust.

This was 1985 and by then the Holmes à Court name had an electrifying effect on politicians. Janet readily gave her name to what excited her. The assumption was often made that this would mean millions would be thrown at the venture, but that was not the reality. All Janet's causes had to be supported by the community if they were going to work as they were intended. They were not clubs for wealthy individuals, like opera or art gallery boards, where bequests were the name of the game. Janet's ventures were associated with grass roots movements growing out of someone's passion, and she gave her time and energy, shared in the excitement and involved herself in the evolution of those causes. Janet threw her support behind PICA which, when it opened, had 60,000 people attending its exhibitions in the first year.

When PICA was established, Noel Sheridan, a Dublin artist, came to Perth as its director. His response to Janet was instantly positive, like Brian McKay's had been. He too felt Janet's tremendous energy, enthusiasm and support and thought, 'If you have to give a great deal of money to someone, this is the person to give it to. She was easy to talk to, she encouraged you to be yourself and there was no bullshit'. Noel found Janet 'very Australian', 'very brave'. Janet invited Noel to view the Robert Holmes à Court Art Collection of Aboriginal paintings, and he was amazed. He found them radical and powerful and believed Robert's concept of engaging with the Utopian Aboriginal women artists in such a comprehensive way was very far-sighted. His view of Robert when he met him at an exhibition opening of PICA was that 'it was like meeting a Cardinal'. He said, 'I thought of the Scott Fitzgerald observation that the rich are different'. Noel never spoke to Robert on a one-to-one basis but he was very intrigued by him.

Sheridan saw 'immense vulnerability' in Robert. One day, Noel was speaking at PICA about an exhibition. He was talking about the complexity of the art and how artists illuminate truth and how knowledge is accumulated over time. During his speech he made eye contact with Robert who was towering over the crowd. He said:

I really was thrown. He looked at me and I felt looked in. I felt everything was different, the opposite of what I thought I would be looking at. The man's sensitivity – words are no good on this one. We never spoke. He never said, 'I agree with you' or anything, but it was astonishing . . . There was a shyness, a softness, this immense vulnerability, the reverse of the legend – the exact opposite of everything you were expecting. It was really only there for a moment and then everybody went back into their roles and we do have to play roles in life . . . I couldn't tell you anything really about Robert Holmes à Court, but for a moment something flipped and you saw its opposite and it would be the exact opposite of everything that you were expecting and dealing with.

Perhaps what Noel saw at that moment was a side of Robert to which usually only Janet was privy.

Janet's interest in art involved more than being involved in community action. Her parents had always fostered cultural values in their children. Although they had little money and lived a very simple life, they valued cultural artefacts and creativity. Janet had been protected from what her family viewed as the crass products of popular mass culture and she admired the best achievements in all fields of artistic endeavour. When she was first married and moved to Darlington, she was twenty-two. Darlington was heavily treed, undulating, hilly, bush country with a natural beauty similar to where Janet had grown up, and it attracted artists.

Each year the artists held an exhibition and it was here that Robert and Janet began to buy paintings. A first purchase was a work by Guy Grey-Smith, who was to become a distinguished Australian contemporary painter. Another was by Wim Boissevain, an attractive Frenchman with whom Janet had become friendly. As a young girl on the way home from school, she would stop to talk with him as he was painting by the side of the road. When she was about twelve years old, Boissevain painted a portrait of Janet and her school friend Dale for an art competition. When Janet was at university, and her boyfriend Peter was going to Oxford, she asked Boissevain to do a crayon drawing of her which she gave to Peter to take with him. The painting Robert and Janet bought in Darlington by Boissevain was called *The Hunter* and still hangs on a wall at the Stud. The original intention in buying art was to do just that, hang the paintings on the wall. Robert would say, 'Janet and I buy what we like; we have no regard for whether a piece is seen as important by the art world, or of particular value'.

But soon Robert and Janet began to go to Christie's auctions in Sydney and Melbourne. Around the galleries Robert was conspicuous. Tall, elegantly turned-out and quietly spoken, he had the manner of someone who would buy art. The Holmes à Courts began to be deluged with art mail and, although they did not give the idea much thought or discussion, decided that if they were going to collect art, they needed to employ someone to work on the collection. In 1980, Robert appointed Roderick Anderson as curator of his collection. As registrar of the Art Gallery in Perth, Roderick had been part of a small, but dedicated, team who had begun to research Western Australian artists during the middle seventies. He had been working on the restoration of, and had a great passion for collecting works by local artists. Western Australia was well behind other states in collecting information about its living and past artists, and the team he was involved with worked in very inadequate conditions to find, restore and preserve for the future, works which were in danger of deterioration from age and neglect.

The idea of documenting and preserving Western Australian art appealed to Robert and Janet. Robert liked to have a plan and a purpose. He liked the idea of a good, representative, didactic collection that could be used by other people. Janet was a conservationist at heart. With this focus, they were not only buying the best of an artist's work, they would buy a group of etchings or paintings that would tell a story of the development of the state's art. The Holmes à Courts' interest caused people to look again at their household junk to see what they could find in their bottom drawers or their garage – a filthy rolled up canvas might prove of value. As a result of the Holmes à Courts' archival interest and aesthetic hobby, much art which would have been lost has been preserved. By 1988, the Holmes à Courts owned the best private collection of Western Australian art in the country. The status of art from the west grew, and collecting it became fashionable.

When Roderick Anderson became the curator for the Robert Holmes à Court Art Collection, Robert and Janet had already acquired eighty-eight pictures, the majority of which, in Roderick's opinion, were of sentimental value only. However, there were five Drysdales, three Dobells, an English John Gould, a Sali Herman, a Jon Molvig and an E. Phillips Fox among the paintings. By the time Roderick left the job in 1988, there were 2,000 works in the collection.

Roderick worked from the house at Osborne Parade, where he saw Janet and the children daily. At that time, Janet was busy with a household of children, including those from the preschool in the grounds. The house was always full of clutter and Roderick particularly remembers the dishwasher as being very old. He found Janet very down-to-earth and her friends were ordinary people. He describes their relationship as 'very personal'. He watched the kids grow up and saw the family's lifestyle change across the eighties. He did not see a lot of Robert. When they spoke, Robert expected Roderick to know what he wanted, to find it and to get it at the right price. There was never a rationale for the collection except in relation to Western Australian art and, later, Aboriginal art.

The art collection became a major interest for Janet. She would read the books and catalogues and discuss ideas with Roderick. When she travelled they spoke daily by phone. He would prod and remind Janet, nagging about potential buys he thought would suit the collection. If Robert didn't like a painting very much, Janet would leave it propped up in the house, hoping it would 'get into his blood by osmosis'. On occasions, paintings would be around for months waiting for a 'yay' or 'nay' from Robert, who was often very preoccupied with other matters. Robert had the ultimate say on purchases. Anderson says, 'To Robert, art was property, everything was property. It was all his'. Roderick would put forward a proposal with photographs through Janet, and she would talk to Robert. Janet was the gatekeeper with the task of getting the art in front of the man with the money. Occasionally Robert would call Roderick in to talk about art. Like many people, Roderick was taken with his charisma and 'felt honoured to be whispered at'.

Because Robert Holmes à Court was such a name and such a good customer, it became easy to do deals. Artists wanted their work in the collection and dealers wanted to sell to the collection for prestige. Roderick learnt that Robert didn't like nudes, black-and-white wood cut engravings (Roderick found him 'uneducated in such things') and he didn't like abstracts, particularly surrealism. Roderick had, he says, a 'fiendishly difficult' job.

Once or twice Janet would approve a purchase alone, but that was rare and the art would be inexpensive. On one occasion at a function at the Western Australian Art Gallery, Robert admired a painting in the foyer by Brian Blanchflower and asked Janet to find out who owned it. She responded, 'You do'. Janet had bought it when she couldn't get Robert to say yes. He was amused.

Because of Robert Holmes à Court's social position, he and Janet moved in circles where they met and came to know contemporary artists, and were able to talk about art. Janet also had her friends through Tony Jones and the Claremont Art Foundation and through Brian McKay and PICA. Art and creativity were central and important interests in her life so, not surprisingly, Janet became the driving force behind the Robert Holmes à Court Art Collection and she became very knowledgable about art. According to Roderick, 'She had the interest; Robert had the say'.

In 1981, Robert bought a full collection of Papunya Aboriginal art entitled *Mr Sandman*, which was then on tour around the world, simply on the basis of seeing the photographs. Brought to her attention by Anderson, Janet loved them and from then she was hooked on Aboriginal art. Apart from the sad life of Albert Namatjira, the recent history of contemporary Aboriginal art only began with the emergence of the Papunya Tula movement in 1971. In the fifties and sixties, work focused on the bark painters of Arnhem Land. It took a decade for Papunya art to attract a significant audience and market and it was only in the eighties that the Aboriginal art movement began to develop and flourish on cultural grounds. It has since become a multi-million dollar business. The Holmes à Courts were early buyers and saw the potential before the unique and radical nature of Aboriginal art was generally recognised by the market.

As the collection grew, Janet and Roderick became frustrated that they had no gallery in which to exhibit the works, and Roderick was frustrated that he could do little to promote the collection. He could spend $1.5 million on paintings, but he wasn't permitted to spend $20,000 on a book about the collection. Roderick was the only private curator in the country, giving him status which he enjoyed, but he had no space to show his treasures, and the Gallery of Western Australia at that time was not interested in Western Australian or Aboriginal art. Robert's position as chairman of the Western Australian Art Gallery board made it more difficult for him to push his own interests and exhibitions.

In 1986, Roderick fulfilled his ambition to publish a catalogue about a selection of early works on Western Australian art from the Robert Holmes à Court Art Collection, for an exhibition which was to be first shown at Sydney's Blaxland Gallery in October 1986. Janet opened the exhibition, which received widespread publicity, and gave interviews about the collection, revealing her knowledge and strong interest in particular artists. She was, she said, intrigued by the paintings from the thirties and forties, pictures about social issues such as war, poverty and unemployment, pictures where artists were making a strong statement. She also liked having to figure out what contemporary artists such as Fred Williams, John Firth Smith and Bob Jacks were getting at. She liked Brett Whiteley and admired Lloyd Rees with whom she developed a relationship through correspondence, eventually meeting him in 1986. She said, 'It was love at first sight'. (One of Lloyd Rees's best late-stage paintings of Sydney Harbour hangs in the family's Melbourne Spring Street apartment.)

Offers of paintings were coming in to Roderick daily and they were being acquired at the rate of one every one-and-a-half days. By 1985, the collection was valued at $10 million, in 1986 at $14 million. In 1985, Janet and Robert began to acquire French Impressionist paintings and sculptures. These included one from the Monet haystack series for which Robert paid $US3 million; and a Pissaro, *Le Pere Melon Sciant du Bois Pontoise* (1879), first owned by Paul Gauguin, for $665,000. Both paintings were bought in a splurge at a Christie's New York auction of French Impressionists where he also bought paintings by Munch, Soutine, Boudin, Bonnard and Gleizes. They bought sculptures by Gauguin (including *Ovari*), Poden, Rodin, Henry Moore and Picasso. Robert snapped up Australian masterpieces, including *Settlers Camp* by Sir Arthur Streeton, for $800,000 in 1986. He also purchased two works by Arthur Boyd, *The Hunter* and *Early Murrumbeena*, the cost totalling $285,000. They were intended to complement the $313,500 Boyd painting *Melbourne Burning*, which had been bought at Sotheby's in 1985. Robert's buys were often unpredictable and traditional, including a record price of $176,000 for a Hans Heysen watercolour of gum trees. His purchases pushed art prices to levels which Patrick McCaughey, the director of Victoria's National Gallery, publicly criticised, arguing Robert was forcing public galleries out of the market.[2] But Robert believed he should buy art the public galleries couldn't afford, and then lend the paintings to the galleries.

When Robert was appointed chairman of the Western Australian Art Gallery, he said he could see no conflict arising between private acquisitions and the unsalaried post of chairman, which would not involve supervising acquisitions. He said:

The role of public and private collections is very different. Great public collections have the responsibility of acquiring important pieces, those which represent a fair sample of whatever school is under attention. Some plan must be adopted. Private collections – whether the great ones or those like mine – have another role reflecting personal taste, a touch of the idiosyncratic. Perhaps they may dart down little side paths, exploring areas which a public gallery cannot always do. Thus the private collections have a very important part to play, especially if they are frequently displayed.[3]

But the full-time curator of the Robert Holmes à Court Art Collection felt constrained. He believed the Collection was on hold during Robert's term as chairman.

In an interview, Roderick emphasised that all the works in the Collection reflected:

the boss's likes and dislikes. If he thinks a painting is worth more than the market does, he'll probably spend the money. If he thinks it's not worth that much, no matter what the rest of the world tells him, he wouldn't spend the money.[4]

There were ongoing discussions between Janet and Robert about acquiring a building for a gallery, as they owned enough paintings to fill the Western Australian Gallery. The problem was to find the right property and to justify the expense. To Robert, art was an investment, money in another form – a gallery would not return its investment. It was a curious contradiction in Robert. He would spend unlimited amounts of money on the studs and his car collection, the hobbies from which he gained the greatest pleasure, but was less hurried about housing his growing body of art work, Janet's great pleasure, in its own gallery. In this case the price had to be right. There was no attempt when Robert was alive to acquire a gallery to exhibit the collection.

But neither Robert nor Janet wanted the art locked away. It was a public collection in private hands. In 1986 the paintings were on display in twenty-two separate locations, ranging from old people's homes and hospitals to Bell Group boardrooms. Some were on loan to public galleries or in travelling exhibitions. Three Heidelberg School paintings, including *Settlers Camp*, were part of the *Golden Summers* exhibition. The Monet was lent to Victoria's National Gallery and travelled to Perth to be on exhibit at a dinner Janet organised to raise money for the University of Western Australia. The Pissaro hung in the Museum of Art in Washington. The art works have always been available to scholars for study, research and for photographic purposes.

On 28 April 1988, the day before Robert sold the bulk of his holdings in the Bell Group to Alan Bond and the West Australian SGIC, an exhibition entitled *European and Australian Paintings* attracted wide interest at the National Trust's SH Irvin Gallery in Sydney. While Robert was no longer stalking BHP and frightening the financial and industrial institutions, his art collection had no parallel in Australia. In June 1988 a major retrospective of Guy Grey-Smith's work from the collection opened in the Blaxland Gallery. This was the first time this artist's work had been brought to the attention of the eastern states.

In the two years before Robert's death, seven exhibitions were mounted from the collection, which by now included three major Australian divisions: a general Australian collection; early and contemporary West Australian art; and the very extensive Aboriginal collection from three regions (the Kimberley in the north of Western Australia, Arnhem Land and an area near Alice Springs); along with some notable European paintings and work by Mexican-American painter Frida Kahlo.

After Robert's death Janet maintained the lending philosophy. In January 1991, a thematic exhibition called *Images of Women* opened at the SH Irvin Gallery, with paintings by artists ranging from Charles Conder, Rupert Bunny and Grace Cossington Smith to Henri Matisse, Camille Pissaro and Pierre Bonnard.

Apart from the purchases Roderick instigated, Robert and Janet would buy from catalogues. It was something Robert and Janet enjoyed doing together. Janet loved the excitement of buying art on the phone at auctions and often spent time thumbing through catalogues looking at what they might buy. The routine often required them to wake up at maybe 3.00 a.m., whereupon Janet would talk to one of the employees at Sotheby's. Robert never spoke to them directly. Janet was always in the middle asking Robert if he was going to bid and not knowing if she was going to miss out on an art work she wanted. They would sometimes joke that perhaps the person bidding against them was Alan Bond who lived a stone's throw away across the Swan River.

On one occasion, Janet was bidding for a work by Frida Kahlo. Janet had read her biography and was fascinated by the woman and her paintings. The Mexican artist had had an obsessive relationship with the great Mexican artist Diego Rivera. She had also spent much of her life in bed after an accident and numerous operations. She would paint small pictures, including meticulous self-portraits. One of Janet's ambitions was to own one of Kahlo's self-portraits and finally one came up for sale. It was a marvellous picture and the estimate was in the order of $US300,000. Robert agreed that if they could get it for $US400–500,000 they would. The telephone rang from New York around 3.00 a.m. and the bidding started. When the bid was at $US1.3 million Robert said to Janet, 'Well, do you want it? Do you want it?'. This was a most bizarre experience for Janet. She was holding the phone bidding for a picture she loved and the price they expected to outlay was a maximum of $US500,000. The bidding had gone to $US1.3 million and Robert was saying to her, 'Quickly, make a decision; if you want it, bid now'. It was too much for Janet who decided, 'No, don't be stupid, we can't, it's silly'. But Janet knew she could have had that painting, she could have had any material thing she ever wanted. Robert was generous with her and with the family although there is not much evidence of philanthropy outside the family. The singer Madonna eventually bought the painting. Later, Robert did buy two of Frida Kahlo's still-life paintings, which Janet sold after he died.

These were heady times for Janet. Robert was acquiring horses, cars, property, houses and very expensive art. As for Aboriginal art, they continued to buy that as if it was going out of style. In 1988 they employed a curator, Anne Brody, who held a senior position at the National Gallery of Victoria and who had qualifications in anthropology, to organise the Aboriginal collection. This appointment and other difficulties led to a falling out with Roderick Anderson, after eight years in their employ. Roderick began as curator for the Robert Holmes à Court Art Collection in 1980 on a salary of $22,000 a year, and in eight years had had only a $2,000 increase. Over his time as curator of the Collection, Roderick had seen Janet and Robert's life change. He says:

Robert got busier; Janet's clothes became more fashionable; there was more jewellery. The circle of acquaintances became more elite and Janet had less time to mix with ordinary people. The house became more ostentatious with the move to Peppermint Grove. It was all done to Robert's taste. There was more and more money to spend.

Janet and Anne Brody moved the focus of purchasing to Aboriginal art, until the Aboriginal Collection made up nearly a third of the total number of paintings acquired.

She acquired a group of eighty-eight batiks on silk painted by the women of Utopia.[5] Later, the same group of women were supplied with a set of canvasses and painted on canvas for the first time. This set was entitled *A Summer Story* and included the first work on canvas by Emily Kane Kngwarreye who by the time she died in

1995, aged well over eighty, had become internationally known, with her pictures in high demand. The other women could not understand why Emily's pictures were more highly valued than their own. Rodney Gouch, their art adviser, provided them with canvas and suggested they produce a work like an Emily painting. This they did, but Emily's painting stood out. Janet purchased this group of paintings to keep the work together. All three sets of this historic art remain in the Robert Holmes à Court Art Collection.

Janet gave *An Aboriginal Dreaming* to Yoko Ono, whom she admired and met when Robert was negotiating the sale of the rights to all The Beatles' music, which he had acquired through ACC. Michael Jackson, the purchaser of the music catalogue, also received a gift of Aboriginal art from Janet.

Robert and Janet's biggest art splurge came after the stock market crash in June 1988. They were returning home from London in Robert's private jet with Jon Elbery and Alan Newman. Because of the need to work out business details at the end of the financial year, Robert, Jon and Alan had to be in touch with offices around the world. After a drama in Egypt involving a failed engine, they found themselves waiting in Athens for the engine to be repaired, trying to avoid the stifling heat. While Jon and Alan sunbaked, the Holmes à Courts studied the Sotheby's and Christie's catalogues. Janet says, 'Robert went mad with those phone calls', but staff observed they had never seen Janet and Robert so affectionate as during those days. Staff thought Robert indulged Janet. While eating a room service meal, Robert sat nodding and grunting while Janet, speaking with the art auctioneer, got more and more excited. Robert was converting money to art; Janet was buying paintings, and in three days they bought $35 million worth, including works by Claude Monet, Henri Matisse, Pierre Bonnard, Berthe Morrisot, Maurice de Vlaminck and Vincent Van Gogh. It was an unusual situation for Robert to be in. He did not go on holidays (they bored him) but in isolated Athens there were not a lot of meetings he could hold. His chief advisers were with him and they could spend time on the phone. There wasn't much to do, so why not buy art? He rarely got so carried away.

Robert had been fascinated by the fact that art purchases had proved a most successful investment for the British Rail Pension Fund. Janet believes he might have thought this was an opportunity. The major works they bought were to become a millstone around Janet's neck when, overvalued in Heytesbury's books, she had to sell them after Robert's death to reduce debt. They did not prove to be good investments after all. The art market was a very different one in the nineties.

In the end, Robert tired of his wife's approaching him to buy more and more paintings. He demanded to hear a rationale for the Collection's use, but she was never able to articulate one to Robert's satisfaction. She wanted a collection which, although privately owned, was publicly accessible. There were works that public galleries couldn't afford, but Robert could. Janet wanted a dynamic gallery where exhibitions would change regularly. She wanted the Collection to be personal, with paintings she enjoyed, and she was not concerned about making sure all artists were represented. She also wanted to explore certain artists in detail to show the history of the development of a particular artist so ultimately, when she had her gallery, there would be specialised exhibitions.

When Janet fell in love with Aboriginal art there was no painting she saw that she didn't like. Her mother's views about the Aboriginal people stayed with Janet and she saw their art as an opportunity to develop their self-esteem. She hoped, as later she hoped with the Black Swan Theatre Company, that if the world's attention could be focused on the creativity of indigenous people, their cause would be helped.

Robert had supported an exhibition of Aboriginal contemporary art from his Collection touring the US in the year before his death. It went first to the Carpenter Centre for the Visual Arts at Harvard University, then to the University of Minnesota and the Lakewood Centre for the Arts at Lake Oswego. A major exhibition had also gone to the Pompidou Centre in Paris. The exhibition made a significant impact and requests to see the exhibition grew after Robert's death. In 1995–96 an exhibition of Aboriginal art toured twelve European cities over fifteen months, for the Department of Foreign Affairs in Canberra.

Unable to persuade Robert to buy more art, Janet started buying herself. When Robert acquired Bell Bros back in 1983, he had given Janet $1,000 to invest, which she put into the Bell Group. She never sold a share and reinvested the dividends in Bell Group. Mrs Holmes à Court couldn't possibly sell a Bell Group share. At one point, the $1,000 investment was worth $5 million. When Robert sold out of Bell and Janet did as well, the $1,000 investment returned $600,000 and it was that money she used to invest in art. After Robert's death she came to understand how Robert must have felt about her insistent approaches to him to buy more art. When the decision to buy was hers solely, she came to feel the same way about the curator Anne Brody as Robert had felt about her. She wanted to cease acquiring more and more works for the Collection and for Anne to focus on rationalising the art the family owned. It was Darrel Jarvis who first imposed discipline on the art collection and, as Janet says, 'stopped these two wild women buying everything they saw'. The excessive buying ceased and in recent times the art purchases have been very selective, although Janet still acquires Aboriginal art and the occasional painting which she thinks should be in the Collection.

Since Robert's death the Collection has been rationalised. Janet was concerned initially that every sale of an art piece was interpreted by the press as a sign that she was going broke, but apart from selling major art works to reduce debt, there was a need to rationalise the Collection. Janet says she and Robert had always bought art with the intention of standing back one day, rationalising their choices and choosing the best buys of a particular artist's work. Belinda Carrigan joined Heytesbury in July 1995, in the role of manager of the Collection which had, up until then, been curator-driven. Now curators are employed as consultants. Belinda's role is, firstly, to provide cultural support to the Heytesbury enterprises and to ensure the paintings on the walls keep changing; secondly, it is to oversee exhibitions for the general community. There are currently 3,690 pieces in the Collection and 1,500 are Aboriginal art works on bark, textiles, paper and canvas – together valued now at $22.5 million.[6] As part of the process of refining the Collection, the scale of the Western Australian Collection has been reduced and the works of many artists represented have been culled to dispose of lesser works.

Currently the Collection is housed at the Stud in Keysbrook, in the vast air-conditioned corrugated iron shed shared with what remains of the car collection. The art collection is supported by three staff and costs around $500,000 each year to maintain. The plan is that once gallery space is available, there will be changing exhibitions on public display of different Aboriginal communities; of specialised artists like Russell Drysdale, Brian McKay, Howard Taylor and John Peart; of Australian print making; of paintings of wildflowers; of the history of the development of Perth, and so on. Probably more than anything else acquired through the empire, the Robert Holmes à Court Art Collection represents Janet Holmes à Court's greatest passion.

While the acquisition of art on the scale Robert and Janet pursued it could only be the hobby of the super rich, Janet gave as much of her time to less fashionable causes in the health and welfare sector.

Janet joined the Cancer Foundation of Western Australia in 1981. In September 1980, prior to Janet's appointment, the Cancer Foundation employed Dr David Frey to research the need for a hospice in Western Australia. The study found that 1,680 West Australians were dying of cancer annually and, of these, 65% died in hospitals which were ill-equipped to care for terminally ill patients whose medical, emotional and spiritual needs were often neglected and whose rights were not always respected.

Hospice philosophy argued that patients should have a right to make their own decisions about the treatment they received and where they would die – at home or in an institution.[7] Opponents of the hospice argued that it had the potential to become 'a ghetto of the dying'. There was an argument between the proponents and the opponents about cost and whether a hospice/palliative care service would mean an added drain on resources. When Janet joined the Foundation, the debate was in full swing. Janet enjoyed a good fight and when a cause was one she believed in, she gave the fight her best effort. At the time, there was very little debate about the issue of euthanasia, and the notion of separate palliative care was itself at the cutting edge of medical thinking.

Janet says, 'It would be false to say I was the driving force behind it, but there was a contributing role because I was on the board encouraging the men to spend some of the ever-growing funds they had'. The choice of a site in Claremont for the purpose inflamed the local residents, who called a public meeting arguing they would be 'living on Death Street' and the value of their houses would be lessened. Janet helped steer the meeting toward a positive result, moving and opposing motions that eventually resulted in a vote that the Claremont Council exercise 'every discretion that it possibly can to see that the project can go ahead'. A vote of confidence in the Cancer Foundation was also carried.

Ultimately, bureaucratic delays by the Claremont Town Council and a range of problems, including lack of support from Dr Blewett as Commonwealth Minister for Health meant the hospice did not proceed on the Claremont site and it was 1 March 1987 before Australia's first purpose-built, free-standing hospice was opened. Janet had played her part by going to Ian Taylor, the Minister of the day, and threatening that if funds were not forthcoming she would take out an advertisement in the *West Australian* newspaper. The Minister knew that she would. The Commonwealth gave a once-only $200,000 allocation. Janet remained a member of the board until 1987 when the hospice was opened. This fight for the first hospice in Australia was only one of Janet's activities in the health area.

In 1983, at the instigation of Dr Alex Cohen, Janet became chairman of the Diabetes Research Foundation Fund Raising Committee – a position she also held until 1987. Although Robert never publicly disclosed his own diabetic condition, Janet was well informed about the problems of sufferers and was able to contribute and assist the Research Foundation, particularly through the TVW7 Telethon.

The Telethon was another project Janet and Robert could do together. Robert liked to open and close the Telethon and Janet was the Vice Patron. Kevin Campbell, then general manager of TVW7 (and primary school boyfriend of Janet's), said 'she always helped out with donations. She was a good contributor, not just a figurehead; she worked; she was a great negotiator'.

In 1983 Janet took on her first national role, joining the board of the Australian Children's Television Foundation. In 1984 she became chairman of the Save the Children Fund and in 1985 the Western Australian Minister for Health asked her if she would help establish a Health Advisory Network to advise him on the planning, policy and administration of the State's health care services and to act as a health issues forum. There were representatives of some 200 organisations with an interest in health issues affiliated with the network, which was to give them a channel of communication through to the Minister.

It was Janet's job to chair the Consumer's Council of the Network and to hear the people with their problems. She was the facilitator, not the strategic thinker. It was a time-consuming task and although she had little experience of chairing meetings she was a sympathetic listener and her instincts led her to fight for the underdog. Frank Parker, the Network's executive director, said 'people appreciated her style'.

In July 1983, Janet joined the board of the King Edward Memorial Hospital for Women, but resigned in November 1986 after a dispute over the way the death of a baby at birth and the mother's grief had been handled. She was to return as chairman of the board from July 1988 until September 1990, appointed by the Minister. As with all the jobs Janet took on, she worked hard. She missed few meetings, attended staff presentations, helped raise funds, judged the baby quest and at functions she would work the room and speak to as many people as she could. She was gaining experience in running meetings, learning how organisations worked, and developing her natural communication skills.

In 1984 Janet became a member of the Senate of the University of Western Australia (UWA), another experience she thoroughly enjoyed. Although not an academic, Janet involved herself in the intellectual life of the University. She had a strong emotional attachment to the institution as she had spent happy and exciting years there as a student, and had first met Robert there. She was later to choose the University and Winthrop Hall as the sites for Robert's memorial service. She was interested in the University's art collection and became a member of the Art Collection Board.

The University had a good collection and Janet believed they needed a gallery to house the works. Robert suggested to her that they have a public fundraising as the Senate was not interested in committing the University's funds to a gallery. Bob Smith, the Vice Chancellor, put together a committee (including Janet) to do the job. Janet and a friend, Juanita Walsh, organised a spectacular fundraising launch and dinner dance in Winthrop Hall, with Rod Kelly (an interior decorator who was later to have a serious falling out with her over the Blue Princess necklace) doing the decorations. Robert lent the Monet haystack to be displayed for the event. The people invited were those in the community with money. Janet found it a very moving event, for many of the people who had the money in the eighties had little education and most of them had never been in the University before. 'These people were not aware that they could walk in the beautiful University grounds any day of the week, that the grounds belonged to them.' They'd driven past for forty-five years and never seen the University as a public facility and were slightly intimidated about entering Winthrop Hall on this occasion. Lawrence Wilson, of Wilson Car Parks, gave a million dollars, and the Gallery was named after him. Robert gave a quarter of a million dollars, and a lecture theatre in the Gallery was named after Janet. Westpac made a substantial contribution and with other donations the money was raised and the Gallery built. Janet's vision for the Gallery was that it would become an integral part of the University, part of the teaching facilities. She envisaged the architecture students having lectures and exhibitions there; she saw engineering students coming in to be taught aesthetics, the language departments becoming involved.

But the Gallery did not live up to Janet's expectations. The exhibitions were disappointing and two years after opening the Gallery had had only 20,000 visitors, even though it had a captive population of 10,000 students. The performance of the Gallery under the direction of Sandra Murray, who was appointed as curator, remained a contentious issue for Janet and one which would bring her into public conflict with Sandra.

In 1990, Janet was appointed the first woman Pro-Chancellor of the University and when the Chancellor was overseas for three months she became the first woman to chair a Senate meeting. She was extremely nervous. Among the members were the Chief Justice of Western Australia and another judge; there were members who had actively campaigned against her getting the position and those who saw themselves as aspirants to the job of Chancellor in the future.

Robert was in London. She phoned him and said, 'I've got to chair the Senate meeting tonight. What if I don't remember the standing orders?'. Robert's response was, 'Just remember you're the chairman; you're in charge. You can do anything you like. If you get out of your depth, close the meeting'. Although Janet knew she couldn't do that, Robert's words gave her confidence and she enjoyed the role immensely. Through the University Senate she also had her first experience of exercising power and thinking afterwards, 'Christ that was too easy'.

The AMP had offered the University what Janet considered was an important sculpture, *Black Stump* – a seminal work in Western Australian art – by Howard Taylor, when they were refurbishing their environs. Janet thought it would be wonderful in the University grounds. The decision to accept the gift had to be made by the Senate – which Janet was chairing. Janet had a great ally on the Senate, Barbara Hamilton, a senior lecturer in politics who had become a firm friend, one who had lobbied on Janet's behalf for her to become Pro-Chancellor. Her other ally was Jim Watson, the chairman of the Art Gallery board at that time and who had been a great supporter of the University art collection. When it came to the discussion, it was obvious to Janet and Jim that they had three in favour and a large majority opposed. Jim said, 'Madam chair, on an issue like this, as you have been so involved, we should break with standing orders and you should be allowed to speak from the chair'. Janet spoke from the heart, put the vote and found she had turned the meeting completely around. The vote was won, twenty-three to three. Janet said:

I actually felt weird. As it has turned out that sculpture has never looked better. People had such ludicrous arguments against it. It's called the Black Stump. *Someone said it's an urban piece. How can it be an urban piece when it's called the* Black Stump? *It's supposed to represent a piece of burnt-out bush. But it was a bit scary to me that it was quite easy to turn them around. I remember thinking, 'What if I'm wrong?'.*

Janet was beginning to see the effect she could have on a group, the powers of persuasion that seemed a natural attribute. While the experiences she went through during the eighties transformed her social skills and her confidence in dealing with people, her work with charitable groups and organisations like the King Edward Memorial Hospital, the University of Western Australia Senate and the Australian Children's Television Foundation, allowed her to participate in financial decision making but with a minimal degree of financial risk involved.

These organisations were hardly a training ground for the tough financial decisions she would have to make when she took over Heytesbury. But the years spent working with them taught Janet that she could inspire loyalty in others, that she could open doors, that given the right lines to speak she could be very convincing. They were skills she would call on and master when she took over the chairmanship of Heytesbury, and increasingly the lines she spoke were her own.

The children meanwhile were at boarding school and growing up seeing little of their parents. Their absence from home meant Janet could devote all the time to Robert that he required. She moved into his office and took a closer interest in the day-to-day business. The years when all their children were at Geelong Grammar became the period of his greatest financial success. While Robert believed the experience of boarding school was character-building he acknowledged from his own experience it wasn't easy growing up in such an environment. He spoke of having to eat black porridge every morning and taking the plunge into cold showers each morning in the middle of winter.

But he didn't mention beatings, and probably didn't know that both Peter and Simon suffered indignities and abuse of the kind that one might have expected in nineteenth-century England, not in an Australian school in the eighties. It was the common practice at Geelong Grammar School for the older boys to beat and humiliate the younger boys, the strong to bully the weak and the group to victimise the individual who was different or had parents who were different. Robert and Janet were certainly different.

Peter was tall and lanky, awkward, slow to mature. As he also played squash, which wasn't a school sport, there was plenty for the boys to pick on. Having his father's name in the media every day was not easy for him to cope with. Peter would be referred to as 'money bags' or other names always to do with money. As the boys became older and more sophisticated, so would the names and the physical abuse. Simon was to be subjected to this even more than Peter. The thing that saved Peter, he believed, was that he would make funny cracks when he was being punched, kicked or given a charlie horse – a knee in the side of a muscle that was really painful.

Simon was beaten repeatedly. One boy who went on to become house captain whipped Simon with an inner tube from a bike tyre. He attached the tube to the end of a broomstick to make a whip out of it and tied knots in the end to make it hurt more. Simon had to get on all fours with his head on a chair and if he moved, the whipping would continue. You had to take it without flinching and then they would stop. A group of boys forced one boy down a sewerage drain and then urinated on him; another boy was hung by his ankle from the second-floor window; one boy was beaten because he had red hair. Under threat of being beaten, the smaller boys would queue to buy an ice cream for an older boy out of their own money.

The culture of violence bred more violence. As the victims grew older they turned on the next intake. Even the house prefects getting people out of bed in the morning became a violent exercise if a boy were slow to move. One boy, a regular victim, felt he couldn't be beaten more than he was – there just weren't enough hours in the day – so he documented around twenty incidents involving the same five or six boys. Three of those boys were sent before the Headmaster and given end of term detentions, which meant a half day of manual labour, and one boy was suspended for a week, but, to put that in context, if you were caught with one can of beer you were suspended for two weeks.

Some of the victims Peter and Simon know still struggle to come to terms with what they were subjected to at Geelong Grammar. Catherine escaped all this brutality, but that only served to distance her from her brothers. Paul escaped as well, because he was protected by Simon and because he had a different disposition. He learnt in primary school to ignore the 'rich kid' comments. He was a gregarious boy who found it easy to be on good terms with everyone, regardless of background.

Simon was different: he stood apart from the group, did what interested him. Simon and Paul both recall an incident at the beginning of fourth year, after the year away at Timbertop, when Paul and another boy had to race along the floor with their hands tied behind their backs, elbowing their way along nylon carpet, getting knees and elbows burned by the nylon. Simon remembers the incident as a time he let his brother down; Paul took it more philosophically. Simon had grown into a big strong boy, and the word got around that you didn't mess with Paul any more.

Simon's nickname in school, which he hated, was 'BHP'. Peter had been affected at school by Robert's move on Ansett, and Simon had to live through the BHP takeover drama. Both moves were very unpopular with the Melbourne establishment and Robert received considerable negative press in Victoria. Their school contemporaries undoubtedly picked up negative comments from their parents and they took that out on Peter and Simon.

Most families of the children at Geelong Grammar were wealthy and most had access to more money than the Holmes à Court children whose pocket money was carefully managed; they worked at jobs in the vacation. Peter says:

We were remarkably unspoiled ... growing up sucked, because we got all the downside of having wealthy, high-profile parents, but none of the upside. I never had a new cricket bat every year, the pads and the gloves, never had all the stuff ... which is as much my mother as [my father].

Simon remembers saving up his $3 a week allowance for nine weeks to buy a model aeroplane which he wanted. He built it and Peter flew it for the first time and crashed it. It was not replaced; it was not an option for Simon to buy a new plane. At school, Simon's new stereo was destroyed by someone dropping a cupboard on it after a dead mouse was put in the mechanism. When Simon complained, the response was, 'Oh, just go and buy another one'. This was so frustrating for Simon because the boys had no idea that he couldn't simply do that. Janet suspected what had been happening and wrote to the Principal.

When Simon left Geelong Grammar, he considered suing the school, and the anger remains at the appalling treatment he suffered and witnessed. In 1990, Simon was present when an associate asked Robert what he thought of Geelong Grammar, as he was considering sending his son there. Robert's comment was, 'The foremen are lousy but the factory turns out good product'. Indeed, the four Holmes à Court children are exceptionally fine 'product', but how much credit Geelong Grammar can claim for the end result is highly questionable. Yet those years had a significant impact and the experiences consolidated personality differences in four people whose views now have a significant impact on Heytesbury.

Far more influential than the school years on their character development was their very unusual home life and the discussions Robert held with his children. Robert did not often play with them, preferring to talk while Janet was more a spectator at these events than a participant. Family discussions or debates were quite serious affairs. They would often frustrate Catherine as she felt it would often end up as the boys against the girls. She and Janet would be on one side of the debate and Robert and Peter on the other. Catherine can't remember the detail of these debates, but it typically happened that her dad would bait her mum and she would step to her mother's defence, then Peter would join in. She began to rebel. Unlike the boys, she was enjoying herself at school. She was popular; she saw the relaxed way many of her friends would interact with their parents and she resented the strong sense of conformity and decorum required within her family. She began to shut herself off. She would be admonished by her father for not being part of the family, for placing too much importance on her friends. Between the ages of fourteen and eighteen, Catherine had an ongoing fight with her father about the way she wore her hair. She had a fringe and Robert couldn't stand it. Her hair was an issue at the dinner table. There would be doors slammed and tears shed. Janet would say, 'For God's sake, why don't you just tie it up when your father's around and let it go later?', and Catherine would respond, 'No, it's the principle'. She was not prepared to compromise, and dug her heels in. The fringe probably would have gone quickly if there had been no comment.

Catherine had come home from boarding school one year looking very thin and Robert said to her, 'You look anorexic. Anorexia is a psychological problem. We don't have psychological problems in this family. Eat steak'. And she did. Robert was not one to be defied. No one spoke back to Robert. He had his methods of dealing with such people. But Catherine was strong. She had Robert's genes, but also her mother's. She was fun-loving, vital and she was of a different generation, so her solution was to withdraw from her family and find solace and support with her friends. She recalls the only time her father ever raised his voice at her. Alan Newman, Robert's managing director, refused to fly from London to Australia because it was Christmas and his wife was pregnant and couldn't fly. Robert was furious and was in a very bad mood. Catherine intervened and said she thought he had a point: 'He's got a family; he's got kids. Why should he leave them for Christmas for work?'. Robert raised his voice then. Catherine says she was so petrified she couldn't remember what he said but she retorted, 'Well that's the difference between you and me'.

Simon, like Catherine, was not easily moulded. He was smacked only once by his father, as a young child for being naughty. He raced upstairs then came down to where his mother and father were, stuck his head around the door and said, 'I didn't appreciate that', and stormed off. It was the first time they had heard him use the word 'appreciate' and they were quite impressed. He only recalls being smacked once by his mother, in the kitchen, and he hit her back in the same way she had hit him. Simon recalls:

Discipline was funny. What we were most frightened of were what we called 'lectures' and that was a specific type of lecture from Dad. Quite a few times, ten times or something as a kid, I had these lectures and they seemed to be always in the dining room at 6 Osborne Parade, which was a really dark room. There were only three or four lights around the perimeter of the room and heavy red lightshades and we could never see what we were eating and we used to joke about that. It felt like an interrogation. It was pretty intimidating for a small kid. The table felt really big; the chairs had a really high back; if we could stretch we could put our hands on the top of the back. I always felt small in that room ... I remember kids at school telling me that they were smacked and I remember wishing at the time that I could be hit and that would be it, rather than this psychological drama ...

Whatever their views around the table or in their minds the children knew and accepted that everywhere they went they would have to be on their best behaviour and they were always pretty well behaved, except for Paul and Simon blowing things up and setting fire to the farm. Strangely, they recall no lectures for being pyromaniacs, and for Simon's worst 'crime', the farm fire, the lecture was very restrained.

The other ritual Robert put the children through was a formal reading of their school reports. They were never allowed to read their school reports; Robert read them to them individually. This was a procedure which distressed Janet as she watched her children's discomfort. She would sometimes plead on their behalf but Robert would be more likely to prolong the agony if she tried to intervene. Sometimes reports would sit for weeks. One year Catherine had to go to the Melbourne office on her way back to school because the summer holidays had passed and the report had not been read.

The telephone tended to dominate the Holmes à Court family routine. Robert lived much of his life on the phone. Meals waited, Janet waited, the family waited while Robert talked on the phone. Not only did he conduct most of his business on the phone, he was at his most relaxed on the phone. Both Peter and Paul had their best and most memorable conversations with their father over the phone. Catherine says:

If you go into any house that we've ever lived in there will be a chair where Dad would have spent a lot of time talking on the phone, a particular chair ... Dad would get on the phone and his time frame governed the phone conversation no matter what anyone else had to do. If Dad wanted to talk, he'd talk to you for three hours. He could play a game of chess while he was talking to you on the phone, he couldn't do that face-to-face. I think more often than not he was doing more than just talking to you on the phone.

Television and music were rarely heard in the Holmes à Court household. There just wasn't the time. It was not until Peter and Catherine first came back from boarding school that Simon and Paul were exposed to any sort of popular music. There were a few tapes in Robert's car that he played when he drove to the farm. Johnny Cash, Frank Sinatra, Neil Diamond, 'Stuff that drove me crazy', says Simon. It was very different from the music Janet had been brought up with. She had a tape of Vivaldi's *The Four Seasons* in her car, which Paul would insist was played loudly.

Janet had once sat Robert down and asked him to listen to Beethoven's Piano Concerto No. 5 and ponder on the mind of the person who had put it together, how the bassoon played, the violin, the double bass, the clarinet, how it all came together in a beautiful sound and what a remarkable mind must have produced it. Robert listened for about ten minutes and then said, 'I think I could do this if I really put my mind to it', so Janet turned it off and they never again listened to music. She did not enjoy Robert's taste in Louis Armstrong or Ella Fitzgerald. He called Janet's music 'church music', and such difference in taste meant there was very little music in the house.

On Catherine's sixteenth birthday, Robert phoned her at school to ask her what her favourite Beatles song was. She replied 'Penny Lane'. In fact she didn't know many Beatles songs and wasn't a big Beatles fan. Robert said, 'Are you sure it's not "Imagine" or "Yesterday"?'. She was sure, so Robert said, 'That's a shame because they earn more money. It's not one of the top two but it's up there, so that's all right. You can have it for your birthday'. Catherine still owns 'Penny Lane'. Although after all the children got into debt through some investments made on their behalf, Robert gave the three boys half a million dollars each on their birthdays, but not Catherine. When she asked was she getting money he said no, if she needed $500,000 she could sell 'Penny Lane'. She said, 'It's a present, you gave it to me, I can't sell it'. He replied, 'It's an asset Catherine; if you want half a million dollars, sell it'.

Equally, Robert could do something generous and charming. Catherine was in London with her father on her twentieth birthday. They were driving to the office and on the way he said, 'We'll buy you a birthday present', and they went to Cartier, where he bought her a bracelet designed like a Russian wedding ring with seven rings. He also organised a small dinner party for her birthday.

Robert tried to instil in the children his unemotional approach to business and the need to honour your obligations – a deal was a deal. When Catherine was thirteen, she wrote out a contract between her father and herself, handwritten, full of spelling mistakes, borrowing $1,500, on which she had to pay interest at current rates. She wanted to buy a horse and when the horse had progeny she sold one and paid him back.

While Peter and Robert had what Peter considered a special relationship and Catherine had a volatile relationship, overall they share common views about their father.

Peter believes he was very lucky to have had the time he had with his father. He felt his father was always available to him and focused on what they spoke about. For the last five years of his father's life he had had 'a solid relationship with him, been in dialogue with him, spent more time with him than ever before in his life, so I was the luckiest. I realised that at the time, Simon, Catherine and Paul hadn't had the opportunity that I had had'. The death of any parent is traumatic for any family and any child but in the case of Robert Holmes à Court there were massive financial and emotional ramifications for each of his children as well as his wife.

It would be some years before the Holmes à Court children as shareholders would participate in the business decisions of Heytesbury but inevitably these strong individuals, brought up in a most unusual environment, a product of exceptional and different parents, would have their say.

BHP AND THE CRASH

Australia scoffed at Robert Holmes à Court's first bid for BHP through the Western Australian caterpillar tractor company, Wigmores Limited, which Robert had acquired only days earlier. Wigmores was capitalised at only $6.7 million. It was to be a cashless share swap, two for the price of one, with $1 cash and a $2.50 option. It was, journalists said, an attempt by a flea to rape an elephant. Robert responded calmly, 'The ant always eats the elephant in the end'. While Robert's greatest indulgence in business may have been his media interests, his greatest challenge was undoubtedly BHP. He had kept his eye on BHP since his university days, when he had propounded a theory for gaining control of BHP to fellow law students.

He had developed an extraordinary capacity to keep many complex financial deals in his mind at the one time. By the early eighties Robert Holmes à Court was the most brilliant financial strategist Australia had ever seen and few in the world could equal him. He made share market trading appear effortless and Robert's personal style reinforced that view. He always seemed laid back, but the guise concealed enormous mental effort and hard work by Robert and his team.

Charles Bright, a junior executive with Potter Warburg knew Robert well and understood better than most Robert's methods and the way they had developed over the years. He first came into contact with Robert when, one day, he picked up the phone in the office of Laurie Muir (the senior partner in Potters) and found Robert on the other end of the line. It was a chance meeting after which he became a confidant, and from that time on he had almost daily phone calls from all over the world from Robert. Charles was then in his late twenties and though Robert had been seeking the senior partner, he was satisfied with the conversation and they developed a productive association. Sometimes the enquiry would be for a share price, sometimes to discuss an all-embracing strategy, sometimes the discussion would be nothing to do with the market. In regular communication, they spoke almost every day. When he phoned, Robert had no regard for time or the day of the week.

In the early eighties when Charles was in London he went to the theatre with Robert to see the play *Anyone for Dennis*, which was a send-up of Margaret and Dennis Thatcher. In the play, when anyone shook hands with Dennis, his leg lifted up and shook. One night after Robert had met the Thatchers, Charles's home phone shrilled at 3.00 a.m. Robert simply said, 'The leg shakes', and hung up. It took Charles all night to understand the context, but he didn't resent the interruption. Over all the years the dialogues took place, he never felt any imposition on his time. The calls 'were always immensely interesting', sometimes 'extremely focused', sometimes 'relaxed and eclectic'. When Robert died, Charles's sense of loss was very deep.

He found Robert complex, extraordinarily open-minded, with no baggage to weigh down his thinking; everything with him was new and fresh. Robert had the boldness to consider quite outrageous ideas such as a company like Wigmores bidding for BHP, a notion that the financial institutions found incomprehensible. While Robert and Charles spoke of many things, the discussion was always intellectual, not personal. Robert never spoke of his health or the way he felt. They both shared a schoolboy sense of humour and would often engage in verbal one-up-manship. Charles rejects the view of Robert as shy or dark. He thinks he was 'a normal human being. Unusual, different, non-conforming, irreverent but not strange'.

Charles described Robert's approach to business as 'highly individualistic and unconventional'. While 'brilliance' and 'genius' were applicable words, Charles saw the major ingredient of Robert's success as being hard work. He said, 'I suspect Rob spent many hours thinking and reading and working at things and then made them sound as if they were a moment of inspiration'. And he achieved what he achieved through debt financing equity. That was the efficient way to spend money in the eighties when there was high inflation. The borrowings would reduce as inflation increased the value of the equity investment.

The idea of a company having an in-house research capacity to analyse companies and their balance sheets was brand new in the seventies. The Bell Group was one of the first, and when Robert expressed what might appear to be a flight of fancy it often proved to be the result of painstaking, lengthy analysis and research. Having done the research, there would be marathon staff meetings chewing over plans and gambits while the idea was examined from every perspective. Then an action would be initiated and invariably thrown out, as Robert devised a different course. The degree of flexibility in Robert's approach was unique. He would talk with Charles, with journalists, with contacts all over the world in the network he had developed, operating at different levels, trying out ideas. In the implementation phase, pressure might need to be exerted, opponents sounded out, options opened up – the conclusion could never be predicted. The major difference between Robert's approach and that of many other entrepreneurs was that he maintained flexibility throughout every stage; there was no rigid sequential thinking.

In 1979, when he launched the bid on Ansett, Bell was a relatively small company with just 5 million shares on issue. When he came to the east coast from the west, Potters identified potential new shareholders and Robert would go to see them. In 1981, Charles and Robert repeated the same process for London and Europe. They did the same in the US, raising institutional awareness of Bell with the money managers.

Robert recognised very early the need to communicate with people who managed money and to communicate with the press. To the business establishment, Robert was an upstart. He had risen from nothing and, even worse, had come from the west; he needed to establish his credibility with the financial institutions. Robert's first placement of shares was done at a premium. That was unheard of and he achieved that by burning leather and meeting and talking to people. Robert's genius was firstly in his analysis and reading of the market. Secondly, it was in his ability to conjure up long-term strategic aims which might take thirty moves, in his grand, chess-playing style. These moves would be unfathomable to other people. For a company the size of Bell Resources to dominate a market, and to dominate a company whose share register was the size of BHP's, was an amazing feat – yet it was not what he did but how he did it that was more remarkable.

Robert had been studying BHP for several years before he made the first cheeky bid through Wigmores, a bid which even he jokingly referred to as 'Wig who?'. He acknowledged it was 'a cheap way of increasing the capital of Wigmores'[1] which later, in September 1983, became Bell Resources when Robert paid $40.01 million for the assets of Wigmores in a tidying-up operation. But BHP, despite its size and icon status, fitted all Robert's ingredients for a takeover target. The slump of 1982–83 which saw BHP take a loss in its steelworks jolted the near century-old company, then capitalised at barely $2 billion. The issues involved were for Robert no different from those with WA Woollen in 1970. The assets were underperforming and undervalued.

Robert Holmes à Court was the entrepreneur who demonstrated most effectively the strength of shareholder power against complacent boards of management. Up until the eighties, shareholders had limited influence on the way large Australian and international companies did their business. Most shareholders didn't trade in shares, and money institutions were passive. The change which occurred in that decade meant shareholders began to demand results and boards of underperforming companies had to smarten up their act or risk being thrown out or taken over.

In the early days of his takeover of ACC in London, Robert had sent a memo to Derek Williams, one of his analysts in the UK, saying simply, 'Please analyse BP'. Derek thought, 'This man doesn't know that BP is the biggest company in Europe'. He sent a memo back to Robert saying, 'This is too big for us to consider'. Robert responded, 'Nothing is too big for me to consider'. It was a typical Robert test. He didn't want to know about BP; he already knew all about it. He wanted to know what Derek knew about BP.

This exchange of memos occurred when Robert was seriously analysing BHP and planning his strategy. He was convinced the gigantic Australian company should be doing much better than it was, that it had grown too big and should be broken back down into its component parts – steel, petroleum, oil, gas and so on. Robert used to say he was going to write the story of BHP and he was going to call it *Colour It Grey*. (Years later BHP indeed published a history of the first 100 years with a grey cover.) Robert laid a $50 bet with John Reynolds asking him to guess which company he intended to take over next. John, who knew Robert well by now, thought of the most outrageous possibility and said BHP. John won the bet and kept the $50 note he received.

But Robert was more tight-lipped about his plans with his board. John Studdy, a partner with Coopers and Lybrand, the auditors of Robert's companies, had joined the Bell Group board in July 1983 when Robert wanted a director from the east coast – obviously in preparation for his expansion east. John Studdy learnt of Robert's bid when he received a telephone call from one of Robert's executives to inform him that the company of which he was a director had made a bid for BHP. He could not believe what he had been told and took some time to come to terms with what was happening.

The bid by Wigmores on 15 August 1983 for BHP was important in getting the ball rolling. 'There were 800,000 acceptances of the

Wigmores offer but those sellers were people who in total held 70 million BHP shares, Robert says'.[2] Although acceptances totalled less than 1% of BHP's capital, they gave Robert 'about 1,000 individual shareholders and some major institutions, most of which retained the bulk of their BHP stakes',[3] and were able to compare the performance of Bell Resources and BHP.

The bid was audacious or courageous depending on your point of view. Tandberg published a cartoon of Sir James Balderstone the chairman of BHP saying, 'A bid for BHP? Pull the other one'. In the next drawing Robert was pulling his other leg, which Sir James was holding out, and the leg was coming off in Robert's hands. In another cartoon Sir James was saying, 'It's a Clayton's bid' and then turning round and saying, 'Pass the Brandy'. Robert and Janet named two horses Clayton's Bid and Pass the Brandy. (Clayton's Bid became a champion and Robert gave the mare to Janet.)

After the initial sneers at the Wigmores bid for BHP in August 1983, Robert demonstrated with a dawn raid on Weeks Petroleum that Wigmores was not to be laughed at. After doing his homework and quietly accumulating stock, he used a Bermuda-based subsidiary of ACC (in Bermuda there were none of the restrictions of the London or Australian takeover codes to prevent a lightning raid), to make his move. While America slept, Australia was preparing to sleep, and in London they were just beginning to go to work, Robert got control of the $900 million Weeks empire in twenty minutes. The target was 15 million shares. They got 12 million in twenty minutes and had 15 million before the day was out.

By early 1984, the Bell Group had significant interests, through TVW and ACC, in Jabiru Prospect (10.3%), Weeks Australia (10.3%), Weeks Petroleum (51.2%), Fleet Holdings (9%); through Bell Bros Holdings, Western Australian Onshore Oil NL (18.7%), Mincorp Petroleum NL (20.86%), Fremantle Gas and Coke Co Ltd and through Bell Resources Lt, Utah (5%) and BHP (2.3%).[4]

A few months after his initial bid for BHP, Robert was able to demonstrate to institutional investors that Wigmores shareholders had done four times better than BHP shareholders, and Bell Group shareholders had done thirty times better than BHP shareholders.

Robert placed Bell Resources stocks with an influential block of BHP shareholders and began to demonstrate that BHP's divisions of oil, minerals and steel would be worth much more individually than as a whole under BHP management.[5] Robert was building up Bell Resources to be not a mirror image, but a better image of BHP. He was demonstrating in effect that he had a mini-BHP that was outperforming BHP and that he could absorb BHP. Robert was enjoying himself immensely.

One shareholder at BHP's annual general meeting said that BHP should appoint Holmes à Court chief executive and pay him $1 million a year. Robert said, 'He had the right idea but the price was wrong'.[6] The ant had begun to eat the elephant. The assumption by the BHP board that Robert wanted a quick profit and would exit was a near-fatal error. Robert wanted BHP more than he wanted West Australian Newspapers and he had the patience to wait for both. The fundamental error made by the BHP board, its chairman, its managing director, and later John Elliott, was to assume Robert was not to be taken seriously. They misread his intentions and the scoffing and derisive public comments made about Robert rankled with both him and Janet.

Had they studied Robert's takeover record over the previous decade they would have found a consistent pattern. With the exception of the Elder Smith Goldsbrough Mort bid in 1981, which Robert sold out of because he believed the bid would threaten Bell, the entrepreneur stuck to his stated intentions. He had certainly moved in and out of investments to take a profit and thus build up his cash and funding base, but his main targets – Bell, UK Associated Communications Corporation, Ansett and the Herald and Weekly Times – were targets he wished to control and he demonstrated patience, resilience and tenacity as he stalked his prey. But BHP chose to label Holmes à Court as a 'greenmailer', a practice considered repugnant by the Melbourne establishment who thought Robert was simply looking to work himself into a position where they would have no option but to buy him out to his profit. Possibly the wisest thing the board could have done would have been to try to pay him off as quickly as possible, as the board of Greenbushes Tin had done in the seventies when they handed Robert a profit of $500,000 to get him off their share register.[7] In the case of BHP there was of course no guarantee that he would not be back.

Robert returned in 1984 with another scrip offer. This time he offered Bell Resources shares and options in return for BHP shares. BHP blocked the bid in court but Robert had picked up 7.5 million shares. Throughout the BHP saga Robert was surrounded by his team of analysts and lawyers, many of them young. He would have lunch with the team in the Bell Melbourne office conference room and often dinner in the Melbourne Spring Street penthouse at the end of the day. As his major focus was in Australia and he had little action in the US, his young staff from the New York office joined the Melbourne team. They became devoted to Robert and relished the experience he gave them.

Katherine Bialo from New York, who joined Robert from Weeks Petroleum, was part of the group. She found the experience 'very exciting'. She said:

> Robert obviously enjoyed the spotlight. He enjoyed having people wonder what he was doing and what he was going to do next ... He was really always the same, very cordial, very quiet ... he would always go 'mmm, mmm', there'd be long, long silences that were hard to take until you got used to them and then you'd learn to sit there; you weren't supposed to fill up the time by yakking, saying something that you didn't need to say. Eventually you got comfortable with the fact that if he had something that he wanted to know he would ask you, and if you had something you needed to tell him you would tell him but otherwise there would be a lot of long silences and a lot of 'mmms'.

For Janet, so much was happening in these years that they are something of a blur. The children were at boarding school but she would try to keep in touch. She was packing and unpacking and making seemingly endless cups of tea. She was the wife of the chairman; that was her role. She had no authority and although she was moving in and out of rooms where the discussion was going on she would follow much of the saga by reading the newspapers. At Spring Street Janet would play the hostess. She would be at the apartment when everyone arrived. They had a resident cook who prepared beautiful meals and Robert would invariably avoid the grains, vegetables, salad and fresh fruit. Katherine Bialo had the impression that 'Janet was walking on eggs with him'. She saw Robert explode at Janet once or twice for:

something that seemed relatively trivial — not having made an appointment or something and he really blasted her in the presence of everyone sitting at the dinner table ... She was obviously embarrassed but took it with whatever good grace she could ... There was clearly a lot of anger directed at her without regard to the fact that he was in a room full of people and that it was inappropriate behaviour.

Nevertheless, the admiration his loyal staff felt for Robert was not diminished by such outbursts. They admired him; they enjoyed working for him. He was cordial and respectful to them and to the younger ones quite paternal. He conveyed the feeling that he cared for them. They in turn felt privileged to work for him and to be exposed to his intellect and his thinking. They were prepared to put in very long hours for Robert and he was very demanding. He wanted report after report on BHP, on the various sectors of the operation, the steel business, the coal business, the coal acquisition, all sectors. Typically he wanted a lot of information in a very short period of time.

Steve Johnston, who worked with the BHP team and was later invited to join Heytesbury, said of his time with Robert:

We worked long hours but I enjoyed it; no regrets — it was good experience for me. I was a young guy who was fortunate enough to get the exposure that I did and I made the most of it; I was very dedicated ... He was a good teacher for me. He taught me a lot about business, about assessing companies. He gave me a lot of feedback ... He taught me a helluva lot.

During the takeover process Robert's share market strategists developed a complex computer program which combined stock with put-and-call options in a formula which meant Robert was trading at a 'no loss' base and whether the shares went up or down he made money. Janet would ask why she couldn't do that with her shares and Robert explained she could if she had a billion-dollar share base. The financial journalists had no idea that Robert had been manipulating the BHP market for some time.

In *The Bold Riders*,[8] Trevor Sykes describes the complicated behind-the-scenes dealings Robert had with Spalvins of Adelaide Steamship. Robert began to write call options on BHP shares and did a deal where Adsteam agreed to sell 70 million BHP shares to him in August and September 1986 at $7.11 a share, compared to the current share price of around $5.50. The deal concealed from the market the fact that what appeared to be happening was the reverse of the truth. Robert delivered his stock as options expired and appeared to be selling as his holding dwindled from 6% to below 5%. Spalvins, who had to build his holding to reach 70 million, appeared the big buyer. BHP chiefs were fairly relaxed because they felt that Spalvins was unlikely to make a takeover bid.[9]

In August 1985, *Business Review Weekly*[10] named Robert Holmes à Court the $300 million man, the new king of Australia's rich. It had taken fifteen years. In the year up to August, Robert's wealth had increased by $2.6 million a week or $15,475 an hour. He owned 44.6% of his Bell Group and had enjoyed a busy twelve months raiding Asarco in the US for a 10% share, pursuing MIM holdings and achieving a stake of 44%, indulging in minor power plays in David Syme and Elders shares, while all the time focusing on his major target interests: the Herald and Weekly Times and BHP. He was involved in as many takeover battles in the courts as he was on the bourse and accumulating further lifestyle assets – horses, cars, art and houses – in his spare time.

It was not until October 1985 that Robert returned to the market to buy heavily into BHP call options as well as buying 10 million shares at $8.50, taking him above the 10% level, which made him a substantial shareholder under the law and therefore forced to make a substantial shareholder statement. The $500 million option deal with Adsteam had to be disclosed. Sykes says, 'Not only was it the biggest option deal in Australia's history (some would call it the biggest bet) but it presaged a serious bid for BHP'.[11] Robert then began to woo the media openly and gave extensive interviews on the record. In December 1985 he gave his most extensive and comprehensive interview to the *Australian* journalists David Potts and Hamish Fraser over three evenings in Perth and in his Melbourne penthouse, with a final session going from 5.00 p.m. to 5.30 a.m., an exhausting marathon which Janet battled out at Robert's side although she had a full day ahead of her. The journalists described Janet as:

> *anxious as Robert to see that we understand the issues and the man. She thinks some of the material we drafted is incorrect, some out of context and some plainly offensive. She bridles at parts of the draft ... 'It's important to realise', she says, 'that Robert realises the importance of BHP to the Australian economy'. Let there be no mistake she is saying that all the implications of the BHP takeover have been considered. This is not just some old share plan.*[12]

This interview was part of a public relations campaign by Robert to convince the financial institutions of his serious intent and his value to BHP.

Robert drew on Janet, who was his greatest public relations asset, more and more frequently. She was the warm, human face of Robert Holmes à Court. She knew the value 'of a well-placed letter or story defending Robert, promoting his business or discussing their art collection ... In contrast, one can't imagine a female face of BHP. Lady Balderstone? Mrs Loton? No. BHP is the Big Australian Male'.[13]

Janet was there when Robert dealt with the unions. Her background was a useful foil. The unionists regarded Robert with great suspicion, but in having a wife with a very left-wing political background he couldn't be all bad. In addition Robert's history and role in the Bell Bros dispute with John Holland was known among union leaders and Robert began to make some ground in building up union confidence.

Janet increased her media exposure as Robert capitalised on her public relations value. She appeared at the Melbourne Stock Exchange to observe the bourse in action. When interviewed she said, 'I'm just watching myself lose $20,000'. 'One doesn't need to be Einstein to figure out that Mrs Holmes à Court holds a useful 100,000 Bell shares. When asked, "Did she think hubby would get control?" "Eventually", the lady confided. "They've brought it on themselves"'.[14] Regular snippets began appearing about Janet's life and views. In March 1986, at the height of corporate warfare between BHP and Robert, when Janet attended the Victorian Supreme Court with son Peter to watch Bell Resources QC Alan Goldberg in action withdrawing the Bell Resources present offer, Janet revealed 'Robert and I have been in Melbourne since the beginning of February ... been back to Perth on the odd weekend [the house at the Stud was being built].' They had not eaten out or gone to the theatre or done anything of note. 'Very dull and boring really'. Despite the bid, life had proceeded 'much the same as normal'. She did not know when they would return to Perth. 'I take the travel arrangements from Robert. When he says "pack the bags" I do it'.[15] And pack the bags she did. Not only did she carry them in and out of airports across Australia but around the world as well, as the second prong of Robert's public relations venture was to tour the financial capitals of Europe. His story was that Robert Holmes à Court would be good for BHP and good for Australia.

The institutions were beginning to agree that Robert may be good for BHP. Bell's performance was demonstrable, investors in Bell Resources were doing better than they were in BHP. Robert was demonstrating the individual divisions of oil, minerals and steel were worth more individually than as a whole under BHP management. But the board of BHP was unmoved. They became increasingly paranoid and intransigent. At no time did they ever ask Robert what his intentions were. They hoped by ignoring Robert he would somehow go away. The moves they made to try to resist Robert's takeover would entangle BHP in a damaging financial imbroglio. Brian Loton, managing director, and Sir James Balderstone the chairman were (in the view of Robert Gottliebsen, managing editor of *Business Review Weekly*),[16] 'in the matter of takeover ... out of their depth'. At the annual dinner of the Sydney Stock Exchange, Brian Loton couldn't bring himself to mention his largest stockholder by name.

Prior to Christmas 1985 Robert called on Sir James to advise him of his general intentions. He said he had no specific plans but would increase his shareholdings. He was considering many alternatives. On the morning of 4 February, Robert met Sir James to tell the BHP chairman he would be making a further offer that afternoon and that he wanted a seat on the board. The Bell Resources partial bid of $7 a share was the third bid for BHP. Robert was told BHP would be opposed to his presence on the board. David Adam, BHP director and executive general manager of Corporate Affairs, and Brian Loton were particularly intransigent. Robert was told they would oppose the bid in every way they could.

Robert withdrew his February bid in March and renewed in April. During this time BHP was working to put together a defensive deal with John Elliott at Elders. The reverberations of the deal, which was reported widely, were felt for the next eleven years. Saturday 5 April 1986 was a home game for the Australian Football League (AFL) team, Carlton. Brian Loton attended as a guest of John Elliott who was the president of the Carlton Football Club. They had a congenial time and enjoyed watching Carlton's victory over Richmond. John Elliott had been trying for months to persuade BHP to invest in Elders. Over the next five days Elliott's Elders executives worked day and night to stitch together $1.8 billion in finance.

On the morning of 10 April 1986, a representative of Elders attempted to contact Robert with an offer to buy his holding in BHP but Robert could not be enticed to the telephone. He wanted firm details on the price. On the same day Elders launched an on-market raid for 19.9% of BHP at $7.36 a share. 'It was the most spectacular one-day raid in world history.'[17] Elders spent nearly $2 billion in twenty-four hours to pick up $225 million worth of BHP shares at

$7.36 each. If the BHP board couldn't get Robert out, this was the next best alternative. The Elders board meeting which approved the purchase of 19.9% of BHP also approved the issue of redeemable preference shares to raise $1 billion with related options. It was not revealed until Monday 14 April that these preference shares had been issued to BHP. On Saturday 12 April, Robert met with John Elliott at his Toorak flat. Elliott wanted Robert to sell his shareholding in BHP. Robert said no, he would be buying more shares and asked Elliott if he would sell. The reported answer was 'No'. Elliott 'couldn't sell his BHP shares and still do business in this town'.[18] Both men met again on 29 April when both reiterated their positions. A further meeting took place on 7 May when Elliott offered a $400 million profit for Robert if he sold his BHP holding. Robert responded he would be happy to take over Elders. He could not be seduced. But the BHP board remained unrelenting in its opposition to Robert.

Janet showed her fire as well as her loyalty when she rose to her feet to speak to the Annual General Meeting of Bell Resources on 29 May 1986. She was described by John Hamilton as a tall figure 'in a flowing black dress with flying wild ducks ... whose eyes flashed as brightly as the cross of diamonds on her wedding finger'.[19] Robert acknowledged, 'The lady in the front row'. 'Janet' [Hamilton said], 'chose her words carefully with controlled fury'. 'We have been subject to the most amazing paid press and media campaign trying to damage our company and Mr Holmes à Court', said the wife of the multimillionaire. 'There are twelve directors of BHP. They have spent an enormous amount of their shareholders' funds on this campaign.' She paused to emphasise her point. 'Only three of these people have even met Mr Holmes à Court. I think that is an amazing corporate mistake.' She went on quietly, as the packed and stunned meeting of shareholders hung on every word. She said that if the position had been reversed in the takeover battle, 'I believe Mr Holmes à Court would at least communicate with them'.

A moustached gentleman leapt to his feet to congratulate Robert on 'a wonderful choice of an excellent wife'. There were 700 eager shareholders at the media event and Robert used the forum to put his view that with $3 billion invested in BHP he thought 'they should just hear me'. The next day Janet's impassioned statement was featured in every paper across the country. Robert's human face had made an impact.

By now under serious threat, BHP was putting pressure on the Hawke Government to intervene, a move that backfired when Robert appeared before a panel of seven cabinet ministers chaired by Bob Hawke and satisfied them that a public inquiry was not warranted. In contrast to the army of executives and lawyers who appeared before the ministerial committee on behalf of BHP, Robert appeared alone, pulling an envelope from his pocket on which he had jotted some notes. The ministers were impressed. The ministers were persuaded. Earlier Treasurer Paul Keating had rung Robert (whom he had never met) to say he'd like to talk to him. They met in Melbourne. With pad in hand he said, 'Now tell me all about it. What's this all about? What do you want to do?'. Robert laid out his plans and the Treasurer said effectively, 'Go for it'. The two men developed a respect for one another and on hearing of Robert's death Keating said, 'He was a prince of the corporate play and he is a great loss to corporate Australia'.[20]

Robert and his directors decided to improve the current offer in May to $9.20. Geoff Cornish, who was company secretary of all the Bell companies from March 1982 to August 1988, was responsible for getting the offers out to the shareholders and processing the acceptances. Bell's share register was around 20,000, but BHP's register was 180,000. Informing them was a massive task. When the decision was made to increase the offer, timing was critical but Robert's team were excited, stimulated and committed. They were all working very hard, long hours on a demanding task but the hours were never an issue. With Robert's latest offer, a twenty-page document had to be finalised, printed and distributed. Following the morning decision the lawyers had the document finalised by 6.00 p.m. The pages were faxed to the printers in one of the industrial suburbs, who then set about typesetting. Geoff Cornish liaised by phone and at 11.00 p.m. he went to the factory to proofread the document. The changes were complete by 2.00 a.m. and then the print-run started. The first copies were available by 10.00 a.m. A job that didn't seem possible was accomplished in less than twenty-four hours.

The bid acceptances began to trickle in and on the last day there was an avalanche. Robert's offices in Melbourne, although not the official drop-off point, were besieged by shareholders waving their share certificates and acceptance forms and virtually everyone in the office was accepting the forms. Hundreds of people came in and Robert walked through them with a big smile on his face, greatly enjoying the shareholders' enthusiasm for the bid.

By the end of the month Bell had 28% of BHP but still no control. Robert sought a truce on the unnecessary corporate warfare. He met with Brian Loton and they agreed there were only three logical alternatives: that Robert gained control of BHP; that Bell Resources remained a shareholder and there was a truce; that Robert sold his shares. Brian told Robert that 'the first two options were not worth talking about'.[21] John Elliott meanwhile either wanted to be managing director of BHP or pursue other plans. He was not a man to sit quietly for long.

Janet found it extraordinary that the BHP board would embrace John Elliott rather than Robert. At the height of the stand-off between Robert and the BHP board, Janet was sent a note which listed all Robert's characteristics on one side with Elliott's down the other side. The note said, 'Which of these two men would you think the Melbourne establishment would prefer? The ocker, beer-drinking, Elliott or the rather urbane, sophisticated, well-educated Mr Holmes à Court?'.

Behind the scenes there was not complete trust of John Elliott. The board was concerned that if BHP did nothing, the ocker Elliott and the urbane Holmes à Court might well do a deal. Robert very astutely underscored the point when in July he handed over his proxies to Elliott for the company's 23 September annual general meeting. While it was a flamboyant move it demonstrated that the two men between them controlled BHP's destiny. So peace talks began. On 15 September John Elliott and Robert were given BHP board seats in exchange for pledges not to buy each other's shares unless they made an offer to all BHP shareholders at the same terms.[22] Both men accepted the offer, acknowledging that the situation could change in the future.

The BHP annual general meeting was held in the Melbourne Exhibition Building where 3,000 people turned up to give the chairman a hard time. At the start of the meeting a shareholder moved that Balderstone should step down as chairman and let Robert Holmes à Court take the chair. He was ruled out of order. It was not a day Sir James Balderstone enjoyed.

Robert Holmes à Court's profile was high. *Business Review Weekly's* 15 August 1986 edition listed the Rich 200. Robert's wealth was estimated at $600 million. That year Robert had been named one of Australia's best dressed men by *Mode* magazine, an ironic contrast to the code name 'warthog' given him by his opponents in the BHP takeover battle. His shareholders had lionised him. During the year he had purchased Double Island off Cairns in the Whitsunday passage for $645,000. He had 2,000 tonnes of silica sand brought in from Cape Flattery on the mainland to improve the beach that he would visit only twice, and on the side, while his BHP manoeuvres were taking place, he dabbled in the Coles takeover of Myer to walk away with $10 million. He had also played the role of white knight to protect his principal banker Standard Chartered which was threatened by Lloyds Bank.

Through it all Janet was his loyal attendant. She resented the year of ostracism they had gone through in Melbourne and on publication of the Rich 200 she protested:

[The list represented] the gross invasion of privacy ... you say that Mr Holmes à Court's wealth has increased by $2,604 per minute based on a forty-hour week and four weeks' annual leave. In the twenty years since we married, Robert has never worked a forty-hour week. Ninety would be the average and one hundred is quite common. Also, in this period he has not taken a total of four weeks' leave, let alone four weeks a year ... May I suggest a follow-up article which details firstly, how hard the people named work to achieve what our society deems success

and secondly, how many people they each employ or how many Australians directly or indirectly owe their livelihoods to them.

An interesting study could be in Albany in Western Australia, for example, where almost all local industries except the Albany Woollen Mills have been closed down and so many of the people depend on the Bell Group and its subsidiaries for their bread and butter.[23]

All the publicity was grist to Robert's mill and he enjoyed himself immensely on the BHP board. His close exposure gave him a chance to evaluate the talent of staff and board members. He was very disenchanted with the board members but impressed with some of the people working for BHP, including John Prescott who was to succeed Brian Loton as managing director. Some of the BHP staff let it be known that they welcomed Robert's role on the board as he delved into the minutiae and challenged their thinking. Robert had obviously done his homework, and read their reports and recommendations. He was regarded as a good contributor.

By February 1987 financial journalists were reporting there was 'a quiet revolution' going on within BHP and that Holmes à Court was enjoying 'a surprisingly warm relationship with former arch foe' Brian Loton.[24] They reported that Elliott was 'looking the more likely seller', as his interests were taken up with his newly acquired London-based Courage brewing group. Robert's quick grasp of BHP led to a growing consensus that he was making a valuable contribution to the board. The betting was on another bid from Robert. He was in *de facto* control of BHP. Bell interests had something like 30% of the issued shares (which normally of itself did not grant control) but the next largest shareholder [after Elliot], the AMP Society, had around 5%. This made Bell's interest six times larger than the next biggest shareholder. At board meetings Robert had a lot of say over what did or did not happen so, while not exerting the total influence he was seeking, he was guiding the Big Australian in the direction he wanted it to go.

Ironically, as Robert got closer to controlling BHP he began, in conversation with Janet, to ask whether this was what he really wanted. He was starting to realise the magnitude of running BHP.

But in the end he did not have to make the final decision that, despite his momentary doubts, he now believed would be inevitable. Fate was to intervene.

On Tuesday, 20 October 1987 Australia woke to learn that the US market had closed down 508 points, or more than 22%. The Dow Jones industrial average tracks the share prices of the thirty largest US corporations. Why it should have fallen on that day by so much and what triggered the huge sell off is not easily explained. But a large proportion of the share market is in the hands of a relatively few institutional players and so a panic is easily instigated. The crash hit Australia harder than any other industrialised market, and billions of dollars – the estimate was $55 billion – vanished that day.

Robert Holmes à Court lost more than any other investor internationally. Earlier in the year *Business Review Weekly* had estimated Robert's worth at $1.4 billion. He peaked before the crash at an estimated $1.5 billion. A year later Robert's estimated worth was $550 million.

Initially Robert thought he was secure. When asked how the crash would affect his operations, he responded with confidence that despite his billion dollar loss he had a $1 billion line of credit in place with a major US institution, Merrill Lynch. The deal had been done precisely in anticipation of a crash, an event which was increasingly being talked about. But Robert, distracted by his BHP dealings, had waited too long. What in normal circumstances would have been a done deal came undone.

Robert was at the BHP board meeting in Wollongong a few days after the crash when he was called out. He returned to say Merrill Lynch did not intend to go on with his underwriting. This was the cash he needed to fund his BHP stock. Robert had been confident that he would be protected by the Merrill Lynch transaction, which had been concluded by his staff in London several days before the crash. They had been congratulated on a fine deal, on what they believed was a done deal. But the investment bank had in its contract a trigger point where they could cancel the transaction in the event of a war or a major world occurrence in the stock market. Merrill Lynch claimed the crash qualified and entitled them to call the transaction off, placing enormous financing obligations on the Bell Group. The BHP shareholding, 36% by now, caused a massive debt burden for Bell following the crash. This was the end of Robert's bid for BHP. He was forced to sell out of BHP for a low price and a substantial loss. Five years of intensive strategising were over. The disappointment was profound. But BHP would not be free of the ramifications of this period in its history for eleven more years.

BHP bought out 19% of Robert's BHP holding for $7 a share, a bargain for BHP, but also a good deal for Robert who was struggling to save his empire from ruin at the time. John Elliott did not survive his rescue mission but BHP remained locked into Foster's Brewing Group, a business outside BHP's expertise. Additionally the Big Australian's reputation and credibility were damaged by its engagement in transactions that came to be questioned in terms of the Companies Code. In the end BHP just made it through the regulatory maze. The financial cost was reckoned at $750 million. Had the return on its Foster's investment been equivalent to its average dividends from its resource operations, the company would have generated $5 billion in additional wealth to shareholders.[25] The defence offered for paying such a price was 'that Robert would have broken up BHP into several smaller companies to finance his debt-fuelled takeover binge' and 'that as part of the final settlement BHP effectively bought back 40% of its capital'[26] and that investment paid off handsomely.

Robert's argument that it would be more profitable for shareholders in BHP and more efficient for the company to separate the divisions reared its head again in August 1997 when the head of BHP Petroleum John O'Connor left BHP because of irreconcilable differences after he had proposed floating off one of the parts of BHP. Breaking up BHP was still anathema to the board of the company. Following O'Connor's departure, two other division heads left also, causing the major shareholders in BHP to call for a full and frank review of the company. The ghost of Robert Holmes à Court must have been smiling his enigmatic, whimsical smile.

In 1997, ten years after the crash, financial commentators were asking 'Was Robert Holmes à Court right?'. BHP's 'score card in the past decade shows more failures than successes with lack of proper due diligence a common theme that has cost shareholders up to $20 billion in lost value'.[27] The languishing BHP share price, which fell to $12 in the crash of October 1997, has led again to talk of breaking up BHP's business units into single entities. Alan Kohler claimed that Brian Loton and his chief financial officer Geoff Heeley never got back in control of the business groups after his attention was diverted by Robert Holmes à Court.[28] In 1997 BHP found itself once again in a classic takeover and break-up situation, and the managing director, John Prescott, fell on his sword in 1998. The chairman of the board, Jerry Ellis, will leave to make way for National Australia Bank chief executive Don Argus in 1999. A new chief for BHP, American-born Paul Anderson, was announced on 3 November 1998. One of Anderson's first actions after assuming the managing director's role in December 1998 was to unwind Beswick, the eleven-year-old takeover defence vehicle that had been put in place to protect BHP from Robert Holmes à Court. Anderson said, 'the structure was so complex I couldn't understand it, so we had to get rid of it'.[29]

The impact of the crash on Robert's business aspirations was terminal, although many commentators view his rise from economic ruin as his greatest coup of all – a better indication of his skills than his earlier takeovers. Others say he died of a broken heart as a result of the crash and his failure to achieve his great ambition with BHP.[30] Robert's BHP strategy was probably one of the most brilliant takeover plans in corporate takeover history and he was not criticised or found to have breached the law. Robert checked every move he wanted to make with Raymond Schoer at the Australian Securities Commission and was impeccable in ensuring the legality of his plans. Raymond, who was executive director and chief executive of the National Companies and Securities Commission (NCSC), said Robert:

was an honourable sort of person. He wanted to know how far he could go, where the boundary was; there was never a debate. He really wanted to know what did the rules permit ... If we said the line's there, he would just accept that and we never argued.

Janet believed the crash hastened Robert's death. She would say to the WA Inc Inquiry that 'her husband had only hoped to leave his position as Bell Group chairman in 1988 with his life'.[31] But Robert's health was such that his life was destined to be shortened. During the NCSC hearings in Melbourne in May 1986, after months of intense activity dealing with BHP, Michael Meagher described Robert's appearance:

The man seemed to have aged ten years in thirty-three months [since the Wigmores bid]. The face ... showed jowls hanging from a puffed languid face. Much of the sparkle had deserted his eyes. His hair had greyed noticeably.[32]

In August 1983 the cameras 'captured an elegant, boyish, bright-eyed executive'. That man had disappeared well before the crash.

Robert's health had always been a worry to Janet, his children and some of his executives. But there was a feeling he'd be one of those people who would break all the rules and last forever. Robert spent most of his time indoors; walking outside was unusual. He would sit and think and work. Increasingly his poor health showed. His complexion was pale, puffy and blotchy. He chain smoked his Henry Winterman long panatellas, an extreme nicotine addict. For someone so much in control of most aspects of his life, this was Robert's Achilles heel and his behaviour regarding his health was as idiosyncratic as everything else about him. Janet lost track of the number of cigars he smoked in a day: 'thirty, forty, heaps'. One of her nightmares was her responsibility to have cigars on hand at all times. She had them stashed everywhere. Robert consumed them. He would have five alight at once around the house.

Janet once persuaded him to give up smoking. They were out to dinner in a favourite Perth restaurant called the Bohemia Cafe eating spicy garlic sausages when Janet said, 'It really does worry me enormously that you smoke so much'. Robert replied, 'Oh, does it really? Oh well, I'll give it up'. He went out to the car, put his cigarettes in the boot and didn't smoke for around four years, until one night when he was away from Janet, John Reynolds gave him a cigar. She said, 'He virtually never had a cigar out of his mouth from then on until he died'.

Janet bought them almost by the truck load, for if Robert didn't have them 'he was unbearable'. Shortly before he died Robert even sent his London chauffeur to Amsterdam to the Henry Winterman factory to see if he could get some cigars, because they were no longer being imported into London. He returned without them and Janet paid for the airfare after Robert's death. Like all addicts Robert was into denial. When he had shocking fits of coughing he would dismiss them by saying, 'I'm getting a cold' and 'After all I don't inhale cigars you know'.

Robert managed his diabetes in his own way and was as self-sufficient with his illness as he appeared to be in all things. He didn't want his disease to influence or have any adverse effect on anything he was doing and he didn't want anyone else to know. He wanted no fuss. As his children had never been told of his condition and, at the time of his death, Catherine was the only one to have worked it out, they were entitled to feel some anger. For it is a fact that as the offspring of a diabetic they had a 20% higher possibility than the normal population of inheriting the disease. Janet ensured they were provided with a healthy diet and she encouraged them to lead healthy lifestyles. But she loyally kept Robert's secret.

It was Janet's job to conceal and dispose of Robert's syringes. He didn't like doctors telling him what to do so he had no one regularly monitoring his diabetes. It was only when there was a medical crisis that he would see a doctor. Rex Hughes, his doctor in Perth who had been a neighbour to Janet's family in Greenmount, and a friend to both, had a sympathetic view of Robert's approach to his disease. He said of Robert's lifestyle, 'It was not an unintelligent decision ... he never spoke about getting old ... he was going to enjoy life to the full while he could ... it was more a game ... that was very hard for certain members of the medical profession'. A specialist physician who treated Robert was quite horrified that he would not take advice to help alter the prognosis but Rex Hughes said he and Robert talked at length about this and Robert knew there was no very great evidence to show that the complications of diabetes could be altered. 'Instead of dying in 1990 he might have survived another year or two but there's no way of guaranteeing that and he was aware of this.'

In 1975 Robert was informed he had the first sign of diabetic eye complications. In 1983 and 1985 he was given laser treatment on his eyes for retinoculty. His visual acuity was severely compromised and ultimately he would have been left blind or near blind. Rex Hughes saw him five times in 1983 – but then only once in 1988 and once in April 1990. At no time did Robert complain of chest pains, shortness of breath, swelling of the ankles – the symptoms of heart disease – but he did have diabetic vascular disease, where the arteries in his legs were blocking up and causing pain in his legs when walking.

Despite these symptoms, Robert wouldn't undertake any major activity that might have altered the outlook. This was very difficult behaviour for Janet to understand. She did everything she could to get Robert to live a healthier lifestyle, to no avail. She felt anger, frustration, guilt and hurt that he would not try to alter his ways for her or his family. While the campaign for BHP had been in full flight the adrenalin flowed freely and Robert's stamina astonished those around him. Janet found his staying power then to be unbelievable – he could just keep going hour after hour. But the crash, the resultant stress and the need to drive himself as hard as he had ever done to survive the economic disaster took an even heavier toll on Robert's health.

Once Robert found out Merrill Lynch had pulled the rug from under him he recognised immediately what needed to be done. He had to sell. Take his losses and cash up. He was convinced, as others were not, that there would be no quick recovery from the crash, the effects would be felt for years – and he was right, the crash preceded a recession that would last several years. Janet and Robert went underground and over the months that followed until Robert succeeded in selling out of his public company and securing his private family company Heytesbury, Janet never left Robert's side. She continued her role as telephonist, tea-maker, lover, communicator, protector, postman, but this time there was an added dimension. Robert was depressed, stressed as he had never been before and stretched to his limit. There were rumours that he had suffered a nervous breakdown and it seems he came close. At the very least he suffered severe depression.

Without Janet it would have been much tougher. She gave him strength and they were never closer in their married years than when they worked together to survive the impact of the crash. There were times they believed they would not make it and would walk round and round the garden at the front of the Peppermint Grove house discussing how they would get the children out of school and go bush if things did not work out. The children themselves were scattered and Robert and Janet hardly saw them. Peter was in America. Simon and Paul were at Geelong Grammar. Catherine, although living at home, was preoccupied with her own life. Catherine turned eighteen that year and she vows she didn't get a birthday present, it was such a very busy year.

Although they did respect each other's space, Catherine was able to observe her mother and father's relationship, something she had not been able to do before. She reports that it was:

a fascinating relationship. They were totally dependent on and driven by each other. Obsessed by each other almost ... No one would have done for someone what she did for him unless they were uncontrollably attracted to someone ... She loved him. She absolutely adored him. She woke up every morning for him. That's why she did what she did ... He was a very powerful, very strong man who actually had a very powerful, strong woman, but he controlled her. He wouldn't have done what he'd done without her.

Dad was a moody person; he had very dark moods. I saw Dad treat Mum so badly – the constant undermining, the constant talking. I suffered from it; my confidence within myself was very stilted as a result of how Dad talked to me and how he had made me feel when I expressed an opinion, how he could just chop me down so you got to the point where you didn't express opinions. The boys didn't get that, so *they didn't see it, so I don't think they understood that side of how Dad treated Mum ... But he could also be very warm and witty. He developed Mum and he gave her opportunities to develop herself as well.*

I think he really knew that Mum was an integral part of his team, that he relied on her ... but I think he always knew that she could survive without him. I don't think he liked knowing that at all, but he did know it and it was very, very real.

Janet was never more important to Robert than she was that year following the crash. Maintaining secrecy as to what Robert was trying to do was critical. It would have been easier for Robert to sort out his affairs without press scrutiny, but for the man who had manipulated the press to his own ends there was no escape. Every move Robert made was recorded for the world to read. There was no privacy. In the UK the press was particularly negative and foreign investors bailed out promptly. In Australia the financial journalists who had made their reputations with stories fed to them by Robert now savaged the tattered empire. The difference was that Robert was not talking to any of them – Janet kept them at bay.

In terms of support for Robert during this period there was only Janet and Alan Newman, his CEO.[33] 'My God', she said later, 'we were on our own'. The board of Bell Resources and the Bell Group were also little involved in the fire sale of assets. Robert and Alan were locked up doing deals as quickly as they could. No time was wasted. It was a traumatic experience undoing the years of success and to those who did observe Robert at this time he was not the same man.

As a director of the Bell Companies, John Studdy kept in touch by phone with Alan Newman, Janet or Robert, but while Robert would say what he was doing, he would not confide in anyone. Whenever John Studdy spoke with Janet she would know exactly what he was ringing about and what was going on. Post-crash, he would more often speak to Janet than Robert. Janet was more involved in the dealings of the Bell Group than she had ever been.

On 9 December 1987, fifty days after the crash, Robert had to face up to the Bell Group annual general meeting. Janet had insisted

Robert spend some time in the sun to develop some colour in his face. Her mother, Bern, cut his hair. The meeting, held in the Merlin Hotel, Perth, was packed out with the overflow crowd watching on closed circuit television. All Robert's directors from TVW Enterprises, Bell Group, Bell Resources and Bell International were in attendance. Janet sat in the front row with her mother.

After sixteen years of continuous growth and profit Robert had a different story to tell his shareholders. The meeting resolved to accept the Directors' and Auditors' Report and then Robert asked for the re-election of his senior directors Frank Downing, deputy director of the Bell Group, aged eighty and John Murdoch, also aged eighty. They had been Robert's sounding boards since his initial takeover of Bell Bros and he did not want a change now. After a challenge from the floor about the need for younger directors, the meeting re-elected both of them. Ironically, Frank Downing was to resign in protest over Robert's sell-out to Bond four months later.

Robert addressed the meeting with the patience, courtesy and aplomb he had always shown. Despite the traumatic time he was experiencing, he appeared in control. The words he chose were, as usual, very carefully considered. They were, he said, 'in much better shape than the market gives us credit for but in a far worse state than they were'. The value of Bell shares had fallen by 80%. They were 'in the eye of the cyclone'. They had moved quickly, taken hard decisions and 'taken the medicine'. They had made $1.4 billion sales of investment assets from Bell Resources and there would be more. They had taken a loss of $70 million on Pioneer Concrete. All sales had been voluntary and at their discretion. To date no operating companies had been sold but TVW7 Perth was to be the first. He said, 'The core and heart of the Bell Group remained' and that they were never given credit for their operating companies that would earn $300 million that year. But significantly Robert said, 'No firm and complete plan has been devised for the structure for the future'. This was the most telling comment for the day.

In summary Robert said that the Group had responded quickly and well, that his confidence lay in his people. The Group – comprising some 200 companies at the time of the crash, including single-purpose companies – might look conventional for a while but it would remain flexible and virile, he said. He stressed his team was committed and determined to drive this company forward to the growth and performance of the past.

Analysing Robert's comments in retrospect, knowing the care with which he always chose his words to say exactly what he meant, there is no personal undertaking evident on that historic day. The suggestion is that the team will take on the job of rebuilding. Few noticed any special import in his words, except for some staff and directors. As he had always done, Robert this time also made a comparative assessment of Bell share value. The investor who made a $10,000 investment sixteen years earlier would have had a holding of $30 million one year earlier – but the value that day on 9 December 1987 was still a healthy $8.07 million, which represented a growth of 52% per annum.

The shareholders gave Robert rousing applause and from the floor came suggestions that Bell shareholders should go out and buy more shares to restore confidence; that they should forego the next dividend. They wanted to know how they could help. John McIlwraith thought the annual general meeting was Robert's 'greatest performance'. Company shares had fallen catastrophically yet 'they cheered him to the roof tops and he made a stirring speech ... not promising anything'.

When the meeting closed and people were exiting the room Robert's voice was heard over the still open microphone saying, 'It's like being in intensive care'. Robert's critical Bell Group annual general meeting was over.

He had built up Bell Resources for the BHP takeover. Bell Resources was cash rich, while the Bell Group had no cash. The business solution was obvious: the two companies should be merged. Although highly geared with debt, the Bell Group included some extremely good businesses including TVW7 Perth, a concrete quarrying business in Western Australia and Queensland, and the UK Stoll Moss theatres. To bring the Bell Group together with the financially robust Bell Resources would have resolved the debt problem in the Group. Robert's team had begun the preparatory work on the merger and the proposal was then taken to the shareholders of both companies. Robert, the major shareholder, was prohibited as a related party from voting, and the shareholders, including Kerry Packer and Sir Ron Brierley, rejected the proposal.

Robert was very annoyed with his shareholders and described the institutions as 'butterflies'. He felt the institutions had done so well for so many years out of the companies he had run and he had never asked for their support before, but the first time he did they rejected him. He was a disappointed and angry man and he now thought he had nowhere to go. He was mentally and physically exhausted, the effects of his diabetic disease on his body were increasing and he had no vision or drive left for his public company. His main motivation was to salvage what he could for his family and move into a private company. He wanted a rest.

The steps he took to achieve this were the most controversial of his career. The lingering criticisms of Robert Holmes à Court stem from the deals he did to establish Heytesbury and from the belief that he deserted his shareholders. The god-like figure, the hero who could do no wrong, it was suggested, had abandoned his shareholders for his own family interests. As with most deals involving Robert Holmes à Court, the facts are more complex than they might first appear.

Robert persuaded the Western Australian Government to buy several city properties at what Alistair McAlpine describes as 'high, inflated prices'. McAlpine blames the Western Australian Government's 'bail out' of Robert Holmes à Court as the single move that 'brought about the virtual collapse of the Western Australian commercial economy'.[34] This had resulted from the Government moving into the property business, competing against the market with the advantage of access to money in the various State pension funds and the ability to move government tenants at will from the buildings of commercial developers to their own.

The Western Australian Government bought three buildings and 2.5% of BHP shares from Robert at around $50 million, a most unusual thing for a government to do. But the Government's activities throughout the late eighties were controversial on many fronts and led to the WA Inc Royal Commission in 1991 – an inquiry where Robert would have been required to give evidence had he lived. One of the issues before this inquiry was the Government's role in the rescue of Rothwell's merchant bank, which Laurie Connell had launched in 1982; and the link between Robert's role in the rescue of the bank and the Government's subsequent purchase of Bell shares through the State Government Insurance Commission (SGIC).

Pierpont wrote in the *Bulletin*, 'In return for subscribing $5 million to the rescue and leaving $50 million on deposit temporarily with Rothwells, Robert struck himself a good deal'.[35] The Government's purchase of Bell's BHP shares and its CBD properties in Perth followed the Rothwell rescue. While Robert:

> told Pierpont he had no idea that the SGIC and Bond had been acting in concert [when they bought Bell shares on the same day] ...Laurie Connell claimed in evidence to the 'WA Inc' Royal Commission that Bond and the SGIC were in concert and Robert knew all about it.[36]

The evidence does suggest it did not prove difficult for Robert to entice Alan Bond into the deal to buy the Bell Group. Bond had approached Robert several times about buying the Group and Robert was aware Bond was desperately in need of cash, so he was able to sit back and wait for Bond and his friends in Western Australia to work out how a deal might be done. Robert of course drove a hard bargain.

Robert spoke to both the Bond Corporation and the Western Australian SGIC about their interest in acquiring his Bell Group Limited (BGL) shares. Through his family company Heytesbury Investments, Robert controlled 43% of the BGL, which in turn owned 40% of Bell Resources. Robert made it clear to both parties that he would not sell his BGL shares unless he was able to sell all of his shares along with two tranches of convertible bonds that had been issued by various Bell companies. The details of the approaches made by the SGIC and the Bond Corporation emerged later in evidence before the NCSC when they were endeavouring to establish if the parties had acted independently of one another. The NCSC inquiry revealed there was a series of meetings between Alan Bond and Robert Holmes à Court in March and April 1988 where Robert told Bond that he was negotiating with others, including the SGIC.

The settlement of the sale of 19.9% of BGL at $2.50 per share took place at 2.00 p.m. on 29 April and the settlement with the Bond Corporation to buy 19.9% of BGL at $2.70 per share took place at 6.00 p.m. on the same day. The takeover law required that anyone who bought 20% or more of a company must make an equivalent offer to the remaining shareholders. Bond was experienced in evading this law, as Trevor Sykes has outlined.[37] So unloading a 39.8% shareholding in equal tranches to Bond Corporation and the SGIC – a deal which Sykes said 'reflected no credit on Holmes à Court ... He sold out to Bond on conditions which gave them [the shareholders] no right to the same price he received'[38] – was a deal which was within the law.

Robert did the deal personally with Bond. John Studdy, who was still a director of both the Bell Group and Bell Resources at the time, read about Robert's sell-out when he walked into the newsagency at Palm Beach Sydney on the evening of 29 April. He was hurt and disappointed that he had not been informed. A few days later when the Bell Group board met, Robert told the board that he was convinced Bond would have to offer the same price to the other shareholders. Frank Downing QC, the ageing director Robert had argued should remain on the Bell Group board four months earlier, was most upset and told Robert in front of the other board members that he considered he had done the wrong thing. They clashed, Robert was clearly angry and in the end Frank Downing resigned.

The press said the deal smelt and although legal events did unfold as Robert said he believed they would, Ray Schoer said Robert was 'drawing a long bow' to assume that the outcome was inevitable. Schoer did act quickly to call a hearing. On 2 May the NCSC sought assurances that Mr MRH Holmes à Court and his board would remain in control of the company and that there would be no new appointments during the next two weeks prior to a hearing. At the same time the NCSC stated, 'While the Commission's enquiries are not completed it has not found evidence of any breach of Section 11 of the Companies (Acquisition of Shares) (Western Australia) Code'.

After a review of the evidence the NCSC did come 'to the tentative view that there might have been some understanding between the SGIC and Bond Corporation in relation to the future management control of BGL, in particular that Bond Corporation would assume that control with at least the tacit acquiescence of the SGIC'.[39] Alan Bond pre-empted any final view by announcing on 2 June 1988 that Bond Corporation would make takeover offers for all of the ordinary voting shares in the SGIC not already held by it, or by the SGIC, at $2.70 a share, the same price paid to Robert. The NCSC was satisfied the requirements of the code had been fulfilled. The benefit derived by Robert was to be offered to all, and wise investors took advantage of the offer, which stayed open for the minimum time allowed by law – the four weeks from 31 July to 29 August. When the bid closed, Bond Corporation held 68% of the Bell Group. The offer had cost Bond Corporation a further $520 million.[40] It was the deal that broke Alan Bond. He had not expected he would have to make the same offer to all shareholders as he made to Robert. He eventually got into fatal difficulties trying to raise the money.

The deal that would break Bond gave the Holmes à Court family company Heytesbury a cash injection of $340 million. Robert had sold out to Bond Corporation Holdings at $2.70 a share and to the SGIC at $2.50 a share. The market price was $1.70. Robert retained a 6% holding and was to stay on as chairman. He wanted to tidy up the transfer of the assets he was acquiring for Heytesbury from Bell as well as oversee the Bond offer to his old shareholders, although this transitional arrangement left him open to further criticism as cash began to flow to Bond via Markland House as loans made by Bell.[41]

As far as Janet was concerned she thought Robert's exit from public life was the best thing that could have happened. At last they could be private people again – a real change of direction after seventeen years of Robert working for his shareholders. She said,

'Because of his ethics, he really did feel he had to put 100% of his time into his shareholders, and having aimed at BHP, there's a certain lack of excitement for him in Bell'. They were sick and tired of the media with their concentration on the private aspects of their lives. Janet said to Robert after the sale, 'This really is the first day of our new lives'.

Robert stayed on as chairman of the Bell board after all his BGL directors resigned on 26 August 1988. Robert called his directors to say he'd had a call from the Bond people 'to get rid of those outsiders' which included John Studdy, Alec Mairs and John Dahlsen. The directors left with few regrets. Bond had begun to acquire funds from Bell Resources from May 1988 when the management fee charged to Bell Resources jumped from $416,667 in April 1988 to $5,924,915 in May.[42] Robert stayed on, resigning on 21 October 1988, a year and a day after the crash, but he was chairman during a large part of a period – from 29 August when Bond's people first controlled the board until 3 November – when $607 million was shifted out to the Bell Resources Group in back-to-back loans through Markland House,[43] a small Sydney-based merchant bank.

Robert left the position of chairman on 21 October before the biggest transactions took place. By 29 October Bell Resources had placed its residual holding of 5.5 percent of BHP on the market. 'The four men [the board] decided that Bell Resources would "lend" Bond Corp $700 million ... Over the next four days [prior to October 29] Bell "lent" Bond Corp companies a total of $502.5 million'[44] including $55 million to Alan Bond's private company Dallhold.[45]

As Pierpont says, 'Robert had certainly gone to sleep at the tiller by then [the time he left]. Nor did he raise the alarm after leaving the board. But by then he had reached the lifeboat'.[46]

Before Robert retreated finally from his role as chairman of the Bell Group he completed his deal with Bond, which ensured he could buy back his jet, Grove House in the UK (both straightforward buybacks) and the Stoll Moss Theatres, which found their way back into Robert's control via Christopher Skase. The few loyal employees who knew the details of these deals are adamant they were legally sound but they are unprepared to go on the record discussing them.

Alan Newman, Robert's CEO had known Robert well over many years.[47] The two men fell out in the year following the crash and there is much hearsay about what went wrong. Within the Heytesbury office Alan was critical of Robert following the crash and Val Pitman who was normally very discreet about what she saw and heard, wrote down Alan's comments and showed them to Robert.

Derek Williams, the UK managing director, had a generous service contract which said that if Robert ever ceased to be chairman of the Bell Group UK, then Derek's contract would be paid out in full for the whole term. He reports that Robert, who was in the habit after the crash of going to his office for a chat, told him he was thinking of relinquishing the chairmanship of Bell and selling out to Alan Bond. He then told Derek he wanted him to start up again with him in Heytesbury. Derek asked Robert how many people he had invited to remain, to which Robert responded, 'Just you. I don't want Alan Newman'. Derek asked what they would be doing and Robert responded vaguely, 'Well, I have a deal with Alan Bond. I can take people from London I want and the assets I want. So shall we take the theatres? We need something to strengthen the balance. I want to live in Grove House. And you choose which people you think you need for the UK office'.

Suddenly Derek had a lot of friends. He picked his team, including Oliver Graham who remained as treasurer; Steve Johnston, another of Robert's chosen people, appeared on the scene as Robert's number two.

In evaluating Robert's business revival there is still community gossip in Perth suggesting that the wealth Robert's wife and family inherited was the SGIC's loss and that the motorists in the state paid a levy of $50 on their motor vehicles to fund that deal. However, as the history of the Western Australian Government and WA Inc unfolded through the Royal Commission, it seems the bail-out by the Western Australian Government of Robert Holmes à Court was motivated more by a desire to assist Alan Bond and Laurie Connell than Robert.

While Robert maintained that he was not aware that the two parties, Bond Corporation and the SGIC, were associated, Ray Schoer believes that 'with his skilled background he doubts that he would have believed that', but Robert wasn't breaking any laws. It is not unlawful to sell shares; it is the buyer who is constrained by law. 'Of all the entrepreneurs of the eighties', Schoer says '[Robert's] relations with the regulatory authorities were the best'. Schoer found him a different man after the crash, less confident, more seeking of approval. Although he had done nothing unlawful, he felt the need to justify his actions to Ray and seek some form of acceptance, something he had never done in the past.

Robert had set up Heytesbury well. His collectibles had always been in the family company and he had the lifestyle he wanted – his Peppermint Grove house in Perth, the apartment in Spring Street Melbourne, the house at the Stud, tropical Double Island off Cairns, the Wallan Stud, Grove house in the UK and the 727 jet. He had a good cashflow business in the London Stoll Moss Theatres, as well as the status the theatre business brought with it. He also had the cash to look for further investments. And the Sherwin properties, the cattle stations covering 1% of Australia, provided an appealing target. They fitted Robert's criteria. They were run down and undervalued. Janet loved the idea of running cattle properties and for Robert the purchase said to Australia in general and the business world in particular, 'I'm back. I'm back in business in a big way'. His recovery in such a short time, when most other Australian entrepreneurs were only beginning to realise the impact of the crash, was complete.

Yet the life Robert Holmes à Court was to lead in the final eighteen months of his life did not satisfy him. He attempted to find an interest through the Robert Holmes à Court Foundation, but could not identify a satisfying focus. Despite his health Robert could not resist share trading and doing deals; he thus returned to his major interest, the thing he was best at, and soon his borrowings equalled his assets once again.

Robert's ability to assess a company, to time his entry and think strategically were unimpaired. He bought Jaguar shares when the company was crippled with debt, performing very badly, and losing market share with industrial problems and bad management. It had all the hallmarks of a company going downhill. Steve Johnston,

Robert's UK financial analyst, couldn't see the value but Robert said to keep buying. Jaguar shares were trading at between £1 and £2. Then all of a sudden the Ford Motor Company came in and bid £8 and Robert made a killing. He bought Christie's shares at an undervalued price and sold to Robert Maxwell's superannuation fund.

In the 1989–90 financial year Robert had to find $30 million to balance the books; he finally achieved $32 million with his deals on Christie's International and Wilson and Horton. Trading was one thing but takeovers another. A lot of time had been spent analysing Dalgety PLC and courting Elf Aquitane in France. The staff had researched and explored the way Dalgety could be broken up. They were ready and raring to go but Robert wouldn't take the next step. There was disappointment in the team and some people thought Robert had lost his nerve. This was definitely not the Robert of the pre-crash era.

With the major exception of his horses, Robert's focus throughout his life had been business and share market trading, so he was not well equipped to switch his attention to possibilities such as community affairs and charitable work. Although he became involved in these activities, the two forays he had made both ended ignominiously. He was persuaded by the Premier, Sir Charles Court, to chair the Joondalup Development Corporation and later became the chairman of the Western Australian Art Gallery.

Joondalup involved a plan to transform raw land north of Perth into an ideal, planned living environment. The Corporation's secretary was John Reynolds (who later came to work with Robert, first at the *Western Mail* and later at WA Newspapers). John was joined by Robin Wright who agreed to take on the role of chief executive early in 1986. Robert took his role as chairman seriously. His vision was to create a vibrant city that gave a quality of life for people in the northern corridor but one that was developed on sound economic grounds. Robert carefully monitored and managed the funds of the Corporation for many years so that it was virtually self-funding and, according to Robin, 'did some really interesting things'. The government wanted to wave the flag and make a fuss about progress for electoral advantage but short-term superficial signs of progress didn't encourage the sale of land. Robert had a tit-for-tat approach with the government – we'll do this if you do that. You lend us $2.7 million interest free to be repaid when the Corporation deems it appropriate. We'll build a bus depot and you can wave the flag.

The government agreed and Robin Wright spent the two-and-a-half years he was with Joondalup telling Treasury:

'We're not ready to pay you back the $2.7 million yet and according to the minutes that the chairman arranged at the time we don't have to.' We used to get right up their nose because they knew they had effectively paid for Joondalup. But Robert made it work and then he used that money; he had it invested in solid investments, quietly monitored by himself and John Reynolds and all under Treasury guidelines, but he made it work.

Robert was conscientiously abiding by the Act of Parliament that governed the Corporation but the Labor government of the time, the post-crash government, didn't want him around. He was criticised in Parliament for not attending meetings. Robin checked the record of meetings at the time and found Robert chaired 55–60% of meetings and when he was absent his views were always represented in advance.

It was, Robin thought, the way Robert oversaw Joondalup rather than his lack of attendance at meetings that enraged Premier Peter Dowding, who wanted returns from the land which the government owned. Robert had said to Robin, 'We've got a lot of big parcels of land and we haven't the resources to develop everything. If we could make a good sale of one parcel of land, that would inject some money in to enable us to extend the golf course and do things a little bit better'. They therefore proposed to sell a parcel of land in a non-traditional way without a tender and without negotiations. The rules were set and the land was sold, as a house would be sold; no one was told the price until the sale day and the first purchaser to meet all the requirements at the announced price got the land. It was a standard offer and acceptance deal.

The cowboys in Western Australia who liked wheeling and dealing did not like this approach. They felt deprived of an opportunity and didn't believe the deal was straight. The parcel of land yielded in the region of $6.5 million, three-quarters of a million over what the market expected the best price to be. The golf course and other amenities were funded as a result, but Premier Peter Dowding was most unhappy. He called Robin Wright to his office. He lectured him on what Joondalup could and couldn't do and objected to spending money on the golf course. Robin pointed out that was a condition of the sale. He believes if it were not for the strength of Robert and the board (two businessmen, Denis Whitely and Barry Waldeck, and two councillors, Nick Trandos and Jim Turley), the Government would have sold the land off to twenty builders for $20 million to get the cash. But they couldn't. The management was sound and proper. 'That's Robert's legacy', Robin says.

Robert officially resigned at the end of 1987 and his contribution was not referred to at the opening of Joondalup in October 1989. Tom Stonnage, in his history of Joondalup, said Robert 'neither trumpeted his own successes and satisfactions nor bemoaned his failures and frustrations. He went silently and generously'.[48] He had much work to do post-crash but he was pushed and he could not afford to be involved in a bun-fight over an issue like Joondalup. Janet retains some bitterness over the government's treatment of Robert. 'Chairing the Joondalup Corporation', she says, 'is one thing Robert did voluntarily. He put lots of time and effort into endless meetings and there is not one street named after him. It's a pretty poor show'. Sir Charles Court commented in the foreword of Stannage's history:

> it should be borne in mind he [Robert] was doing this as a community service and not for his own financial gain. It is amazing that he stayed with the project so long and gave so much of his time when he was under such national and international pressure and had to cope with so many conflicting views and ambitions from within the project. It can be fairly said he kept the real aims and objects on course.[49]

Robert remained as chairman of the Western Australian Art Gallery, which he believed would be less contentious.

But that position was also ended ignominiously by the Western Australian Government. And nor was his role here viewed favourably by his chief executive, this time a woman, Betty Churcher. There are not many opportunities to evaluate Robert's general attitudes to women. There were few women in his business life and most who worked for him were in middle management roles. His association with Betty, director of the Gallery of Western Australia when Robert was chairman, was unique. The relationship between the chief executive and chairman of a public body where both are appointed by a government minister is very different from that of employer and employee. It was not a relationship either was comfortable with and, as a woman, Betty's up-front approach was not accepted in the same vein as was Robin Wright's at the Joondalup Corporation.

Through his role with the Gallery, Betty was able to observe, with feeling, the life Janet led with Robert. She grew to respect Janet and her knowledge of art and her acumen in the arts, which she believed was greater than Robert's. She watched Robert listening to Janet give advice and felt he relied on her for many things; but Betty also saw the pain Janet endured and the torture he put her through, of a kind not unrelated to what she herself experienced from Robert.

Betty had been interested in the job in Western Australia as gallery director only because Robert was chairman of the board. She was impressed by him and thought the opportunity to work with him would lead to an exciting gallery for Western Australia. Janet was sent to meet Betty at Phillip Institute in Melbourne – she was then Dean of the art school – and Janet conveyed Robert's view that he thought the Gallery should concentrate on Aboriginal and contemporary art, which were exactly Betty's interests, so she was excited about the job. In retrospect she recognises there were warning signs indicating this was not going to be an easy relationship. She was kept waiting an inordinate amount of time after the headhunter's approach to be invited to Perth for an interview, then kept waiting an hour and a half outside the boardroom to be invited in – Robert's typical ploy – then everyone sat in silence embarrassed, rustling papers until Robert finally spoke and said, 'You'll be happy to know you've just been appointed the director of the Art Gallery of Western Australia. Is there anything you'd like to ask?'. Betty responded that while she'd been at the Gallery all day and learnt a great deal about the Gallery and its operation, terms and conditions had never been discussed. A look of irritation crossed Robert's face. 'Oh', he said, 'plus a thousand'. Betty replied, 'That's good, what's that?'. Robert answered, 'I don't know'. It was an extraordinary job interview.

It was early 1987 when she went to Perth, a significant year for Robert with more drama involving BHP to occur prior to the crash. Betty says:

I don't think there was anyone I wanted to please more than Robert Holmes à Court. It was almost like an albatross around my neck, wanting to please, yet wanting to succeed in the job and wanting to do a good job and thinking that would please him. What I think he really wanted was absolute obedience and absolutely undivided loyalty.

Betty found that pleasing Robert and running the Gallery were not congruent objectives. She kept telling Robert that she had to work for the artists' community, the general public, the public service commissioner, the ministers, the board and the chairman. She would say:

'I've got many masters, not just one', but he didn't like that because as far as he was concerned I had only one master and that was him and if I wavered from that I think he saw me as disloyal.

Over her three years as director of the Gallery, her relationship with the chairman did not improve. After making the mistake early on of believing silence meant assent, she gradually learnt to read Robert's ploys. He would never say 'No, he couldn't do that', he would just never be available on the numerous dates put forward. He didn't forgive or forget quickly and Betty knew 'of no one who could express displeasure without saying a word in the way that he did'. He never explained and when he applied silence, you would wait and wait and wait for a response. He was also never on time for a meeting.

Robert urged Betty to put a fund-raising foundation together for the Gallery. Betty then approached Ivan Hoffman who had successfully raised money for the University of Western Australia, but he said he would only agree if he could pick his own team. He wanted Kerry Stokes as chairman as he believed he would get a million dollars out of him to kick off the foundation. But Robert wanted the chair himself. Ivan's response was:

> Forget it. I know Robert, I like Robert, I respect him but you'll never have a meeting; there'll always be a reason why we can't do this or that. He will not ask for money. He will not give money.

When Betty tried to progress the foundation Robert quietly unpicked everything she tried to do and it never happened.

Gallery board meetings would last for hours. They would begin at 3.00 p.m. and sometimes everyone would still be there at 10.00 p.m. On one occasion Betty asked if he would mind if she rang Roy, her husband, at 7.30 p.m. because he was waiting and didn't know where she was. Robert replied that he would mind: 'Janet's been in the car park since five; Roy at least is at home'. Betty thought:

> no man was blessed with a better wife than he had in Janet. She was his support. I don't think anyone's ever had anything like that, perhaps in previous centuries but not in this century. I think he realised it. I think he understood what he had. But he could be just as cruel to Janet as he could with me.

Janet once said to Betty, 'Don't cross him, he'll destroy you', and Betty believed her. Robert reminded her of a Japanese Samurai:

> With one swipe of the sword he'd dissect you, but you would never quite know when that sword swing was going to descend; it might be

*two or three years later. I didn't feel scared but I realised that he had
absolute power, that he could have disposed of me in an instant. I
think he would have when my term came to an end.*

Betty also knew Robert had great power over David Parker, the
Minister for the Arts, who at that time looked as if he would still be
in power when her term was up. Parker's fear of Robert became
clear following the sale of the Perth Entertainment Centre when
Kerry Stokes got the nod over Robert from the Minister to buy the
Centre. Robert was furious. Parker was to open an exhibition in the
Gallery; invitations had gone out with his name on them but Robert
phoned Betty to insist she phone the Minister to tell him he was not
opening the exhibition. Reluctantly Betty phoned and said, 'Look
I'm terribly sorry, David, but the chairman has changed his mind on
this matter and now does not want you to open the exhibition'. The
Minister went into a tailspin of panic. He asked Betty to come
around immediately although it was 10.30 p.m. and she lived in
Fremantle. He wanted to talk and he was so nervous his hands were
shaking and his cup was rattling as he tried to pick up a cup of tea,
which he quickly put down. He wanted to know Robert's words, the
actual words he had used. She then resolved that if Robert had such
complete control of the Minister, the Government, the Gallery, the
purse, she could not operate as director.

When the offer was first made for Betty to go as director to the
Canberra National Gallery she said no as she still wanted to set up a
working relationship with Robert. But now she met Robert to tell
him she had tried but the relationship was not working. Robert told
her she was 'very wilful', then was silent. He rose to leave and said,
'I'll let you know'. Betty recalls that as 'the most chilling thing I've
ever heard and I thought, "That is it. We can never work together,
not possibly"'. She then went to see David Parker to tell him she
could not work with Robert. His response was to go:

*into this extraordinary, I can only describe it as a sort of maniacal
tirade against me ... He was literally frothing and shouting to the
embarrassment of his staff who were there, his extreme response again*

pointing to the fact that there was something very much deeper than I have any idea of.

Churcher called Canberra and said, 'Count me in'. It was a career move she never regretted and Perth had provided an experience she would never forget. Robert had taught her timing, patience, to pace herself, to present an idea. She had never known a more self-contained man, someone with such presence. He'd walk into a room and everybody, even the people with their backs to him, were conscious of the fact that he'd arrived. Giving away very little:

he'd make a gesture with his hand and suddenly you'd feel so blessed that he was including you in this sort of beneficence. He had everyone just absolutely cupped in the palm of his hand. I've never known anyone with a charisma equal to what he had ... I had unbounded respect for the man, but unbounded hate as well because of what he'd done.

Just as Betty had come to the conclusion she could never win with Robert, she felt that Janet must have thought at some stage in her life that she had to go along with Robert 100% or move out. 'As a very intelligent woman she would have decided there were no half-measures. "I'll just do precisely what he says"', and Janet's rewards, she thought, would be to live with an interesting, fascinating and exciting man. Betty says, 'When he was relaxed and just talking about this or that he would've been marvellous and she must have had a lot of that'.

When Robert's first term as chairman of the Gallery was up, David Parker was no longer the Minister for the Arts. Kay Hallahan was, and she was part of a government that was trying to distance itself from the Western Australian businessmen who had been part of WA Inc. Robert was advised his chairmanship would not be renewed. He was furious and he gave a television interview where he said he had been 'treated discourteously'. It was rare for Robert to make such a pointed, if restrained, public comment.

These negative experiences in public roles did not motivate Robert to look further in that direction. But there was the question of what to involve himself in next. His dream of controlling BHP no longer a possibility, having retrieved his financial position and no longer head of a public company, Robert began to implement plans to establish a charitable trust. For the first time he began to think about the wider social contribution he might make. Janet was excited. She hoped for a future where Robert might share more directly in the causes to which she was committed.

I was invited to become a trustee of the Robert Holmes à Court Foundation along with Janet, writer and management consultant Edward de Bono, former High Court judge Sir Ronald Wilson, Sir Michael Clapham, a Zambian lawyer Dr Rodger Chongwe who had studied law with Robert in Perth, and the Deputy Vice Chancellor of UWA, Dr Robert Parfitt. The first meeting took place on Friday 28 and Saturday 29 October 1988 in Perth. Robert's initial memo to the trustees stated that he wanted an entity that had:

its own vigour and energy and skills ... It must not simply be a channel through which money is passed on to other organisations. It must develop a superior management team, conduct its own research and go some way towards implementing its own projects.

He did not want to exclude any idea, any ambitious human endeavour or activity; as well he wanted to encourage research of all kinds. Two broad areas of focus were to be initially on youth through a project Janet chaired, titled Westrek, and through an early childhood television program I had proposed. He said, 'We should cross geographic, racial, political and national boundaries because that is the way the world should be'.

Westrek had been established in 1985 in Western Australia when Peter Dowding was Minister for Employment and Training. Dowding, Janet's old friend from university days, had asked her to chair this work skills program for unemployed youth. It was another idea that appealed to Janet's social conscience. The Westrek program aimed to provide its participants with the opportunity to learn new life and work skills through involvement in voluntary work projects throughout Western Australia. Participants were between seventeen and twenty-five years of age and were usually long-term unemployed. Projects were run on a residential basis over an eighteen-week period, seven days a week. All food and accommodation costs were met and an allowance of $30 per week paid. On completion of the project, participants received an honorarium of $500 and a certificate of achievement, as well as assistance with subsequent placement in employment. A board was formed, with Peter Sherlock employed to run the project. The Government injected $251,800 and in the first six months there were six projects running in different parts of the State. Janet threw herself into Westrek; she travelled to all project locations, meeting the young people, and had 'a fantastic time'. She was excited to see the effectiveness of the scheme. Projects were selected on the basis of three principal criteria: they must be a priority for the local community, usually of a conservation/heritage nature; they must be able to be completed within eighteen weeks; and they must provide a variety of opportunities for skills learning. Peter Sherlock and Janet worked to get local communities involved. Initially the participants were paid the dole, but Robert suggested they should be paid a little more than the dole to differentiate them from others who were unemployed and not working.

The project aimed to teach social skills, care for others and self-respect, as well as provide work experience and training. Despite the high ideals of the program and its apparent early success, money was difficult to come by. Every time someone came off the dole and into the project, it saved the Commonwealth the dole equivalent and it cost the State Government the dole equivalent. But the Commonwealth Government would not support the Westrek project – the concept of working for the dole was not government nor union policy. In August 1987, Westrek was incorporated as a foundation and vigorously sought funds from a variety of private and corporate sources. Westrek, like most of Janet's causes – the organisations she chaired – needed money. Although she gave her time and was willing to pursue financial support through Government and private sources, when the Stock Market crashed, funds were very hard to come by. Westrek struggled through each year and Janet shared its struggle. She was delighted when Robert wanted to fund Westrek through his Foundation.

Robert had often said Janet behaved like a mendicant in relation to Westrek, and that Patricia Edgar did the same for the ACTF. Before I knew of the plans for the Foundation, Janet informed me that Robert had proposed he take over the funding of the ACTF through his Foundation. He believed it was a waste of my time continually chasing funding through the States and the Commonwealth. In 1988 when the approach was made, however, I felt the ACTF's funding was secure. While we had gone through several years of insecurity and there was always one State or another threatening to drop out, we had settled into a relationship with the Commonwealth Department of the Arts which understood and supported the work we were achieving. I also had not forgotten the words of Sir James Cruthers regarding Robert and I was wary of being placed in a situation under his financial control.

My counter suggestion was that if Robert wished to be generous, then the ACTF should take on a special project that we would not be able to do with our current funding. I undertook to put together a proposal for Robert, the development of an Early Childhood Program that was to become 'Lift Off'. Nothing of any significance had been developed for television anywhere in the world for young children since the introduction of 'Sesame Street' in the late sixties. Much had been learnt since then through research into child development, so I believed such a project was timely. The Robert Holmes à Court Foundation was finally launched a year after the crash, with a dinner held on the evening of Friday 28 October, featuring Donald Horne as speaker. Those present were mainly Janet's friends from her wide range of associations.

At the first meeting the board was asked to ratify the commitment of $500,000 to Westrek to maintain its activities for approximately twelve months and the donation of $250,000 to the UWA's Art Gallery Appeal. On the agenda for discussion was a contribution of $250,000 to the Murdoch University Law School, the proposal for the ACTF to develop a preschool program, donations to the University Flying Club which Robert conceived in 1963, and various other small sponsorships. As well, Robert wanted to discuss his Foundation's involvement in the UK. At the meeting, Robert was vague about the amount of money that would be available to his new Foundation but had initially deposited $2 million. I was asked to further develop the preschool proposal. The tax status of both the Robert Holmes à Court Foundation and the ACTF in Australia was problematic. An approach to Treasurer Paul Keating for exempt status for Robert's Foundation had been rejected, and the ACTF could only receive tax exempt donations through the Australian Elizabethan Theatre Trust, and not in its own right.

The story of the Foundation is illustrative of the very complex nature of the relationship between Janet and Robert and indicative of Robert's apparent inability to separate philanthropy from a business deal. Both the ACTF and the Westrek Foundation were dear to Janet's heart. She was excited and pleased that Robert was showing such an interest in her projects. My assessment is that for his part, Robert had little idea of what it was he wanted to achieve through the Foundation, other than wanting it to be different from others and dynamic in its processes. Meetings were subdued, with trustees uncertain about what was expected and Robert typically giving little lead.

At the second meeting of the Foundation, on 1 February 1989 in Perth, I presented a nine-year-plan for the proposed Early Childhood Program. Robert then asked me how much money I wanted from the Foundation. I had absolutely no idea of the level of funds Robert had in mind. I did not know whether he was thinking $100,000 or $1 million so I knew I must not name a figure, I must endeavour to draw it from him. I'm sure much smarter people than I had tried that tactic. While all other trustees sat silently, Robert asked gently and persistently for me to give him a figure and each time I declined and there would be silence. In the end, Sir Michael Clapham broke in and said, 'I think we should give Patricia $2 million. That should be sufficient to test further funding'. I was watching Robert's face as I kept mine motionless, concealing my delight. There was no reaction of any kind from Robert. Then he inclined his head, nodded slightly and said, 'That seems the right amount'.

The development of 'Lift Off' commenced, but it took seventeen months to get Robert to a function where the $2 million could even be announced. He declined to make any such announcement himself and finally said if Prime Minister Bob Hawke would announce it, he would attend. This took some engineering, but with Hazel Hawke's help Bob, Hazel, Robert and Janet were all present at the media launch of 'Winners Series 2, More Winners' – an anthology of children's television programs – on 14 June 1990, when I announced Robert's $2 million contribution to 'Lift Off'. In his speech, Bob Hawke spoke of Robert's generosity. Robert did not speak, but thoroughly enjoyed himself in the Great Hall of Montsalvat, Melbourne, where the function was held. He found himself at the centre of an admiring group of journalists who revelled in the opportunity of a face-to-face encounter with Robert. This was to be Robert's last public attendance at a gathering in Australia before his death.

Next day I met with Robert and Janet to discuss progress on 'Lift Off' and when we might expect to receive the funds, as the ACTF was financially extended with the development of the project. Robert was immovable, to both Janet's and my surprise and distress, and despite Bob Hawke's appearance and the public announcement, it looked as if the money was not going to be forthcoming. Robert was to think further about it. He told Janet after the meeting, 'No wonder Phillip Adams called Patricia a centurion tank.'[50] I had pushed him hard, to no avail, and it was clear he didn't like it.

Janet was worried. Robert's response to the financing of 'Lift Off' and his changing attitude towards Westrek gave neither of us cause for confidence. At the same meeting where 'Lift Off' was supposedly approved, there were indications that the enthusiasm for the Westrek project was not as strong as it had been initially and the director of the Robert Holmes à Court Foundation, Greg Pearce, wrote in his report to the board that there had been 'considerable discussion on the Foundation's relationship with Westrek, its philosophy and objectives and ways in which it could be determined if these objectives were being achieved'.

At that meeting Robert had been quite voluble in expressing reservations about Westrek and the other trustees had sat rather silently. It was embarrassing to them (as it was to me), to see Janet put through such discomfort. This was Janet's project which, at Robert's suggestion, had come under the auspices of his Foundation and Robert was now raising questions about the way it was being run. He wanted Westrek to make a full report to the next meeting, together with financial statements, so that trustees had 'adequate information on which to base decisions concerning the Foundation's involvement in Westrek'. On the face of it, this procedure was perfectly proper, but Janet had been involved with Westrek for more than three years and nothing had changed in her view. She did not understand Robert's motives or intentions. She was clearly hurt and confused. But she knew that Robert was capable of a complete change of heart and there were certainly precedents of such changes involving other projects of Janet's.

One of these involved Paula Dawson, an artist whom Janet regarded as a great talent, 'a holographer extraordinaire' who understood laser physics. Janet was introduced to Paula by a friend, Margaret Carnegie, went to visit Paula's studio and became very excited about a project Paula wanted to create called *Absent Friends*. Paula had developed an idea for a grand hologram, which was a piece about memory and the nature of nostalgia. The idea was to create a hi-tech hologram with the appearance of a cheap and nasty seventies bar overlaid with memories and regrets for times past. Paula imagined the installation operating as a real bar where people could meet regularly and become a part of the work themselves.

At the time of Janet's first meeting with Paula, she was working at the forefront of art and technology. She already had the reputation of making the world's largest holograms and there was commercial potential in the work. Janet persuaded Robert to back the project and a company within Bell Resources was created for the venture. Paula estimated that it would cost about $1.25 million to complete the work. She was given a laboratory with state-of-the-art equipment and thought all her Christmases had come at once. The Bell Group, meanwhile, gained the image of being an art patron, as well as the potential commercial payoff from hologram development. This was the type of situation and result Janet liked to work for and believed in – she had brought together an innovative artist and Robert's financial resources.

Janet and Paula developed a friendship as Janet took a close interest in her protege's work. She found Paula great fun to be with. Robert had not met Paula when the deal was decided. He was initially happy with the oral reports from Janet and the written reports that came to him from Paula. She would sign off with a big lipstick kiss and Robert was amused. But following the October crash, and during Robert's negotiations with Alan Bond, the hologram project manager Ian Wildy approached Paula to see if she would be prepared to work for someone else. Paula said no, she did not see herself as an employee of Bell Resources; she had gone into the relationship only because of her rapport with Janet. So the company was devalued to around $25,000, bought from Bell Resources by the family company Heytesbury Holdings, and with the name changed to Heytesbury Holographics the show went on.

In September 1988 Robert met Paula for the first time when he made a visit to her laboratory. Paula has been described as a cross between Plato and Jeannie Little.[51] Petite, blonde and wackily exuberant, she is possessed of a nasal voice and a high decibel laugh. Robert was not impressed by the person, nor by the art and he pulled the plug. Janet was devastated. Already more than half a million dollars had been paid out. As Janet says:

> It was terrible. The art world just thought that it was the pits. I was incredibly embarrassed but in an awkward situation. Piss-weak I suppose I was. I just had to go along with what Robert said. He was sick of the money going out when he couldn't see any money coming in. He expected her to be making small holograms that we could sell to pay for the work on Absent Friends. I couldn't have argued with him or done anything about it. That would have made it worse for me. It was just awful. It all collapsed and went bad.

In her embarrassment Janet cut off communication with Paula Dawson, as she had done with others in the past when things were beyond her control. There were moves to junk what had been made for *Absent Friends* but Janet intervened and had the pieces mothballed. The project has not been revived, the only record of the grand piece being a film of the work in progress made by Film Australia.

Janet continued to divert her energies into other projects, though she felt responsible for Paula's disappointment. Whenever she could, Janet stayed with the projects she committed to as she did with Westrek, but where the project relied on Robert's resources and he changed his mind there was little she could do. She had learnt long before that she could not take Robert on and win and the resulting discomfort was more than she could bear.

With Robert's Foundation she hoped both their interests could be served. The third meeting of the Foundation was held on 15 May 1989, in London at Grove House, the magnificent Regency Villa situated on the west side of Regent's Park. Built between 1822 and 1824 on four-and-a-half acres of private parkland, Robert had bought this house in 1986 for £10 million and Janet, with the help of Rod Kelly, had restored and refurnished it meticulously to all its former glory. The property is held on direct lease from the Crown Estate. The house extends to approximately 12,300 square feet, and contains spectacular murals by the Edwardian painter Siegmund Goetze, who owned the property from 1909–1939. It is one of the purest of the surviving villas in Regent's Park, with the largest garden area in London outside Buckingham Palace. The interior of the main house had been improved extensively. Janet arranged and supervised all the renovations and Robert gave her free rein. He wanted the best. He was very proud of Grove House and he loved to stay there. It was certainly a fitting place for a meeting of Robert's charitable Foundation.

A stay at Grove House when in London on ACTF business gave me the opportunity to be around Robert at close range for an extended time. Janet warned me not to be surprised or offended if he didn't join us or if he walked out of a meal or discussion. I'd had dinner with

Robert before and found him very good company, charming, sociable and challenging. He liked a good debate and so did I. Robert enjoyed setting up parameters to the concepts we discussed and I enjoyed challenging those parameters. At Grove House that particular week he was well-behaved – no sudden exits, no silences. He was relaxed, sat around in his dressing gown and watched the boxing on television. Janet teased him and was in a playful mood. Together the three of us discussed many issues, including one of particular interest to Robert – whether women were capable of very tough decisions, whether they could prevail to get what they wanted. The debate was always logical and illustrative; the argument progressed step-by-step. But clearly Robert had significant reservations about the ability of women to be tough and to make the hard decisions, Margaret Thatcher being the obvious exception in his opinion.

One night, Robert announced he was getting out the Rolls to take us to a play he had already seen and enjoyed and thought I might like. We sat in a box where he liked to sit, though Janet preferred the stalls. He enjoyed the sense of occasion and he found pleasure in sharing that. I could see without any difficulty the brighter side of life between Robert and Janet, even if the earlier Foundation meeting had revealed another, darker side.

The minutes of meetings of the Foundation were always interesting. When I once questioned Greg Pearce, the director, on the words used, I was told they were Mr Holmes à Court's and he was always very precise in his choice. The full report on Westrek was provided to the third meeting. By now Janet knew that Robert had changed his view on Westrek. Robert led the trustees to the conclusion that 'Westrek had not generated as much momentum of its own within the community as could be expected and appeared to have misunderstood the basis on which funds had been provided by the Foundation for the 1988–89 year'. The sum provided was to be $250,000, far less than the amount needed for the project to be viable.

The outcome was again humiliating for Janet. Her response outside the Foundation was to help Westrek fight harder for further independent funding. She did not lessen her commitment and passion for Westrek. Although she did not say so, Robert's actions probably strengthened her resolve to make the project work. At the next meeting, in October 1989, Robert's Foundation resolved to support Westrek on a project-by-project basis. Support was wound down further. Despite Robert withdrawing funds, with Janet's help Westrek did consolidate its financial position by attracting public and private funds from other sources for its projects. She did not desert this cause as she had been forced to do with Paula Dawson.

After Robert's death, when Janet had to relinquish much of her committee work, she chose to stay with Westrek. Westrek continued to survive, making its money by running training programs for people who could afford to pay. That money was used to subsidise training programs for people who couldn't afford to pay. It was one of few such projects in Australia and the philosophical assumptions appealed to Janet. Helping train the unemployed was a worthwhile endeavour.

Robert continued to dabble with his own Foundation. He stepped in to rescue the British Theatre Association's (BTA) collection of British theatre memorabilia and underwrote the rehousing of the historic collection. This became a business deal, as Robert proposed the BTA be charged a rent which would be offset by an equal donation from the UK Holmes à Court Foundation. Further small projects were assisted: the funding of two Aboriginal artists for twelve months including Emily Kame Kngwarreye, a National Aboriginal Art Award and the Guy Grey-Smith Memorial Travel Grant. Other larger schemes brought to the Foundation by Rodger Chongwe, Sir Ronald Wilson and Edward de Bono did not fire Robert's imagination. Greg Pearce resigned in January 1990 and his replacement, Jane Gilmour, did not join the Foundation until May. After an initial interview, she did not have time to meet with Robert before he died and the Foundation did not meet formally again. I believe Robert lost interest. He could not reconcile his philosophy of business with the philosophy of a philanthropic trust. The cultural divide was just too great, as evidenced by the final negotiations on 'Lift Off'.

Robert directed Janet and me to meet with Jon Elbery regarding the $2 million investment in 'Lift Off' following our June launch and discussion. At that meeting, Jon told us Robert was now proposing to lend the ACTF the money. Robert had moved from a donation to an investment, and now to a loan. I responded that the ACTF could not possibly consider accepting a loan as we had no means of repaying such a sum. Janet was wide-eyed with horror at the proposal. As with Westrek, Robert seemed to be trying to make life difficult for Janet by undermining another of her projects. Although Janet and Robert had been married for over twenty years, she still found his responses unpredictable.

Grove House was another example. With the house interior, money had been no object, but when it came to the grounds Robert took a different attitude. Janet invested a considerable amount of her time (with Robert's encouragement) finding a suitable landscape gardener and spent many hours of her time planning the proposed changes. She was ensuring that the meticulous attention given to the inside of the house would be given to the grounds because she thought that was Robert's wish. When Robert saw the quote for landscaping of £12,000, he vetoed further work. Janet felt a fool and thought the landscape gardener would think she was a greater fool, spending time, getting enthusiastic about something her husband would not ultimately do. But she defends Robert's response saying, 'I do sometimes get carried away and when people see the name Holmes à Court they just add a few zeros to the bill'. Apart from some minor repair works, the Grove House grounds remained as they were.

In the last year of his life, Robert took to spending more and more time alone in London, staying at Grove House while Janet remained in Australia. He felt comfortable in London and he enjoyed the house. It is also likely that Robert felt more comfortable where he was away from the prying journalists he once cultivated and away from the country where he had experienced his greatest disappointments. Now rejected by the Western Australian Government as chairman of the Art Gallery and the subject of criticism for his newly acquired wealth, London, the Stoll Moss Theatres and Grove House were a refuge.

Robert was brain-tired. He had never spent much time in the past on social chit chat. But this became his habit. He would invite his senior employees back to Grove House for company in the evenings. Staff found him very sociable and more reflective than they had known him to be. He would be discursive about the crash, why it happened, how Japan would emerge. If there was any boxing on television, everything would stop so he could watch. He would then either talk about the fight for days after, or get on to his other favourite topic, horses.

Derek Williams believes that in the last months of his life Robert was a lonely man who desperately needed company. In the office around half-past-four each day people would come past Derek's office and say, 'Have you been invited back?'. Derek may have been to Grove House twice that week but when Robert dropped by and said, 'Doing anything today Derek?' plans for the evening would be cancelled. They would drive back to Grove House in the chauffeur-driven Rolls Royce, have a drink, Robert would change, then drive the Rolls to a back street where they would go to an Indian restaurant. The staff at Grove House, Phyllis and Peter Williams, would have a meal ready and not know what to do with it. Robert was totally unpredictable.

Derek saw Robert for the final time in mid-1990. Derek was then over sixty. They were at Grove House when he told Robert that he ought to think about finding a replacement as he wanted to retire within a year. Robert insisted that he did not want Derek to retire. He would not hear of it. In the course of conversation Derek asked Robert why he wanted to continue to work and he replied, 'I don't have anything else to do'. Robert went on to say, 'You know I haven't even made a will'. To Derek's response of disbelief that a solicitor would not make a will Robert said, 'If I make a will I think it's inviting the inevitable'.

Derek felt sure Robert knew that he was not going to live long. He thought he was just filling in time. So much had happened in two-and-a-half years – the crash, the careful sell-off and recovery, the move from Bell to Heytesbury, the purchase of enterprises and the challenge to get them running as productive businesses, the accumulation of assets and debt. Phyllis and Peter Williams used to see Robert sitting alone at dinner in Grove House just staring into space. Several people were to wonder if Robert had had a doctor's warning that something could happen. If he had, he certainly hadn't changed his habits. He still smoked his cigars heavily, ate stodgy food and didn't exercise.

Strangely and unexpectedly, Robert agreed, with no further argument, to the investment of $2 million in 'Lift Off', through a letter signed by Jon Elbery on 29 August 1990, three days before he died. It was Janet who insisted on honouring that agreement after his death. The Robert Holmes à Court Foundation did minor business after Robert's death, mainly in the UK. Janet did not have the time initially, nor the interest, to devote to it, with the new demands of running Heytesbury. And then the financial resources were not there.[52]

Jon Elbery rang Derek Williams to tell him of Robert's death. It was a curious phone call. Robert Tranded was the name of Robert's chauffeur. He had shot himself in a suicide attempt the week before. He had failed to kill himself and was in intensive care in hospital. Derek had been keeping in touch with his progress. Jon called at 5.00 a.m. London time to say, 'Derek I have to tell you that Robert died.' Derek couldn't understand how Jon knew this for as far as he was aware the chauffeur was still in intensive care the previous night. Jon said, 'No, Robert Holmes à Court.' Robert's chauffeur died the same morning.

No financial journalist or writer since Robert's death has attempted to evaluate his overall impact on corporate life. When I asked Terry McCrann why not, he replied that it would have to have been a collaborative effort and journalistic rivals did not cooperate. The obituaries acknowledged Robert was a great man of immense personal charm and intellect, adored by his shareholders and his loyal staff, but utterly ruthless in business whenever he thought necessary. He was a very controlled man; he revealed little of himself or his feelings.

His play for BHP was his moment in the sun. Whether he would have enjoyed running BHP as much as he enjoyed the process of acquiring it is doubtful. His great satisfactions in life seem to have been the doing of the deal and perhaps his horses. Robert died an enigma to most who knew him. Of those who admired him and those who reviled him few can claim to have known the whole person, except perhaps Janet. She views him today as an accident of nature. Yet he was someone attractive enough for a strong and resolute woman to subjugate herself to and devote twenty-four years of her life to.

When Robert died, Janet wanted to be rid of Grove House. It did not represent her personal style. She didn't want to live there and she didn't want the worry of looking after it. Robert had enjoyed the trappings of his success. He was the great acquirer, buying the grand houses, the grand cars with the chauffeur, the staff to wait on his every need. Janet shared his exciting lifestyle with enthusiasm as his loyal wife, managing the houses, the domestic staff, the properties, the art and primarily managing Robert and ensuring his every need was met.

Robert's death brought about a huge stocktaking in Janet's life, in what she owned, in her lifestyle, in what she valued and in the way she wanted to work and spend her time. So many of the things that they had acquired together were, she found, simply a burden, a worry she could no longer afford and she found she had no sentimental attachment to them. They were the accumulated possessions which came of having so much money.

She had once said to Robert, 'These things are called possessions because in the end they'll possess us'. She was to find over the next few years how prophetic her statement had been.

JANET TAKES CHARGE

The day after Robert's funeral Janet woke early, if indeed she had slept at all. She rang Val Pitman at 7.30 a.m. with the instruction to clean out Robert's office, as she would be moving in that morning. She wanted to see the interior decorator that day to select furnishings to redecorate Robert's sombre office. The heavy leather couches were not to her taste and she would transform it to be more in tune with her own personality. Dressed in a bright tangerine-coloured jacket with a white blouse, and with her face carefully made up, the 47-year-old widow looked very much alive and ready for action.

Her first meeting for the day was with the children and the family lawyer. Robert had died without a will. This had been discussed before his death and Robert's view was that he did not need a will, reasoning which Janet never fully understood. Without a will her task was made more difficult, and several people felt it was a deliberate action on his part. Under Western Australian law, she inherited one-third of the estate and the remaining two-thirds were divided equally between the four children. None of the houses in which she lived with Robert were in Janet's name, so they now belonged to the family as a whole. His mother Ethnée received nothing. As the recent inept performance of young Warwick Fairfax in his handling of the family media business was fresh in the minds of the banks and the media, Janet was concerned that full control of the company was seen to be in her hands. Already a press release had been issued without her approval, stating that she would take control of the company, 'assisted by' son Peter. Tim Treadgold, who issued the release, considered it was Peter's right to be mentioned in this way, and it was also Peter's wish. As the oldest son, Peter felt he had been groomed to succeed his father, though he was daunted by the prospect and actually preferred to stay with his studies at Oxford University.

In the event, the children all agreed to sign over control of Heytesbury to Janet, although Paul at only seventeen was not legally old enough to make the decision until he turned eighteen. When the meeting concluded, Simon and Peter said they were going down the street to get T-shirts made saying 'I'm no Warwick'. Papers would be prepared for signature the next day. Janet then drove to the office. She had a cold, but she swept in with energy. The staff were amazed, first that she was there at all and secondly that she was taking charge with such authority.

She addressed the staff for the second time since Robert's death[1] and reiterated her intention to run the company and retain the enterprises. She had no intention of selling up and sitting in the sun. During this address, the senior accountant John Frame, in an aside to another staff member, asked if 'Jon Elbery knows what is going on?'. Having overheard him, Janet turned and said, 'I am running this company, not Jon Elbery'. Jon Elbery's response to Janet's initiative was positive. He hadn't known what to expect and was worried that people would just drift away. He was relieved by Janet's display of leadership. He reassured her that John Frame was important to the company because he didn't automatically trust everyone, was very good at analysing accounts and also at sniffing out trouble – in short, an excellent accountant.

Janet stayed very late at work that day. She met individually with the managers of the major divisions of Heytesbury and asked what they saw as the major issues for them, what the financial situation was and where they thought things were going. She wanted two written pages from each of them by the end of the week summarising these issues. She was excited by the possibilities now before her; the adrenalin was flowing. She had a challenge and an opportunity unlike any that life had offered her before. She later observed that for some people the experience of death can be energising; for her, this was certainly so.

Janet had feared that the staff who had worked for Robert might not want to work for her but, regardless of their personal views, most of them in effect said, 'They had worked for the family and would like to continue'. Derek Williams stressed his support, although privately he considered Janet would be better off selling the assets in the UK. Janet instructed him to disband Robert's UK board, which had advised him on the London Stoll Moss Theatres, and to sell Grove House. He acted diligently to carry out her orders.

That evening, a group of senior staff had gone out to dinner to discuss their surprise at the way Janet had handled her first day and the way staff had settled down so quickly. Janet meanwhile had dinner with Simon, Catherine and Peter and reviewed her day. Catherine had been in the office organising mail and drafting letters in response to the hundreds of personal letters of sympathy and good wishes which had already arrived. She had dressed very smartly to go to the office, something she had never done before. She wore a skirt instead of her more usual trousers; she looked the way Robert would have liked her to look. Janet's second son Simon and Will Holmes à Court, who had come to Perth with his wife Jane for the funeral, had cleared out Robert's study in the house and organised his papers, which had been removed from Robert's Heytesbury office to make way for Janet. Peter was looking after friends of his who had arrived from England but he also dropped into the offices of individual employees to chat and make himself known.

Meanwhile, the media were preoccupied with scoring the first interview. They questioned whether Janet could fill Robert's seat. What did she know about running a business – after all she was merely the chairman's wife? Did she have the fire in the belly, the killer instinct? Was she tough enough, ruthless enough, cunning enough to run the second-biggest private company in Australia? How would she have time to run an $800 million business and keep up her voluntary work? It was my job to help keep the media away from Janet on those first days, having flown over as soon as I heard of Robert's death. Those who spoke to the media on Janet's behalf – Will Bailey, the chief executive of the ANZ Bank, Bruce Vaughan, the Sydney-based chairman of Dalgety Farmers Ltd and Fay Gale, the Vice Chancellor of the University of Western Australia – said they believed she could do the job, but they saw an essential difference between her and Robert. While he was never concerned as to whether he upset people, Janet was more sensitive and humane. Robert may have had the financial skills, but Janet had the people skills necessary to run businesses after they had been acquired. And Janet did not believe Robert's enemies had to be her enemies, a decided plus for future relationships and strategies. From Janet's point of view she didn't know whether she could run the business successfully or not, but she was going to give it her best shot.

In February 1992 Janet was to tell the WA Inc Royal Commission that she 'didn't sit in on the business discussions at any time because I was the chairman's wife, not the employee'.[2] But at the time of Robert's death this was not the best message about her business experience to put out. Managing the media to ensure positive coverage was part of the effort to maintain the confidence of the banks, something Janet was going to learn a lot about in the coming months. For now it was one step at a time.

On the second day after the funeral, Janet issued a press release about her plans, detailing the committees she intended to resign from to give her more time to run Heytesbury. She announced she would remain as chairman of the Australian Children's Television Foundation and as Pro-Chancellor of the University of Western Australia, organisations with which Robert had been closely connected. In the case of the Foundation she said that she was very proud of its achievements and wanted to remain and see through the projects that he had invested in; furthermore, she wanted to continue in a role she had been in for seven years and which had seen the growth of a unique and successful organisation. In the case of the University of Western Australia, she had a commitment to education and wanted to be part of the changes that were being made there. The press release included the line, 'That was where I met Robert and that was where I said goodbye to Robert'.

Tim Treadgold, handling the media release for Heytesbury, objected to Janet's wording. He told her she should not speak of Robert in that way. 'That's the past', he said. 'You're dealing now with the financial press'. He insisted that she must be very careful, that the only audience of any significance was the banks and the financial world. She must address them and she could not address them in such terms, terms which, he said, 'Looked weak and womanly'. But Janet insisted the line remain. She was not Robert; she was going to do things differently. Treadgold's response was indicative of the culture among Robert's people. In his view, there were certain rules and expectations in the world of men's business. Treadgold's sympathies were not with the matriarch; he felt for 'the boy', Peter. He felt so strongly that he said to me, 'The boy wanted his name in [the press release] and I thought that was right. I put his name in and I could see he was going to have to come back to pick up the bones'. Although the press release was issued as Janet wished, the next day Treadgold continued to hammer his point. He again told Janet she'd done very well that day, but it had been a big mistake to include the line about where she met Robert and where she said goodbye to him.

But Janet was satisfied with her two days' work. Legal matters surrounding Robert's will were resolved; she had resigned from the committees that had complemented her role as Robert's wife, so as to make time for the business of running Heytesbury; staff were back to work and she had in hand written reports from her managers to read at the weekend. She had made crucial progress. Staff were relieved and, although in a state of shock, expressed enthusiasm and willingness to apply themselves on the family's behalf.

On Friday evening, dinner at home was very lively. Peter, Catherine and Simon were in good form, cracking jokes and enjoying themselves. Will and Jane Holmes à Court joined in. Janet decided to go to the Stud for the weekend. When she reached the farm, she drove straight to the horses' stalls to see the newly-born foals, then entered the house and sat in the large bedroom with its beautiful drapes, canopy and chairs decorated in bright, patterned material, the room where Robert had died. I was still with her, and we talked of the events of less than a week before, events that had changed her life dramatically. Her role as the dutiful, self-effacing wife of an Australian tycoon had suddenly and dramatically ended. She was now the head of a dynasty encompassing 9 million rural hectares carrying sheep and cattle, London theatres, a freight operation, an impressive art collection, vintage cars, horse breeding, publishing and share trading. So smooth had been the initial changeover that, after less than a week, share trading was the only division on hold. Janet had already hit her stride.

The task facing Janet was an extraordinary one. Her administrative and management experience was limited, but she had determination, tenacity and strength and she had twenty-four years of observing a brilliant mind at work. It had required an enormous amount of strength to be married to Robert, and she now turned that strength on Heytesbury. Jon Elbery confirmed to the press that Janet 'was participating four to five hours after Robert's death'. He said, 'Her comment to me was: "We have a huge responsibility. It is not just one family which has been affected. There are all the other families who rely on us for their livelihoods"'.[3]

Janet's first difficult business decision had to be taken on the Monday after the funeral. Clearance of the Loreto Convent site, originally planned for their new house, had begun the previous week and the Loreto Chapel was due to be demolished. The Art Deco Society claimed it was a building of national significance, and there was an Aboriginal claim that the land was sacred as the home of a Dreamtime serpent which followed the Swan River. The site was to be prepared for residential development. The press had been debating the issue for some time.

It was one thing for the cold-hearted Robert Holmes à Court to be demolishing an historic building, it was another for Janet the art lover and friend of the Aboriginal people to do so. Janet took the decision to proceed with the demolition that Monday as planned. The old Loreto Convent bell tower was later reconstructed by Heytesbury and John Holland on the site of the new tax office building. The idea for the restoration had been approved by Robert, but kept secret until the tower was reconstructed.

The future of Carisbrook was also a high priority. Carisbrook, Heytesbury's share-trading subsidiary, was the area Janet was most wary of. She knew that those in the company who worked on the share plays worked under Robert's personal direction. Each day and night, Robert issued detailed instructions on what to buy and sell, and even those who took his instructions often could not see what Robert saw. When Robert died, he had a 6.6% stake in Andrew Lloyd Webber's Really Useful Group (RUG), 5.3% in Dalgety PLC and $5 million in Fairfax junk bonds. Heytesbury's US subsidiary had recently embarked on a number of share operations, including $US10 million of stock in the Denver-based copper giant Cyprus Minerals Corporation. Janet's initial thought was that she would allow trading with a small amount of money to see how the team went, but she soon decided to get out altogether. So complete has been her rejection of this activity that, in terms of its trading potential, she hasn't looked at a share price to this day.

Janet was left with a mess, huge assets and massive debt. Robert, the supreme business strategist, knowing he was unwell and not likely to recover, made no plans to assist his family to manage his legacy. He left no instructions, no structure, no will, nothing, and no one in place to succeed him. The people who were there represented the old regime, one she did not trust without Robert to make the decisions. And they viewed her, the tea maker, with considerable apprehension. These males did not respect Janet for her business ability or her style of operation.

From the first day after Robert's death, she was required to demonstrate credibility with the business community, the banking community, the media and her own staff. Janet needed to have her own group, whose advice she could take, whose advice she trusted on a personal level, people with whom she could feel comfortable. Instinctively she wanted people around her who were able to separate her from Robert and not see her in the role of the appendage to which she had been relegated for so many years.

To help her bridge this gap, she asked Will Holmes à Court to come to Perth as her personal assistant. Will was a graduate in engineering and commerce and had been planning manager with Capita, a big insurance and funds management group. He and Jane agreed immediately to Janet's proposal. Will had a high regard for both Robert and Janet and loved the children, whom he had known for some years. His father had worked for Robert in New York and Will knew that Janet would need support and someone she could trust, someone who did not have a vested interest, someone with an objective view from outside the organisation.

Will's mother had died two years before from cancer and he had some experience of handling death and grief. He recognised the company was in corporate mourning, that staff felt they had lost their leader and there was a vacuum in their lives. He knew that, from an operational point of view, the corporate staff had never been taught to be managers. Will said:

> [Robert] had his thirty or so people who didn't know how to run a business to save themselves. Basically they were great providers of information, but he only kept people who wouldn't make decisions. So they were absolutely the wrong people to have in place ... Robert had the people who suited him but simply didn't suit [Janet] in any shape or form ... There was a lot of shock, a lot of inability to look at the world in an objective way and I enjoyed being there for Janet, to be a shoulder to cry on, to be there to be a comfort, for a knowing look in a moment of grief rushing back ... I tried to provide the environment for Janet that Janet had provided for Robert and not make any noise about it.

Janet also turned to Katherine Burghard,[4] the lawyer in the New York office and one of the few senior women in Heytesbury. Robert had kept the office in New York although there was not much going on there except share trading. He would visit perhaps twice a year and the staff comprised of only an analyst, an accountant and Katherine. The business in New York was a branch of the London costume company Bermans and Nathans, which owned 800,000 costumes and had been operating for 200 years. Katherine admired Janet and Janet liked the idea of a woman on the board she could talk to, so she invited Katherine to join the Heytesbury board. In the end, Katherine was too far away to offer much to Janet and it was only a matter of time before the New York office would be closed, the costume business and the spectacular Manhattan apartment, high above the Museum of Modern Art, sold. Katherine was the last one out the door.

Janet knew what she wanted to do – to run productive enterprises. She did not want to engage in share trading, and the further accumulation of 'goodies'. She did not put value on wealth for its own sake. Although she wanted to retain the Stoll Moss Theatres and rejected all offers to buy which came in over the next week and throughout the following months, she did not want to live in London or spend as much time as Robert had in London. Janet was more interested in Asia, and Perth was a better base for that.

When Robert chaired Bell Group, all his private non-performing assets were in Heytesbury – the Stud, the car collection, the art. When he moved from a public company to a private company, all his private non-productive assets were in with the business enterprises. Together, all Heytesbury assets were capable of generating about $30 million cash a year, but the cash requirements of Heytesbury were $60-$70 million. So the enterprises by themselves weren't capable of servicing the debt that had been amassed to acquire them. The growth in Robert's portfolio had accrued very rapidly. Although badly injured by the 1987 stockmarket crash, when Robert extracted himself from the Bell Group he accumulated debt again very quickly. John Frame, the Group's treasurer, described the growth prior to Robert's death as 'a feeding frenzy'.

Heytesbury had never been a highly profitable company; it tended to just get there each year, with Robert generating the balance through his dealing. There was around $350 million debt. Without Robert, the strategy Janet and Jon Elbery applied to Heytesbury was sound – firstly to sell off non-productive assets and secondly to replace Robert Holmes à Court with a cash-generating business. Stoll Moss generated cash, but the pastoral group was marginal, needing work and reorganisation before it could become a reliable cash business.

Action was needed on every front, but it is very difficult to change the culture of an organisation. Janet had no hands-on management experience. She had to rely on Robert's managers who were all good people, but also still finding their way. It took several months for the severity of Heytesbury's financial position as a company to emerge.

Robert's horses were his indulgence. Where a business deal would be managed and argued down to the last dollar, money spent on the horses and the Stud was not an issue. While his greatest racing and breeding triumph materialised when Black Knight won the 1984 Melbourne Cup, he also made some costly purchases such as the yearling Paint the Stars, reflecting the highs and lows of racing. Robert was philosophical about such setbacks. He bought horses from all around the world and it did not take long before Heytesbury's performance in breeding winners was recognised nationally and internationally and in the inaugural Western Australian Racing Industry Awards announced in October 1985, Robert took out the honour of the Achiever of the Year.

And Robert's plans expanded exponentially. He acquired Trelawney Stud in New Zealand and Wallan in Victoria. Janet located Wallan, which she and Robert always felt would be a very good real estate proposition, and they spent 'unbelievable amounts of money on the property'. It was to be the best stud property in the world. There were 65 kilometres of white post-and-rail fencing. There were more garden staff working there than horse staff. It would take three days to mow the lawn from the front gate to the back gate and once finished they would start again. Wallan had to be developed in a grand manner.

By 1985 Robert had two broodmares in Ireland, two in the United States and seven highly bred fillies which he purchased at the premier yearling sales at Newmarket, England. He was planning to extend further his UK operation. As his horsebreeding spread around the world and the number of properties he owned increased, so the lifestyle on the studs was steadily upgraded. A $2 million house was built at the Keysbrook Stud in 1986, the year Robert and Janet were very preoccupied in Melbourne with BHP.

The ultimate plan at Keysbrook had been to build a sprawling Australian colonial family home. The site had been chosen early on. It was a one-level structure with a shingle roof, limestone walls, verandahs on all sides, and rough bush posts as supports. There was also a poolhouse, gym, sauna and squash court, with a separate guesthouse with four large quarters and ensuites built around a central loungeroom and kitchen. The builder estimated the floor area at one acre.

Plans had been drawn up for another grand house on the property at Wallan.

When Robert died the horse business was in a serious loss situation. Janet had inherited 165 brood mares, 45 horses in training, four stallions, the Trelawney stud farm, the large property at Wallan and a property at Benger in Western Australia. Janet considered the horse operation a shambles. She had never been enthusiastic about Robert's interest in racing horses in England and America because the cost was so outrageous. She didn't see the pleasure in writing cheques for something you could not enjoy.

After Robert's death Janet stopped the racing in the UK and the US. She sent the horses from Wallan to Trelawney. Janet had always felt Wallan was too cold for horses. She greatly reduced the number of horses in training. It was costing $12,000 a year to train a horse and very few of them were in profit. If a horse hadn't won a race, training ceased. She felt 'It was a mug's business to have so many horses in training'.

Nick Poser and Mick Sheehy have been employed at the Stud with both attempting to turn the horse business into a profitable operation. By the time Sheehy arrived in January 1995, Benger and Trelawney had been sold, Wallan was on the market.[5] The number of mares had been reduced to 35, with three stallions.

The only operating property was Keysbrook, with the focus on improving efficiencies and profitability. It was apparent that there were underutilised facilities at the Stud and there were services that could be offered to the thoroughbred industry other than just breeding.

These services involved the preparation of horses for sale, the breaking-in of horses after they'd been sold and the educating of horses prior to racing. So Heytesbury was to become a one-stop-shop which could offer all the services an owner would require within the industry, except for training horses to race at the racetrack. It was decided not to venture into this area as many clients were trainers and it was preferable to complement their clients, not compete with them. This approach overcame the seasonal use of facilities linked only to the breeding season. Where Robert had been a 100% owner of his stallions, Mick Sheehy looked into stallion syndication.

The Stud remains a beautiful property with its now very well-established trees, its white painted fences, bitumen roads, attractive buildings and lush pastures. There is nowhere better to see the horses and enjoy the environment. It has been Ethnée's home for twenty-six years and is Janet's favourite resting place. Heytesbury Thoroughbreds is now a separate enterprise, reporting to Heytesbury Pty Ltd,[6] managing its own cash flow and reporting obligations. John Holland advised on the construction of the racetrack at the Stud, which was completed May- June 1995.

Janet stays at the Stud as often as she can, eight to ten times a year, and spends Christmas and Easter there. She loves the farm and is very supportive of the change in direction which has sometimes been in conflict with her personal preferences. Some of her beloved trees have had to go to make way for the racetrack and selling yards. The farm is more of a public place than it used to be. Janet resents the intrusion into her private spaces. So there is a balancing act on both sides.

From the point of view of the shareholders, Catherine retains the most active interest of the four children in the Stud. Although they all have happy memories of their childhood activities on the Stud, it was Catherine who took most interest in the horses and became the most proficient horsewoman. She races horses and has done outstandingly well. She also worked with the yearlings, in the business. Catherine bought a mare from Peter which produced a champion. Peter always regretted the sale. After Robert's death Catherine worked at the Stud for a time and in 1997 she purchased a share in a stallion, which gave those working at the Stud a great morale boost knowing a shareholder was taking such an interest.

The monument to Robert Holmes à Court looks down on the property. It stands tall, strong and solid in amongst the jarrah, blackbutt and redgum bush high on the windswept escarpment at Heytesbury Stud. The timber, which Janet found in Tony Jones's workshop, came from an old bridge which was demolished in the South West of Western Australia in the early nineties. Janet thought it a most appropriate sculpture for Robert as the South West was the part of Australia where Robert had his business beginnings at the Albany Woollen Mills, an area of which he was fond. It was also appropriate that Tony Jones, who was a fellow boardmember when Robert served as chairman of the Art Gallery of Western Australia, created the sculpture with assistance from Brian McKay, Matt Dickmann, Greg Powell and Mike Elms.

Brian McKay routed in the inscription which Janet had found after an extensive search. The words are by Lord Byron.

I stood among them but not of them.
In a shroud of thoughts which were not their thoughts.

The sculpture is a large wooden construction, made of historic beams that had served a practical purpose. In shape and style their formation was an accident – as Janet believed Robert was an accident of genetics and environment – a fitting tribute to a unique human being.

Along with the Stud, two other major non-performing assets had to be sorted out following Robert's death: the vintage car collection and the Vasse Felix Winery.

The car collection was Robert's idea. He loved cars. When Janet met Robert she drove a £150 Standard Ten which she acquired with a loan from the Bank of NSW (later Westpac) at Nedlands – the bank manager was her boyfriend's uncle. Robert drove a VW beetle, which Janet later purchased from him for £350. It was her second car.

They started married life with a Porsche and a Karmann Ghia, two pretty classy cars at that time. Robert and Janet were amongst the first to use vintage cars at their wedding. Cars were another interest Janet and Robert had in common throughout their married life.

When Robert died, reducing the car collection proved to be an easier exercise than Janet expected. She has had so many very nice cars she forgets many of them, but she did like Porsches. Early in the eighties Robert bought Janet a Porsche for her birthday and she didn't like the colour. He changed it immediately for a colour she did like. It finished up in the car collection and was the first car to be sold after Robert's death. Janet's sons were disappointed because Robert had gone to so much trouble to get the car for their mother, but she saw it as a symbol of a time that was now finished and felt they had to get on with the new phase of their lives.

The car collection which numbered 45 was rationalised, with 20 cars sold. She retained single examples of cars which told the story of the development from the horse-drawn carriage to the steam car and the internal combustion engine. She kept one electric car. She sold all the grand cars except for one Packard, sold the Mercedes, and added to the Jaguars, using the money from the sales to buy cars where there were gaps in the collection. The cars are now used for Heytesbury promotional purposes, taken to rallies and driven by the employees as team-building exercises. They have also been displayed at the Vasse Felix Winery.

The Vasse Felix Winery was also a candidate for serious attention as part of the clean-up. It had been acquired in 1987 almost on a whim. One morning Janet was flicking through the paper while she and Robert were enjoying their first cup of tea for the day. An advertisement for the sale of the Vasse Felix Winery caught her eye. Janet said, 'Vasse Felix is for sale. That would be a fantastic thing to own'. Robert liked to purchase assets which he thought were the best of their kind. Trelawney Stud in New Zealand was a premiere stud. Grove House was one of the best houses in London, 99 Spring Street was the penthouse at a sought-after apartment block in Melbourne and Vasse Felix had a very good reputation for making excellent wine. Robert replied, 'Let's do that'. Janet says, 'I think probably less thought went into that decision than any other he ever made'. The price was around a million dollars.

Vasse Felix was the first commercial vineyard and winery in the Margaret River region. The area had been identified by Dr John Gladstones, who wrote, in the *Australian Institute of Agriculture Journal*, December 1965, of the suitability of the climate and soil for the production of high-quality table wines. Tom Cullity, a Perth cardiologist, bought a small area of land and spent his weekends and holidays establishing a small vineyard, living under difficult conditions in a tin shed. The winery was named after a seaman, Vasse, from a French vessel which had charted the waters of south Western Australia in the eighteenth century. Vasse lost his life while trying to return to his ship, which was anchored in Geograph Bay near Busselton. 'Felix' is Latin for 'fortunate' or 'happy'.

In 1973 David Gregg, a British dairy technologist, arrived in the area. He had tasted Tom Cullity's wines and an association developed which led to David Gregg becoming wine maker and manager. In 1980 the crop averaged seventeen tonnes per hectare and they had run out of space for the material. When Robert bought the winery David Gregg stayed on as manager.

The small business experienced increased demands from its new owners. Robert decided that he would like to see Vasse Felix grow substantially and injected capital. The reporting and accounting functions also needed radical improvement. But Robert visited Vasse Felix only once and divisional accountant Bob Baker says he 'wasn't particularly taken by it at the time. He didn't think it looked like an efficient production operation and didn't view it as a serious business vehicle'. Vasse Felix was considered in the same breath as the other collectibles. And it was also considered 'Janet's thing'.

While Vasse Felix had virtually been an indulgence, a gift from Robert to Janet, it was to prove to be a model enterprise for the new

Heytesbury. The winery, like every other enterprise, was required to improve performance. During the year after Robert's death when Bob Baker and David Gregg went to board meetings with Janet, Jon Elbery, John Frame and Ian Wildy, frustration was expressed by the board with management's inability to produce its budgeted profits. The Forest Hill vineyard Robert acquired in 1989, and Mount Barker forestry operations (also under the responsibility of Vasse Felix management) were sold and there was no further capital investment in the winery.

Soon after Darrel Jarvis became deputy managing director of Heytesbury, Bob Baker was appointed general manager. The vineyard was placed within Heytesbury Pastoral Group as an agricultural business. Bob Baker then analysed the organisational problems Vasse Felix faced, conscious that given the problems of the Heytesbury Group, Vasse Felix was potentially expendable.

The winery had been overstocking and there was production in excess of sales. There were problems with the product range and there was a need to improve the quality of the white wines. A restaurant had been built in 1988–89 and opened for the summer season of 1989–90. Its purpose was always as a marketing tool for the wine but it was not a success. As the remedial process began, Clive Otto, who had been David Gregg's assistant, was appointed winemaker and he and Bob set about reducing stocks and generating cashflow. They sold a lot of wine in bulk and to the theatres in London. They also sold into Japan under a variety of labels almost at cost, just to convert stock to cash which could go back to the then-financially troubled Heytesbury Group.

By increments Vasse Felix began to achieve improved results, which were visible through 1993 and 1994. The business plan was for the winery to grow to a 400-tonne capacity. Distribution was sorted out and the returns on capital were good. As the fortunes of the Heytesbury Group turned around, Vasse Felix turned around at a faster rate. In 1995 Bob discussed with the Heytesbury directors the 400-tonne limit, which he thought was too restrictive. He considered Vasse Felix capable of growing to 500 tonnes over the rest of the decade and he went to the board with a plan presenting the capital investment that would be required to achieve that growth. In 1996 Vasse Felix crushed 730 tonnes. The directors approved the reinvestment of Vasse Felix's profit, which was no longer required for the Group. Vasse Felix thus became self-supporting, paying a respectable dividend to the holding company.

In 1997 Vasse Felix celebrated its thirtieth anniversary, and its tenth under Heytesbury ownership. In the years since Robert's death production had grown to the point of winery capacity and profits grown to record levels so that Vasse Felix had become the best performing enterprise in the Heytesbury Group. There are plans now underway for expansion. As well, a beautification plan for the property is well advanced, which makes Vasse Felix a most striking vineyard to visit. The marketing of Vasse Felix wines is helped by the fact that Margaret River is a very popular tourist destination, meaning there are strong cellar door sales.

Bob Baker is now managing director, rather than general manager. Janet says proudly:

Vasse Felix makes a small number of very high-quality, prize-winning wines; they taste pretty good and they all sell. It's a great success. Vasse Felix is a microcosm of what we'd like the whole of Heytesbury to be. It has really good management, a really wonderful team of people in place, it makes a fantastic product which the public seek out . . .

While Vasse Felix in time became a model enterprise for Heytesbury, the same period saw some dramatic highs and lows for Janet as she struggled to remould the Heytesbury enterprises into viable working concerns. Apart from revamping the non-performing assets in the Stud and the Winery, what Janet needed for Heytesbury to succeed was a cashflow business. Robert was no longer there to do the deals and make up the shortfall on the company's interest payments.

Under Jon Elbery's direction, the Heytesbury team set about doing what they knew best – identifying undervalued companies that were ripe for takeover. John Holland, Australia's third-largest construction company, looked like a good contender and it was going at a bargain price. Robert had considered John Holland as one of many possible target companies in the year before his death. The association between Heytesbury and Holland went back to the days of Bell Bros. In 1978 Bell was subcontracted to Holland to work on the earthworks of the Wungong Dam, south of Perth. Heytesbury research had revealed that if Holland could be separated from the majority shareholder Pennant, which was having significant financial difficulties, it would be good buying, but Robert didn't like the figures and had not pursued the acquisition.

The company had been founded by John Holland, a construction engineer, in April 1949, and had gained almost icon status in Australian business. The young Holland had been inspired by successive pictures in the daily press of building progress on the Sydney Harbour Bridge. Following six years of war service, where he blew up bridges rather than building them, he returned to Commonwealth Oil Refineries and was appointed construction engineer for Australia. But in 1949 he decided to form his own engineering construction company, accessing capital through Stafford Fox, a 40% shareholder who later became managing director of BP Australia.

His philosophy had been to build a company of quality and reliability, working on community projects of significance, staying on schedule, paying accounts when due, and dealing fairly and firmly with both employees and the unions. He achieved all of this through one of the most dynamic periods of development in Australia's history. Post-war, there was a need for infrastructure, new city buildings, dams, roads, ports, factories, mines and airports.

But in the sixties and seventies came the minerals boom and 'some of the less attractive practices adopted in the USA spread across the Pacific'.[7] Funding operations began to change. It was no longer possible to just call the bank and gain a performance guarantee. John Holland ran into financial difficulties in the eighties. It had had severe problems even before the bankruptcy of Pennant Holdings, when Janet took over the company. Construction companies generally in Australia had become very aggressive and adversarial about the way they did business, fighting with their clients over payment. The aim was to win a contract and solve the problems afterwards. In Janet's view the corporate culture in this industry (including that of John Holland) was macho, aggressive, smug and inward-looking.

Janet decided she was interested in the construction business and the Heytesbury team re-examined John Holland. When the first budget projections came through there was a projected cash surplus of $30 million. It appeared that John Holland would be able to balance their books, and so initially it looked like a very good idea. When Janet announced the acquisition on 6 December, the business media was impressed. Just three months after his death, Robert's widow had made a major corporate move. Robert Gottliebsen wrote in glowing terms of the strategy behind the deal:

> *The Holmes à Court dynasty is emerging as a unique and powerful force in the business community ... Janet Holmes à Court has not only taken over the reins but set the family business on a path towards accelerated growth ... she boxed the banks into a corner and pulled off a remarkable coup, subject to John Holland shareholder approval.*[8]

The strategy of this takeover had been to bypass the share ownership stage and buy the asset from the banks, who were wanting to cut their losses from their own wild and extravagant spending during the eighties. Unfortunately, the problems evident with John Holland when Robert looked at the company had grown progressively worse. Its main shareholder, Brian Johnson's Pennant Holdings, was in receivership and could not finance continuing ownership. John Holland had been severely mismanaged. It had moved into the USA with little operating knowledge and suffered major losses. It had put equity into property it was constructing and lost heavily when property values dropped. The banks had guaranteed the US venture to the tune of $100 million, which they had to honour when the venture failed. The banks had guaranteed a second $100 million of John Holland performance bonds. The winding down of a construction company is a tricky business and the appointment of a receiver would undoubtedly have meant the full loss of this guarantee.

Heytesbury was not the only company that appreciated the banks' dilemma, as Gottliebsen said, but Heytesbury also appreciated John Holland's potential. They were currently building a $65 million office development in Perth for Heytesbury which was to be let to the Taxation Department. John Holland had a good name in Australia and Asia, and a qualified team of engineers. The deal Heytesbury offered involved only the payment of $500,000 deposit and 50% of the profits up to 30 June 1991, plus 10% of the profits in the 1991–92 financial year. Heytesbury also agreed to inject $15 million into the new company to provide working capital. A new joint venture company (Keatsmanor Pty Ltd) was formed, whose only asset was John Holland construction business. Gottliebsen predicted 'The most Heytesbury can lose if things go wrong is the $15 million working capital injection'.

Heytesbury had refused to inject more capital so, being the only bidders, the bank had to take the deal or leave it. Jon Elbery said, 'We won't be doing much to change John Holland's method of operating. The core operations have been and continue to be profitable'. He said he expected to 'grow the business by expanding the books rather than further acquisitions'.[9]

The banks and the family shareholders agreed to the offer in February 1991. The *Heytesbury Herald* reported the deal:

With the acquisition of the core business units in Holland came 1,600 employees, more than $700 million in ongoing work and projects spread across Australia and right throughout South East Asia ... Major works include the massive redevelopment of the famous Melbourne Cricket Ground, a power station in Thailand, airport hangars in Bangladesh, water treatment plants in Malaysia, contract coal mining in Indonesia and office blocks around the region.[10]

Heytesbury believed it had a cash cow and John Holland believed it had a white knight. The John Holland network in Asia was seen as having immense value and would in the longer term assist in the Heytesbury cattle and transport operations.

Janet and the Heytesbury team were very enthusiastic about the deal they had done. However, in the work undertaken by the team of analysts the long-term strategy for John Holland was not at all clear. One member of the later Heytesbury financial team, Peter Wood, recalls that 'the issue of a quick sale was always being floated' and 'towards the end of the negotiating process that took on, certainly in Steve's [Johnston] and Jon's [Elbery] minds, a bigger element in their thinking'. One of the reasons Robert had not been interested in John Holland was the very complicated legal issues involved with this bankrupt company.

The Heytesbury team had, however, done the legal work required to extricate John Holland from Pennant Holdings. The banks had appointed a soft receiver to John Holland. All the contracts had default clauses in them, so every bank guarantee the banks had out would have been called in if John Holland had folded. The company was unsaleable. The leverage in buying John Holland was that Heytesbury would assume the outstanding bank guarantees on the projects. The banks were left with an $80 million debt, but also the comfort of knowing that the extra $100 million in bank guarantees would not be cashed.

It was thought, therefore, that John Holland could be sold at a profit but no one had spent much time on how to manage it or how to make it work as a business. In relation to overall strategy for the company, it was considered a natural fit for the other highly capitalised businesses. The overall objective from Jon Elbery's standpoint was to generate roughly $10 million from Stoll Moss, $10 million from Pastoral and $10 million from John Holland. But this theoretical objective was very difficult to achieve.

The Heytesbury bankers were not aware that Heytesbury was looking at John Holland. Suddenly they found that not only did they own it, they were banking Heytesbury into John Holland. At the time, Heytesbury was banked under a negative pledge negotiated by Robert where all the companies were tied in one group, so with John Holland in the group there were no financial restrictions on John Holland.

John Holland was, of course, due for a big shakeup. When Darrel Jarvis became deputy managing director in November 1991, within three weeks he was in Melbourne with Janet addressing the problems of John Holland. Graham Duff, the managing director of John Holland, departed and Bob Nordlinger became managing director of John Holland on 1 January 1992, appointed by Janet.

The earlier analysis had fallen well short of understanding the existing projects on the books and the cash flow implications. The cash Heytesbury hoped to find in John Holland was not there. As well, the company had to be 'cranked up' as a going concern. There were no new projects in the pipeline. There was no confidence in the organisation and it wasn't winning jobs. The analysts had looked at projects being completed but hadn't examined what would be involved in keeping John Holland afloat. Nor had they calculated how long it would take to get it moving again as an operating business.

It was meant to be a zero balance sheet. Peter Wood said the Heytesbury team:

> tried to disassociate themselves from some bad projects, but in the end a couple of significant things went wrong. One was that they had to accept a number of completed projects where there were disputes and rather than getting a cash settlement on day one to bring assets and liabilities to a zero position, they had to accept soft assets as a settlement against the deficit. Those projects included the Princess Theatre renovation in Melbourne and a host of other disputed claims. John Holland had done a complete refurbishment of the Princess Theatre for Marriner and Company and on their books it was a $12 million receivable; they had in fact spent $13 million. In the end, Heytesbury agreed to value the Princess Theatre claim at $4.5 million.

Another technical project, International Railway Systems (Electronics) Pty Ltd (IRSE) for Australian National Rail, was also in trouble and Heytesbury had to take that on. Peter Wood said:

> In effect what happened was, the analysis said John Holland needs $15 million worth of working capital. There was in fact a $16 million deficit from day one in that we were forced to take on assets we didn't

want, so immediately the $15 million was $30 million. Over and above that, there was $30 million where it was just bad analysis.

The significant cash flow problems of John Holland were now apparent and the need to win new projects, restructure the organisation and get it moving again was urgent. But from the outset Janet was clear in her view. She did not want to sell John Holland as Robert might have done; she wanted to make the business work. The trouble was, John Holland had the potential to bring Heytesbury down.

Bob Nordlinger was not the answer. He resigned in the same year, after six months in the job, and Randolph Creswell, who had a long history with the company (most recently as director of the engineering and construction arm) and nearing retirement, took over until October 1994. During his tenure, the group was restructured along geographic and discipline lines. Mechanical and electrical divisions were separated. Malaysia became the head office in South-East Asia, specialising in civil engineering. Thailand was the base for mechanical and electrical engineering, with railways in the Philippines and contract mining in Indonesia. Turnover increased in 1994 from $619 million to $751 million, but it was a tight, highly competitive market; the jobs that were won in 1993–94 were won by aggressive bids, typical of the whole cultural ethos in the construction industry that Janet wanted to change. This gung ho approach rebounded on Janet in the Mobil refinery project for Toyo Engineering later on.

Not only were there unforeseen financial problems that impacted on Heytesbury and its relationship with its banking syndicate, there were work practices and cultural problems which were deeply entrenched in the business and incompatible with the way Janet wanted Heytesbury run.

Roz Chalmers, formerly secretary to Keith Drew, managing director of John Holland, had a long but interrupted association with John Holland lasting from 1979 until she rejoined the company in 1989–1996, and had seen the company culture change dramatically. In the old days as an engineering firm, it was 'a boys' club'. There had been some change when she returned in 1989, but she was most struck by the effect Janet had made.

The old boys were so condescending when she came in. I used to hear the talk that would go on in the staff room on a Friday night when they'd had a few drinks ... My first introduction to her was at the takeover cocktail party when she'd just taken over the company ... She walked in and she was beautifully groomed as usual and the men, the look on their faces, and the wives. She has the ability to look people straight in the eye. For the first six months she was here the men couldn't cope with that confrontation. You used to watch them back down, then go away into their little rooms and have their sessions. Quite amusing. Of course we girls were thrilled, we were absolutely thrilled to watch it all going on ... This glamorous woman appeared on the scene, this educated, glamorous woman, and they were in awe.

By 1994, both the restructure and the corporate culture change process were bearing fruit. John Holland formed a 50–50 partnership with the Malaysian manufacturer Humes Industries Berhad, which is 44% owned by the Asian conglomerate Hong Leong, rated among Asia's top ten companies. The two companies had worked together for several years in Sabah, on the privatisation of the water supply in the Malaysian State.

The restructured John Holland focused on the projects the company was experienced at, and then targeted specific customers. Instead of being all things to all people they became more specialised. The company refocussed from turnover to profit and cash and changed its risk profile. The five areas of construction focus in John Holland are: building, civil engineering, heavy engineering, operations and maintenance and railway construction and maintenance, which is a small industry at the moment but seen as having potential.

Janet and Darrel Jarvis, who took over from Jon Elbery, recognised that the construction industry was going through a very difficult period and if John Holland was going to change, they needed a managing director who could make that occur and who had the same approach to business they did, both in terms of ethics and customer focus. Keith Drew was selected from a short list of five applicants as the experienced all-rounder to take on the task of restructuring. He commenced with the John Holland Group in December 1994 as managing director. An economist and mechanical engineer, he had gained considerable experience in the construction industry in a range of consulting and executive positions. As managing director for John Holland, Keith is responsible for all operations of the group within Australia and South-East Asia and its staff of 1,200 in Australia.

When Keith joined John Holland, he understood Janet's appraisal that she 'was unhappy with the way the company was going'. Keith said Janet wanted the group to be:

more client-focused, going back to what John Holland used to be in the sixties and seventies — she was very keen for the ethos of the company to change and for it to become more shareholder responsive.

During his interview, Darrel had impressed on Keith that major change had to occur, but Keith was not prepared for the extent to which that was necessary. Janet's aim was for a company that had repeat business, where clients wanted to do business with John Holland because of performance – working with the client to achieve a result in the interest of all – with shareholder and client satisfaction. This meant a staff restructure was imperative. New people were selected to drive the new culture and several middle managers left the company. In the construction business, a large company takes time to change direction and business must keep moving on. Ghosts from the past can continue to reappear for some years as projects move through the pipeline. And in Toyo Engineering there was a large ghost which had the potential to bring down Heytesbury itself.

With John Holland in the bag, and before the emergence of the problems its purchase brought, Janet also focused her attention on the other enterprises. Among these was the London theatre group, operating under the name of Stoll Moss.

Stoll Moss has a long and rich history in the theatre world and the company today owns ten theatres in the West End, making it the largest single owner/operator of theatres in London. The two founders were Sir Oswald Stoll and Sir Edward Moss. Born in the mid-nineteenth century, the two men were both raised in the world of entertainment and were the same age when they acquired their first theatre, each in partnership with one parent. Oswald Stoll was born in Melbourne in 1866, and at the age of fourteen sailed to England to help his mother run the famous Parthenon Theatre in Liverpool. He prospered rapidly and acquired the Cardiff Empire by the age of twenty-three before joining forces at the turn of the century with Edward Moss, who had founded Moss Empires.

Theatre historians claim that Oswald Stoll was responsible for changing the direction of theatre entertainment. Historically, the 'music hall' was perceived as a bawdy, working-class tavern or saloon associated with cheap drink and immorality. Stoll made the music hall respectable for all the family. He helped London establish itself as the mecca of the theatrical world.

As their respective theatrical empires grew, the two men decided to pool their resources, rather than compete. On 15 December 1899, they formed Stoll Moss Empires Ltd and incorporated their many theatres throughout the country, including music halls in Edinburgh, Birmingham, Newcastle and Liverpool. As well as staging productions that people wanted to see, the company had the business acumen to design and build theatrical palaces of unimagined luxury. Some of these buildings still grace the London skyline, such as the Palladium and the Coliseum. By 1905, Stoll Moss were directly employing nearly 600 artistes, 100 musicians, 2,000 stagehands and entertaining nearly 100,000 people a day throughout the country. In later years, as styles in entertainment changed, the company acquired smaller, more intimate theatres. Throughout its history, the company has brought the very best live entertainment, in various forms, to Great Britain.

Today the Stoll Moss venues range from the grandeur of the Theatre Royal, Drury Lane, Her Majesty's Theatre and the London

Palladium to small intimate theatres, such as the Duchess, the Garrick, and the Queen's. The strength of the company is that it can provide a theatre to suit any production and cover a wide range of entertainment possibilities.

Not only was Stoll Moss Theatres Ltd an excellent business, the theatres represented an important slice of British history and British culture. Sir Oswald Moss's colonial origins were long forgotten when a new Australian entrepreneur, Robert Holmes à Court, arrived on the scene to take over ACC. Robert's interest was primarily in the fact that ACC was an undervalued company. It was to become his first international takeover, one which was to arouse the interest of the British takeover panel.

When Janet succeeded her husband as chairman of Stoll Moss Theatres, she became the first woman in history to control the majority of London's theatres. Having maintained an interest in theatre and culture from her childhood, this was not an asset Janet intended to give up, as both Stoll Moss staff and the industry were quick to discover. The London theatre community had not had time to assess Robert Holmes à Court and his plans for the historic theatres but, given his reputation, they were deeply suspicious of his motives. One of Robert's last interviews, his last in the UK, was given to the *Evening Standard*.

The journalist was seeking to establish Robert's plans, given his highly publicised disputes with Cameron Mackintosh and Andrew Lloyd Webber, the two pre-eminent London players in the theatrical world. The *Standard*'s interest in Robert's plans had also been sparked by his appointment of four new staff to Stoll Moss. There was speculation that whatever Robert did would not benefit London theatre. Robert observed to Robin Stringer, 'I enjoy what I do. I would be less interested in building shopping centres and office buildings than preserving and developing theatres, but I would not overstate it. It's just gently worthwhile'.[11]

He explained that he was embarking on a program of restoration and modernisation, computerisation, and the acquisition of properties adjoining theatres like the Coliseum and Palladium so as to extend facilities; he was also making his first tentative investment in a production, *Show Boat*, which was opening at the Palladium in August.

Despite making these investments, Robert told the journalist, 'I was once told that you will not sell an extra ticket by repairing the carpet or making the seats more comfortable. People will come to a good show and they will not come to a bad show. That is all it is about'. But Robert was bringing a change to that philosophy. He said, 'I am saying we have to service the producer and the theatregoer if we are to remain the rightful custodians of these wonderful assets'. But in such service, Robert made it clear he was 'in the theatre business not for charity, but for commerce'. He would be seeking commercial rents and he wanted to buy more theatres. The *Evening Standard* reserved judgement.

The contrast in styles between Robert and Janet Holmes à Court is nowhere better illustrated than in the story of these theatres and in the way they approached their relationships with other players in the theatre business, especially the two outstanding English producers, Cameron Mackintosh and Andrew Lloyd Webber.

When she came to Melbourne to announce the acquisition of John Holland, Janet attended the Melbourne opening of *The Phantom of the Opera*. It was the first time she had met both Cameron Mackintosh and Andrew Lloyd Webber, the musical producer and the creator of *Phantom*. She spent time with both of them at the after-show party and travelled back to London on the same plane as Cameron. He came and sat on the floor of the plane at Janet's feet and they spoke at length about Robert and the dispute they had had over theatre rental and the interest earned on pre-bookings for Cameron's *Miss Saigon* which was playing in a Stoll Moss theatre. It had been a bitter dispute, Cameron having formed the view that Robert was making more money than he should from the arrangement.

Cameron and Robert had met to discuss the dispute at the Stoll Moss board room, with Derek Williams present. *Miss Saigon* had just opened and was such a success Cameron wanted to reduce his theatre rental. Derek Williams said the conversation at the

David Parker, Kim Rooney, Janet and Robert in 1988
in front of Monet's *Haystack,* which was owned by the Holmes à Courts.

At the 1988 Royal Variety Performance, the Theatre Royal, Drury Lane.

Bern and Fred Ranford in the late 1980s.

At the launch of the ACTF's 'Winners' program, 1990.
Photograph courtesy of the Herald & Weekly Times Photographic Collection

Patricia Edgar, Janet and Hazel Hawke at the 'Winners' launch.

The Holmes à Court family at Robert's funeral, 4 September 1990.

At the memorial to Robert.
I stood among them but not of them.
In a shroud of thoughts which were not their thoughts.
Robert Holmes à Court 1934-1990

The Room at the Top Conference, held by the
Office of Women's Interests, December 1990.

Catherine's graduation, March 1991.

Janet, in her role as chairman of the Black Swan Theatre Company, with Ken Dray, the general manager, and Andrew Ross, the artistic director, 1991.

Patricia Edgar, Paul Keating, Janet and Wendy Fatin, at the launch of 'Lift Off' in 1992, which was also a celebration of the ACTF's tenth anniversary.

Patricia Edgar and Janet at
the celebration of the
ACTF's fifteenth
anniversary.

Photograph courtesy of Greg Noakes.

Janet celebrating her
fiftieth birthday with
her mother, Bern.

Janet and Sir John Gielgud at the renaming of the Globe Theatre to the
Gielgud Theatre in October 1994.

Janet, Freda Glynn and Hazel Hawke at the first World Summit on Television and Children, held in Melbourne, March 1995.

At a Westrek presentation.

World Summit on Television and Children, 1995.

Janet and Bern at Peter and Divonne's wedding, June 1995.

Janet with Sir Cameron
Mackintosh, 1997.

Catherine, Janet, Katrina, Simon, Peter, Divonne and Paul at
Simon and Katrina's wedding, Hydra, Greece, June 1997.

Simon, Peter, Paul and Janet at the wedding celebrations,
Hydra, Greece, June 1997.

With John Holland staff members at Port Hedland, 1997. Janet wears
the fake 'Blue Princess' necklace made for her by the staff.

Celebrating the victorious conclusion to the Constitutional Convention, February 1998.

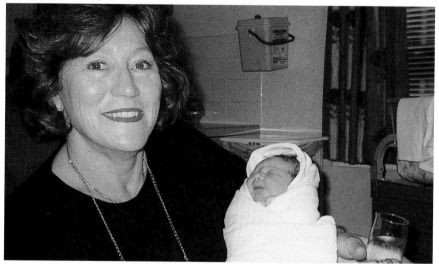

Holding Emma Bern Mather, Janet's first grandchild, January 1999.

On being awarded the Veuve Clicquot Business Woman of the Year Award.

meeting began with pleasantries and preliminary talk, with Cameron telling Robert that he had started out in the theatre world in Drury Lane as one of the backstage people. They soon got down to the business at hand. Derek's recollection of the discussion is substantially as follows:

CM: It's totally unfair, you shouldn't be making all this money.

RHaC: But I've got a contract that says I'm entitled to it.

CM: I know that contract. I had it put in front of me by Louis Benjamin [previous managing director of Stoll Moss]. I just signed it; I didn't read it.

RHaC: Well Mr Mackintosh, you should have read it – that's what contracts are for.

CM: No, no, no. That's not the point. We've been doing business for years and this is totally absurd and if you do this I'm going to withdraw the merchandising rights and the brochure rights and all the other rights.

RHaC: Well I don't think you can do that; you've signed the contract and you're going to be bound by it. But while you're here, Mr Mackintosh, I notice that down the road for *The Phantom of the Opera*, which you also produced, I'm not getting very much rent and that show's been running for seven or eight years.

CM: Well, we're not talking about that Mr Holmes à Court.

RHaC: Oh, I think we are, Mr Mackintosh. I think we're talking about the whole scene. Now I'm sure that if we could come to some arrangement about *Phantom* . . .

CM: I'm not having that. Do you know who you're talking to? I'm the most successful producer in London. [Becoming very heated.]

RHaC: Well, I'm sure we could have a contract which agrees to vary both of those contracts to our mutual satisfaction, but otherwise I don't think there's anything more we can say.

CM: Is that your last word Mr Holmes à Court?

RHaC: No, my last word is, if things go badly for you, you can always get your old job back.

According to Derek Williams, Cameron then walked out and slammed the door. Later, there was an exchange of letters about another related matter. Cameron wrote:

Regretfully, stubbornness may be the only thing we have in common. As long as you retain your position over the sharing of box office interest, it is unlikely that we will do business again. My grandmother warned me that tough cookies were bad for the teeth.

Robert responded:

I hope we don't have to commit to never doing business with each other again as I am sure that we would both be losers in that event . . . Should there ever be a reversal in your fortunes I would like you to know that your old job at Drury Lane is still available to you. I am sure your grandmother would like that.
My kind regards, MRH Holmes à Court.

After a nine-month dispute with Cameron, Robert invited him to dinner at Grove House to bury the hatchet. By then Robert realised he was up against a fighter, a worthy adversary, one he respected, and there was more benefit in their working together. He agreed to sort out the contract. Now friends, they spoke about wide-ranging issues, including the burden and responsibility of wealth. What did one do with the amount of money they each possessed? What about the problems that could be created by destroying the independence of others? The dinner took place during the last months of Robert's life and he told Cameron he had made no will, but had no intention of dying. Cameron found Robert charming and engaging, yet distancing at the same time. He said, 'I saw glimpses of why Janet loved him'.

Janet had never seen value in Robert's argument with Cameron and resolved to start on a positive footing. She became good friends with Cameron, inviting him to stay at her Double Island resort and travelling to New York to the opening of Cameron's production of *Miss Saigon*. Their friendship has developed over the years. Cameron finds her 'extremely engaging, straightforward, immensely practical and winningly charming, in no way snobbish and not at all duplicitous'. He adores her as a great friend, and although he is not uncritical of some aspects of Stoll Moss and the way Janet runs the business, he recognises that it makes sense to work together constructively.

Sir Andrew Lloyd Webber, like Cameron Mackintosh, had also been in serious conflict with Robert when Robert bought shares in his company, the Really Useful Group (RUG). He had done this hoping he could use them as a lever to force Lloyd Webber to sell him the Palace Theatre, which Lloyd Webber owned and where *Les Miserables* was playing. Lloyd Webber had decided to privatise his company and wanted to buy Robert's shares back. Robert refused and said he would only sell the shares if Lloyd Webber would sell the theatre. Lloyd Webber was deeply attached to the theatre. He had restored its terracotta facade with money from the National Trust and it was a theatre with great character.

Lloyd Webber had spent more than $100 million building up ownership in his company and his personal holding stood at around 82.5% in March 1990 when Robert acquired his parcel.[12] He needed a little over 94% to claim RUG as a private company, but if he could not achieve that level then his debt would have to be financed more expensively and he would remain bound by statutory regulations governing public companies.

Robert was interested in owning as many London theatres as he could. The year before he had made a bid for the Maybox theatre chain, dropping it when there were threats of a referral to the Monopolies Commission. Lloyd Webber was hoping to get support from the Commission if Robert attempted a similar takeover. But Robert remained an irritant. In July, when Lloyd Webber had acquired 90% of RUG, Robert opposed plans to pay off directors.[13] Lord Gowrie, the Group's chairman, was to be paid £25,000 as compensation for loss of office. Lloyd Webber was also proposing to pay three other directors £10,000 each. In a letter dated 27 June 1990, Derek Williams, also a director of Robert's Stoll Moss Theatres Ltd wrote, 'As the holder of a 6.6% minority interest in your company, we oppose the enforced resignation of the non-executive directors and the proposed payments for loss of office'. While Robert couldn't stop the payment, he threatened to seek redress through the courts as an aggrieved minority shareholder.

Andrew Lloyd Webber did not need a long and costly legal battle, but Robert was making it clear he would not walk away without a substantial premium to the price he paid for his shares. Lloyd Webber had not had a good year generally. Apart from fighting with Robert, he was losing staff from his company and had split up with his wife Sarah Brightman and taken up with Madeleine Gurdon, a champion horsewoman. It was hardly surprising then that Lloyd Webber was receptive to Janet, Robert's conciliatory widow.

Janet thought the stand-off was rather stupid and saw much more productive business sense in working with Lloyd Webber. He was a creative producer; Janet was a landlord who owned theatres. He created programs; she needed good clients. So she agreed to sell back to him the 6.6% parcel of shares Robert had been holding in the RUG. He won control of his company (which he later sold in part to Polygram) and Janet forged a good relationship with a top London producer.

It paid off handsomely when Lloyd Webber brought *Joseph and His Technicolour Dreamcoat* to the 2,222-seat Palladium. Starring Jason Donovan, the show was financially the most successful ever to run in the West End, playing for two and a half years. It was profitable for Lloyd Webber and very profitable for Stoll Moss at a time that was very tough for Heytesbury.

Janet had said at the time of Robert's death that his enemies weren't her enemies and she saw no reason why they should be. Andrew Lloyd Webber and Cameron Mackintosh remain major Stoll Moss clients. As a measure of the new relationship, Madeleine, Lloyd Webber's wife, held a cocktail party for Janet in London where she had a very unpleasant encounter with Robert Maxwell. (This experience convinced Janet that Maxwell later died in the same way as Robert Holmes à Court.) For several months Maxwell had been attempting to meet Janet, she thought it was because he was interested in buying Stoll Moss. The day after Robert died, there had been soundings from within Stoll Moss 'to get the

Australians out'[14] and bids from outsiders, from those waiting in the wings to pounce with indecent haste, including Lord Delfont, Trevor Chinn of Lex Services, Chesterfield Properties and Andrew Lloyd Webber. The response to the bidders was swift. 'The theatres are simply not for sale. No bids. No management buyouts.'

Maxwell orchestrated the meeting with Janet at the cocktail party, which was also attended by Andrew Lloyd Webber, Jon Elbery and a few others. He sat next to Janet and gave her the third degree about Robert's death. Coming only three months after Robert had died, Janet found this not only tactless and tasteless but distressing as well. He wanted to know all about Robert's lifestyle. Did he exercise? What did he eat? Did he smoke, drink? Was there tension in his life? Was he stressed? He went on and on and on. Maxwell didn't raise the Stoll Moss Theatres for discussion. It was the lifestyle of the entrepreneur that obsessed him. Soon after that meeting Maxwell died mysteriously at sea. He had become incredibly hot, gone up on deck to cool off, had a massive heart attack and fallen overboard. That is Janet's belief, despite all the media theories about spy connections and murder that followed Maxwell's death.

The overall Heytesbury UK operation was run by Derek Williams. As one of Robert's men, he knew very little of Janet. She was the voice who always answered the phone and they exchanged courtesies about the weather. Derek thought of Janet as 'a very hospitable lady who made us all feel comfortable ... Although we knew she was on the board, I didn't think she knew what was happening here (in London)'. Derek went to Australia for Robert's funeral and when Janet addressed the employees Derek knew the UK office's main function, which was takeover activity, could not continue, but learnt quickly that Janet intended to stay with the theatres. Derek's role after Robert's death was to scale right down to the core of the Stoll Moss business. He remains on the Pension Fund board.

The people who had run Stoll Moss over the previous decades had, in Janet's view, 'forgotten they were actually landlords and no refurbishment and practically no maintenance had been done for many years, so I inherited these theatres in shocking shape'. Robert had recognised the need for a maintenance program for the theatres, but

Janet implemented it. The first theatre to need an expensive refurbishment was Her Majesty's. The lease was about to expire and could not be renewed without the work being done. Around £5 million was spent renovating it. The copper dome on top hadn't been touched since 1892. The effect of pollution meant it fell to pieces in the hands of the workers as they tried to bring it off the roof. The toilet and bar facilities were appalling and needed complete renovation.

Janet says, 'The managers were not responsible for their theatres; they were treated like glorified ushers'. She had been told a story by Mark Hayward, the manager of Her Majesty's where *The Phantom of the Opera* was showing. Louis Benjamin, the previous managing director of Stoll Moss when Robert acquired the theatres, did not know that his theatre manager was not an usher. One night the Queen Mother was coming to see *Phantom* and Mark Hayward was called down to Louis Benjamin's office. He thought, 'This is great – I'm going to be presented to Her Majesty', but no, there was a hole in the wallpaper in one of the corridors and Benjamin wanted Hayward to stand in front of it so the Queen Mother wouldn't see it. Mark Hayward later became the manager of the Theatre Royal, Drury Lane, overseeing a staff of 120.

The style of management at Stoll Moss Theatres, however, had been undergoing change. A new managing director, Richard Johnston, had been employed by Robert two months before he died, but while Robert had spent some weeks in London before his death, it was not long enough for Richard to be fully initiated as one of Robert's men. The other innovation much needed in the theatre business was a computerised ticketing system. There had been computerised systems in Australia for many years, but in London manual systems still prevailed.

So Stoll Moss was ripe for renewal and reform. Janet loved the theatre; it was a business very dear to her heart and one that would hold Heytesbury together through difficult times. While the theatres may have been run down physically, the theatre business itself was booming.

Richard Johnston had been chief executive of the Contemporary Dance Trust, the largest modern dance organisation in Europe, and before that he ran the Birmingham Hippodrome Theatre, one of the most successful theatres outside London. He had taken it from a run-down state into a very successful position. Like Darrel Jarvis, Richard had been approached by headhunter Lloyd Smith on Robert's behalf. Typically, his first meeting with Robert was a two-hour chat about this and that. Richard liked Robert and had no difficulty communicating with him. He thought Robert:

very, very keen to bring people in who could bring about positive change for Stoll Moss, to try to flush out the old hierarchy. There was a culture that was essentially looking back to the mid-fifties and there were people running the company then who basically didn't think Robert should own the company and they carried on running it in the way it had run for the last twenty years.

Richard believed that because Robert wasn't particularly good at dealing with people and was not close enough to the senior people to know their style and capabilities. For instance, when Louis Benjamin retired, Roger Filer, who had been with Stoll Moss under him for many years, was appointed by Robert to the position of managing director and Roger and Robert did not get along. Richard joined Stoll Moss and was appointed operations manager. By 11.00 a.m. the day he started he was operations director, and by 2.30 p.m. he was joint managing director – with Roger, in the rather invidious position of sharing a role and having to sort out exactly what that role was. Richard says, 'Robert was a Darwinian, so he was chucking me in there to see how I got on with Roger and what happened'.

Richard enjoyed his brief working relationship with Robert and, as the latter spent much of his time through July–August 1990 in the UK, and Richard was part of the Grove House dinner club, he had enough time with Robert to be impressed with the same traits that impressed others: anything was possible for Robert, the kind of fantastic ambition Richard had seen in artistic and creative people was possible in business with Robert, and he admired Robert's mastery of lateral thinking. Richard also found that Robert loved going to the theatre and he believed that Stoll Moss had the best selection of theatres in the world. Robert enjoyed opening nights and was a good first-night participant. Richard says, 'You might not have thought that, but he got stuck in, had a good laugh and was a real good supporter, as of course is Janet'.

But Richard was not at all sure that Robert knew what to do with his theatres. One scheme he had was to put *The Phantom of the Opera* into the Palladium, which Richard thought 'from a financial point of view initially might have stacked up, but in the long-term was probably not such a good idea'. He thought it would have been fascinating [to work with Robert], 'completely different'.

It is within the Stoll Moss theatre enterprise that it is easiest to evaluate the impact of Janet – her ethics, her values, her vision and her cultural influence over her first five years as chairman of Heytesbury Holdings – and to contrast Janet's approach with Robert's. Stoll Moss enjoyed boom years during the nineties. Johnston says the company was 'absolutely flying'. The theatre business performed extremely well during a difficult time for Heytesbury and was a major factor in the survival of the group. It was a good cash business for Heytesbury to be in. The focus for Stoll Moss was therefore on building for the future rather than radical restructuring.

After Robert's death, when Janet went over to the UK in November, she was an unknown quantity. Within Stoll Moss, as well as in the wider theatre community, Janet, like Robert, was viewed by some as an interloper. For Stoll Moss, meanwhile, it had been business as usual. Unlike the Heytesbury UK Investment Group, the theatres were not affected by Robert's death. Nor were they so affected by the financial fall-out of the late eighties. There must have been some querying as to what she could contribute that wasn't already being done.

In the first year, Janet's visits to Stoll Moss were to do with specific business issues. She curtailed the rumours that Stoll Moss would be sold and authorised the plans that were under way to computerise the ticketing system and refurbish the theatres. It was not until after the bank crisis, at the end of 1991, and after Darrel Jarvis became deputy managing director of Heytesbury, that a staff restructure occurred and Richard Johnston took full control as managing director of Stoll Moss. He developed a closer working relationship with Janet and a stronger focus on building and developing the company.

Extensive research was put into the computerised ticketing system. Loretta Tomasi, financial director of Stoll Moss, was impressed by the fact that although Heytesbury was in financial crisis, the major investment in computer technology for the ticketing operation and the commitment to the refurbishment continued. Tomasi says:

If I was asked what is the most important thing that Janet did in the early stages, it was to actually allow that commitment to continue. In five years from when Janet took over, we've spent something like £7.7 million on refurbishments and we invested nearly £3 million on a ticketing system at a time when really the group was pretty close to saying, 'How are we going to continue?'. [Janet] had a serious interest in theatre and she was able to convince the same group who were sceptical of Robert that she was not just an Australian there for a short time having a good time.

The changes in Stoll Moss provided the evidence of a committed owner. Tickets could be booked to all theatres in London and there were plans to extend ticketing services more widely. As with all Heytesbury enterprises with a short supply of capital, emphasis was placed on its people and finding ways to manage more effectively with a view to growing the company. There is a finite number of seats in theatres but keeping the venues open with diverse, lively and popular theatre is the challenge. With the expertise that has been developed in theatre management, Stoll Moss is looking at running theatres outside the group and acting as a consultant.

Nica Burns started at Stoll Moss on 1 February 1993. As an independent producer, she had perceived Stoll Moss as 'a very unsympathetic commercial company that didn't really care very much about its product and didn't work very closely with producers ...'

Her brief is 'to make Stoll Moss the company of choice for all our clients and all our employees'. In that process she sees producers' shows on the road as she scouts for talent. Stoll Moss has become flexible in terms of the financial deals it does when producers go through bad patches. They work in partnership with their clients. The proof that this is a more effective way to work has been in the financial results. Since Stoll Moss has been more flexible and sometimes given money back to producers, Stoll Moss has actually improved its bottom line.

One of Janet's initiatives has been to break down the British class system as it applies to theatre management, to provide for a career path where there had been none before. A technical manager can now move to senior management or a theatre manager can train managers. Previously people could move from theatre to theatre, but not up the hierarchy. As well as developing Stoll Moss's staff, Janet tries to meet all staff. She instigated a meeting with the senior technical people about safety, which is a big issue in the construction industry but hardly thought about in the theatre industry although theatres are extremely dangerous places.

Janet's greatest publicity coup was to rename the Shaftesbury Avenue Globe Theatre the Gielgud. There had been a public press campaign to persuade Janet to rename the Queen's Theatre after Sir John Gielgud in honour of his ninetieth birthday. But the Queen's Theatre was used predominantly for musicals and Janet did not think it an appropriate theatre to name after a great dramatic actor. At the 1994 Olivier Awards, held in the Palladium Theatre and televised on the BBC, Sam Wanamaker was to be recognised posthumously for the work he had done building a replica of Shakespeare's Globe Theatre on London's South Bank. His daughter Zoe, an actor, was to receive the posthumous award in honour of her father and his contribution to the theatre. Following this award, Janet announced on stage that Stoll Moss, in recognition of both Sir John Gielgud's ninetieth birthday and Sam Wanamaker's Globe Theatre, would rename the Globe, the Gielgud, ensuring there would be only one Globe Theatre in London. It was a great idea, an idea which Richard Johnston had put to Janet. It captured the imagination of the theatre world and turned critical opinion around in her favour.

Both Richard and Nica pay tribute to Janet for the restoration and revitalisation of Stoll Moss. Richard says:

She is one of the best networkers I've ever seen and in our business there is real value in that ... When she comes, by the end of the first day her diary's packed, including weekends and evenings, and quite often I will be concluding some business I started on the first day, on the last day, driving her back to her house or going in the taxi somewhere – that's the nature of the beast, if you like.

With Robert it would be totally different, 'There'd be lots of papers flying backwards and forwards, financial information happening ... more formal communication'.

In public recognition of Janet's achievements in her five years at the helm of Stoll Moss, she was nominated by ten prominent business, political and industry leaders for the prestigious Veuve Clicquot Award for the British Business Woman of the Year and received the honour in 1996. The judges said that Janet had instilled a renewed sense of pride in Stoll Moss and Janet repeated a now common theme in her public speeches: 'We believe not so much in the power of one but the might of many'.[15] In addition to Janet's achievements in pioneering computer technology for ticketing, in customer services, staff training, the creation of an active production strategy, and a program of building repair and maintenance, Stoll Moss's operating profit over the five years of her chairmanship had increased 107%. Within the ticketing division 11 million tickets had been sold, an increase of 43% on 1994. In 1995, the number of dark (closed) theatres out of a potential 520 performing weeks a year was 25 weeks, the lowest number on record.[16]

In the same year, the first two co-productions between Stoll Moss and independent producers – *The Live Bed Show* and *Fame* – had been well received. Staff wrote warmly in support of her nomination and press clippings were admiring of Janet's achievements through Stoll Moss. Janet attributed her success to her 'Australian approach to business',[17] her 'belief that everyone is a fundamental cog in the wheel'. She acknowledged Darrel Jarvis and

Richard Johnston and 'all the people at Stoll Moss who transformed the company'.

Stoll Moss was to be the jewel in the Heytesbury crown and a respite from the trials and tribulations in Australia as Janet came to terms with the financial chaos and mounting debt that was to consume her energy and attention in what came to be known in Heytesbury as the 'war years'.

CRISIS WITH THE BANKS

Throughout the first six months of 1991, less than a year after Robert's death, the wheels had begun to fall off the Heytesbury Group. John Frame, the financial controller, who was watching the figures very closely, became the voice of doom. By April/May, he was asking Linton Byfield, the Group treasurer, whether Heytesbury had the facility in place to cover its growing debt. Will Holmes à Court said, 'He kept trying to point out the problem but did not seem to be able to get his message through'. Janet thought him negative and, as management was not used to giving the boss bad news, his was a lonely voice. Management also thought they could fix the problems and, if not, there were always the enterprises to sell to reduce the debt. In this way they felt the situation was salvageable. But the debts were mounting because the existing interest payable on the debt was not being met.

Over these initial months, as Heytesbury's financial problems became apparent to everyone, Janet grew closer to Darrel Jarvis. And over the next seven years Darrel's involvement with the Holmes à Court family would dominate the history of Heytesbury.

The year Robert bought Sherwin Pastoral Company, its financial performance showed a $10 million loss. The stations had been overstocked and neglected, but the analysis by Robert's staff showed Sherwin to have potential.

Janet believes Robert bought the cattle stations for her. One day while they were on their 22,000-acre property at Joanna Plains, Janet said, 'I love Keysbrook, I love the studs, but this to me is real farming'. Robert replied, 'What about cattle stations; would you like some cattle stations?'. Janet said she would 'absolutely love to be involved in the pastoral industry and own cattle stations', and Robert said, 'Oh well, we'll get some'. Shortly after that conversation, he acquired Sherwin for $80 million.[1]

But Sherwin was technically bankrupt. At least this was the opinion of Darrel Jarvis, the man who developed the methodology to audit Sherwin for the public float in 1986. Darrel did not consider himself a cattleman so he was surprised and flattered when he received a call from Lloyd Smith, a headhunter employed by Robert, to help him find someone to clean up Sherwin.

Darrel Jarvis joined Heytesbury in November 1989. The company had had a controlling stake in Sherwin since May, but little had been done to restructure it and improve the pastures. On the board of Sherwin was Shane Noble, who had come up through the ranks of Heytesbury to be acting general manager and was expecting to become general manager. Darrel remembers Shane barely bothering to get up out of his chair to shake his hand when they were introduced. This was not a good start, as Darrel was not a man who liked to be ignored or treated discourteously. Within a month Shane had gone. This episode set the tone for Darrel's time with Heytesbury.

Darrel started visiting the stations and in the process, he said, 'started to spook Heytesbury Holdings'. Early on it became very clear that he had a very different way of operating compared to the genteel culture of Heytesbury. He was to go far with Heytesbury, ultimately becoming the managing director and Janet's right-hand man, but it was to be a stormy journey.

Darrel was born at Mount Hawthorn Hospital in suburban Perth, on 7 January 1947. He was the youngest of four, significantly younger by five years than his brother and two sisters. He was spoilt and aggressive and he got away with being so. His father was a tradesman, a mechanic who worked for himself and later went truck driving. Darrel had no expectations of being able to do anything. A Jarvis couldn't expect to go to university. His mother was a housewife. She was, according to Darrel, 'a very emotional woman', while her husband was 'a raging bull'. Darrel says he inherited both temperaments.

At the end of year four at Tuart Hill High School, where science and maths were his strongest subjects – his speech impediment affected his performance in English – he went to Agricultural College. His first job was as a rural officer with the Commonwealth Development Bank. At the same time he decided to do a part-time land valuation course through the Royal Melbourne Institute of Technology. At twenty-three, after three deferments for studying, Darrel was called up to do National Service. He had married Irene, his girlfriend since the age of nineteen. He made the decision to do officer training and was selected to do a six-month crash course at Windsor, Sydney.

'Having a punch-up in the army was no big deal' for Darrel. He was aggressive and he had the appearance of someone you wouldn't want to tangle with. He went straight to a rifle battalion and he was given the anti-tank platoon. This suited him perfectly. The stint in the army gave him the opportunity to go to university, as he won a bursary from the army.

Darrel did a Bachelor of Commerce with a double major in economics and accounting and worked for the Commonwealth Bank, where he fell out with the branch manager for not following the rules. In his final honours year he was employed at Hutton's pushing meat into bags, boning out pig carcasses, working on the shop floor. There was no prejudice against his speech impediment on the shop floor, but he wanted to get back into agriculture.

He eventually gained employment as a farm management consultant for Australian Agricultural Consulting Management at Merredin in the eastern wheatbelt of Western Australia, 260 kilometres east of Perth. Darrel worked for this company for the next thirteen years. He gained a reputation as a mediator, facilitator and mentor for family partnerships. He was an expert at assisting troubled family companies and helping them restructure.

In this job, as in others, he had his tussles with managers but in the end no matter how difficult they thought him to be, they recognised the results he achieved. He was given the top job of managing director and turned the company around, from a loss to a profit, in less than twelve months. He joined the company in 1976, moved to the Perth office in January 1980, became manager for Western Australia in 1982, and a director and shareholder in 1984.

By 1989, Darrel was bored. All that was changing were the people in front of him. He was also confident about his knowledge and his capabilities, although he was still sensitive to the way he was sometimes treated because of his speech or his background in agriculture. He had learnt to trust his antenna and his 'flashes' where the answer came before the logic – the reasoning would be developed later.

Darrel was a mirror opposite of Robert in most respects: in style, in interests, in method and manner, in temperament, in speech and in the way he dealt with people. The Western Australian entrepreneurs were of little interest to him. He had never bought a share in his life. He was in small business and considered himself to be a student of management who happened to be operating in the sphere of agriculture. And he had learnt that the little boy inside who lacked confidence, who had developed his own style of working, was often right.

In November 1989, Darrel was in his early forties, at his peak, fighting trim; someone needed him and they had a mess on their hands. It looked like a lot of fun for him. As the new managing director of Heytesbury Pastoral Group, he immediately set about visiting each station and assessing the managers. He found that most of the managers who, in his view, weren't up to the job, had been employed recently by Heytesbury, not by Peter Sherwin. He had to create an effective team very quickly. He understood that a good way to do this was to create a common enemy and the Heytesbury head office with its rule book approach became that enemy.

Depending on his mood, 'they'd get the finger sign at the very least or they might get more'. He was starting to clean out Heytesbury people from the properties and was getting a reputation as an extremely difficult person. In his view he was doing a job for Robert Holmes à Court.

The first board meeting Darrel had to report to went very well and initially Robert and he seemed to hit it off. The board comprised Robert, Janet, Peter Holmes à Court, Ian Wildy, and Jon Elbery, with Peter Morris and John Studdy as the two outside representatives. It was a friendly, warm party down at the Stud for the first meeting and it was his first meeting with Janet. He remembered her as 'a nice lady who didn't sit down much at the meeting'. She 'played the housewife, or the entrepreneur's wife rather than the director'. He was not used to mixing in this type of company – 'it was all a bit unreal in this flash house; this was not DAJ's place in the world'. Janet saw him to the door after the meeting and Darrel expressed his pleasure that the meeting had gone so well.

The second board meeting was a different story. Darrel hadn't done any budgeting up to this point; he was still travelling around the stations getting teams in place and making some basic decisions. Sherwin was still managed out of Brisbane and the Brisbane group had come up with figures that showed a profit in the order of $20 million for the next financial year. This was the figure Robert expected to see, based on the analysis his team had done, which showed potential returns on capital of 22% when he had purchased Sherwin. Darrel refused to accept that figure as a realistic measure of potential performance. His response was:

Robert, this is bullshit stuff. You've got raped assets out there; you don't even know what your assets are in terms of the number of cattle. You've got a company that has been trading at a loss. What's happened between now and then to dramatically change this company?

The best that could be achieved, Darrel said, was a profit of $8 million. Robert did not like the figure and the board meeting turned quite unpleasant. Darrel said, 'Robert got grumpy, angry, got up, walked out in his quiet anger. Anger is not intimidating to me. I can match anger with anger and sometimes even value-add. So the more angry he got, the more angry I got'. When it was over Darrel flew down the highway at 180 kilometres an hour back to Perth releasing his pent-up aggression.

Darrel's predictions proved to be correct. In the end Sherwin came in that year with a profit of $7.5 million. But he had lost Robert. The relationship between the two men was never the same. Darrel felt there were many signs that Robert was determined to make life difficult for him from then on. His monthly reports were never acceptable. They would be sent back to be rewritten because Robert couldn't understand them. Jon Elbery would give him advice. Darrel had a lot of time for Jon, and thought him amazing in the way he could handle Robert. 'He poured a lot of oil on troubled waters', and ironically Jon played a big role in persuading Darrel to stay in the job from where he would ultimately replace Jon.

After the third rejection of his monthly report, Darrel gave up trying to get it right. Then Ian Wildy, who had worked for Robert for thirteen years, was appointed as interpreter. Instead of Darrel writing a report to Robert, he would write it for Ian to rewrite. As well as the indignity involved in secondhand reporting, he had to put in an internal application to Jon every time he wanted to fly to look after the 80 million acres.

In Darrel's opinion, Robert was trying to reform Heytesbury and make it an enterprise-based company, but Robert was hedging his bets, since he bought asset-rich companies like Sherwin and Stoll Moss which, if they did not perform, could still be sold. But he believes in the end it was the deal, the play that Robert loved and he could not let go of the idea of the company as a trophy in a cabinet. When they were trophies he had to keep and run as businesses, the task became much more difficult. Darrel says:

Robert was on about wealth generation. He would operate on the cash side but every time he generated cash he'd buy something – art, property, the Pastoral Group, Stoll Moss. So much of his portfolio was aimed at asset growth. They had a low return on capital but a reliable track record in terms of asset growth. Unfortunately, the goodies – the art work, the tropical island, Grove House, the properties – weren't only incapable of generating cash, they were cash negative; they needed cash to maintain them.

Darrel believed the Sherwin Pastoral Group had been a trophy to put on the shelf and Robert didn't know what to do after the deal. And when Robert was running out of deals to balance the accounts – which Darrel maintains is what he was doing – he wanted to see profit from the Pastoral Group. Despite the projected low returns on Sherwin, Robert still wanted to expand, and there were strict instructions that he was to be advised of any above-average properties that came on the market. There were two memorable deals which taught Darrel a good deal about the Holmes à Court style of negotiation and the power of the name in the marketplace. The first property which came up for sale was Young River, one of the best properties in Western Australia. The word around town was that it would go for around $10 million. It was thought possible to buy it for $7–7.5 million. Verbal approval was given to Darrel to bid. He attended the auction and put in a bid when bidding reached $7 million. The other two bidders stopped immediately and Heytesbury had the highest bid. The agent said 'If you go to $7.5 million you'll get the property'. Darrel urged Robert to accept the offer, 'It's a very attractive property; it meets all your criteria', but Robert withdrew the authority to bid higher.

That night, at a meeting with Jon Elbery, Darrel threatened to resign, but Jon calmed him down. Next morning Robert arrived and wanted to discuss the property. The agent arrived at Heytesbury at 10.00 a.m. to see what was going on and Robert, Jon and Darrel disappeared into the boardroom. Robert said to Darrel, 'Talk to me about Young River'. Darrel went through the projections for the property's performance. Then Robert said, 'I think we might buy that'. Darrel thought, 'So that's that', but Jon didn't move. Nor did Robert move, and it started again. Darrel did not understand that Robert used to think out loud when he was working his way toward a decision – it was his way of testing the water. Those who knew him well knew how to differentiate a decision from a process of examination of the issues. Jon knew what Darrel did not. Robert said once more, 'Tell me about Young River'. Darrel went over all the projections again for another half to three-quarters of an hour and Robert said, 'Yes, I think we might buy it'. Darrel thought, 'I'm a slow learner, but I'm not that slow', so this time he just sat there. Then Robert said, 'Mmmm! Tell me about Young River'. Darrel, on the spur of the moment, changed the story and said:

Oh Rob, we'll sell everything, we'll sell all the stock off it and set it up as a beef operation. We'll transfer all the steers from the north; we could probably do 20,000 a year [some outlandish number like that].

Robert became excited. The agents were still waiting. They had been advised the bid was $7 million. Robert wasn't shifting. At 1.30 p.m. Robert said, 'We're buying it', and they signed at $7 million.

Robert later said, 'Well, Darrel, you learnt something from that, didn't you? We got it for $7 million. Always be prepared to walk from a deal; there's always another one'. And Darrel had learnt the lesson. That night Janet rang Darrel at home and began chatting. He was flattered to hear that Robert wanted to speak with him. Things were looking up. 'That was a pretty good deal Darrel, wasn't it?', said Robert, and Darrel knew this was a rare event. Robert did not often compliment his staff.

Another learning experience for Darrel was the purchase of Glenprairie, a property in North Queensland. His instruction was to bid to a limit of $7 million. At that level there was another buyer and Darrel went to $7.05 million. To go beyond the level Robert had approved was life-threatening, but the name Holmes à Court frightened off all other bids once again and no one bid any further. Robert was happy with the deal.

Darrel found the mixture of communication and withdrawal of communication from Robert confusing and frustrating. Robert went to Victoria River Downs (VRD) only once. He spoke about visiting the stations, but didn't go. Darrel's speculation is that Robert 'would have been uncomfortable on the stations in terms of playing the power game. It was unfamiliar territory'. Robert's shyness aside, he was by now also very limited physically by circulation problems in his legs. He could not walk any distance without having to stop, and the lifestyle on a property may well have revealed that.

In 1990, when Robert was spending long periods of time at Grove House without Janet, Jarvis was asked to come to London. Robert was involved with Elf Aquitaine in France as part of his relationship with Dalgety's. He had a stake of 20–25% with Elf Aquitaine and other private French partners in food processing plants making cattle feed products. Heytesbury's involvement had been through the UK operation, but Darrel understood that Robert wanted to make it part of the Pastoral Group's operation. Darrel went to Grove House for dinner with Robert and to discuss his thinking. He then flew to France with Derek Williams, who was a director of the French operation, to check out Elf Aquitaine. In his assessment, the physical structure and the management of the cattle were fine. Their breeding program with blonde aquitanes was innovative.

They had a board meeting in France, but Darrel was unhappy with the financial performance of the French feed lot. He upset the French at their meeting. Derek was quite shocked by Darrel's manner. It was the first time he had met Darrel and he said to Robert of Darrel, 'I don't like that guy'. Robert replied, 'Nor do I, don't worry about it. He's got a use for me to deal with Sherwin cattle'. Derek continued to operate the Elf Aquitaine joint venture, called Como, out of the UK. It eventually went into liquidation after Robert died.

There were times when Darrel felt he got on well with Robert. 'It wasn't all cold war stuff. It was when we got down to business methodology that the roughness would start.' Val Pitman said Robert thought Darrel was a good operator who needed to be controlled. She was unaware of any falling out between them, but said people often thought that they were being singled out for special treatment when in fact Robert treated everyone the same way. He simply wanted to talk to them when he was ready and when he wanted to speak to them. They might be thinking, 'Oh, I'm in the bad books; I've done something wrong', but it was simply the way Robert operated. Darrel had very firm views, put them strongly, and winning was important to him. Robert had few people around him who were competitive and challenged his views. But despite Darrel's bravado, underneath he wanted approval, and he resented the way Robert treated him.

Darrel heard the news of Robert's death from one of the station managers who phoned and asked what was going to happen. To that Darrel replied, 'No he hasn't. I haven't heard anything'. 'Well, he's dead', was the reply. After hearing the news, Darrel didn't feel he could ring Janet. He didn't feel part of Heytesbury. When he went to the memorial service at Winthrop Hall he sat with the Wesfarmers' people, not with the Heytesbury people. In the gardens afterwards he held back. He didn't know if he should be there, so he was the last to go into the receiving line. He shook hands with Janet who said, 'Oh Darrel, we have to catch up. I need you'. Darrel was surprised. He never considered that he was someone Heytesbury would need. Janet doesn't remember what she said to Darrel. She was no doubt feeling that she needed all the help she could get and Janet could always make people feel needed.

Darrel had not had the opportunity to show Robert his detailed plan for the Pastoral Group, but thorough work had been done. It was a good blueprint for the sale he expected would be made. Instead, it became the blueprint on which to build. Darrel's assessment of Robert reveals the complex relationship the two had had over twelve months; despite the resentment, he found much to admire. Like Derek Williams, he thought Robert a person of limitless boundaries. It would not cross Robert's mind that something wasn't possible. Darrel learnt from Robert not to think in terms of boundaries. Assets and liabilities were a professional accounting concept: look at them differently and they change shape. Change your approach and a liability becomes an asset. Robert gave Darrel confidence to run with his ideas, an experience he would later draw on for Janet. They had both learnt from a master tactician.

Depending on one's position in the company, there were varying views on the state of Heytesbury at the time of Robert's death.

Contrary to Darrel's view that Robert was running out of deals, one of the senior people said:

> If Robert had lived, there were enormous opportunities because Australia was in the depth of a recession. The Fairfax thing was restructured and done; Robert would have been involved in that. He would have been involved in Western Australian Newspapers. As we came out of the recession there would have been a flow of deals that would have created significant value for the group, but Janet wanted to move away from that and move into core businesses.

Given the timing of Robert's death, there remained much work to be done to build and strengthen the Heytesbury enterprises. Robert had left Janet a substantial debt, the Stoll Moss theatres in need of extensive repairs, an over-grazed group of cattle properties, and an unlikely asset in Darrel Jarvis.

During the months before Robert died, the Pastoral Group had been working on a marketing strategy to develop pride in Heytesbury beef. Darrel had wanted to have a beef-tasting night but Robert wouldn't have a bar of it. He also wouldn't allow Darrel to get the managers together for a Group meeting, but Janet liked both ideas. The day after Catherine's twenty-first birthday, 24 November 1990, and just seven weeks after Robert's death, Darrel organised a beef tasting. Janet had a marquee set up on the front lawn of the house in Peppermint Grove. There were butchers and cooks preparing a variety of meat cuts – roasts, steaks and sausages from northern and southern animals, each labelled with a coloured flag. There was an informal vote at the end and the result pleased Darrel. It was a 60–40 vote in favour of the northern animal, based on flavour. Darrel said, 'It was a great night'.

A managers' conference took place at Glenprairie in March 1991. The theme was 'Cows, cows, cows, calves and bulls'. Darrel organised all the details the way he wished. He didn't want a conference room; he wanted it run on the veranda of the homestead, which was on a hill with a view for miles around – a fabulous spot where Peter, the eldest son, would later be married. Darrel arranged 'for a booze-up at the pub the first night so the managers could bond'. They met more formally next morning to discuss theoretical matters and in the afternoon they went on field trips to the CSIRO's Belmont Research Station, a local meat export works and a bull selection demonstration at a Brahman stud. The emphasis was on workshops, the interchange of ideas and a spirit of teamwork. Social events added to the feeling of family and friendship. It was an event Robert would almost certainly have never participated in.

Darrel had arranged for all support staff from Perth to attend the conference, to overcome the 'head office syndrome'. With Janet's full support, Darrel wanted to get across that the Pastoral Group had come from being an ill-managed, loss-making company to a good position in a little over a year; that they were going right to the top as an Australian pastoral company through the performance of the cows; hence the theme 'Cows, cows, cows, calves and bulls'.

This conference also involved a memorable conversation between Jon, Darrel and Janet. They walked up behind the house before everyone arrived. Janet was discussing a speech she would give and she spoke of her 'vision'. Jon was uncomfortable with those sorts of terms, and thought they shouldn't talk 'like missionaries'. But Darrel thrived on that sort of language and felt that Jon wasn't showing Janet respect. He believed that what Heytesbury needed most was a vision for the future, a view he did not hesitate to express to Janet. Janet participated in all the sessions, writing down key words which were used throughout the week. At the end, she spoke about the Heytesbury Pastoral Group, the HPG alphabet, listing key words from A to Z. Her talk was well received. The conference ended on a high note with a barbecue at Rockhampton. Janet's education in the pastoral industry had grown; she spent time observing Darrel, how he ran the meetings, how he handled people. She was very excited about the Glenprairie meeting and her confidence in Darrel was growing apace. I met her at Perth airport when she flew in from the meeting and she was bubbling with enthusiasm about Darrel Jarvis.

She had another landmark conversation during that week. She spoke to Rett Joyce, who had been with the company when Robert died. He told Janet that when the word of Robert's death had gone around on 2 September, they had all thought that was the end of their jobs. Janet was stunned by that. She couldn't understand why they would think that way, but it reinforced for her the importance of her having gone into the office on the Tuesday after Robert's death and saying to staff, 'I have got a vision and we'll do it together'. It reinforced her determination to succeed.

Darrel next persuaded Janet to travel with him to the US to study the cattle industry – Darrel had never been there and was interested in learning from the country which is held up as the pinnacle of world beef production. The trip further cemented the relationship between Janet and Darrel and her respect for his knowledge and experience.

Darrel had been a consultant to the retired managing director of Cargill's, Pete McVay, who organised the tour. Cargill's is a highly successful company with many interests including the production of cattle and beef. Darrel's goal was to market and brand Heytesbury beef in Asia. They visited one of the largest abattoirs in the world, where 5,000 cattle a day were slaughtered. Nearby was a feedlot with a capacity of 100,000 cattle being fattened up for the Japanese market. Janet says of that time, 'That was a great experience because Darrel and I were like sponges learning about the American beef industry … I was intrigued and Darrel and I got on extremely well'.

While Janet was away, there was a crisis at home. When she left Australia she'd asked Elbery to put together a package for the banks to report on Heytesbury's financial performance. He did this and forwarded Janet a copy, which did not please her. But when she phoned, she found it had already been sent to the banks. Elbery thought it a routine matter. Janet instructed Elbery to get the report back.

Janet was finding Darrel was including her in the business in a way that Elbery and the others never did. While Darrel couldn't be more unlike Robert in appearance and manner, she thought their way of thinking very similar. Both men could never stop thinking and analysing and she would be surprised at things Darrel would say that she believed Robert would have agreed with. She began to confide in Darrel and he began to advise her on matters beyond the Pastoral Group.

Darrel, Wim Burggraaf and David Clapin had been tracking the Heytesbury group and like John Frame they were thinking there were a lot of problems. The Pastoral Group had been very concerned about the purchase of John Holland. At the time, Darrel had asked Janet, 'Are you buying what you think you are buying?'. Janet believed she was; she believed in the team of analysts assessing John Holland. On another occasion, Darrel had been to Janet's office to speak to her about the direction in which she was taking the company and had been reassured by Janet's response: 'I want to run enterprises. I can only have so many paintings in my room, and own so many houses'.

Darrel reassured the Heytesbury Pastoral Group and in turn built Janet's confidence in herself. Janet says:

The other people did nothing for my confidence and they did nothing for my knowledge. It was a relief to be able to go out on a station where Darrel actually wanted me to participate, to be with the managers and not be in the background ... Rather than Robert making a speech when we got somewhere, or Darrel making a speech, I would have to do it. And there was respect for what I could do. I was given the feeling that it was important, which I hadn't actually ever had before.

Janet had a natural talent for speaking warm-hearted words. She revelled in the new experience of being involved, being central to the business and of having her words make a difference. Darrel was the main person building her confidence. Janet therefore sought Darrel's advice about the report Jon Elbery had prepared for the banks. Darrel told her, 'Janet, *you* have to run this company'. At home in Australia, some members of Heytesbury were beginning to gossip about the relationship between Darrel and Janet and there was concern about his influence over her. It was, at bottom, a concern about Darrel's style, which was radically different from any other in the Heytesbury culture. As well, several of Janet's friends were concerned by what they saw as Darrel's defensiveness, his aggression. Darrel for his part was aware there were growing problems in Heytesbury and believed he was trying to pose solutions and help Janet. The management problems in Heytesbury were also becoming apparent to Will Holmes à Court, but he was not as forthright as Darrel in pointing them out to Janet, or in dealing with them. Will thought Janet didn't understand how best to manage. Her model was Robert, who made all the decisions himself and never stopped working. Will was trying gently to persuade Janet that she needed to employ good people to run all the operations, give them a set of objectives and the authority to follow those objectives. Will had suggested someone he had in mind to come in and run the company, but the idea went on the backburner.

Will had worked on a plan for a structural reorganisation of Heytesbury and Janet had the papers with her when she went to the US. The plan was reworked by the time Janet and Darrel returned. Will says of Darrel's role:

> *There was a power vacuum; there was an enormous strain on Janet ... all of a sudden, here's someone else who can provide an answer. Big bandaid on the pain, fix a whole area of your life that you know is really hurting because the company was in trouble. The financial controller was calling up all sorts of problems, but because he was seen as pessimistic they kept shooting him. He was just calling the truth, but because there'd been so much sadness around, they didn't want to hear the bad news and quite understandably.*

John Frame was telling Will, 'I can't get anyone to understand'. And Will felt, 'I was in a predicament where I didn't know how much to heal and hold and how much to lead. I took the soft option'.

Darrel felt there was jockeying for position throughout this period. He describes two significant board meetings. The board members included Jon Elbery, Peter Morris, Ian Brindley, John Studdy, Peter Holmes à Court and Janet. The first was the one at Canterbilling Springs when his figures for the Pastoral Group were in contention. Darrel says one of the board members took the view that management were 'jiggling the figures' to the extent of $11 million.

At the next board meeting at Young River, Darrel believed there was an attempt to split Jarvis and Janet, the first of many he would notice in the coming years. The temperature was around 42°C and Darrel felt he had the homeground advantage. He saw this meeting as a watershed. The argument was over the valuation of the cattle and the composition model being used, which came back to the method by which the $11 million had been arrived at. If a calf born was valued at $100 book value and ultimately realised a sale of $800, the profit was $700. The issue was how the animal was carried in the books up to the point of sale. Money is being invested in the animal continuously and the animal is changing. The way to give Robert (now Janet) the additional money needed for the balance sheet was to declare the full profit across all animals, about 280,000 head at that stage.

With such a large herd there was ample room to move, completely logically, and it satisfied the auditors, but there was also ample room for argument. There was suspicion of manipulation and there was distrust, which could only finally be resolved by Janet placing her trust with one side. She decided to side with Darrel, which ultimately meant a rift with the independent board members. The result for Darrel was the consolidation of his position.

The Pastoral Group's financials were still problematic. The investment was $180 million and the group was generating $9.5 million, only a 5% return. The cost of the funds was around 13–14% so it appeared that Heytesbury could not afford the Pastoral Group. Darrel thought a section of the board wanted to sell the Group – a legitimate response given the financial predicament but not the response Janet wanted. People were not listening to her. They were not accepting her vision, so they were pursuing a different strategy. These people saw Darrel as the problem, but did not see that Darrel's strategy was to try to meet the chairman's vision. Jon Elbery wanted to sell the Pastoral Group to reduce overall debt. But Janet was feeling less and less confident about his advice, which ran counter to her own desires and instincts.

In the eighties, bankers had behaved as speculators, not bankers. They had fed the boom and in turn been severely damaged by the crash. $30 billion had been written off in a decade.[2] At the time of his death Robert had eleven banks in a consortium servicing his companies' needs. They included: the State Bank of South Australia (SBSA), Tricontinental, Toronto Dominion, Security Pacific, Standard Chartered, the Commonwealth Bank, Westpac, ANZ, Societe Generale, Rural and Industries (R&I) Bank WA and Citibank. Two of these banks, SBSA and Tricontinental, were bankrupt and two others, Toronto Dominion and Security Pacific, wanted to stop operating in Australia.

In 1991, the banks in the Heytesbury consortium were getting edgy and the reports at the end of the 1990–91 financial year resulted in a major crisis. Jon Elbery had overseen the preparation of the financial reports and Janet was not pleased with them. With Janet's confidence in Jon diminishing and her confidence in Darrel increasing, there was a concurrence of causes. The attractive, vivacious, elegant widow with the vision, will and determination to keep her family empire together and build operating businesses on three continents found the ally she needed in the stocky, rough, hard-hitting, agrarian economist – the strategic thinker and fighter who loved an impossible challenge and who wanted 'to help this nice lady achieve her aims'. He had done it before, but never with companies of this dimension, never in such company. He was raring to go.

Janet had seen the respect people they met in the US showed Darrel. She knew the respect and the confidence he gave her. She was immersed in the business in a way that had never occurred before. Neither Derek Williams in the UK nor Jon Elbery, both Robert's loyal men, ever went beyond seeing Janet as Robert's widow. They had known the loyal, attentive wife. She did not persuade them in her role as the company chairman. Derek and Jon thought it much more realistic to sell the enterprises than run them.

Darrel was made a director of Heytesbury Holdings in August 1991 along with Derek Williams, UK general manager, and Katherine Burghard, former president and legal counsel of Heytesbury New York. Janet assumed the title of managing director of Heytesbury.

At the time Janet said the appointments reflected the reshaping of Heytesbury Holdings and its greater focus on operational enterprises. The confrontation with the banks precipitated the direction Heytesbury would take.

A commitment had been made to Tricontinental, which was in liquidation, that the $50 million owed them would be paid back at the end of January 1992. Jon Elbery had confirmed that the money would be paid. SBSA had lent the Group a further $25 million so were owed $75 million; Standard Chartered had provided the Group with $15 million of bank guarantees to support John Holland. Heytesbury was on track for a financial disaster. Darrel says:

> I have no idea where management thought they would get the money. If they were pursuing Janet's vision they would not be selling one of the enterprises to do it, but there seems to have been no other option for their thinking the money would be available. It seemed they did not take Janet's plans seriously.

In fact, corporate management simply did not believe the enterprises could be retained in the long run. Where Darrel was taking Janet's vision as his bible to develop his strategy, Jon viewed Janet's vision with much scepticism.

On the morning of 26 October 1991, Darrel had gone to Janet's house in Peppermint Grove to collect mangos brought from the station at Victoria River Downs to deliver to staff. He was driving a company car that was only two years old. The car broke down close to Janet's so Darrel walked back to ring the RAC. Janet insisted that Darrel take Catherine's Saab, which was parked in front of the house on the sloping drive.

Darrel went inside to make the call and suddenly heard Janet screaming. She had leaned inside the car, put the keys in the ignition and turned the engine on. The car had jumped backwards, knocking her over and under the wheels, which rolled over her legs. When Darrel came outside, Janet was on the ground. A neighbour called the ambulance, which took her to hospital.

Janet was shocked and bruised but no serious damage was done. While in hospital, she had a meeting with Jon Elbery, Linton Byfield and Darrel about the banking arrangements. Darrel says he was 'totally, utterly, amazed, shocked, disturbed by what they were telling her. It was tell the boss no bad news stuff ... I thought, hey Janet, you're copping one helluva snow job here'. The three returned to the office, then Darrel returned to the hospital:

Janet, this is bullshit. Janet, this company is in trouble. Janet, I can't do a thing about it. You're the only one who can do anything about it. I know you've been run over, but for you to stay in this hospital means we're dead. I suggest you get out of your bed. I suggest you ring the SBSA. We are dead unless you take control of this company.

The SBSA was due to be repaid the additional short-term loan of $25 million it had advanced Heytesbury.

Janet dressed, Darrel took her home and she started phoning people. At that point she took control and was very decisive. She reassured the SBSA that she was seriously committed to asset sales and that obligations would be met. She then prepared for a meeting with all the bankers in Perth on 8 November 1991. Derek Williams and Richard Johnston flew from London representing Stoll Moss; Katherine Burghard flew in from New York; Graham Duff, managing director of John Holland, came from Melbourne. Darrel was there representing the Pastoral Group, Jon Elbury represented Heytesbury and Linton Byfield represented Treasury. There were ten banks represented along with Olaf O'Duill, the Irish banker representing Tricontinental.

Janet spoke of her vision for the company. Each managing director gave a presentation on progress within their enterprise. Linton Byfield spoke of how they would make money in Treasury and Jon and Derek gave a corporate report. Jon said that 'hypothetically' the company could achieve a certain level of debt reduction and the word did not go down well – the bankers wanted definite commitments. They certainly did not want to see another company fall over and did not want to desert Janet Holmes à Court, who was very much admired for the way she had conducted herself following Robert's death. Her growing public image was Heytesbury's key asset.

Janet invited Olaf O'Duill and Darrel to her house following the meeting. The details of both of these meetings were subsequently leaked to Robert Gottliebsen and Janet found herself on the cover of *Business Review Weekly,* with the headline, 'What the Banker told Janet Holmes à Court'. O'Duill had the contract to recover as much as possible of the merchant bank's $3–5 billion loan portfolio on behalf of Victorian taxpayers and he wanted to get the $50 million back from Heytesbury, not lose it. Gottliebsen said:

> *The banks had not singled out Heytesbury for special attention, but loans were due to be rescheduled just as Heytesbury was predicting that in the year ahead it would not cover its interest bill with cash profits, excluding asset sales.*[3]

The company's attention had been focused on the problems with John Holland and asset sales were slow. The bankers wanted quicker reduction of Heytesbury's debt, quicker sales of assets.[4]

O'Duill was forthcoming with his advice. He spoke to Janet about what Heytesbury needed to do and what Janet needed to do. He told her that 'if she failed to make the right moves or hasten the asset sale process she might fall into the hands of bankers like himself'. He also suggested Darrel could help her achieve what was necessary. His advice differed from other bankers who saw Darrel as a cattleman – acceptable in that role but not elsewhere in the company. They underestimated him, but O'Duill did not.

On Saturday 9 November, Janet called a board meeting. She made it clear to Derek Williams and Katherine Burghard that she wanted Darrel to replace Jon Elbery as managing director. They both accepted her view. Derek, who had worked alongside Jon, was surprised and thought in hindsight, as a proper board member, he should have had more information about what Jon had done, but this was Janet's company. Janet wanted the change, so he agreed. He still believed that with the offers for Stoll Moss coming in and 'knowing that Heytesbury was very stretched, the bankers were calling for their money', his last task in the UK would be 'to deliver Stoll to somebody, take the cash and allow her to repay the debts'.

Katherine Burghard had a pragmatic response. It was obvious Janet didn't have confidence in Jon Elbery, but did have confidence in Darrel. Darrel's main qualification for the job was, in Katherine's opinion, that Janet was comfortable with him and was prepared to take his advice. The fact was Darrel was there; he had demonstrated his ability in the pastoral company; Janet trusted him and he was decisive.

On Sunday, Janet asked Jon Elbery to come to see her. He was surprised and very upset by the meeting and immediately left Heytesbury. Darrel began at 8.00 a.m. Monday morning as deputy managing director under Janet. His first meeting was with the internal auditor, who was understanding of the situation. Darrel went through the week, meeting after meeting. Gottliebsen reported, 'Eight others departed and although events like this are taking place in executive suites all around the country, it was completely outside the normal Holmes à Court tradition'.[5]

Janet was still recovering from the accident with the car, from a year of traumatic events and emotional highs and lows. She did not speak with any of the staff who left at that time other than Jon Elbery. There was some bitterness about the way things were done. From Darrel's viewpoint, 'It was war and time was of the essence'.

Whereas Robert dealt with people by sending them to Coventry over an extended period – and in one instance gave a senior executive of a company a job operating the boomgate at the same salary level to break his morale and avoid the redundancy payment which would be incurred if he were sacked – Darrel did not delay and did not mince words. The people who went were Robert's people. At the end of the week Darrel organised drinks to settle people down and reassure them that the restructure was complete.

The company at this stage was surviving financially on a day-to-day basis. Meetings between the bankers, Janet and Darrel became very frequent events. They were running Heytesbury with a $500,000 reserve, transferring money rapidly around the world 'to hit the hot spots'. Janet and Darrel agreed on a ten-year-plan. Janet wanted to retain Stoll Moss, the Pastoral Group, and John Holland – three large enterprises operating in the UK, South East Asia and Australia – as well as Vasse Felix, Key Transport and the Thoroughbreds. Darrel's assessment to Janet was that their probability of achieving that was 80:20 against. He believed, 'If the company went into receivership it was dead: the company would go into liquidation'. He believed that the only way to achieve the goal was by unorthodox methods and therefore they must keep control. The way to keep control was with Janet's charm and reputation, combined with Darrel's rough-and-gruff style and with the help of a few independent board members.

The company was two months away from receivership, so a debt reduction program was put forward. They were given until the end of February by the banks to achieve a debt reduction of $20 million. The banks wished to appoint an outside consultant to report on Heytesbury. Westpac, the largest debtor, wanted to appoint a representative from Peat Marwick, a receiver manager, to do the evaluation. They met with Westpac and the man the bank wanted to do the job. Janet says:

> It was the worst professional meeting you could imagine. This man was supposed to be our banker: he was telling us we were naive, he was telling us we didn't understand. It was just appalling and we left shaking with rage ... We were at our wits end with the amateurish treatment that we received in that meeting.

Darrel was determined this known receiver should be kept out of Heytesbury. If he were seen in the building the rumours would fly.

Janet sought the help of senior executives in Westpac, the ANZ; and Olaf O'Duill. In the end she managed to split the opinion of the banks and it was agreed Janet could make the appointment of the consultant. The terms of reference were agreed between Heytesbury and the banks, and Arthur Anderson was appointed. Arthur Anderson reported that Heytesbury couldn't meet its interest payments. On management accounts at 30 September 1991, the Group had net assets of approximately $474 million and debt at around $390 million. On a worst-case forced short-term sales basis, the Arthur Anderson report stated the equity position would be negative $6 million. In other words, as Heytesbury was unable to service its loans, if the banks did not continue to support the company and forced a fire-sale, the banks would recover their money but the shareholders would be left with nothing.

Darrel was livid. It was the first time Janet had heard him use obscenities. He believed the banks would panic when presented with such a report. But the banks were reassured. Such a fire-sale situation was not an acceptable option for the Group or the bankers. Their preferred option was to achieve debt reduction through asset sales but they wanted to see results relatively quickly. The mood of the banks improved further when $20 million debt reduction was achieved by the end of February. It was important if the enterprises were to survive to keep up the level of confidence.

Heytesbury came to a standstill arrangement with the banks whereby the company agreed to reduce its debt from $420 million to $225 million in two years. Throughout that two-year period (1992–93), Heytesbury never missed an obligation. They met every debt reduction target, met every interest payment and did not sell one enterprise to achieve it. The aim remained as Janet wanted: theatre, pastoral and construction enterprises on three continents, with a debt level which could be serviced from operating profits. There was always a contingency plan that one enterprise could go, but it was never called on. No bank lost any money, with the exception of Security Pacific, which decided to sell its debts to Bank West at a discount, but that was their independent decision.

In the context of Janet and Darrel's ten-year strategy for Heytesbury, the first three years (1992–94) were Darrel's 'war years'. The strategy was to sell assets, downsize Stoll Moss and the

Pastoral Group, capitalise John Holland, get some working capital and achieve debt reduction in the first twelve months of more than $100 million. With Janet and Darrel working frantically, seemingly against the world, they achieved their targets. They won this particular war. Their success in their asset sale, debt reduction program, was a significant achievement. The book value of many of the assets they sold was based on old valuations and the economic times were much tougher than the affluent eighties, when the world seemed to be Robert's oyster and he was the great acquirer. Janet and Darrel's efforts saved Heytesbury from the receiver.

Janet and Darrel saw 1995–97 as the consolidation period when there would be reinvestment in the enterprises, a repair of any damage done during the war years and further work on changing the culture, the ethics and standards of Heytesbury. Unfortunately this later plan would come unstuck; but, in the meantime, Janet set about using her considerable people skills to sell the style she wanted for Heytesbury. In the *Heytesbury Herald* she outlined her plans in a letter from the chairman, saying the Heytesbury of old had gone. She began:

> *Times of change can be upsetting to some people. To others such times represent great opportunities. I would like to think that after a difficult year, most of us in the Heytesbury Group can start to see the benefits that will come from our reorganisation and the opportunities that will be available.*
>
> *You will have read and heard much of what we are doing in Heytesbury. Some is true, much is gossip. Let me now tell each and every member of the group, be they in a capital city office, on an outback station, in a London theatre or on a construction site, just what I want to achieve.*
>
> *The Heytesbury of old has gone. We are no longer a share trader and investor. When we did those things, we were among the best in the world and we were led by a man, Robert Holmes à Court, who excelled at what he did.*
>
> *I have no desire, and certainly not the ability, to copy him in the world of investment.*

But, I do have a clear picture of how we can operate and build on the business enterprises that have been acquired and developed within Heytesbury.

Excellence in performance will be one of the few links to our past. Where we were once the best investor, now we will be the best in operations . . .

I want Heytesbury to become a group of companies with clearly defined goals of excelling at their chosen pursuits . . .

The first steps down the path of re-direction can be painful. We have lost the services of some good people, but people who largely represented the old, investment-driven Heytesbury. We have also taken painful actions in selling assets that once seemed to represent the best of Heytesbury.

These actions are essential for Heytesbury to achieve my vision. We have to use our capital better and more creatively in our operating business units. Capital liberated from a poorly performing asset can transform other parts of the group.

The job of re-directing Heytesbury is not complete though everyone should now have a clearer picture of where I want to go and how I want to place absolute emphasis on operations and management excellence.

As we make changes, and as we boost our financial performance, we will create new and more rewarding job and career opportunities for everyone in Heytesbury.

I look forward to working with you to achieve those goals.
Janet Holmes à Court.[6]

Janet threw herself into a program of visiting all her enterprises and making personal contact with people. She thereby gained enormous respect and support for her plans.

Selling assets was a very difficult process. Heytesbury maintained a confident public front which was necessary for success, while within the company the teams were hard at work selling assets and turning around the enterprises. During the boom of the eighties, the Holmes à Courts' acquisition of art, horses, jewellery, tropical islands and property were typically the sorts of investments made by entrepreneurs. For a time their value appreciated, but when the recession hit they were depreciating in value and absorbing cash. There were now not so many buyers looking for depreciating assets. But Robert's portfolio was so large that there were many options.

Darrel and Janet took charge of the asset disposal program. They compiled a list of $250 million worth of assets and with every sale they would triumphantly rule a line through that item. Team members assisted in all the enterprises with sales, but meeting the targets required Janet and Darrel's commitment. New skills were needed. Darrel said, 'I had no idea how to go about selling a Van Gogh; I couldn't even pronounce the bloody name'.

Janet recalls some of the advice they were given by the banks regarding asset sales:

> as [being] high school stuff, pathetic. One bank put forward its long-term plan for Heytesbury – included in the projections was a profit in one of our enterprises (Key Transport)[7] of $500,000 – in a couple of years' time. We were already making a million dollars, why would we make less? It was so bad it was unbelievable. And those were the people who were advising us and had our destiny in their hands.

Peter Wood, former finance director for Heytesbury with responsibility for keeping the shareholders and banks informed and for tax planning, was involved primarily in selling assets and said:

> they all took a long time; they all took a lot of hard work ... You certainly can't show any sign of weakness and you need two or three buyers. It's difficult to hold your nerve with only one buyer on the line ... In the early days there were enough things for sale that if we played bluff and it didn't work on that particular asset we had to play bluff on another one.

The team generally achieved very good value for their efforts. The *West Australian* wanted to buy the *Collie Mail* for $900,000 and then $1 million. Heytesbury sold it over a two-year period for $2 million. The sale of the Coliseum in England was a good deal. Stoll Moss was receiving a peppercorn rental on a lengthy lease to the English National Opera. Heytesbury owned the freehold. There was an election coming up and the Thatcher Government wanted to do something for the arts, so they approached Stoll Moss to sell the theatre. The sale was approved by Parliament with little debate, and at £16 million it was a very advantageous sale for Heytesbury at a point in time when Janet was wondering 'Will anything ever go right for us?'. Grove House meanwhile sold for £10.2 million.

The sale of the Australian Tax Office building in Perth was another success story for Heytesbury. The building was not complete but the banks wanted it sold. A figure of $41 million was mentioned. The banks were prepared to sell it $10 million short of its value to diminish debt, but in the end Heytesbury was able to net $58 million when the building was complete and fitted out, with the tenant in place. With that sale, Tricontinental left the syndicate.

One of the great asset sales was of 50% of John Holland Asia, a sale for $22 million which achieved the objective of reducing debt and the strategic objective of having a strong local partner, Humes, in Asia; this was a strategy that at the time seemed worthwhile regardless of the asset sales program. As well, Wim Burggraaf and David Clapin sold Trelawney Stud in New Zealand and some of the Pastoral properties including Cluny, Springvale and Diamantina.

Added to the banks' concerns regarding the pace of asset sales was a contingent liability with a foreign exchange contract which was a hedge for the UK balance sheet which Peter Wood says none of the banks understood. The banks wanted to crystallise it at a loss of $15 million but Heytesbury Treasury was able to convince them to go another six months. At the time, the contract resulted in an $11 million loss. Within weeks the dollar had contracted against the pound and the position could have been closed for a $6–7 million loss, but the banks were too nervous to wait.

Peter Wood's evaluation of the strategy to save the company was that there were only two options. One pursued the sale of assets – the other could have been the sale of enterprises. He believes they could have been sold to repay the debt, still leaving a significant portion of the art in place. But as with the assets, speed would have been critical. There were definite buyers for Stoll Moss and John Holland in 1991. Peter says Janet's strategy was 'a much more exciting strategy'. He saw the culture of Heytesbury change. Peter says, 'it was a lot of hard work but it was Janet's natural ability and enthusiasm and pleasure in dealing with people that really made the difference and made the change possible'.

He remembers the first time he met Janet. As a Canadian he had never seen her photograph, so didn't know what she looked like. He says:

> [I] saw a six foot by six foot Aboriginal canvas walking past my office door about a week after I joined and this head poked out around it and she said, 'What do you think?'. We discussed the art and had a bit of a laugh and carried on. I thought she might have been the decorator. Five minutes later John Frame came back and said, 'Peter, I'd like to introduce you to Janet Holmes à Court'. That's always highlighted the type of person she is. She's very easy to get along with and I think her style then made it easy for Heytesbury to embark on a change, such a dramatic change in culture, where you had a few people guarding their cards, guarding their power with Rob, which was an investment-based structure, to one that revolved around people'.

Alongside the debt-reduction program, the enterprises each required significant attention. Regardless of whether it was to be sold or retained, John Holland had to be capitalised. To do that, both Stoll Moss and the Pastoral Group had to be reduced. Both were valued at around $180 million and the aim was to reduce them to around $140–150 million and use the revenue raised to provide much needed working capital for John Holland.

The beef herd was reduced from 280,000 to 230–240,000 and Janet and Darrel convinced the banks that the reduction should be regarded as a normal operation for the Pastoral Group, not as an asset sale. In 1992 there was a drought, something else Heytesbury didn't need, so it made sense to reduce the herd. The normal sale program at 60–70,000 head of cattle a year was large enough, and selling 100,000 was a huge logistical exercise. Darrel said:

You couldn't have thrown anything more at us. Between foreign exchange losses, the drought, high interest rates, the goodie market collapsing – you just couldn't sell the stuff let alone know what it would bring – and here we were trying to unload 100,000 head of cattle in drought conditions which had forced us to adopt new and untested radical weaning techniques.

A road train of three trailers is around 200 feet long, and weighs 150 tonnes. It has six decks, two decks per trailer and depending on the size of the animal can fit 35–40 animals per deck. So on one big metal creature you can fit 220–240 animals. To sell 100,000 cattle, in addition to the normal transfers between properties, was an enormous job. Darrel says: 'The Pastoral Group did a great job that year but also took on baggage that cost us afterwards. All through these war years we always said our enterprises were taking damage'.

But what Heytesbury did have going for it was the boom conditions in the Stoll Moss theatres that year. The sale of the Coliseum improved cash flow for Stoll Moss, but while the theatres were showing improving profit and loss, the asset as such had been deteriorating through a long period of minimal maintenance. There was no choice but to inject cash into the theatres. Heytesbury could not afford to allow them to run down any further, so the refurbishment program continued.

Jason Donovan as Joseph in *Joseph and the Amazing Technicolour Dreamcoat* came to the rescue. Jason was the popular lead in the Australian television soap 'Neighbours', which had gained a huge following in the UK. The advance ticket sales of £4 million were a record for London's West End. The Palladium was booked out for every performance. In addition, Stoll Moss theatres were running other hit shows including *Miss Saigon, The Phantom of the Opera, Five Guys Named Moe* and *Return to the Forbidden Planet.* The success of *Joseph* provided a solid test for the new box office ticketing system which had been installed by Stoll Moss.

Janet's vision was for a corporate whole, enterprises which were linked to each other in the minds of the employees, not competing in terms of capital. Darrel would describe Janet's vision as a constellation by analogy:

> I keep saying to our engineers or our theatre people or our cattle people, 'You are us, we are you'. This is not about little boxes with lines in between. Heytesbury is a solar system with Heytesbury Corporate as the sun in terms of gravitational force, then the Pastoral Group is Jupiter with its fifteen moons [properties] around it; John Holland is Saturn with lots of projects around it, a lot of rings around it; Key Transport is Mercury – transport, the wings; Vasse Felix is Pluto; Stoll Moss is Mars; we exist not being tied in together ... we are a free-floating force if you like but we exist together, and the interrelationships of the planets is very much there; take one out and the whole system has to reposition itself'.

The other favourite analogy Darrel employed was of Heytesbury as a forest:

> Stoll Moss is the oak tree; John Holland is the conifer. The Pastoral Group is the big eucalypt; Vasse Felix represents the bees, the cross-pollinator. Heytesbury Corporate represents the foresters nurturing the forest but wanting the trees to grow ... We have the watering cans, the secateurs to trim, the firefighting equipment. The forest is a good analogy of how Janet wants Heytesbury to operate ... We don't want to have a plantation; we want a living organism. She wants to operate in a total ecosystem rather than in a green desert.

From 1998 to 2000, the third stage of the ten-year plan, Heytesbury intended to reap the benefit of all the seedlings planted in stage two. It would be 1997–98 before Heytesbury would emerge from financial crisis but their family politics would contribute to further upheaval. On 22 December 1993, right on target, Janet, Darrel and Heytesbury achieved debt reduction to a level of $223 million. This was $27 million less than the original goal of $250 million. There was champagne in the office that day – it was a great achievement. But the banks weren't ready with a facility to support Heytesbury through the next stage. It had been agreed with the banks that Heytesbury would come out of the standstill arrangement and that the banks which needed to exit – Toronto Dominion, the Security Pacific, the Tricontinental and the SBSA – would exit, with the remaining banks forming a new syndicate.

However, the lead bank, Westpac, whose managers Darrel believes did not agree with the plan even though they had signed off on it, did not have the new facilities in place, so the exiting banks could not leave the syndicate. Heytesbury went into yet another crisis. This period, at the beginning of the calendar year, was the time of the group's greatest need for working capital. The problem for Westpac was a difference in view from Heytesbury about the debt level they believed Heytesbury could sustain. The business plan set out a sustainable debt level of $180 million but Westpac thought the debt level should be no more than $140 million. Westpac said that the exiting banks could not leave the standstill arrangement because Westpac could not arrange $225 million worth of longer-term facilities. Their view was that the banks remaining as Heytesbury bankers could provide $200 million and the SBSA, who were to leave the syndicate, would need to provide the further necessary $25 million.

During the war years Westpac had played a key role in binding the banks together, and at times during those two years Westpac came in and provided bank guarantees when nobody else would. But it seemed to Janet and Darrel that by insisting SBSA remain in the syndicate, Westpac were ensuring there was no let-up in pressure on Heytesbury – the banks wanted ongoing focus on the debt problem. Additionally, Heytesbury needed working capital of $30 million whereas the new facilities proposed only allowed working capital of $10 million. That amount would not get Heytesbury through the next four months.

Janet and Darrel were feeling exhausted and fragile. Darrel said, 'The general was stuffed. You can only keep the troops at war at the frontline for eighteen months'. Once again he had threatened to resign. He felt he could not go forward without the correct facilities in place. Janet refused to accept his resignation. It was February 1994, Heytesbury was in cash crisis, there were no facilities in place, the SBSA wouldn't agree to an increase in the working capital arrangements and then the banker from SBSA went on holidays. Another month went by with no facilities and the SBSA would not delegate anyone else to make a decision. At his wits end, Darrel flew alone to Adelaide for a meeting with the SBSA. He describes the meeting as rough, but he got a further $20 million working capital and lunch at the end. Another crisis came to an end and Darrel was back in the job. It was, Janet says, 'a pretty traumatic time'.

Under the new facility the aim was to reduce debt to $190 million by the end of 1994. They actually achieved a debt level of $193 million, a further $30 million reduction. But the task of debt reduction through asset sales was becoming more difficult; there were fewer assets to sell. During the cash crisis, Heytesbury's creditors were fully stretched, with debts blowing out to 45–60 days or 60–90 days in some instances. Each time that was done the tolerance of creditors became more limited. John Holland's creditors started increasing their prices as they knew the payment terms were bad. The creditors had suffered in 1989–90 with the public company Pennant Holdings, then at the beginning of 1992 and 1993 they had suffered with Heytesbury, so the cash crisis in 1994 created real operational difficulties. This was also mid-winter, when the theatres in London have their quietest time of the year. Furthermore, it's the wet season in the north of Australia, which means trucks can't get onto the properties to reach the cattle to take them away for sale. The transport industry slows down. (Indeed, only Vasse Felix, the winery, does well at this time.) Money was borrowed from John Holland Asia and operational capital stretched to its limits in every possible way until the crisis was resolved by the showdown between Darrel and the SBSA. With a new facility in place, Heytesbury set about restoring their payment terms to industry standards and regaining supplier confidence.

Janet says of the bank crisis and her experience of the bankers, 'some of those people were so insulting'. At one of the first meetings she was asked, 'Why don't you just sell everything, pay off all the debt and go and lie on the beach. Then you wouldn't have any worries'. She never considered that an option. The challenge was so great she was motivated to prove that it could be done and she says, 'We were on our own when we were at those meetings, by God we were'. But unlike her experience with Robert post-crash:

> we were not on our own in Heytesbury . . . We had 350 people out on the stations who were working like mad to help us. We had Richard Johnston and all the people in Stoll Moss and thank God we had Joseph. We had the John Holland people. John Holland was our biggest problem because our banks hated it, and they hated us doing business in Asia. That was extraordinary to me. The Prime Minister and the Government were encouraging business to operate in Asia. All our banks said there were problems in Asia — terrible, terrible, terrible. I thought that was pathetic. They were fearful of construction companies. They actually didn't like agriculture very much. They'd seen what had happened to wool and they forgot that cattle didn't actually grow wool. They didn't look at the individual businesses. They were most unprofessional in their behaviour. So, although we were on our own when we were in those bank meetings and we'd fly back to Perth absolutely exhausted, we were not on our own in Heytesbury.

While all this behind-the-scenes activity was going on, Janet found it irritating to be referred to constantly as 'the richest woman in Australia'. Trevor Sykes, a financial journalist who understood her difficulties, dubbed her 'Poor Little Rich Girl'. He wrote, 'Janet Holmes à Court is asset rich. But she's probably going to stay cash poor for a year or two yet'.[8] He was correct in his prediction.

Those years, the change in her fortunes and the experience gained brought about a dramatic change in Janet. She was no longer, in her terms, 'a phone answerer, a tea maker, a lover, a mother, a communicator, a protector, a policeman, a postman, a telephonist, those sorts of things'. She was the key person driving change. She was like a gutsy butterfly emerging from the cocoon. Previously sheltered, constrained, sometimes uncertain of her ability, she grew in confidence. It could be seen in her face, in her bearing.

The capacities that had always been there, but held in check by the demands of her role as Robert's wife, burst forth. Her social skills, her interpersonal charisma, her ability to make people feel listened to and important, and her capacity to engender loyalty and devotion among her now huge staff became key assets of Heytesbury in a way that parallels the capacity of Robert to make up a deficit by successful deals on the stock market. Always perfectly groomed and well-dressed, Janet nevertheless did her own hair, wore the same black skirts with a few well-chosen jackets, the only sign of ostentation the wide, sculptured gold bands she wore on her fingers. She was recognised by almost everyone in Australia, her face constantly in the press, her name often mentioned in relation to the Reserve Bank, the new programs of the Australian Children's Television Foundation and her links with Paul Keating.

What kept the legend fascinating was the amazing combination of apparently enormous wealth and her down-to-earth, unassuming and genuine approach to every person she met. She was becoming a legend in her own time. But she was not herself fooled for a moment. She knew the fragility of the structures she was defending and while at times she was completely and utterly exhausted, she was exhilarated by the challenge and her growing power and confidence. She knew she was a force to be reckoned with in her own right.

In 1994, when the focus was on restoration of the companies, one bonus occurred with the banking fraternity. The Chemical Bank of America approached Heytesbury saying they had been watching John Holland and they liked what they saw. They banked construction companies, were coming into Australia and they didn't want to join a queue in three years' time when things had picked up for Heytesbury to then ask to bank them. So they bought out the SBSA long before Heytesbury thought they could be ready to take in a new bank and before they thought anyone would be interested in taking them on. It was a great boost for morale. Since then there have been several offers to bank Heytesbury, which in 1995 still had six banks (ANZ, Chemical Bank, Westpac, BankWest, Standard Chartered and the Commonwealth Bank).

When the cash crisis was over, Darrel and Janet called all the managing directors, the finance directors, the general manager of Key Transport and Alec Mairs, board member of Heytesbury Holdings, together to introduce them to one another's enterprises and get on with building the Heytesbury forest. This meeting commenced in Australia, then continued in the UK. This was to be a repeat, on a wider scale, of the style of the Glenprairie conference of property managers. But it was a traumatic meeting, lacking the good feeling experienced at Glenprairie. The troubles in John Holland had not been resolved. According to Darrel, the old club of engineers were unhappy with the shareholder (the Holmes à Court family). Heytesbury was not the white knight they expected. A campaign began when the managing directors were visiting VRD to change the shareholder. Previously Stoll Moss management had indicated a willingness to depart from the Heytesbury stable as well. These were old enterprises and Heytesbury was young. Times had been tough in large part because Janet wanted to keep all the enterprises. Darrel says:

> Our most threatening task wasn't the banks and the financial position; it was in fact this mismatch of Heytesbury and Janet wanting to do something alive and go somewhere but with cultures that were quite stick-in-the-mud sometimes. They could only focus on capital as being their saviour ... a people company is where we in fact have plugged the brains of our people into a network and our resource is our brains, not our capital base.

Darrel's message to the enterprises was that they had to perform and then they would have the capital they wanted. But they saw the only solution to their problems as being given more capital. They were fed up with the constraints of Heytesbury debt. Darrel says:

> The allocation of blame, of capital being a restriction on performance, is a part of the culture we had to really shift. I think it comes out of the eighties when the era was very much focused on the manipulation of capital and the generation of wealth via inflation. They were perceiving

the failure of John Holland to be more a failure of the shareholder. It's an interesting phenomenon where management assumes ownership. The shareholder's having a rough time so ... they want another shareholder, another owner. The fact that they failed and sold out seemed to go right over their heads.

The unhappiness with the shareholder also extended to unhappiness with the managing director. Janet was lobbied by the disgruntled directors and told she was being badly advised. So Darrel walked out. These were emotional times. On top of two years of warfare, under siege from the banks, Darrel was now being challenged by his own troops. He went home, collapsed, rested and then came back recharged.

He flew to London for the next stage of the meeting.[9] To prepare himself, and release aggression, Darrel took his Lexus and raced around roads in the Lake District.

When the meetings started the engineers came in with the same arguments, and Darrel cut them off quite harshly. He said that what they were trying to achieve was not open to debate; the only question was *how* they were going to achieve the goal. The group was divided. Darrel was very disappointed that day that some of the Pastoral Group colleagues that he had brought to Heytesbury sat on the fence, and waited to see the way the discussion would go, without coming straight in unquestioningly to support him. But they were all tired after a very hard two years and in Darrel's words 'they could see some cracks developing around DAJ that they hadn't seen before'.

Still, the managers had by now seen the pattern in Darrel's behaviour. He was a brilliant strategist but he was not an engineer. Theatre often bored him and they saw Jarvis's pattern of recurrent over-the-top emotionalism as a symptom of his inability to take criticism or advice regarding Janet's (and increasingly his own) vision. But Darrel set about trying to restore harmony. He talked with Janet and asked her to speak to the managing directors about herself, 'her background, what drives her, why she is prepared to take risks and give things a go when logic says don't do it, to talk about her plan, her idealism, her hope for a better way'.

Darrel then spoke about his philosophy on business, his view that labour means teams, enterprise is the courage to be different, profit maximisation is non-sustainable. He spoke about the strategy for Heytesbury and how they were applying these philosophies. The group adjourned and drove to Bath in two cars. Darrel insisted they stay together, which they managed to do. They bought ice creams and when they returned to the meeting the atmosphere had changed completely.

It was another watershed for Heytesbury and for Darrel. But 1995 wasn't over. At no stage was it to be an easy year. Darrel was increasingly doubting his ability to lead Heytesbury after the war years and to change his mode of operation. Even before Heytesbury he had been employed as an agent of change. He would manage a client, a family, through a change and then move onto the next restructure. He didn't ever get through to the stage where he could be 'coach'. His self-doubt and his volatile emotional state led to tensions not only with Heytesbury staff but also with Janet. They were both exhausted from the stress of Heytesbury's financial crisis.

Darrel went in search of a consultant who could help him address his personal dilemma and his relationship with Janet. He settled on a couple in the UK. Janet and Darrel interviewed Marsha George and Adrian McLean together and, late in 1995, began the process of working through the issues they faced. It was a traumatic and exhausting experience but they made progress. Darrel and Janet then followed up the sessions in the UK with a further meeting in Australia in January 1996, inviting Marsha and Adrian to a meeting with the other shareholders, Janet and Robert's children, who had largely been protected from the turmoil of the war years. Their assets had gone from zero value in 1991 to a capital base of around $250 million in 1995, but they weren't fully aware of the human cost involved and they were forming strong opinions. Given the opportunity to put their view about the company and assets they had inherited from their father, the children asked questions Darrel did not appreciate. So Darrel walked out again. The facilitators at the meeting had helped the shareholders to unload their views, but no one anticipated the result. In retrospect Darrel said of the meeting:

When you take people to the rubbish tip, they are going to unload, but you have to finish the meeting with a kick-up at the end, and it didn't happen. It just went to a low, got really into the mud and then stuck there and there was no kick-up. So it was a topping off of a grim year. It blew the stuffing out of Janet.

While it indeed blew the stuffing out of both of them, it wasn't to be the last time this shareholder unrest would surface. The Holmes à Court family members were no longer school and college students. They were independent, strong-minded individuals who would in the end assert themselves as shareholders. They wanted their inheritance protected. They wanted to know what was going on. They were forming their own individual views about Darrel Jarvis.

THE NEW JANET

By the end of 1994, Janet's dignity in the face of Robert's sudden death, and her subsequent noble battle to transform Heytesbury from a hierarchical company led by a sole, brilliant sharetrader who viewed his assets and his balance sheet as the scoreboard, to one where her vision was to grow diverse businesses, provide services and meld the employees into a team, had earned her a high public profile and an admiring and sympathetic following. She grew into a popular Australian icon in her own right. When she entered a room, people angled to be near her. She was viewed not as an ordinary woman, but more like a pop star, an actress or a sporting hero. There appeared to be something special about her business feats, although few would have known much about what was going on inside Heytesbury and how difficult the struggle had really been.

Initially, Janet did not seek publicity. She knew Robert had manipulated the press to his own advantage, but she still felt bruised from the mauling she thought the Holmes à Courts had received from journalists following the crash. The press had to be managed.

She went with her instincts on the initial press release following the funeral, but heeded the advice of those warning her about the response of the financial world. When she agreed to be interviewed, she stressed that she would not speak about her private life. She would speak for a cause – the Australian Children's Television Foundation, the Black Swan Theatre Company, the environment, Westrek, the Republican movement, peace issues, Aboriginal art and music – all issues about which she was passionate and not reticent to put her point of view.

As Janet grew in confidence, in part due to Darrel Jarvis's coaching and encouragement, and through her tough dealings with the financial world, she shed the restrained guise she had adopted over her years of marriage to Robert and became more like Janet Ranford, the fun-loving, outspoken girl.

At the *Images of Women* exhibition on 11 January 1991 in Sydney, she introduced Prime Minister Bob Hawke, who was to open the exhibition, and publicly told him very firmly she did not approve of his sending Australian troops to the Gulf War.

By October 1992, Janet was publicly speaking her mind about Prime Minister Bob Hawke and his treatment of his wife, Hazel. Her views were not moderated by her focus on Heytesbury's business pressures nor by hope of political favour.

Hazel Hawke asked Janet if she would launch her autobiography, *Hazel: Her Own Story*. Bob Hawke approved of Hazel's choice, but was not happy when he heard what Janet had to say. She praised Hazel's competence, compassion and her honest conversational style, but then she told the gathering at the launch (as she spoke directly to Hazel from the podium) that there were 'many of us here today who can't believe you stayed in your marriage for so long'. She said:

I'll never forget the annoyance that I and many Australians felt as Bob forgot to include you as he received the initial acclamation from journalists and the party faithful on the evening he led the ALP to victory in the 1983 federal election.

Janet said Hazel, rather than being a 'consort to be hidden' (as one of Bob's female friends had claimed in a jealous letter to Hazel) had become 'his greatest asset in office'. Bob Hawke listened to Janet's public words, smiling grimly through his tears.

When Bob and Hazel split finally after thirty-eight years of marriage, and Hazel, with dignity, acquiesced to Bob's demands in the interests of her children, Janet proffered some behind-the-scenes advice to Hazel to get sound legal counsel. But any mention of Janet's name angered Bob. Although a Labor supporter, Janet discriminated between her Labor Prime Ministers and begged no pardon. Bob Hawke was not a man she admired.

In contrast, she and Paul Keating did have excellent rapport from the time they first met. They had come to know one another when Robert invited Paul and Anita Keating to stay at the Stud during Paul's time as Treasurer. Although they rarely met, the bond was strong and Paul phoned Janet immediately after hearing of Robert's death to offer both sympathy and advice. He phoned her regularly after that in the early months, and the media, after his electoral defeat, spread rumours of an affair between them, totally baseless and annoying to them both. After Paul Keating became Prime Minister, Janet was appointed, in August 1992, as the first female member of the Reserve Bank of Australia. The Reserve Bank board had approached Treasurer John Dawkins to appoint her to the board. John Dawkins tried hard to talk her out of the idea but she said yes. When asked by journalists what she would bring to the position, Janet responded, 'humanity', a comment she later regarded as inappropriate, but others at the Reserve Bank did not. She was not one more conservative grey suit. She represented a wider group and she brought with her a social conscience. She made the board more relaxed and asked commonsense, perceptive questions which set the technocrats back on their heels. Her approach encouraged others to do the same. While Janet was not an expert in the arcane aspects of monetary policy, she helped the economists sort out the wood from the trees and provide the checks and balances commonsense and experience can bring. Staff at the bank saw Janet as extremely well-qualified for the job and not a maverick choice by a friendly Prime Minister.

Janet worked hard at the job, attending all but one meeting in five years – a better record than any of the men. She read her papers, sought to understand the issues and asked questions when she did not. She was always a fast learner and she earned the respect of Bernie Fraser, the Reserve Bank Governor, who shared Janet's social values. She enjoyed the position and contributed and learnt a great deal concurrently.

Darrel Jarvis was always there in the background for Janet, guiding, prompting, influencing her views, her thinking, and often her speeches. Janet admired Darrel's intellect, his strategic thinking, and the bond between them continued to grow through the rough times they weathered. There was little he would not do for her. He was a loyal and obedient CEO, but he was also having the time of his life. The young, insecure boy from Tuart Hill High School had come a long way. He was not only running a pastoral company with vast Australian landholdings, but also a construction company and a large chunk of London's theatres. He had ample opportunity to test his theories, and a glamorous, high-profile and socially-accomplished chairman to stand behind on the occasions when he felt out of his depth. Janet trusted him and they worked well and very closely together. Her social skills and charm facilitated Darrel's strategies, as they had for Robert, and were a major asset for the company. They orchestrated the good guy/bad guy routine in crucial meetings as they devoted themselves to the work of Heytesbury. Together they were a unique and formidable duo.

Janet evolved as chairman of Heytesbury and Darrel exposed her to the workings of John Holland, Stoll Moss, the pastoral industry, the transport industry, the winery, the whole world of business. And as she gained recognition from her male peers in business, she transformed both inwardly and outwardly. The pain and grief caused by Robert's sudden death receded. She rethought her partnership with her husband and began to speak publicly about her revised view of their relationship.

On 27 October 1993, three years after Robert's death, Janet was asked to present the HC Coombs Lecture at Perth's Government

House. She spoke of what had occurred in Heytesbury following Robert's death:

> When Robert died, Heytesbury consisted of Sherwin Pastoral Group, Stoll Moss Theatres, some trucks, a winery, 250 horses and four stud farms. Masses of non-income earning things – paintings, houses, sculptures, etc – things that were collectible. And lots of debt which needed servicing.
>
> Heytesbury's method of servicing this debt pre-1990 was for Robert to ring stockbrokers and do deals. In this field he had few peers. There was no necessity for managers of the divisions to make profits; they simply had to make Robert happy. Robert Holmes à Court was the most profitable division Heytesbury had.
>
> After the shock of his death, I found myself with an inherent belief that he had put together the seed of something very good. However, the seed was unsustainable without him. My strong desire was to nurture it and take it forward myself. I made the decision not to accept the recommendation to sell everything, pay off the debts and go lie on a beach.
>
> But at that time I also made a first mistake in not assuming a full leadership role. Looking back, I can see that my belief in Heytesbury was undermined by a lack of confidence, particularly in my own financial and accounting skills, and I delegated too much of the leadership function to others who thought that they had Robert's skills so that the company could carry on as before.
>
> I always knew that change had to happen. The conflict was that the company tried not to change. The people believed the power had simply transferred to them and they paid lip service to the required change. It took a shock which dragged me away from the day-to-day running of Heytesbury to show me that the lack of required changes had meant that the successful germination of the seed was in severe jeopardy.
>
> The shock was that I ran over myself – which is quite easy to do. The trick is to do it and survive. After a short trip in an ambulance and a short stay in an emergency ward, I ended up in Bethesda Hospital. From this peaceful haven I was able to take an outsider's

view and see that Heytesbury was in a crisis situation and urgent change was required.

Janet then went on to speak in the metaphors of Darrel Jarvis:

Our response was to go to war – not easy for a self-confessed pacifist. Some soldiers were brought in and a battle plan formulated on the principle that the best form of defence is attack. The first step was to rally the troops by exciting them with the plan – that is, telling them about the seed and how they could participate in its germination and enjoy its growth towards maturity.

Armed with this knowledge, Heytesbury was protected from doubting Thomases, stray opinion, gratuitous press speculation and panicky financiers.

Once our defences were in place, the second part of the plan involved sending a spearhead through those resistant to change, to capture the seed and begin the germination process. I have to say, and in some respects sadly, that the plan has worked. I say sadly because I seem to have confirmed the oft-made analogy between management and warfare. How many of us in management have been urged to read the ancient Chinese book The Art of War? *I cannot help reverting to my pacifist roots – there must be a better way.*

From that time – the silence broken – Janet spoke often about her life with Robert and her revised view of that life. She began to recognise that public sympathy for her was huge. Robert (unlike Alan Bond) had not been a popular man, and her servile devotion to him had puzzled many. It made sense that she would now see her past in a different light.

By 4 October 1994, in an address to the Australian-Israel Chamber of Commerce, she had honed her theme. Using Bryce Courtenay's book title *The Power of One*, she compared the power of one to the power of a team. She said, 'the power of one cost me a husband'.

The thing about a one-man-act is that it is unsustainable and it cannot be duplicated. This was the root of my problem in September

1990. What I inherited was unsustainable and unstable because the whole equation relied on one ingredient to determine success or failure – Robert Holmes à Court. By definition it failed as soon as he exited the equation.

The sustainability of the power of one is a mirage. It doesn't exist. Robert taught me a lesson. If I was going to accept the challenge of making something out of the inheritance, I would not repeat the constraints of a one-man-act. The antithesis of one is a team. The team is the basis of the strategy I adopted.

She then spoke more strongly than previously about the internal opposition she encountered within Heytesbury:

I always knew that change had to happen. The conflict was that the company tried not to change. The people believed the power had simply transferred to them and they paid lip-service to the required change.

She referred to Darrel's crucial intervention in pointing out the problems with her other managers, their 'battle plan' and the war years. She concluded, 'If we had to do it again – we'd do it better. But we did it! *We* being the operative word. The power of one? Give me the might of many!'. The 'many' Janet was referring to were the employees of Heytesbury, but in vision and strategy Janet and Darrel were two halves of a whole. He now held enormous power but he knew his limitations and Janet's strengths, the social skills he did not have. He nurtured Janet's strengths because he understood that the big difference between Heytesbury and any other company running close to the wind financially was Janet. If Heytesbury was to maintain control of its own agenda Janet was the key. He could devise the strategy but it was Janet who would win the individuals over to her side.

Janet began to take charge of the publicity she received, particularly in the UK. As a foreign owner of a unique cultural enterprise – London's major theatres – she needed to improve her image, and turn around the antagonism of the theatrical establishment which Robert had engendered by his perceived harsh treatment of Lord Lew Grade. Australia's richest woman had to earn their respect for the sake of the Stoll Moss business. What did an Australian know about London? Theatre owners were thought to take without giving, and this one was not only a colonial but also a woman! Janet hired a publicist, Peter Thompson, and under his expert guidance began a series of strategic interviews in 1994, aimed at showing the human face of Stoll Moss and demonstrating that the company under her regime was user-friendly and culturally aware.

Always irresistibly charming when she set her mind to it, Janet won over the journalists she spoke to and some of the most frank interviews Janet had ever given began to appear. She was disarming, talking about the filthy state of the Stoll Moss theatre loos, and was more revealing than she had ever been about her life with Robert.

Michael Thompson-Noel described her as 'Powerful, glamorous and beautiful'.[1] Charles Spencer called Janet 'the Queen of Shaftesbury Avenue', 'warm', 'unpretentious', 'exceptionally likeable'.[2] She was described as 'a formidable motivator of people',[3] as 'a hard-working businesswoman'.[4] The publicity was effective and she very quickly won over the West End London theatre world.

She told journalists Robert's death was more of a shock than a surprise, as he didn't look after his health. 'He smoked like crazy and worked like mad, got absolutely no exercise. He'd smoke six cigars before breakfast. He was addicted to nicotine', but her loyalty did not allow her to mention his diabetes. She spoke of the help she had been given on his death by a writer who spoke of grief and the need to remember the person as they really were, 'warts and all, because then you're remembering a true, rounded human being. If you remember someone that you put on a pedestal it makes it much more difficult'.

She also spoke of the fact that Robert always came first and took priority over her children in her life. She said:

That's where a husband should come, because if you do things correctly, your children grow up and leave. The birds push their babies out of their nests and the objective should be to make your children *independent, to be stand-alone people who will find their own partners and carry on . . . And I did look after him. Yes, I really did, especially in the later years because of the smoking and the strain, the tense existence. He worked incredibly hard . . . I constantly tried to make him lead a healthier life, but he was a very independent, private person . . . People would say to Robert, 'What do you do for relaxation?' and he'd say, 'I go and do a bit more work'.*

Lynda Lee Potter said, 'Her enthusiasm, direct approach and lack of grandeur is disarming, but there is steel behind the charm'.[5] In fact, there always had been.

Janet said to Sue Summers:[6]

As time passes I begin to see my husband differently. I always realised he was a loner. Now I see how negative that was and that it was really rather sad. Would he think I had changed? I suppose he would, because I might not be prepared to do some of the things I used to do, like pick up his dirty underclothes and lay out fresh clothes for him every morning. I don't regret having done it, but I'd never be that sort of wife again.

Janet found it liberating to acknowledge the role she had played in the past and how different she had become. The years since Robert's death had been exciting. Darrel welcomed Janet's public critique of her past life. She was, he said, 'letting go of the ghosts of the past'. Darrel did not hesitate to convey his own strong criticisms of Robert, and he provided words for Janet around her theme, the power of many versus the might of one.

Together, they were leading a very different Heytesbury from that which existed in Robert's day. Neither of them had expected to play such a role in their lives and they found excitement on a world stage. They had one another for company on their travels, and they both loved the challenge. The boorish but shrewdly clever boy from the backblocks now had some of the power formerly enjoyed by Robert. But unlike Robert who had exposed Janet to a breadth of diverse experience, he built Janet's new belief in herself. While he shored up her confidence in making bold business decisions, at the same time he was instrumental in everything the new Heytesbury did. He often reminded Janet, however, that it was *her* vision they were achieving together. Such an approach displaced his own responsibility as chief executive officer for the actual running of the business, of which Janet was the chairman. A division of opinion was growing about Darrel.

Some of Janet's friends and staff felt he was isolating her and saw him as ruthless in getting rid of any internal opposition, thus forcing Janet, more and more, to see him as the one indispensable figure in her life. Janet did not agree. She was enjoying the praise and adulation of others who appreciated the new energy she brought to Heytesbury, but she felt she owed her new status and confidence to him. She repeatedly stated, 'I could not have done what I have done without Darrel'. Others felt she should not feel so indebted. Janet maintains, as does Jarvis, that she was the driving force, he was not manipulating her, he was doing her bidding. In the London theatre world, at least, Janet earnt her stripes through her own merits and the views of those in the theatre world attest to this.

Michael Owen, chief arts correspondent of *The Evening Standard*, London, spoke to me of the growth of his affection for Janet from the time she had engendered suspicion from London's theatre people as an outsider, simply using the theatres as a plaything. He first met her in Perth at the Perth Festival of the Arts. She reminded him of Joan Sutherland – large, big-framed, open. He was struck by her down-to-earth openness and caring, and the way she instantly sought to embrace friends. He credits her, not Darrel, with a revolution in Stoll Moss theatres. She made a profound mark, he believes, and changed the face of theatre-going in London. She attended to the state of the lavatories, the quality of the fabric on the chairs, the service of staff. She themed her theatres and made them friendly and welcoming. He finds Janet warm, generous, lots of fun to be with, always laughing her loud and healthy laughter. 'She brings Australia with her. I feel freer in her company.'

Michael Owen believes Janet to be:

the most appreciated theatre owner who has been around in the twentieth century. From the day she renamed the Globe Theatre after Sir John Gielgud, she was regarded with new esteem by the theatre-going public. For those who know her privately, she is life-enhancing. She throws open her house and makes a party happen. The lady in glowing red satin can touch base with anyone, from any level of society.

This sort of love for Janet is shared by many who know her.

Janet's publicist, Peter Thompson, and his partner Stephen Barton, are equally admiring and both say they 'feel nothing but the utmost love and respect for her'. They joke with her in a way Janet enjoys. On one occasion Janet had tripped and badly twisted her ankle in London. She commented to her publicist, 'I hate thick ankles. I feel I'm just like a fat, old ex-school teacher'. He replied, 'Well you are aren't you?'. They tell another story with great amusement of a weekend when they took Janet to stay with Cameron Mackintosh at his country estate. Cameron has a large dog and, together, they were touring the grounds, admiring the fountains and the grotto. As Janet put her foot forward to enter the grotto, Cameron yelled, 'Get off there, you fat bitch!'. Janet thought he was speaking to her, not the dog, and they all fell about laughing.

Such glowing opinions of Janet and of the fun they have in her company are common feelings among her friends – the people she likes and chooses to spend time with. These people are genuine, uncritical and very defensive of Janet. She truly inspires incredible love and loyalty, which she returns unless she feels she is betrayed.

Janet's status in the UK had never been higher than at the beginning of 1996, having been named the UK Veuve Clicquot Business Woman of the Year. But this was also the year of John Howard's federal electoral success in Australia and the landslide victory of the Liberal Coalition. Paul Keating was no longer Prime Minister and Janet was quite devastated by the election result. She had believed in Keating's big picture – his insistence that Australia face the future of globalised trade, repositioning Australia as a European nation in Asia, its need to define a new national identity as a Republic no longer tied to Britain's coat-tails. She had shared his passions for the Aboriginal reconciliation process, for equity, tolerance and the finer things in life.

Paul Keating was now a feather duster, consigned to the scrapheap of political history after one of the most comprehensive political defeats in Labor Party history. When asked in London about her response to the election result Janet said, 'If you live in a democracy you have to expect governments to change. What disappointed me was the success of racists and bigots' (having in mind Pauline Hanson and Graeme Campbell). The journalist filed the story and quoted Janet as saying, 'A lot of very racist and bigoted people were elected'. Her comment received wide news coverage and came to the attention of new Prime Minister John Howard. It touched a sensitive nerve.

Two days before the election, Paul Keating had announced Janet would chair the Centenary of Federation Council, a job which excited her. He did not follow the normal protocol for such appointments during an election and John Howard, as leader of the Opposition, was not consulted. Once elected, he soon made it clear that Janet was not his appointee and should resign, sending a message to her via the bureaucracy. Janet requested a meeting, which Howard agreed to, saying the meeting would not change his mind. Her resignation followed the meeting with Howard and she maintained her silence, although Phillip Adams wrote a full account of her dismissal in the *Australian*.

In many ways the 1996 Australian federal election was a turning point for Janet. It signalled the start of an *annus horribilis*, and perhaps the end of her dream run with the Australian media. John Howard was intransigent in his view of Janet Holmes à Court. She was not reappointed to the Reserve Bank board, despite representation from the Bank on her behalf. She was also initially denied another job she was eminently well qualified for, and interested in doing, as chair of the Western Australian Symphony Orchestra, but Richard Court, the Premier of Western Australia, intervened and Janet was appointed.

Politically, Janet was out in the cold with the Australian Federal Government, an experience that took her back to her childhood and the memories of her parents' radical beliefs. Although by no means a political radical in the same manner as her parents, Janet remained outspoken on the Republic, on the need for a new flag, and on the race issue. She publicly criticised John Howard for not speaking out against Pauline Hanson, the independent Queensland MP from Oxley who was leading a racist and xenophobic social movement called One Nation. Janet took every opportunity to speak out against the Hanson dogma and had made hundreds of orange ribbons to pin on lapels which she distributed to those she met to symbolise support for multiculturalism.

At the same time as Janet Holmes à Court fell from political grace, Heytesbury had a very bad year and journalists began to sniff blood. Despite putting on a brave face, and repeated denials from Janet and Darrel that their ongoing asset sales were a reflection of trouble with the banks, media reports turned from unbridled admiration for her and Heytesbury's achievements to a more cynical and suspicious tone. The negative probing by news journalists gathered momentum following news that Heytesbury had sold pastoral properties in Queensland and Western Australia. 'What will be left?' asked the *Herald Sun*.[7]

James McCullock[8] linked Janet's financial woes to the loss of the contract at the Altona oil refinery and threw doubt on the sale of Double Island because of a Mabo claim by the Yirrganydji people. In a four-page feature article Neil Chenoweth and Karen Maley of the *Financial Review* pulled together a foreboding picture of the Heytesbury empire and its future. They began with the observation that:

By last Monday it was looking as though someone in Janet Holmes à Court's sprawling Heytesbury empire had dropped the ball ... From the moment late last Friday when project manager Toyo Engineering [Corporation] gave notice that it was terminating John Holland's $250 million [$45.4 million][9] contract on a catalytic cracker unit, it was clear that, one way or another, this dispute was going to cost John

Holland money. Probably a lot of money. In fact, it was a variation of one of the conundrums of the nineties: just how bankable is Janet Holmes à Court?[10]

The writers observed that Janet 'has always had too much charm and assurance ever to raise serious doubts about her liquidity'. The article quoted supportive comments from some of her unnamed bankers, but the thrust of the article was very negative, with the journalists concluding Janet had 'performed an elegant impersonation of someone dog-paddling gamely on, nose just above water, hoping not to run into any waves'. They went on to point out that with net assets in December 1995 of reportedly $240 million, net bank debt down to $183 million and profit at $11.6 million, almost every cent of cash flow was going into debt repayment. Despite Janet's new spending on a Cessna Citation V executive eight-seater jet, a new house in Perth and a $2.2 million revamp of Vasse Felix winery, they said, 'around last June, the corporate style grew a bit less expansive'.

The *Financial Review* listed 'a string of other asset sales ... all reported to be the "last major asset sale"'. – They included Double Island (around $4 million), the Blue Princess necklace ($2 million), the Wallan stud in Victoria (around $10 million), [the family's] Peppermint Grove house ($4 million), and two more cattle stations at Joanna Plains and Galways Downs (about $6 million).

There is no doubt that the Altona project came at the worst possible time for Heytesbury. They had been relatively successful in reducing risks and exposures of John Holland and this project appeared on the scene when the company was experiencing difficulties in its beef markets. The project had been won by John Holland, based on a competitive price.

The project experienced a series of adverse influences including: one of the wettest periods of time on record, when the civil works (in ground) were being performed; changes and delays to the procurement program of major pieces of equipment sourced from overseas; a series of Area, State and Federal external industrial actions; and a concerted push by the local Electrical Trade Union (ETU) for a return to a 35-hour week on the site. Mobil had in the past provided a 35-hour week to electricians and this campaign was characterised by the union leadership as gaining what they had lost from Mobil. This site was also subject to three cases of legionella which hospitalised the infected workers and led to site shutdowns for the ten-day disease gestation period.

John Holland experienced difficulties in negotiations with Toyo in part because of Japanese/Australian cultural differences but also because it became clear that Toyo was also incurring substantial losses on the job. The ETU had been undertaking a rolling series of disruptive actions, including not carrying out required tagging of equipment, necessary for Occupational Health and Safety reasons. John Holland was put in the 'no-win' position of either shutting the site because of health and safety requirements or tagging the electrical supply with off-site labour. The major strike which ensued after use of off-site tradesmen caused the whole site to be shut for just over five weeks. John Holland proposed a range of catch-up (acceleration) measures, including nightshifts and increasing the workforce, which were encouraged by Toyo and Mobil. However, it became quite clear that Toyo did not see they had any obligation to reimburse John Holland for these very expensive measures.

Ultimately it was a commercial decision by John Holland and Heytesbury as to whether they would continue to expend substantive amounts of money on acceleration, which were not being recovered through the payments from Toyo. At one period of time the project was losing John Holland and Heytesbury $1 million per week.

It is unlikely that any contractor in Australia, unless they have enormous cash reserves, could withstand that type of loss over an extended period. Given Heytesbury's cash constraints, the project certainly required additional financier support. When all negotiations had failed, John Holland advised the unions, the workforce, Toyo and Mobil that it was no longer prepared to meet the significantly negative cashflow nor accept all the responsibility for the delays to the project and thereby reduced the workforce by half. Toyo terminated the contract and the matter went into legal dispute.[11]

John Holland management had seen the problem brewing and had tried unsuccessfully to find a solution. In the end, they were in a very difficult position as they had to pay their subcontractors, pay the employees on the site or their redundancies and continue with their commitments while the client no longer paid them. The publicity surrounding the termination by Toyo harmed John Holland's position with new clients and they had to work hard at damage control as they went to arbitration on the Toyo project.

Concurrently with the John Holland problem the Pastoral Group had been experiencing difficulties so neither enterprise was performing according to Darrel Jarvis's ten-year plan. The move into the Toyo project was part of a strategy to shift John Holland from the building construction market into energy and resources engineering. John Holland's projected growth would be in this area and Toyo was a key project undertaken with this new direction in mind. The project went wrong very quickly and the cost to John Holland was significant.

At the same time there was a major drop in the beef commodity market for Japox (a 500–600 kilogram animal developed for the Japanese market). The Pastoral Group managers were caught out by this substantial drop in expected returns, so properties went into a loss, which contributed to an additional $15 million debt. Others in Heytesbury attempted to blame the cattleman for the loss. In London, the musical *Oliver* was finishing sooner than had been expected at the Palladium, so advance bookings were not bringing in the badly needed cash. Altogether things were once again extremely difficult. Heytesbury quickly moved from a cash positive position to a cash negative position.

The setbacks in the enterprises and the need to invest in their operational performance meant that the debt reduction program had stalled at close to $200 million for three years. No projections done accepted that level of debt as sustainable. Heytesbury had come out of 1994 owing the banks $200 million. In December 1996 Heytesbury had $2 million in cash on hand and no working capital at their time of greatest need.

1996 had been downhill all the way for Heytesbury. In the view of senior Heytesbury executives during that year, Darrel Jarvis had not been keeping his eye on the ball. He was exhausted, going through a personal crisis and doubting his capacity to lead Heytesbury into his own projected growth phase. He was also negotiating his 5% shareholding in Heytesbury. The businesses were not performing as they should have been. The managing directors complained they could not get Darrel to listen. Darrel's management style had come to be seen as too domineering, too self-assured, too lacking in consultative processes. Several of Heytesbury's senior staff had become fed up with Darrel's aggressive style, believing he dominated Janet's thinking, kept them away from her so she didn't hear an alternative view.

With Heytesbury financially facing the wall and in this mood of anxiety and confusion, Darrel called a management conference of managing directors and corporate senior managers at Karriview in October 1996. Once again he brought in the UK consultants Marsha George and Adrian Maclean to manage the process and facilitate the meeting. The managers wanted a structured discussion, but Darrel was disruptive of the group processes and Janet became irritated by his behaviour. Janet found her voice and spoke openly and frankly about her hopes for the business. People responded. In the end, Janet wrote to Darrel telling him to change his behaviour or he would be gone. Darrel was in a crisis. For the first time he had lost the support of Janet, the chairman, the only person whose views really mattered to him.

Darrel went on holiday and on his return met with Janet and took her back over the events of 1996. He placed the blame for Heytesbury's problems on the budgeting process and reminded Janet that he had held the company together. Darrel was arguing for his survival and he was adept in such situations. Janet was faced with a difficult choice.

In the end she opted for the devil she knew. She was facing another major financial crisis with Heytesbury. She had weathered them before with Darrel's advice. Darrel was telling her the senior managers had it wrong. Graham Scott, an accountant she respected, and Alec Mairs, her independent board member, were telling her she needed Darrel. (Graham was appointed to the board on 7 January 1997.) She also felt very strong loyalty towards Darrel, for all they had achieved over the past five years and for the way he had helped her personally grow and develop.

By the time the shareholders (Janet, her children and – by now – Darrel) met in December 1996, Peter Wood (the finance director) had gone, quickly followed by others who had been at Karriview. Janet's children were not pleased. They, too, had had enough of Darrel's behaviour and while acknowledging his earlier contribution they did not like the risks they thought he was taking now with their inheritance nor did they like what they perceived to be Darrel's control over their mother. They wanted him out of Heytesbury. They reiterated their view at a shareholders' meeting in the UK in April 1997. Janet agreed, but said she would determine when and how Darrel would leave. Heytesbury was in a standstill arrangement with the banks and she would not make any move that would destabilise the company. Darrel was told of these discussions. He remained fiercely loyal to Janet and he swung into action, applying his mind to the best of his ability. Heytesbury had the best year on record. In December 1997 total debt facilities were down from $217 million in May to $148 million with cash on hand of $33 million.

Heytesbury had made the decision to give John Holland a clean start and warranted to absorb the positive or negative outcome of the Toyo project's arbitration on their books. 1996 was the last year Keith Drew, the John Holland managing director, still had 'projects from hell' on the company's books. Quality and ethics were now promoted in relation to all jobs, and Heytesbury's John Holland was now more like the old John Holland when Sir John was running the company. John Holland and Janet promoted a culture of operating in the construction industry with ethics and high safety standards. The view was they would still make a profit and get enjoyment from the company. This is the message which she conveys to her workers. And they listen. Janet's presence on a construction site is something to see. I visited the Blue Circle Southern Cement Berrima Works Kiln Upgrade with her where she toured the site and had lunch with the employees. She spoke of the mix of ethnic groups on site and what pleasure it gave her to see this. The men lined up for photographs with her for their wallets and some were quite emotional. One of the senior men told me he had observed the lift in the morale of the men on site after Janet's previous visit; if she spoke to them individually it meant so much. The fact that the owner of the company was an attractive woman who demonstrated a caring attitude was tremendously important to them.

In 1997 John Holland reported over $20 million in profit for the year to 31 December, and their cashflow came in $15 million ahead of budget. The result was underpinned by a turnover of $807.7 million including $203 million from its Asian joint venture with Hume. 1998 also looked like being an exceptionally good year. High-profile projects including the Sydney Show Ground, the Joondalup and Mount Hospitals for Health Care Australia, the Pacific Motorway, and the BHP Direct Reduction Iron (DRI) project at Port Hedland (which is one of the major developments in Australia – a $2 billion project which at its peak had up to 1,818 John Holland employees on-site) have helped turn around the image of John Holland.

The DRI project was a John Holland/BHP alliance contract (with others involved) and is one of the largest industrial developments ever undertaken in Australia. It produces 90% pure iron briquettes from iron ore which have sufficient purity to feed into an electric arc furnace (not a blast furnace), and represents cutting edge technology. John Holland's work was worth $400 million. They were two years on-site and completed the job within the agreed target. And it is another first for an Australian company. John Holland received a five-star national safety rating on the construction site, with 4 million man hours worked without lost time or injury. Working on this project with BHP to build something of significance, while Robert had fought them for six years, gave Janet a great sense of satisfaction – a vindication of her way of doing things.

The downturn in Asia had been cushioned by John Holland Asia's decision two years previously to sign contracts only with international companies or governments and only in US dollars. Likewise, Stoll Moss Theatres were having a positive run. In January 1998 Janet was named the most significant figure in British theatre by the *Stage* newspaper. The award is based on a survey that assesses the major players and their achievements over the previous twelve months. She rose from sixth place in 1997 to be top of the charts. Stoll Moss's commitment to staging new plays such as *Shopping and Fucking* and Ben Elton's *Popcorn*; extending support to individual writers; backing events such as the Vivian Ellis Prize and the National Youth Music Theatre's production of *Bugsy Malone* at the Queen's Theatre were all factors influencing the survey decision.

The change in philosophy in Stoll Moss had led to an increased demand for theatre and an increase in the bottom line. Stoll Moss's services – Ticketselect, the booking service; Select Theatre Breaks, the accommodation, travel and dining booking service; as well as Class Act, the education service for schools – were all doing well and bringing more people to the West End. There are also plans to redevelop and renovate the Palladium. A conservative valuation of the Stoll Moss enterprise in 1998 was £110 million. Ten years earlier Robert paid Christopher Skase £33 million.

Vasse Felix has become a model enterprise. The winery is expanding with the construction of a new $4 million winery which will increase its production capacity from 500 tonne to 3,000 tonne. New vineyard land was purchased and planted in 1998, which will eventually provide 50–60% of Vasse Felix's total fruit requirements. This new vineyard development is funded by external investors. It is anticipated that a significant proportion of future sales growth will be in exports which will also involve re-establishing supply links with Stoll Moss theatres.

Only Key Transport and the Pastoral Group were standing still in 1998. Heytesbury sold out of all properties in Queensland to repay debt. Janet says:

> It was the correct thing to do at the time. Heytesbury had $50 million invested in Queensland that was not earning anything. Queensland was the beef producer in the group. The Northern Territory and Western Australia were calf factories. We decided to cease production of beef and concentrate on the production of live cattle for export. Hence we sold the Queensland properties.

Heytesbury Beef dismantled the joint venture in Malaysia by selling to their partners – they were out of Asian beef exports by the skin of their teeth when the Asian financial crisis hit. Heytesbury implemented a cost-reduction program on the stations to be more competitive. They battened down the hatches and stopped cattle sales, restructured their capital base and let the herd build up. In 1998 they continued exporting live cattle to the Phillipines and worked on building up exports to the Middle East to replace the Indonesian market, which had collapsed. The capital base of Heytesbury Beef had gone from $150 million to $80 million. The enterprise did feel plundered for the greater Heytesbury good and Janet needed to provide reassurance that she remained interested in and committed to the beef industry.

Darrel Jarvis, as CEO, had spread himself too thinly and did not establish a corporate management structure in Heytesbury with communication procedures that allowed for team management without crisis. Despite the financial turnaround in 1998, the shareholders wanted an expansion of the board with an increase in the number of independent board members. Janet concurred.

David Karpin joined the board of Heytesbury on 18 August 1997. He had retired from Rio Tinto Zinc–Conzinc Rio Tinto of Australia (RTZ-CRA) after a twenty-two year career. His previous roles with CRA included six years as managing director of Argyle Diamonds, commercial director of Hamersley Iron and executive manager (commercial) with Bougainville Copper. He was a well-credentialled, independent board member who came with a reputation as a solid formal operator. He was Janet's choice and he was welcomed by the young shareholders and by the managing directors in John Holland and Stoll Moss. But Darrel was not happy. In the end Janet agreed with her family that the only solution was for Darrel to leave. Janet and David Karpin did the rounds of the banks and the sky did not fall in as Darrel had predicted it would. Fear had been a great rallying call in the past.

Darrel had been the right man at the right time. He had contributed a great deal to Heytesbury and to Janet, but even he doubted his capacity to lead in the long term and provide the stability and wisdom which leadership requires. Darrel's words suggest he was overcommitted and emotionally involved:

I took on too much. I was taking on this big business challenge, trying to keep it all together and doing too many restructurings in one. Then I was taking on pseudo roles of father and mentor, partly in good faith, partly a bit in over-confidence, partly out of loyalty. Mixed emotions through it all, mixed motivations through it all.

Darrel did underestimate the power of the shareholders. He left amid controversy both over the value of his 5% stake in Heytesbury and over whether the family was divided about the decision to sack its former CEO.[12] Heytesbury released a statement on 20 March stating, 'Mr Jarvis's departure followed a unanimous decision by shareholders to seek a new chief executive to lead Heytesbury in its new growth phase'. Janet assumed the role of executive chairman with David Karpin as deputy chairman. A search for a new CEO was implemented, but later abandoned as the divisions among the family about the future of Heytesbury became more open.

Janet was once again drawn back into hands-on work in Heytesbury and intimately involved with planning and policy. This was a wrench for Janet, for although she played the chairman's role in a very high-profile manner she had spent more and more of her time over the previous three years enjoying the excitement of her other activities. The image employed by Neil Chenoweth and Karen Maley of Janet as the 'dog paddling gamely on, nose just above water hoping not to run into any waves'[13] could not have been more off the mark. Janet has an extraordinary ability (learned during her childhood) to compartmentalise her life, which can lead people to wonder if she really understands what is going on. It's a rare and very useful ability and invaluable in generating an air of confidence. A more appropriate image of Janet would be that of a sole canoeist careering through the rapids of a fast whitewater river, stopping now and then to admire the scenery and take on supplies. She has never been so depressed that a good sleep wouldn't recharge the batteries, and 'dog paddling' simply is not the way she crosses a turbulent stream. The weekend after the damaging article on the woes of Heytesbury, Janet was on a paddle steamer on the Murray River between Mildura and Wentworth with forty people celebrating my husband Don's sixtieth birthday. She certainly appeared to be enjoying herself, with little evidence of the concerns of Heytesbury on her mind. She has always managed to do this. She maintains her commitments to her friends, to her committees, and continues to develop new interests despite all that keeps going on in Heytesbury. She is like Robert in that she can focus on the situation at hand. She is unlike Robert in that she finds time for a social life.

Although Janet's voluntary activities were unceremoniously curtailed by Robert's death she soon began to take on new charitable interests and responsibilities which were compatible with her style.

The concept of the Robert Holmes à Court Foundation was not something she enjoyed. She didn't want to sit back and give money away. There clearly wasn't the ready cash Robert had access to any more. She preferred active involvement and working with people to achieve objectives. Although she relinquished several of her voluntary community roles to give her more time to run Heytesbury, it did not take Janet long after Robert's death to find another cause in the Black Swan Theatre Company. The artistic director, Andrew Ross, had a plan to rejuvenate theatre in Western Australia. The Minister for the Arts, David Parker, asked him to come up with a blueprint for change, but Parker left political life abruptly before the plans were realised.

The next Minister, Kay Hallahan, was slower to make decisions, so Andrew Ross took the initiative. He called together an informal group who documented what they wanted, but they needed a board. Andrew had just produced *Bran Nue Dae*, the Jimmy Chi musical celebrating the life of Aboriginal people in and around Broome. Janet loved it and, on the evening of the closing performance, Andrew spoke with her about chairing the board. Janet agreed. As her mother before her, she was inspired by being part of bringing about change in the way white society viewed Aboriginal culture and Aboriginal people.

Andrew Ross credits Janet with keeping the board of the Black Swan Theatre Company focused on the objective of producing ambitious, high-risk ventures. There was to be no compromise. The task was tough. It is a struggle keeping the company alive, but she will not let the company go under. She helps Black Swan financially and in kind. In the first year, Heytesbury oversaw the accounts and payroll, along with the company secretarial and legal assistance. What interests Janet is the notion of something uniquely Australian being developed in Western Australia and productions such as *Bran Nue Dae, Sistergirl, Tourmaline, Dead Heart, Corrugation Road* and *Cloudstreet* fit that bill. Black Swan maintains a particular interest in the work of Aboriginal writers and performers as well as theatre for young audiences and the regional adaptation of classic works. Janet is a vehement defender of the Black Swan Theatre Company and ensures that everyone she deals with who comes to Perth attends a production by Black Swan.

In 1997 Janet accepted the position of chairman of the Western Australian Symphony Orchestra. She has her parents' love of classical music and is a regular attender at the orchestral concerts. She has travelled with the orchestra throughout Western Australia when they have given concerts and on one occasion conducted the orchestra herself. When the orchestra travelled to Melbourne to play in the Concert Hall she hosted a party for the players following the performance in her Spring Street apartment, which lasted until the early hours of the morning, leaving her honey-beige carpet splattered with red wine.

Janet has been widely acknowledged for her contribution to the community. She received her first Honorary Degree of Doctor of the University from Central Queensland University in 1994 and both the University of Western Australia and Murdoch University recognised Janet's contribution by awarding her honorary degrees in 1997. She was made an Officer in the Order of Australia for services to Business, the Arts and the Community in 1995, and was the Veuve Clicquot Business Woman of the Year in the UK in 1996. In 1997 she was awarded the Institution of Engineers Medal, which recognises organisations and individuals who have made a significant contribution to the economic or social development of Australia. In 1998 she was named among the 100 Australian Living Treasures. Despite the damaging financial news that appeared throughout 1996–97 about Heytesbury, the coverage of her other activities balanced the picture, showing a complex person who is not easily categorised and who retains a strong personal following.

Invariably, no matter what was going on in Janet's life or how she was feeling, she always presented herself with great composure and put a positive spin on it all. She ironically described Robert as 'the great acquirer', herself as 'the great disposer'. In an interview with Doug Aiton,[14] he described her very positively as being 'captivating, but she doesn't gush', 'regal without being haughty', 'extremely frank and direct', someone in whom 'You can easily see the fibre that enabled her to take over her husband's vast empire'. Aiton reported her as saying:

> *I'm not conscious of having wealth. I do enjoy the fact that I am able to do things like this, being chairman of the ACTF and the Black Swan Theatre Company in Perth. But I don't have a concept of myself as being wealthy. Except that I have great kids, fantastic friends, good health. I suppose I could have anything I want in the world, but I don't need very much. And I still have my mother, who's a great friend.*

Janet had certainly impressed Doug Aiton. These reported words are a key to the Janet Holmes à Court character. She seems genuinely not interested in wealth as such. What she holds dearly are the interesting people she has met through her position and lifestyle. Important people who make a difference for society, powerful people who want to sit at her side, the whirl of activity, travel, decision-making and the excitement of hard work are what make life meaningful to her.

The real Janet has the strength and the nerve to fight in the face of threat and 1997 was as threatening for Janet and Heytesbury as the early years following Robert's death. Reduction of debt and sale of assets were crucial to maintaining the confidence of the banks in 1997, and Janet did what she could to assist. She also did not hesitate to pursue in court a long-time friend, Rod Kelly, whom she believed had betrayed her trust over the sale of the Blue Princess necklace, nor to sue the Subiaco Municipal Council and its mayor for defamation of her company's reputation. She won both cases.

The Blue Princess necklace saga was stranger than fiction. Though the story had a satisfactory ending for Janet and Heytesbury, it was not without heartbreak and embarrassment. As one press report of the Blue Princess saga put it, 'The legal action revealed a story worthy of a James Bond plot: dazzling jewels, Eastern potentates, shady deals, doubletalk, Swiss bank accounts and a trail that began with a rendezvous in the Middle East and continued across Europe'.[15]

Rod Kelly was one of Janet's favourite people. He had become her friend and confidant during the many years he had advised her on the interior decoration of the many properties for which she was responsible. He had built up a highly profitable antiques dealership in Perth. He was ebullient, a witty conversationalist, full of energy and knowledgeable about his business. He also knew a good client when he saw one. Janet first met him through the Claremont School of Art Foundation, and when she and Robert were moving into 22 The Esplanade, Peppermint Grove, she asked him to help her furnish and decorate the house. She said he 'was absolutely marvellous'. He had also helped Janet with many projects like TVW7's Telethon and the dinner at which the UWA Art Gallery Appeal was launched, where he did 'wonderful, creative flower arrangements'.

When the refurbishment of Grove House in London's Regent Park began, Janet turned for advice to Rod Kelly because she knew nothing about antiques or their value. After Robert's death, Rod helped Janet refurbish her office in Perth and transformed the Spring Street apartment in Melbourne, previously decorated to Robert's taste with sombre grey carpet, grey curtains and dark paintings to match the often grey and gloomy Melbourne sky. Its one touch of colour had been the huge blue Brett Whiteley painting of Sydney Harbour and the Opera House on the main wall. She decided she wanted more warmth and colour.

Rod had very good creative ideas, which suited Janet, and he was quite significant in her life, having created the environments she lived in. When she had her car accident, he came to the hospital several times. He was genuinely upset that she had injured herself. In those days she would phone him every day and he would phone her. They were clearly very close friends. So it was shattering to her when the events surrounding the sale of the Blue Princess necklace were revealed. Janet commented, 'It's very sad to me because I obviously made a bit of a fool of myself with the Heytesbury people ... he was one companion who shared a huge part of my life for quite a long time who just suddenly disappeared. Awful. He used to just make me laugh so much'.

Immediately after Robert died, one of the things on Janet's mind was the Blue Princess necklace. She felt guilty that she hadn't worn it and she didn't like it. Her comment to me when she showed me a picture of the necklace the day after the funeral was, 'Robert must have loved me to have given me this'.

Robert had bought the Neela Rani (Blue Princess) necklace on 11 April 1984, at Christie's in New York for $1.86 million. It had been part of the estate of the flamboyant eccentric millionaire, Florence Gould, and was certainly operatic in its proportions. Gould reputedly draped her Pekinese dogs in pearls, and her taste for a chain composed of double rows of diamond baguettes, terminating in a cluster of three single blue sapphires with a pendant of no less than 114 carats encircled by a white ribbon of round brilliants was certainly different from Janet's. In fact, the necklace stayed in a New York bank vault until 1993, two years after Robert's death, when it was flown to Perth to be put back together, as Janet had taken a couple of stones out.

A year after Robert's death, Janet asked Rod Kelly to help her find a buyer for the necklace. Valuations by Cartier's and Sotheby's in New York were seen to be too low, and he suggested Charles Mills-Edward who worked for Jogia Diamonds, located near his Nedlands antique shop, might have some useful contacts. In fact, Mills-Edward did not work there, was in trouble with the law and had been arrested in April 1992 on charges of fraud, a month after

Janet appointed him as her agent. Basing her decision purely on Rod Kelly's advice, she believed the sale was in train. She agreed to pay Mills-Edward a 12% commission on the sale. By mid-1992, Mills-Edward reported that a person in Singapore was interested in the necklace and they should meet. In need of money himself, he desperately wanted to make the trip and clinch the sale but, because his passport had been confiscated, he was forced to appoint as his sub-agent a Perth diamond broker called Robert Embling. He, too, was a man of dubious integrity, who also came under investigation for fraud and would later flee the country after a $100,000 judgment was made against him over another diamond deal. His whereabouts are still unknown. But at the time he had the needed contacts.

The delay had been annoying Janet, and Rod Kelly told her he would take over. His status as her agent was a key to the later dispute, with Kelly claiming he had merely intended to 'chivvy along' the first agent, Mills-Edward, and suggesting that final responsibility for the sale rested with Robert Embling who took over from Mills-Edward. Nevertheless, Embling and Kelly went to Singapore in July 1992 and reached an agreement with a Dr Hussein Talaat and a Mr Jogani to purchase the necklace on behalf of the Emir of Qatar for $US7 million or $AUS9.8 million. This price was not disclosed to Janet. Heytesbury arranged for Brinks Security to deliver the necklace to Qatar on 20 January 1993. Janet had insisted the payment be made by bank cheque. Kelly took with him to Qatar his own lawyer, Tim Whittington (for a fee of $2,000 a day), and Robert Embling. Here the deception gathered pace.

Dr Hussein Talaat had arranged with his nephew Redha Abdu-Jassem Al Zuhairi, to dress in flowing black-and-gold robes (bought at the local bazaar in Doha, the capital of Qatar), and pose as representatives of the Emir of Qatar. In an extraordinary meeting on 21 January 1993, in the Sheraton Hotel in Doha, Kelly, Embling and Whittington were naively blinded by the apparent power and wealth of these two imposters. Talaat told the Australians that the Emir was too sick to meet them in their private suite and had sent his personal secretary in his place. Kelly and Embling handed over the Blue Princess necklace in return for five cheques, all made out to Kelly.

One cheque for $4.9 million was for Kelly's payment to Janet for the necklace, one made out to Kelly for $2.8 million was to cover his self-determined commission for setting up the sale, and three cheques totalling $2.1 million (which Kelly blithely endorsed over to Talaat) were for his role as agent to the Emir of Qatar. The cheques, which were handed over in a brown paper envelope, were duds, with the signatures forged by Redha. Kelly did query the fact that they were personal cheques drawn on an unknown company, Biyat International Group, but the imposters feigned outrage at the expectation of asking the Emir for a bank cheque, claiming 'It would be like asking the Queen of England for a bank cheque. In any case, the Emir owns the bank on which the cheques are drawn', (which turned out to be Citibank in Dubai). There was no further demur and the conspirators departed in all their finery, having successfully duped the team from Perth. Kelly later claimed, under cross-examination, that he had been out of his depth at the meeting. He was conned, totally and utterly.

Talaat flew immediately to Vienna, drove to Switzerland, and deposited the necklace in a bank vault in Zurich, where it would remain until Heytesbury staff tracked it down. Meanwhile, pleased with their deal, Kelly and Whittington flew to the Isle of Man to bank the cheques in Kelly's account, then to London to report to Janet. But Kelly told her the necklace had been sold for $4.9 million, not mentioning the other cheques. He had no answer to her annoyance that they had not obtained cleared funds via a bank cheque, as instructed. He was even more devastated when the cheques bounced and, when she was informed, Janet's fury hit new levels. Kelly and Whittingham met Talaat again in Singapore on 31 January 1993, to challenge him over the cheques and Talaat smoothly assured them that everything would be all right, with a little patience. He said the Emir had been offended because he had been asked for a special clearance so he had cancelled the cheques.

But months passed with no word from Talaat about the money or the necklace. With the realisation that the necklace had been stolen, an international search began. Lawyer Karl Paganin, acting for

Heytesbury, flew to Austria and Switzerland in September 1993 and offered Talaat $US50,000 cash for the return of the necklace. Talaat said Jassem's price would be $US500,000. But Jassem was arrested by Qatar authorities in October and confessed his role in the scam to police, naming Talaat as the mastermind behind the scam. Paganin hired Austrian lawyers to find Talaat. When police searched his apartment they found keys to a safety deposit box. A negotiation with Talaat's lawyer to recover the necklace led to the opening of the safety deposit box in Zurich and a payment by Heytesbury of $US100,000, an amount equivalent to the cost of a legal tussle if Talaat refused to cooperate. The necklace was recovered after a sixteen-month international search which Heytesbury estimated cost the company $900,000. Heytesbury then issued a damages writ against Rod Kelly in the Western Australian Supreme Court to recover its costs.

The necklace was finally sold at auction in Geneva for $1.9 million and Heytesbury was awarded $633,915 in damages against Rod Kelly, with the Court finding Kelly had breached 'his fiduciary duty to Heytesbury by allowing his personal interests to conflict with his duty to act in Heytesbury's best interests'. With costs and interest, Kelly paid Heytesbury more than $1 million.

Janet was pleased with the outcome, but devastated by the loss of a friend who had been so important in her life. Darrel Jarvis maintained that Heytesbury staff believed Rod Kelly had been taking advantage of her friendship for years but said nothing because she enjoyed his company. It's a patronising view that does not allow for the important personal support Kelly gave Janet in times of great need. The incident, however, was revealing about her because, despite initial advice that Heytesbury should not pursue the matter and should accept the loss, she was willing to face public scrutiny for what she considered were 'the importance of high standards of conduct and ethics in Heytesbury's business dealings'.

Heytesbury did need all the money it could assemble at that time but as well Janet felt utterly betrayed by Rod Kelly. In the end she believed Justice Ipps's decision vindicated her actions and the publicity, which was by no means all negative. At its height, John Holland employees at Port Hedland presented her with a phoney

Blue Princess necklace which a joker had made from steel washers studded with sequins. She wore it with great style and keeps it as a memento.

The saga of the Blue Princess was to contribute to a growing view about Janet that she was a fighter and a woman to be reckoned with. The Subiaco affair was another if less exotic example of her steely resolve. Heytesbury had purchased long-term leasehold property in this Perth suburb in 1988 as a speculative venture for a housing development. Protracted negotiations with the Council to find a solution to the proposed development failed, so Heytesbury decided to build a new corporate headquarters building there. The Subiaco Council denied the planning application. Heytesbury then refused to pay the rent on the leases. Subiaco accused Heytesbury of refusing to pay rent amounting to $1.2 million by June 1997. Defamation action was taken by Heytesbury against both the Council and its mayor, Tony Costa, for describing them in a public press release as 'neither a good tenant nor a good ratepayer'. In the mayor's view, the proposal did not comply with the lease or planning requirements for the area and was rejected, with Heytesbury making 'no effort to put forward an alternative proposal'.[16] In Heytesbury lawyer Karl Paganin's view, they had no obligation to pay since Council had put a stop to any development at all. By June 1997, instead, Heytesbury purchased a major residential development site in east Perth, where it is building its new offices as well as residential apartments. The defamation trial concluded on 12 June 1998 with Heytesbury awarded $5,000 damages after a Supreme Court judge agreed the company's reputation had been besmirched.[17] Litigation continues over the rent.

Fueling the more hard-line Holmes à Court image, the *Australian Financial Review Magazine* presented Janet on the cover in a most uncharacteristic pose, looking very severe but looking like the fighter she is.[18]

For Janet the fight for Heytesbury goes on. Keeping such diverse businesses together will never be a straightforward matter. Her goal is not to build a dynasty as it was with Robert – the goal is to make a social difference. Someone with Janet's social views might have chosen politics to make a difference, but she chose Heytesbury.

Her unexpected inheritance presented her with the vehicle to attempt to improve people's lives through enterprise. And this unusual approach in these tough economic times binds people to her. Keith Drew, managing director of John Holland, says the biggest part she has played is through her 'sheer determination'.

I think a lot of people would have given up and sold John Holland but she stuck with her vision ... I was advising the board and advising Janet of the difficulties that were within John Holland in early 1995. The easiest solution would have been to sell it before they came out and hit the headlines ... John Holland is a group of people, not an asset, not a fixed asset, not a building, it's the people. There were four companies clamouring to buy in 1995 and into 1996 but she was telling the buyers to go away. And that's the difference, that determination, the long-term vision to say no. She's sure you can operate with ethics, with high safety standards.

Janet is not interested in just making more money. The quality of life she is looking for is to own John Holland as a quality company. And she is a risk taker, prepared to take risks with the company assets in pursuit of a longer-term goal. This is what has kept certain senior managers committed to Heytesbury, but it was also what has made her family nervous and ultimately led to Darrel Jarvis's departure and the board restructure.

In recent times she has diverted her enthusiasm for political causes into the move for an Australian Republic. She has long been a supporter of a new flag and she wants to see the Union Jack removed from the Australian flag. At the Stud she flies a blue flag with the Southern Cross only and she frequently wears a dark blue T-shirt sporting the Southern Cross. As a director of Ausflag, she opened an exhibition of alternative Australian flags at the National Gallery in Canberra during the February 1998 Constitutional Convention stating, 'I believe we need a flag which represents us and which people can recognise as being ours'.

Janet led the Western Australian ticket for candidates for the Constitutional Convention. She topped the vote in that State and joined the 152 delegates for ten days in Canberra. Her speech and comments were highlighted in the media and when the final decision resulted in a decision to hold a referendum, an emotional moment for the Republican supporters, Janet's tears were photographed for all to see on the front page of major newspapers in Australia and the UK. In the West, the *Sunday Times*, under the banner headline, 'Janet Call',[19] reported that Western Australians who took part in a national *Quadrant* poll favoured Janet as the first President. She was fourth in a national poll, which was headed by old friend Paul Keating.

Janet will be one of the staunchest supporters of an Australian Republic and one of a few in the business world prepared to take a lead role in the debate. She is passionate about the cause and her emotion surfaces easily. Likewise when she launched the Russell Drysdale Exhibition at the National Gallery of Victoria in December 1997 she described the exhibition as 'The Australian equivalent of the Sistine Chapel' and was moved to tears. In referring to the discussions over the republic, reconciliation and land rights, she went on to say, 'It is the perfect exhibition for us in this country at this time', reminding us of what is quintessentially Australian about this place and its people.[20]

Following the Constitutional Convention, Janet's name was floated by supporters as a more appropriate and more appealing leader of the Australian Republican Movement than Malcolm Turnbull. Turnbull consolidated his support and Janet demurred, but her enthusiasm for the cause is undiminished. She will be there fighting with all the passion she can muster for a new nation in the new millennium.

Meanwhile the future of Heytesbury and its businesses took on a different dimension as the conflicting interests of its young shareholders took centre stage.

FACING THE FUTURE

It was inevitable that Robert and Janet's four children, all of whom had grown up in very unusual circumstances, encouraged to be independent from a very early age, and the heirs to their father's fortune in equal shares (one sixth each with Janet owning one third), would eventually have their say. They were young and inexperienced when Robert died in 1990 – Peter, Catherine, Simon and Paul were twenty-one, twenty, eighteen and seventeen respectively. They had been willing to sign over their voting rights to their mother and leave the management of the company in her hands. By the end of 1996, six years after their father's death, they were all university graduates. Peter was a theatrical producer. He had married New York lawyer Divonne Jarecki on 17 June 1995; she is now his business partner in Back Row Productions based in New York. Catherine, after graduating from Oxford, had remained in London to work and gain experience in the Stoll Moss theatre business. Simon, always a computer buff, was engaged to Katrina von Muller-Harteneck, an Australian musician and student of opera. He was planning to live in San Francisco and work in Silicon Valley. Paul, who had completed an undergraduate degree from Middlebury College in the United States, was dabbling in a law degree which he later dropped when he purchased an old fire station in Cottesloe, Perth, to renovate as a restaurant and artists' think-tank.

Apart from the relationship between Simon and Paul, the children had never been close. They did, however, come together over their opposition to the way Heytesbury was being managed by Darrel Jarvis with their mother's compliance. Over the next twelve months their opposition to their mother's business strategy for Heytesbury would harden as they insisted Darrel must leave the company and that Heytesbury must divest itself of the high-risk businesses of construction and beef. After considerable heartache and grief, Janet faced the reality of their demands and considered her options. She could not continue to operate Heytesbury with the free hand she had had since Robert's death. She had thrown herself into the task and worked hard to consolidate the businesses and divest Heytesbury of debt, which she believed was the best approach for Heytesbury and the family, but that period was drawing to a close.

There are few family companies that survive the passing of the years and the different views new generations bring with their own expanding families and their conflicting interests. Problems that arise over the years include dealing with individuals, solving business problems and rationalising inefficient or bloated structures. In a study of 1,400 family businesses conducted by Victoria University in 1993 only 30% were found to survive to the second generation, with succession the major cause of family business failure.[1] Recently, the Smorgon family sold off several hundred million dollars worth of assets after the family's second generation stepped aside from day-to-day management[2] and Frank Lowy sold a $460 million slice of his company to reduce its interest to 30%, citing the fact that he had 'ten grandchildren coming up through the ranks and they may wish to pursue other opportunities'.[3]

In these family businesses the patriarch had not died and his vision had been well established with the children able to mature and grow into the business under the direction of its founder. Kerry

Packer learnt this way and so have Rupert Murdoch's three children. Robert Holmes à Court had not left a legacy of operating businesses with which his children were entirely familiar. The business talk they heard was scant, and mainly about the bottom line, the only measure of success being revenue growth and acquisitions. This approach was in the air they breathed, despite their mother's diverse social and creative interests. The broader family was not involved and had little practical experience in running business enterprises. The Albany Woollen Mill, Bell Transport, WA Newspapers and TVW7, were peripheral to Robert's main agenda of takeovers and they knew the deal was what he valued. Robert never felt so attached to a business that he would not walk away at the right price. He would not retain a business for sentimental reasons or because he enjoyed running it. He did not have printer's ink under his fingernails.

It was Janet's vision to run the diverse Heytesbury businesses and to build them as successful enterprises by employing people to create wealth through production. Far more than Robert, she was the one who came to identify with each business and the people who ran them. Janet believed she acted in the best interests of her children when she allowed them to make their own career choices, something it is unlikely their father would have done, Robert might not have seen his eldest son as a theatrical producer. But Janet's open-minded approach to her sons' career interests eventually came to be viewed by them as a lack of interest in them.

At the time of Peter's marriage to Divonne Jarecki, the Holmes à Court family appeared as close as they had ever been. Peter and Divonne married at Glenprairie homestead, a plum cattle station property which Darrel Jarvis had negotiated to purchase on Robert's behalf in 1990, during his first year at Heytesbury. The wedding came at the end of the week when Janet had been honoured as an Officer in the Order of Australia for her services to business, the arts and the community. Janet had spent considerable effort organising the wedding and the festivities extended over a weekend. The service was conducted under a clear blue sky with a cool breeze blowing. The speeches were eloquent. Janet welcomed her new and first daughter-in-law and Peter described his mother as 'The most amazing woman who had made this occasion the most perfect wedding'. It was difficult to imagine on that weekend how events would unfold over the next three years for Janet and her family. 1995 had seemed to be a positive turning point for the Heytesbury enterprises. But as the financial disasters of 1996 unfolded and the Karriview management conference at the end of that year fell into disarray, the bottom line on the balance sheet told the story. Janet's family took note and discussions intensified.

Newly-married, Peter Holmes à Court was impatient for success and not interested in working in a hands-on way to learn the theatre business, as someone like Cameron Mackintosh had done. Peter had some tough lessons early. Billy Boesky's[4] rock and roll musical, *Fallen Angel,* was Peter's first off-Broadway show, which he put together in 1994. It stayed open three weeks and lost most of Peter's available capital and that of some investors close to home who weren't happy with the result. He also burst upon the Australian scene attempting too much too quickly with some negative financial results. Peter beat a hasty retreat and, with Darrel's advice, was able to regroup, but he has chosen as his career a very risky business where fortunes may be made or lost quite dramatically. Both Heytesbury and the experience and connections Peter is able to tap within Stoll Moss have contributed to the reputation he is gradually acquiring. He was able to bring Jerry Seinfeld to London where the show 'beat the one-day ticket sales record at London's Palladium Theatre [a Stoll Moss theatre] by £87,000'.[5] Nevertheless, Peter arguably needs access to his inheritance to succeed as a successful theatrical entrepreneur, and sooner rather than later.

Simon was not interested in being involved in the Heytesbury businesses, nor was he in urgent need of funds to run a business but he married Katrina on the island of Hydra, Greece, on 20 June 1997, and they were planning to buy a home in San Francisco. More importantly, Simon was highly antagonistic to Darrel Jarvis and ready to align himself with Paul, especially after the debacle with Darrel which followed the management conference at Karriview. At that time, Paul saw Heytesbury as 'being destroyed by the minute'. He had absolutely no faith in the processes Darrel and

Janet were setting up and, living in Perth, he was in a position to witness Darrel's influence on his mother at close range. Of Darrel he said, 'That man won't change'. The boys came together to rid the company of Darrel Jarvis and to regain the voting shares they had relinquished to their mother.

At the time of Robert's death the shareholding structure in Heytesbury had been reorganised. A private company, Trebor Investments, was established and issued with new A class shares, which held all the voting rights and were controlled by Janet. All of the existing ordinary shares were then converted to B class shares which were non-voting shares.[6] The voting structure could only be altered with the consent of 75% of votes of the B class shareholders, meaning Janet would have to agree to any change. The four children together could not alter the structure as they held only 66% of the B class shares. Janet thus had full voting control of Heytesbury through her control of the A class shares and the ordinary shares were stripped of their voting rights. The Articles of Association were later amended so that if one of the family wished to sell any of their shares in Heytesbury, they had first to offer their shares to the other shareholders in equal proportions; only if the offer was not taken up could they sell their interest outside the family.

The children's view was that Janet held the A class shares in trust for them, while Janet had said she was pursuing the business strategy in the interests of her family. The purpose of the structure at the time was to give the banks confidence that Janet had unimpeded management control. Peter contended that it was no accident that Robert did not make a will. He believed his father intended his children would hold a majority stake and that their mother would not have full authority. But none of the sons appeared to be concerned about the position their father had placed their mother in with his final game after her twenty-five years of loyal devotion to him. Robert, as he had done so often in life, had refused to clarify an ambiguous situation. He had equipped no one to deal with the highly charged and conflicting legacy he left behind. The children and Janet were left to follow their instincts and needs, and these differed greatly one to the other.

As time passed Janet became less interested in establishing a dynasty than she was in the dynamics of the current business operations and in those she worked with. She considered the risks in businesses like construction and beef were ones worth taking. Her sons did not agree and they wanted their voting rights returned to them so that they could have a meaningful say in the future of the Group.

Catherine was the obstacle in the way of their plan. She told her brothers that under no circumstance would she join with them to unseat their mother over the issue of the voting shares but, like them, she had had enough of Darrel Jarvis and his management style. In early 1997 in London, Darrel had met with Catherine and suggested he wanted to restructure Heytesbury and phase himself out in three years time. He appeared to be inviting her to be his protege but she did not want to be sucked into any tactic of dividing and conquering the family. Darrel had laid out detailed financial information on Heytesbury's current situation which she questioned closely, to his discomfort. At the end of their meeting Darrel tore up the paper on which he had been writing into one inch squares. He knew he had lost Catherine. She later agreed to join her brothers at a meeting with Janet to insist Darrel must go.

At this time, April 1997, there was turmoil in Heytesbury. Several senior staff were privy to the boys' plans and the uncertainty about the future was affecting company morale. The boys took action. Coinciding with a shareholders' meeting which was to be held in the UK, they arranged a weekend in the country to meet with Janet. The location was Tylney Hall, a privately-owned English country house in Rotherwick, Hampshire. Faithfully restored in 1985, it had the style of a grand baronial mansion with modern amenities and extensive grounds. Present for the weekend were Janet, Peter, Catherine, Simon, Paul, Divonne (Peter's wife), Katrina (at that time Simon's fiance), Rob Mather (Catherine's boyfriend), and myself. I had been invited by Peter and, knowing the background to the meeting, I was concerned for Janet's well-being and the manner in which they might conduct the meeting. Janet had no idea what was planned.

On the evening of Friday, 18 April, the family dined at a pub some distance from Tylney Hall and on the return walk Janet twisted her ankle sharply. It became swollen and for the rest of the weekend she had to contend with the physical discomfort from her ankle as well as the mental anguish which followed a frank presentation to her of her children's views. Through it all Janet sat with her head bowed; she did not argue, but the physical shock was profound.

Janet and I drove back to London together early on the morning of Monday, 22 April, where Janet met with Darrel and with members of the Heytesbury board, Alec Mairs and Graeme Scott. Darrel sat at the table and after some discussion said, 'You've failed, Janet. You've failed to reach your dream. It's all over'. It was a devastating time for Janet. To top it off, that evening she received a phone call from her son Paul who had returned to Australia to say there had been a call from a man to the Sydney *Daily Telegraph* classified advertisements' section with a death threat to Janet. The police were taking it seriously. It had been an historic week but she was not defeated.

Janet felt guilty about Darrel and her family's determination that he should leave Heytesbury. She felt she had egged him on just as she had Robert and Darrel did nothing to relieve Janet's feelings of guilt. But it could not be said, no matter what Janet's urgings, that Robert and Darrel did not run their own race. Janet agreed with her children that Darrel would go but he would go in the time-frame she determined and that time was not now. By mid-May she had informed the key players it was 'business as usual'. She remained loyal to Darrel long after her family had given her notice.

But the die was cast; the Heytesbury she had dreamed of and worked for was no longer feasible. The boys' larger agenda had been made clear. They would not be part of a company with such a high-risk profile and they wanted their voting rights which they considered belonged to them and so that they could have their say in the running of the company. At their instigation, and within a short time, independent directors joined the board – David Karpin, appointed as deputy chairman on 18 August 1997, was joined by Brian Finn on 14 July 1998, and Catherine, representing the family, joined on 9 April 1998. Peter joined the board of Stoll Moss on 1 May 1998. Darrel worked very hard to restore his position, but left Heytesbury on 20 March 1998. Rowena Stretton, who had made a special study of the Holmes à Court family business, speculated publicly on the reasons, with a little help from an unidentified source.[7] A protracted negotiation followed about the value of Darrel's 5% shareholding. Darrel did not trust the boys to give him a fair financial deal. As a disgruntled minority shareholder, through his lawyer, Darrel wrote a stream of letters demanding information. Janet, who had willingly agreed to Darrel's 5% shareholding reward for services to Heytesbury, wanted the deal honoured. In the end Darrel accepted an offer from her and Catherine to buy his shareholding, and together the two women began to discuss the future they wanted for themselves and Heytesbury with the three boys.

Despite Darrel's departure, Peter, Simon and Paul remained adamant about wanting their voting rights returned to them and about change within Heytesbury. Paul had sold his fire station in Cottesloe in 1998 after closing the restaurant, and enrolled in a Securities Institute course. There are parallels with his father's path in the interests he has chosen to follow, including the running of a restaurant. Several people have commented he is his father all over again (without the patience). Paul became a director of the board of Heytesbury on 2 February 1999.

The plans for a new CEO for Heytesbury went on hold as the family negotiated their different plans for the company and Janet stepped into the role of chairman and CEO. John Holland produced a $25.16 million profit in 1997[8] but the options for the company, which had included public fundraising to finance expansion or issuing bonds, now included Heytesbury's exit from the company. The Asian financial crisis has ensured John Holland Asia will have difficulties for a time (and the crisis has affected the cattle trade adversely). However, Keith Drew, the managing director of John Holland, remains upbeat about it's prospects. John Holland marks its fiftieth anniversary in 1999 and the company will, he says, 'most definitely make a profit, but it will be less than the $25 million for 1997, after mark-downs for Asia ... the company has $1.5 billion of work in hand'.[9] The Stoll Moss theatre business was also swinging along, with the refurbished theatres looking wonderful and a show in every one. The company was supporting new product, new writers, new directors. When Janet attended performances in London people came up to thank her for her contribution to the West End. Vasse Felix Winery was doing very well as the producer of some of Australia's best wine and plans for expansion included a performance space and gallery – a concept that illustrated Janet's belief in the integration of business with the arts.

At September 1998, the Group's net asset position was $267 million, comprised of solid, income-producing assets which were all supported by recent valuations at a conservative gearing level of 1.53 times net tangible assets to debt.

In practical terms, Janet has brought Heytesbury from potential receivership to a position where an orderly disposal of the Group's assets meant all shareholders would be substantial beneficiaries. She has taken risks along the way in pursuit of her vision but she believed in the goals she had set for Heytesbury and she did not spare herself in working for their achievement.

A Heytesbury venture with Malaysian Airlines in November 1998 exemplified what Janet enjoys doing best. Aboriginal art works worth $300,000 – including silk batiks – from Janet's private collection went on show in Kuala Lumpur with musicians and actors accompanying the exhibition, which had been instigated by Dario Amara of John Holland Asia. The mix of art and business continue to demonstrate the diversity of Janet's activities. These are the successes. While Janet was facing the difficult decisions she had to take both as a businesswoman and as a mother, she still made time in late 1998 to fight for the Black Swan Theatre Company, then in a funding crisis; to speak out against the One Nation Party and Hansonism prior to the October 1998 election; and to work for the Australian Republican Movement. But how she would shape the next phase of her life was weighing heavily on her mind.

As I attempted to conclude this story I sat with Janet to talk about where she saw herself after her eight-year journey since Robert's death. I told her about the issues I had been tracking, including the questions outlined in the introduction. She laughed and said, 'What makes you think I know the answers to those questions?'. Unlike most people she does not dwell on such issues.

Janet grew up in a most unorthodox, somewhat bohemian Australian family, her childhood occurred during the Cold War when socialists such as her parents were ostracised and victimised for their strong views. Bern and Fred Ranford were good people, they lived according to their values, committed to the welfare of their fellow human beings. Janet absorbed their beliefs, and she absorbed her mother's work ethic and desire to please others. She also learned to live a dual existence within and outside a family who believed in political views that were misunderstood in the wider world. She moved easily in both worlds and grew in confidence, never questioning her ability to do whatever was needed or to take on whatever opportunities came her way.

She retained the work ethic, despite the enormous wealth and affluent lifestyle Robert provided. She clearly has no desire to stop working, and as a fifth-generation Australian she feels a sense of responsibility and obligation to the community and to her country. She loves the company of others, has a strong need to be loved, and she has a fun-loving nature. Very early in her life Janet developed a liking for men. There was nothing untoward in this. She became attached to several of her parents' friends and enjoyed a closer bond with some of the men than they shared with their own daughters. They talked to her, they encouraged her, they expanded her dreams, and Janet was comfortable with them.

Having lived an unusual childhood and youth, exposed to unorthodox views and values and having experienced a life different from the norm, she was open to the older Rhodesian, the adventurer and loner who challenged authority and broke the mould which characterised most of her peers. She wanted a life with this unusual man. Janet married Robert for the very old-fashioned reason that she loved him passionately and he offered her, a vital attractive energetic young woman, the most promise for an interesting, exciting life. She was so anxious to be the chosen one that she made every effort she could to please him. She ran around after him, waited on him, washed his car, drove him around as if she was his chauffeur, minded his mother. Once married, she had savage lessons in what it meant to be Robert's wife. Her lot was made apparent to her and she accepted it, for if she did not meet his expectations Robert could be incredibly cold and disapproving. He had no need to use words, his meaning and demands were evident. This was the dark side of Robert, the side Janet never admitted existed, which she tried to hide from others. But the rewards were there as she anticipated; life with Robert was indeed rewarding, the world was their oyster.

Like a true socialist and egalitarian Australian from working-class stock, she was never good with delegating tasks to staff, so she personally worked very hard to organise their married life around Robert's convenience. She put in the hours of servitude, no task was too menial for Janet. Yet she did not resent the role she was given. She admired Robert's brainpower and viewed him as a unique man who was worthy of such devoted attention. In the early years they had fun planning their lives (which were always full), planning their homes, their family, their collections, their lifestyle. They had a good time. With so many plans they were never short of things to talk about and never happier than when walking around the Stud together. Janet also kept Robert amused with her laughter and zest for life. It suited him that Janet was a social asset but also a hard worker. And together they worked. They were always working towards Robert's fulfilling his ambitions, with Janet diligently paving his way. Life with Robert was always focused, always purposeful. If he was socially isolated, Janet found her social life, her personal social needs, through daytime friends and voluntary committees. She may have been offered the roles she had in these organisations because she was Robert Holmes à Court's wife, but she used those positions to further her humanitarian causes. Her committees and all she gave them in terms of her energy, enthusiasm, time and commitment, were a kind of balance against the pursuit with her husband of greater glory and success in the business world.

The wealth they acquired did not bother Janet despite her socialist leanings. She did not feel rich and there was never much cash as such. The day came when she understood that there was nothing in the world she wanted that she couldn't have, and that day she ceased wanting things. She dressed simply, often wearing the same clothes over and over for convenience, and they entertained only for business purposes.

Janet was not a reluctant partner in Robert's enterprises. She encouraged Robert and she urged him on to bigger takeovers. She was proud of his pursuit of BHP, the Big Australian. She had grown up in a household that believed that company was untouchable. For Janet it was exciting and stimulating, an extraordinary idea to think that her husband could take over and control BHP, the ultimate company icon to beat all the icons which had born the scars of her husband's assault on them – including the Bell Group in Western Australia, the Herald and Weekly Times, Elders IXL, Ansett. For Janet, the daughter of two socialists, who grew up in a home environment where big business was the enemy and her father used to sing to her, 'Elders Smith the Company Limited/Robbers, thieves and vagabonds', there was delicious irony in all of this takeover activity.

But for Robert, the closer he got to his goal of running BHP the less sure he was that he wanted control. Stalking the prey was fun, if very demanding; the kill less satisfying. In retrospect, post-crash Robert believed that going after BHP alone was a mistake. If he had collaborated with a major Sydney institution – CSR or Boral, for example – the outcome could have been different, he very likely would have succeeded in his audacious plan. But that was not Robert's way. He was a loner in business and in life. Defeated by the October 1987 crash, Robert struggled with fatigue and disease to rebuild his fortune, to create what he hoped would be a family dynasty. His greatest fear, expressed in confidence to Janet, was that he would fail to sort out the financial mess he found himself in after the crash. He did not want to fail Janet and his children. Janet did not leave his side during those months while Robert devised the rise of Heytesbury from the financial chaos, exploiting a flawed system of regulation and accountability to its limits in a way he had not done before. This resurrection of the Holmes à Court empire was regarded by some as his greatest achievement. Financially secure once more, Janet began to expand her interests, thriving on her new challenges. But Robert's health and his spirits flagged. On the last day of his life Janet was still encouraging Robert to take over Fairfax but Robert knew better. There would be no more Robert Holmes à Court takeovers.

Janet had never thought about how she would act or what she would do in the event of Robert's death. It was a shock but no surprise. Typically, she never asked herself if she had the skills and experience to take over a business empire and make it a success. She just threw herself into the task. She worked, as always, on instinct. She had no idea what she would do but somehow she would find a way. She felt there was no option. Only gradually did the size of the mess Robert had bequeathed her become clear. The debt level at its peak was $420 million. She was surrounded by non-performing assets that drained the capital she needed to make the Heytesbury enterprises work – expensive jewellery, studs and horses, a 1,000 hectare property at Wallan into which Robert had poured many more millions than its value on fences and artificial lakes, a private island, Grove House, a Manhattan apartment, cars and art (the only collectible Janet ever genuinely cared for). There were no staff in place who could fill Robert's role or advise her effectively, only his loyal attendants who had waited on his word, and done his bidding. They were of little use to Janet in her efforts to run Heytesbury. Janet was on her own.

Robert had replied, when she asked him what would happen if he died without a will, 'Whatever you want to happen'. He was only half-right. The road taken was Janet's choice for a time. She examined her lifestyle and moved to simplify the manner in which she lived. Acquiring further wealth was always Robert's objective, not hers. Wealth under Janet's control meant that she could employ a lot of people; she did not want the trappings, Grove House, a chauffeur-driven Rolls Royce. She wanted direct involvement in what she owned. She threw herself into her obligations and she did what she had always done, she worked hard for her own satisfaction and for her family's future.

She resolved that Robert's enemies would not be her enemies. She liked people, they liked her and would become a resource for Janet to tap. She knew that Robert always tested his ideas widely in conversation after conversation. And Janet learned to do the same. She soaked up advice from everyone she spoke to and she drew on a wide network of people who were already in place. She was never afraid to bare her soul and when ideas made sense to her she would take them on board and make them her own. At the same time she knew whose help she did not want and was quick to reject advisers who did not suit her. People in the business world (mainly men, who held all the key positions), were generous with their assistance and advice. Her social skills made them feel they wanted to help her. This was her major strength at that difficult time and it was unselfconscious, a natural talent. She astounded Robert's coterie in Heytesbury. They could not fathom her, nor could they gain her trust. The tea-lady was taking charge. Janet had to find her own people, her own trusted advisers and confidants.

When the financial precariousness of her position reached crisis point she turned to Darrel Jarvis, another maverick, another who did not fit the mould, yet who happened to be ready and able. For the first years of the nineties he seemed to be just the man for the job. Janet undervalues her own contribution in the revival strategy for Heytesbury. 'Others did it,' she says. But it was Janet who held the bank syndicate together, not Darrel. The bankers did not know what to do with the charming widow who had wide public empathy and support. They did not want the negative publicity that would go with putting the popular widow out of business and she won enough of them over with her passion and commitment to hold them together. It was Janet who motivated the staff; Darrel, who was also highly motivated by Janet, followed her vision. But Janet does not undervalue her enormous stamina, her great powers of recovery, and the energy she gains from other people. These strengths helped her survive.

Janet is energised by people but energises others. Her charisma motivates listeners as she plays to each audience and they respond. She is a great actress, but she performs without an interval for each individual or crowd she encounters in each day. She presents as a personality, her smile will be the widest in the room, but unlike an actress she lives her role. She inspires those around her but most of them know she appreciates what they do. She understands people's difficulties, she knows how hard they work and they know how hard she works. This dynamic has been a major factor within Heytesbury during its trials and tribulations.

But her children were not so inspired. The single biggest disappointment in her post-Robert life has been her inability to get her children to share the future of Heytesbury as she saw it. They were not caught up in the vision and the direction she wanted to take the company and they have been responsible for initiating the next phase in her extraordinary life.

In the Australian community and in our political, cultural and business life, Janet Holmes à Court is a unique figure. Comparisons are difficult to find. Many in the business community have no idea how to evaluate her business performance. She is lauded and honoured for her achievements at the same time as she is criticised for not maximising returns to Heytesbury and expanding the value of the family company. It is unlikely that she will win over 'the big end of town'. From the perspective of the hard nosed economic rationalists, Janet is flaky. After all, isn't the balance sheet the objective measure? Robert always thought it was and his devotees would agree.

On 16 September 1998 Janet added the International Business Council of Western Australia Business Award to her growing list of honorary doctorates, honours and medals, while the *Business Review Weekly* featured the trials of Janet Holmes à Court on the cover of its 9 November 1998 issue. Tim Treadgold, a former employee of Robert's and the man who issued the first Heytesbury press release following Robert's death in 1990 without Janet's approval, the man who told me 'I could see he [son Peter] was going to have to come back to pick up the bones' – wrote confirming his prejudice of the earlier time:

... the true performance of Heytesbury as distinct from the public images, has been far from impressive ... since the handover, Heytesbury has lurched through a series of crises, and repeated

management changes in the operating divisions. Asset sales, rather than business building, seems to have been the central issue at Heytesbury. Selling another slice of John Holland (after selling half of the Asian operation several years ago, and cattle stations, art, cars, jewellery and property) is another disposal about to be portrayed as a win.[10]

This critical piece appeared the day after Janet received the news that a very good friend and companion had died suddenly and at a moment she faced another dramatic loss in her personal life.

Tim Treadgold and others had no confidence in Janet when she took control and they see themselves vindicated by the relatively static bottom line. But if a calculator is all you use to measure success, it will never be possible to understand the nature of Janet's achievements. More than being all smoke and mirrors, Janet's success consists of this: with no previous direct experience of running businesses or enterprises of any kind she survived, and she did more than preserve the bottom line by her wits and her instincts. The asset sell-down reduced debt and resulted in real net assets with growth in John Holland, Stoll Moss and Vasse Felix. Over a seven-year period Janet had done well. She had no training for the role she found herself in. She was not Robert's star business pupil as many assumed. He did little to prepare her and often belittled her capabilities. He was no role model for Janet in the job she had to take on. As a chairman and CEO Robert was not skilled in many areas that might now be regarded as essential for the successful management of diverse and complex businesses; his chief skill was mainly financial. As a voracious learner, Janet immersed herself in Heytesbury and absorbed knowledge, and because of her style and commitment many people wanted to help, though they would have been unlikely to help a man in her position. She made mistakes; purchasing Bell Freight Lines (later renamed Key Transport) was one of them. But despite the problems that came with John Holland she has turned that company around. She bought John Holland for zero dollars. Then, discovering that the company was not the cash cow it was thought to be, Janet stuck with it and despite the turbulence of the construction industry managed to turn the company around dramatically, improving the bottom line, but also changing the work practices and the culture of the enterprise.

Through it all, Janet kept on keeping on and Darrel Jarvis contributed considerably to her development, as did many others. Her achievements are solid. Stoll Moss is thriving. Janet has become 'the Queen of Shaftesbury Avenue'.[11] Vasse Felix is thriving. Debt is at an all time low and Janet was able to sell off assets at a very difficult time, discovering that if you want to buy something it never comes cheaply but when you want to sell, it's a buyer's market. She has earned the respect of those in business who share her values and ideals. In 1999, she joined the board of Australasia's biggest food company, Goodman Fielder Limited, evidence that she is seen as a valued business contributor.

The drought and the Asian downturn had harmed the cattle industry generally. But Heytesbury Beef is the enterprise that has done most damage to the overall balance sheet. (Heytesbury Beef owned 3.28 million hectares and was the eighth largest agricultural landholder in Australia at the end of 1998.[12])

Janet's contribution has always been broader than merely to business. Her cultural contribution includes the preservation of the art of Western Australia and of Aboriginal Australia. In both cases Robert and Janet helped bring to public attention the importance of Australia's heritage and these collections remain intact while many of the expensive paintings Robert acquired have been sold to reduce debt and rationalise the art collection.

Her focus in Stoll Moss theatres has been on restoration of the historic buildings, alongside active involvement in nurturing producers and their productions. Attending all new performances in her theatres, often seeing a play several times, she enjoys mixing with the artists, the producers, writers and actors. Certainly she can hold her own among this cultured elite. Her policies with Stoll Moss and her presence in London have helped enliven and rejuvenate the West End. Her contribution to the arts in Australia is longstanding through her work with the Australian Children's

Television Foundation, the Black Swan Theatre Company, the Perth Festival and, more recently, with the Western Australian Symphony Orchestra. She led the Western Australian arts community in the call to reassess its support of resident arts companies and venues during their financial crisis at the end of 1998[13] and in doing so achieved an opportunity to restructure those companies with a longer-term plan.

Janet is a cultured person in the best sense, a well-rounded individual who espouses a much wider vision than most of her business peers. She makes few donations that are not integral to her life and work, but she will regularly purchase tickets for her employees to attend Black Swan Theatre Company productions or for John Holland construction workers to attend a concert by the Western Australian Symphony Orchestra in Port Hedland. Yet her vision is difficult to sustain in today's economic climate. And she has struggled to reconcile the seeming inconsistencies and incongruities in her life. In that struggle she is like most people, contradictory. Walt Whitman once wrote, 'Do I contradict myself?/Very well then ... I contradict myself;/I am large ... I contain multitudes.'[14] So does Janet.

The one definite assessment it is possible to proffer with confidence about Janet Holmes à Court is that she has been changing all her life. She has played the cards that have been dealt her with skill and panache, with vibrancy and energy as her engine. From her simple, austere, politically-radical background she worked her way to centre stage as the attractive party girl-cum-campus radical. She overcame the feelings of inadequacy that initially overwhelmed her when she moved outside her parents' circle into the formal dining and social whirl of the Perth middle classes, always retaining friends who were unpretentious. But she became what Robert wanted – a social asset and a model wife. She played that role with more conviction than any wife or mother in the American sitcoms that were rampant on television in the sixties. When the time came she remade herself as the leading Australian businesswoman, in the process grappling with the contradictions inherent in her life experience. She has always held on to the values of her parents which were instilled in childhood – a belief in a better deal for Aboriginal people, reconciliation, support for multiculturalism, an independent Australia as a republic, a sustainable environment, an appreciation of learning and the arts and an egalitarian approach to everyone she meets. People are surprised to find that someone with such a high profile is so down-to-earth and so lacking in the arrogance that commonly comes with power.

Robert was comfortable with a wife expressing these social views, so apparently at odds with his own. As an outsider himself, such a wife added to his mystique and her views didn't cost him any significant amount of money. However, for such values to be propounded by Janet as the chairman of a company that was deeply in debt was a different matter altogether. They did not sit well with the Liberal or the business establishment and Janet was forced to watch her P's and Q's as she moved from wife to business leader. She had to court the banks and her likelihood of winning them over would lessen if she were to lead peace marches down St George's Terrace in Perth.

As the Heytesbury chairman, Janet could not bite the hand that fed her, she had to demonstrate she was responsible, more like one of the establishment. It was fortunate for Janet that there was a Labor Federal Government in power at the time; that the then Prime Minister Paul Keating, who admired Robert, was an ally; that a sympathetic government appointed her to the Reserve Bank – an appointment which, while criticised by the establishment, brought Janet further status, respectability and the opportunity to learn and to extend her networks.

The Labor government of the time was, like Janet, trying to reinvent itself – a government with traditional ALP values but in bed with the corporate world. In that way, Janet's membership of the Reserve Bank was consistent with her expression of the ideals of reconciliation, ecology, republicanism and social welfare. The greater conflict for her came from within Heytesbury where the need to restructure, and later to downsize, meant turning her back on former loyal employees and moving on. It would have been impossible to live with Robert Holmes à Court for twenty-five years as a close observer and participant in his business and personal dealings and not absorb some of his steely resolve. That steel is within Janet, adding to the complexity of her character. If Janet is charismatic, can inspire loyalty, productivity and admiration, she can and also does walk away from people, friends and employees when she believes the situation demands that of her. In a global business world where many business leaders manage by fear, Janet's style is unusual but, on any enlightened assessment, desirable.

There are those who argue this style is flawed, it has failed to achieve results. But history will evaluate these results at the time the economic rationalists fall from grace, as they will surely do. Financial journalists often have short-term memories and short-term visions. They adopt the rhetoric which is fashionable at the time, it's easier to write stories that way. Robert played these journalists like an orchestra when he was at his height and they must claim a large share of the responsibility for making heroes of the entrepreneurial cowboys of the eighties – Skase, Bond, Connell, Herscu, Elliott, Holmes à Court et al. Only in hindsight did those journalists expose their heroes' shortcomings and the damage they did to the social, business and financial systems. Some of these same journalists write just as superficially about today's era of economic rationalism. But a most unlikely critic is now pointing out the social fallout from the damage being done to hundreds of millions of people around the world by the unregulated global capitalist system's manipulation of the market. George Soros, the financier and philanthropist who is one of the biggest speculators and money manipulators, has written recently to warn of the threat to social democracy of the untrammelled market in money. 'As a market participant I try to maximise my profits. As a citizen I am concerned about social values: peace, justice, freedom or whatever. I cannot give expression to those values as a market participant.'[15] He says of publicly-owned international corporations, 'Severe competition will not allow them to pay much heed to social concerns . . . they will not be able to afford to maintain employment to the detriment of profits'.[16]

Janet is wrestling with the same dilemmas of principle. Her vision for Heytesbury as a company which puts people first has foundered because of the pressing demand to grow the bottom line. She wants to manage her businesses in the interest of her employees and the wider community. She believes that profits will follow. Her dilemma is expressed by a growing number of writers, thinkers and politicians who, like her, are searching for a solution, a better way, a third way (as British Prime Minister Tony Blair has expressed it), one which draws on the ideologies of both left and right and attempts to redress the failure of political systems to reconcile social and economic policy.

In Janet's search to make sense of a world where business accommodates her social values, she has turned to the writings of Robert Theobald[17] and John Ralston Saul[18], both leading critics of economic rationalism and the social destruction being caused by corporatism. Theobald in particular, whom Janet has met, presents a view she shares – that of rebuilding communities, of sustainable economic development, of a simpler life which is anti-consumerism and which restores the relationship between individuals and democracy.

Janet would like to be part of a social movement that tries to translate these ideas into action – a movement that is indeed underway following Theobald's 1998 visit to Australia when forty people met in Sydney to establish 'conversations and actions for the twenty-first century'. Janet believes she can help drive social change. Remaining an optimist who believes individual action can contribute to a better future, she is attracted to the big issues, to broad scale world renewal. While the details are for others to attend to, she is quite plainly capable of being an inspirational leader. Underpinning all is a desire to contribute, a need to make a mark. And in the process of exploration, of searching for a future role, once again Janet is changing. Such an ability to change and reinvent herself is rare and has been fascinating to observe. She is a work in progress, someone who cannot be easily categorised, and if she could be, with little conviction that she will stay that way in the future.

In contemporary business life there are few to whom she might be compared, but Katharine Graham comes to mind – the owner of the *Washington Post* who in her autobiography revealed a disarmingly self-effacing person.[19] She too was widowed early, at fifty-four, when her husband, who ran the *Washington Post*, took his own life and was technically intestate.[20] She, too, had to remake her life. In her case, she took over the business of the *Post* and learned to run it successfully, relying on the advice of the strongminded men around her. One in particular, the editor, Ben Bradlee, was to define the course of the *Post's* famous history in publishing the Pentagon Papers and the disclosures surrounding Watergate and the subsequent resignation of President Richard Nixon. Katharine Graham succeeded by trusting her instincts with people, working alongside them and treading a very tough and rocky business path.

Although Katherine Graham, like Janet Holmes à Court, had suffered severe misgivings about her own competence (which were reinforced by her husband), feeling inadequate to cope with all of the problems she faced, and sometimes even feeling that she was being made to pay for surviving, she reinvented herself, becoming one of Washington's major power-brokers. When the *Post* became a public company, Graham confesses she knew little about Wall Street or what was required of her and was fearful of speaking to financial analysts. She made a friend of Warren Buffet (the legendary investor and one of the most wealthy men in the world) who, after he bought into the *Post,* became her confidante and main financial adviser.

Both Janet Holmes à Court and Katharine Graham ably remade themselves, with some help from supportive figures. When Robert died people were primarily interested in Janet because she was Robert's wife. Now they are interested in Janet herself. She has achieved her new authority by force of personality more than any business accomplishments. She has an extensive network of opinion leaders to call on for advice and ideas and she collects ideas like a bower bird. A great proselytiser and champion of the people whose ideas she respects, she will often purchase multiple copies of books to send to friends or clip articles from papers and magazines to spread around.

Janet is a very much more seasoned, confident and resilient person than when Robert died, made of much sterner stuff than her family and colleagues might have imagined. That she can, and does repeatedly, turn her losses into triumphs is no accident. She has not had a run of good luck – quite the contrary. But she has the affection and goodwill of many people for the fundamental reason that she is a genuinely charming, gregarious personality with a love of people and their potential. Hers is an intelligence which happens to have a very different orientation from that of her late husband Robert or his business peers. It is an intelligence that human development experts are only beginning to recognise and study – emotional and social intelligence.[21] Robert, like many men, particularly businessmen of the recent past, was sadly lacking in such fundamentals. Yet with Janet by his side he was far more powerful and competent. The question has to be asked, who made who?

AFTERWORD

In 1997 the Australian Children's Television Foundation celebrated its fifteenth birthday. Don Edgar had seen his wife leave home in a red jacket but had to wait until Patricia and I had appeared together on the *Today* show to know I was in blue. Shortly after our interview, astonishing flowers were delivered to the Foundation offices – red for Patricia, and delphiniums, irises, hydrangeas and agapanthus for me. Patricia's card read – 'To my best mate'. Mine – 'To my best mate's best mate'.

Patricia has written in her foreword that this is a book by a friend about a friend. Friend, mate – Patricia even told me once she was my pal, a word I associate with canine dietary requirements. But friend she has been – twice she has flown across Australia to comfort me on the loss of a partner, and once comforted me at a family meeting I would not wish on any mother.

The writing of this book has been difficult for us both. At times I have had to beg for a rest from the questioning. Attempting to fathom why at fifteen, twenty-five, thirty-five or forty-five I did this or that has been extraordinarily difficult and, at times, harrowing – particularly as I did so little 'fathoming' at the time. I simply followed my nose.

So what next for me? Throughout my life I have held views which have been criticised at the time. I have been labelled as being part of the 'looney left'. I have noticed, however, that many of these views later became part of mainstream thinking. At the moment it is my view that we cannot allow economic rationalism to dominate our thinking into the next millennium. To my great relief there are many who share this view.

I am writing this in December 1998, on the eve of the birth of my daughter's first child, my first grandchild, and my mother's first great-grandchild.[1] I do not wish my granddaughter/son to grow up in a world where the bottom line is king – and where all measurements are in terms of dollars. Perhaps in the new millennium we will find that this particular economic theory has passed into the 'interesting blip' category and my criticism of it will have become mainstream. Perhaps there is a role here for me.

Just as I do not wish the bottom line to be king, I do not want the head of state of Australia to be queen – Queen Elizabeth II – nothing personal, of course.

I want an Australia where every citizen can aspire to become our head of state and which acknowledges prior occupancy by our indigenous people.

I was honoured to have been elected as a delegate to the 1998 Constitutional Convention. There is much work to be done to ensure a YES vote at the coming referendum. I will be pleased to play a role in this campaign.

I hope, of course, to continue my activities with those creative organisations I cherish – the Australian Children's Television Foundation, the Black Swan Theatre Company, and the West Australian Symphony Orchestra.

However, my family, Heytesbury, and those who work within it – my extended family if you like – must occupy most of my time and energy.

No doubt, though, I will follow my nose – it is what I've always done.

Janet Holmes à Court

NOTES

Introduction

1 Stephen Oates (ed.), *Biography as High Adventure. Life-Writers Speak on Their Art*, University of Massachusetts Press, United States, 1986, p. ix.

Chapter 1

1 The list of Robert Holmes à Court's takeovers is detailed in Max Hartwell and Jaqui Lane, *Champions of Enterprise: Australian Entrepreneurship 1788–1990*, Focus Books, 1991; pp. 315–21.

2 Interview with Jon Elbery by Sheryle Bagwell of the *Australian Financial Weekend Review* 7 Sept. 1990.

3 John Fitzgerald Kennedy, *Profiles in Courage*, Harper, New York, 1956.

4 Adele Horin, 'How to handle a millionaire', *National Times*, 4–10 Nov., 1983.

Chapter 2

1 This had been funded by Thomas Peel and other wealthy investors and had landed hundreds of unsuspecting settlers on the beach with their furniture and baggage. No survey had been done, there were no streets, no buildings, little fertile land and no work. The entire colony had been forced to move inland to the sheltered lagoon that later became the city of Perth. The poorer settlers found their lots covered in heavy timber or just barren sand, with no access roads from the better ground of Perth which had been bought up by the wealthier investors.

2 The letters from that time and the papers of the League are based at Murdoch University.

Chapter 3

1 The coat of arms reads: *Grandescunt Aucta Labore* (Increased by labour they grow large).

2 *Undaunted* was the title Ethnée chose for her autobiography, published by Pan Macmillan Australia in 1998.

3 Bruce London, Dai Haywood, David Potts and Hamish Fraser, 'The missing years', *Australian*, 9 Dec. 1985.
4 'The Holmes à Court story', *Business Review Weekly*, 5 Sept. 1986.
5 ibid.

Chapter 4

1 Nicholas Hasluck, 'Practising with Holmes à Court', in *Offcuts from a Literary Life*, University of Western Australia Press, 1993, pp. 30–31.
2 ibid., pp. 34.
3 Trevor Sykes, 'How Holmes à Court made his first million', *Australian Business*, 4 Sept. 1985. This article gives a detailed account of the WA Woollen takeover.
4 ibid.

Chapter 5

1 Adele Horin, op. cit.
2 Sheryle Bagwell, 'Wife who would not weep', *Sunday Correspondent*, 9 Sept. 1990.
3 Michael Meagher and Florence Chang, 'One-Man Bands? How their companies would fare without them', *Business Review Weekly*, 20 Feb. 1987.
4 Deborah Light, Michael Meagher and Alan Deans, 'Road to riches: Into the big league', *Business Review Weekly*, 19 Sept. 1986.
5 Barry Farmer would later move as the racing affairs journalist to Robert's *Western Mail* and subsequently became the manager of the Stud.
6 Brochure *Heytesbury Thoroughbreds Australia* (n.d.), p. 6.
7 Light, Meagher and Deans, op. cit.
8 Pago Pago had sired winners in excess of $5 million before Robert bought him. He was twenty years old but continued his success at siring winners at Heytesbury Stud until his death in November 1988.
9 Light, Meagher and Deans, op. cit.
10 Quentin Falk and Dominic Prince, *The Sinking of Lew Grade*, Quartet Books, London, 1987.
11 Lew Grade, *Still Dancing: My Story*, Collins, London, 1987, pp. 274–5.
12 Falk and Prince, op. cit., p. 135.

13 *Business Review Weekly*, 3 Oct. 1986.

14 *Australian Business*, 19 May 1983.

15 ibid.

16 *Business Review Weekly*, 2 Oct. 1987.

17 Robert Macklin, 'The new baron arises', *Bulletin*, 15 Dec. 1981.

18 ibid.

19 Deborah Light, Michael Meagher and Alan Deans, 'News maker as newsman', *Business Review Weekly*, 2 Oct. 1987.

20 Denis Reinhardt, 'Big Guns in the West under circulation fire', *Bulletin*, 30 Oct. 1984.

21 *Business Review Weekly*, 2 Oct. 1987.

22 Robert Holmes à Court, Graham Perkin memorial address to the Melbourne Press Club, November, 1985.

23 Transcript by Peter Smark from the Robert Holmes à Court files.

24 Jeff Penberthy and A. N. Malden, 'The media wars', *Time*, 2 Feb. 1987.

25 Michael Meagher and Robert Gottliebsen, 'Behind the Fairfax carve-up', *Business Review Weekly*, 2 Oct. 1987.

26 Penberthy and Malden, op. cit.

27 Trevor Sykes, 'Fairfax, the numbers behind the last great media carve-up', *Australian Business*, 7 Oct. 1987.

Chapter 6

1 Adele Horin, op. cit.

2 Geoff Maslen, 'The Big Australian art collection', *Good Weekend*, 16 May 1986.

3 John McIlwraith, 'A user-friendly collection', *Far Horizons*, March/April 1990.

4 Cary Reich, 'Thunder from down under', *Institutional Investor* International Edition, Jan. 1987, p. 55.

5 The eighty-eight artists included major names such as Emily Kame Kngwarreye, Kathlene Petyarre, Gloria Tamerre Petyarre, Lilly Sandover Kjngwarreye, and Lyndsay Bird Mpetyane, the only man in the group.

6 The Robert Holmes à Court Collection has 3,214 works valued at $21,922,766, including 1,062 Aboriginal works. The Janet Holmes à Court private collection has 476 works valued at $2.552 million, including 330 Aboriginal works.

7 Bobbie Oliver, *Towards a Living Place: Hospice and Palliative Care in Western Australia 1977–1991*, Cancer Foundation of WA Inc in association with The Centre for WA History, University of Western Australia, 1992.

Chapter 7

1 Hamish Fraser and David Potts, 'The great chess game – the battle for BHP', *Australian*, 8 Dec. 1985.

2 Jefferson Penberthy and Ivor Ries, 'You hit at dawn', *Business Review Weekly*, 11 Feb. 1984.

3 Bryan Frith, 'The secrets of his success', *Australian*, 10 Dec. 1985.

4 Penberthy and Ries, op. cit.

5 ibid.

6 ibid.

7 Michael Meagher, 'How BHP's defenders misread their foe', *Business Review Weekly*.

8 Trevor Sykes, *The Bold Riders*, Allen & Unwin, Sydney 1994, pp. 413–17.

9 ibid., p. 414.

10 'Australia's wealthiest people', *Business Review Weekly*, 16 Aug. 1985.

11 Sykes, op. cit., p. 414.

12 David Potts and Hamish Fraser, 'Holmes à Court: the man who could own Australia', *Weekend Australian*, 7 Dec. 1985.

13 Valerie Lawson, *Financial Review*, 17 Oct. 1986.

14 *Financial Review*, 5 Feb. 1986.

15 'The uninspiring details of the private life of a predator', *Australian*, 25 Mar. 1986.

16 Robert Gottliebsen, 'BHP's bombshell may be too late', *Business Review Weekly*, 21 Feb. 1986.

17 Trevor Sykes, 'Memories of the biggest share raid ever', *Australian Financial Review*, 6 June 1997.

18 Colleen Ryan, 'Elliott the Lion Heart meets Hacca the Fox', *National Times*, 30 May 1986.

19 John Hamilton, *Courier Mail*, 30 May 1986.

20 *Business Review Weekly*, 14 Sept. 1990.

21 Meagher, op. cit., p. 47.

22 Reich, op. cit.

23 'The Rich 200', *Business Review Weekly*, 10 Oct. 1986.

24 John McIlwraith, Bruce Jacques and Shirley Skeel, 'A raider in the boardroom', *Australian Business*, 4 Feb. 1987.

25 Ivor Ries, 'BHP deal shows saga's full cost', *Australian Financial Review*, 6 June 1997.

26 ibid.

27 John Hurst, Ian Howarth and Christine Lacy, 'The long, slow and painful decline of the Big Australian', *Australian Financial Review Weekend*, 27 Sept. 1997, p. 30.

28 Alan Kohler, 'BHP woes began in Loton era', *Australian Financial Review Weekend*, 20 Sept. 1997.

29 Rod Myer, 'Culture change started at the top', *Age*, 19 Dec. 1998.

30 Ries, op. cit.

31 'Janet Holmes à Court tells: when Bond was dealing, I dealt myself out', *Hobart Mercury*, 20 Feb. 1992.

32 Meagher, op. cit.

33 I tried to no avail to entice Janet to Australian Children's Television Foundation meetings but while she would talk to me on the phone, she was circumspect and unavailable.

34 Alistair McAlpine, *Once a Jolly Bagman Memoirs*, Weidenfeld & Nicolson, London, 1997, pp. 171–2.

35 Pierpont, 'Robert revised', *Bulletin*, 25 Feb. 1992.

36 ibid.

37 Trevor Sykes, *The Bold Riders*, pp. 195–6.

38 ibid., pp. 225–6.

39 NCSC Media Release, The Bell Group Limited, Melbourne, 6 June 1988.

40 Mark Westfield, 'Signposts to a swindle', *Weekend Australian*, 8 Feb. 1997.

41 ibid.

42 Trevor Sykes, 'How Bond stung Bell', *Bulletin*, 27 Sept. 1994.

43 Sykes, *The Bold Riders*, p. 225.

44 Westfield, op. cit.

45 ibid.

46 Pierpont, op. cit.

47 Alan Newman refused to be interviewed for this book. After Robert's death Newman complained to Janet that Robert had made commitments to him he did not keep, although Robert did cut Newman into a lucrative deal through Caterpillar. It was a substantial parting gesture, if not all that Newman expected.

48 Tom Stonnage, *Lakeside City: The Dreaming of Joondalup*, UWA Press, 1996, p. 159.

49 ibid., p. xii.

50 Phillip Adams said on the Nine Network's 'Sunday' program, on 27 June 1982, 'I regard Patricia Edgar as a sort of human tank. Patricia is a sort of centurion in her abilities to kick down doors and push walls over'.

51 Jo Litson, 'Holography's shining light', *Australian*, 1 May 1991.

52 Janet subsequently said to me, 'Thank goodness the Robert Holmes à Court Foundation did not take over the ACTF'. I shared her relief. While Robert generously supported the ACTF with its first project 'Winners', it was Janet who made sure the $2 million was there to invest in 'Lift Off' and I have no doubt that if the ACTF had moved under the banner of the Robert Holmes à Court Foundation, life for its director would have been exceedingly more difficult than it was.

Chapter 8

1 Janet had also gone to address the staff the day before the funeral to assure them she intended to run Heytesbury.

2 David Humphries, 'Holmes à Court widow takes it all in her stride', *Age*, 20 Feb. 1992.

3 Sheryle Bagwell, 'Janet Holmes à Court', *Australian Financial Review Weekend Review*, 7 Sept. 1990.

4 Now Katherine Bialo.

5 The 1,000-hectare property into which Robert poured $30 million sold early in 1997 for $7.3 million to Malaysian billionaire developer David Chui.

6 Heytesbury Holdings Pty Ltd became Heytesbury Pty Ltd on 6 August 1996.

7 *A Constant Challenge – A History of the John Holland Group 1949–1986*, The Craftsman Press, 1994, p. 236.

8 Robert Gottliebsen, *Business Review Weekly*, 8 Feb. 1991.

9 Deborah Brewster, 'Heytesbury gets Holland', *Age*, 7 Dec. 1990.

10 *Heytesbury Herald*, May 1991,

11 Robin Stringer, 'Stages of fright', *Evening Standard*, 12 July 1990.

12 'Holmes à Court calls the tune', *Sydney Morning Herald*, 26 Mar. 1990.

13 *Australian*, 2 July 1990; from *The Sunday Times*, London.

14 According to the *Sunday Correspondent*, City Editor, Margareta Pagano, 9 Sept. 1990.

15 Natalie O'Brien, 'Britain honours Holmes à Court success', *Australian*, 3 May 1996.

16 Janet Holmes à Court Nomination for Business Woman of the Year 1995. Nominated by Thelma Holt, CBE, February 1996.

17 O'Brien op. cit.

Chapter 9

1 Richard Gluyas, 'Holmes à Court hog-ties Sherwin', *Australian*, 27 May 1989.

2 'Top Floor', a documentary by the Australian Broadcasting Corporation, 30 July 1998.

3 Robert Gottliebsen, 'What the banker told Janet Holmes à Court', *Business Review Weekly*, 13 Dec. 1991.

4 Debt was $450 million with an interest bill of $40 million leaving a potential loss of $12 million at year end. Source: John McIlwraith, 'All change at Heytesbury', *Bulletin*, 17 Dec. 1991.

5 Robert Gottliebsen, op. cit.

6 *Heytesbury Herald*, March 1992.

7 Key Transport was sold on 6 February 1998 as the result of poor management. Sixty-three permanent staff were retrenched and paid a three-month redundancy payment.

8 Trevor Sykes, *Australian Business Monthly*, Feb. 1993.

9 This meeting of managing directors included Wim Burggraaf and David Clapin from Heytesbury Pastoral Group, Raldolf Cresswell and Geoff Horsley from John Holland, Richard Johnston and Loretta Tomasi from Stoll Moss, Keith Edwards, general manager of Key Transport, Alec Mairs, a member of the Heytesbury board, and Janet and Darrel.

Chapter 10

1 Michael Thompson-Noel, 'Powerful, glamorous and beautiful', *Financial Times Weekend*, 4 June 1994.

2 Charles Spencer, 'The Queen of Shaftesbury Avenue', *Daily Telegraph*, 14 June 1994.

3 Lynda Lee Potter, 'How the West End was won', *Weekend Interview*, 11 June 1994.

4 Judi Bevan, 'The tycoon's widow takes centre stage', *Sunday Telegraph*, 4 Dec. 1994.

5 Lynda Lee Potter, *Weekend Interview*, 11 June 1995.

6 Sue Summers, 'The toughest takeover', *Mail on Sunday Magazine*, 27 Aug. 1995.

7 'What will be left?', *Herald Sun*, 15 Nov. 1996.

8 James McCullock, *Brisbane Courier Mail*, 27 Nov. 1996.

9 Chenoweth and Maley quote the value of the contract at $250 million (in 'The woes of Janet Holmes à Court, *Financial Review*, 29 Nov. 1996) but the actual size of John Holland's contract at time of tender was $AU45.4 million.

10 Chenoweth and Maley, op. cit.

11 ibid.
   Mark, Skulley, 'John Holland gets marching orders on cracker job', *Financial Review*, 26 Nov. 1996; Mark Davis, 'Things get nasty in Mobil Holland dispute', *Financial Review*, 15 Nov. 1996. The arbitration case is expected to conclude by April 1999. The verdict has significant financial ramifications for the Heytesbury shareholders.

12 Steven Loxley, 'Heytesbury gets rid of its CEO', *Sunday Age*, 22 Mar. 1998.

13 Chenoweth and Maley, op. cit.

14 Doug Aiton, *Sunday Age*, 16 Mar. 1997, on the occasion of the Australian Children's Television Foundation's fifteenth birthday.

15 *Australian*, 16 April 1997.

16 *West Australian*, 11 June 1997.

17 Natalie O'Brien, *Australian*, 13 June 1998.

18 Rowena Stretton, *Australian Financial Review Magazine*, 5 June 1997.

19 *Sunday Times*, 15 Feb. 1998.

20 Robyn McKenzie, 'Drysdale view embraces all', *Herald Sun*, 22 Dec. 1997.

Chapter 11

1 'Families fail to cope with the business of succession', *Age*, 24 Jan. 1994.

2 Ian Porter, 'Smorgan stays private despite public moves', *Australian Financial Review*, 18 Sept. 1998.

3 Robert Harley, 'Family affair: Lowy sells down to 30%', *Australian Financial Review*, 27 Aug. 1998.

4 Billy Boesky was the son of Ivan Boesky, a high flying US financier who fell from grace in the eighties.

5 Alan Deans, 'Running his own show', *Australian Financial Review*, 30 Oct. 1998.

6 Mark Drummond, 'Dynasty of Dissent', *Age*, 19 Sept. 1998.

7 Rowena Stretton, 'The perils and passions of private companies', *Australian Financial Review*, 28–29 Mar. 1998 and 'Float plans on hold as former chief waits on cash', *Financial Review*, 21 Sept. 1988.

8 Helen Shuld, 'Heytesbury plans a strong future', *The Age*, 4 June 1998.

9 Lucinda Schmidt, 'Janet Holmes à Court's biggest fight', *Business Review Weekly*, 9 Nov. 1998.

10 Tim Treadgold, 'A remarkable survival act', *Business Review Weekly*, 9 Nov. 1998.

11 Charles Spencer, *Daily Telegraph*, 14 June 1994.

12 Ben Mitchell, 'Business goes bush, buys up big', *Age*, 19 Nov. 1998.

13 Brook Turner, 'Arts minds join funds call', *Australian Financial Review*, 18 Sept. 1998.

14 Walt Whitman, *Song of Myself*, lines 314–6.

15 George Soros, 'The Crisis of Global Capitalism', Little, Brown & Company, United States of America, 1998, quoted in 'Soros: debunking the market myth', *Age*, 30 Nov. 1998.

16 ibid, 'The Final Crisis', 1 Dec. 1998.

17 Robert Theobald, *Reworking Success new communities at the millennium*, New Society Publishers, 1997.

18 John Ralston Saul, *The Unconscious Civilization*, Penguin, Melbourne, 1997.

19 Katharine Graham, *Personal History*, Alfred A Knopf Inc, United States of America, 1997.

20 She had to go to court to deal with the legal issues involved and gave up some of her husband's estate in favour of the children.

21 See Daniel Goleman, *Emotional Intelligence: Why it can matter more than IQ*, Bloomsbury, London, 1996 and *Working with Emotional Intelligence*, Bantam Books, New York, 1998.

Afterword

1 Emma Bern Mather was born in London on 6 January 1999 to Catherine Holmes à Court and Rob Mather. Divonne and Peter Holmes à Court are expecting twin boys in April 1999.

INDEX

Holmes à Court, Ethnée Celia (nee
Jones) 6, 17, 57, 58, 59, 60–1, 62–3,
65, 67, 68, 72, 74–5, 76, 79, 80, 84, 85,
89, 112, 115, 116, 236, 246
Holmes à Court, Evelyn Spencer 60
Holmes à Court, Henry Worsley 60, 66
Holmes à Court, Jane 123, 124, 125
Holmes à Court, Janet (nee Ranford)
Aboriginal culture and People 325,
336, 345, 354, 362, 363
ACTF 2–3, 166, 224–6, 230–1, 238,
308, 314, 362–3
art 88, 147–8, 149, 150–64, 1689, 216,
335, 345, 354, 362
and Australian landscape 24
Australian Republic 344–5, 354
awards 273, 323, 336–7, 360
and BHP takeover 190–1, 193–4, 357
birth of Catherine 102
birth of Peter 101
Black Swan Theatre Company 335–6,
354, 363
born 20, 30
British Business Woman of the Year
273, 323, 336
business confidence 236–9, 288–90,
291, 293–4, 298–9, 304–4, 307–8,
310, 315, 316–18, 31922, 329–30,
334–5, 342, 344, 354, 358, 359,
360–1, 361, 363–4
Cancer Foundation of Western
Australia 164–5
cattle stations 212, 276, 285, 286, 290,
302–3
Centenary of Federation Council 324
Central Queensland University 336
character and personality 8, 9, 18–20,
21, 22, 23, 27, 35, 43, 45–6, 489, 53,
55, 78, 80, 98, 102, 104–5, 111,
116–17, 123, 148–9, 150–1, 168–9,
237, 240, 258, 288, 290, 291, 302,
307–8, 313–14, 315, 319–21, 322–3,
334–5, 337–8, 342–5, 352, 355, 356,
359–60, 363–8
childhood 21, 22–9, 31, 32–3, 35, 36,
37–8, 355
children 117, 122–3, 125–6, 144–7,
148, 170, 172, 173, 174, 185, 202,
235–6, 330, 346–7, 350–2, 360

at Claremont 47
community activities 146, 148,
148–51, 164–9, 221–2, 229–30, 314,
335, 336–7, 356
at Cottesloe 102, 105
at Darlington 84, 85, 87, 102
Diabetes Research Foundation Fund
Raising Committee 165
Diploma of Education 79
and domesticity 18, 27, 31, 78, 82,
82–3, 85–6, 102, 103–4, 112–13,
115, 116–17, 123, 125–6, 148,
320–1, 356
and economic rationalism 365, 370
education 34, 35, 37, 37–9, 41–3, 45,
46, 47, 51, 79
as an employer 236–40, 259, 286–8,
299, 304, 307, 313, 330–1, 343, 359,
363, 236–40, 366
engagement 82, 83
family life 8, 30, 31, 32, 34–5, 37, 38,
39, 41, 46, 51, 52, 78, 100–1, 104,
116–17, 122–3, 143–5, 147–8, 314,
355–6
and feminism 78–9
and financial decision making 169,
359
on financial wealth 8, 194–5, 307, 337,
355, 356–7, 358
friendships
Cameron Mackintosh 266
Dale Hunter 37–8, 84
Joan Rapley 42–3, 47, 48
John Byrne 49, 50, 55, 83, 91, 95
Leanne Banfield 51
Sandy Stock 43–5, 83, 85
Goodman Fielder Ltd 362
Governor Stirling Senior High School
87
grandparents 29
at Greenmount 22, 24, 28, 32, 41
Guild Council 50, 52, 55, 78, 79
and handcraft 45, 47
health 100
Health Advisory Network 166
and Heytesbury Holdings 8, 15–16,
18–20, 169, 236–44, 250–2, 286–314,
317–23, 325–34, 337–8, 342, 343–4,
346–54, 358, 359–62, 364, 365–6

and BHP takeover 12, 181–234, 357
business meetings 4–5, 120, 124, 129,
  131, 185, 190, 191, 217, 218–19,
  223–4, 229, 263–4, 279–80, 281–2
business ventures 2–4, 6, 11–12, 13,
  58, 69, 70, 74, 77, 85, 88–9, 93–4,
  95–8, 102, 107, 117, 118–21,
  126–42, 188–9, 198, 201–2, 204–8,
  210–12, 233–4, 243, 249, 263, 264,
  280–2, 348, 357
career 71–2, 76, 88, 90–5
car accident 292–3
cars 54, 56–7, 71, 76, 88, 111, 128,
  147, 160, 187, 247, 248
character 1, 2, 4–5, 6, 54–5, 56, 58,
  60, 61, 62–3, 65, 66, 67–8, 69, 70–1,
  75, 76–7, 79, 80, 82–3, 86, 88, 92,
  94, 101–2, 104, 108–10, 111,
  116–17, 124, 125, 137, 148, 151–2,
  173, 174, 178, 175–6, 200, 214,
  215–16, 225, 227, 228–9, 230, 231,
  232, 233, 263–4, 279–80, 281–2,
  286, 320–1, 356, 357
children 117, 122–3, 125, 143–6,
  169–70, 172, 173, 174–5, 202,
  346–8, 350
childhood 58, 61–5, 66–71, 106
Chobe River 58, 75
community affairs 213, 221
Cordwalles Preparatory School
  66–7
death 6, 14–15, 70, 87, 114, 162, 198,
  199, 232–3, 235, 240, 358
diabetes 14, 73, 76, 124, 200
education 54–5, 58, 66–71, 72, 73
as an employer 89, 186, 232, 279–80,
  282
entrepreneur 65, 66, 69, 70, 74, 77,
  85, 89, 93–4, 95–8, 102, 104,
  118–19, 138, 178, 180, 181, 203,
  211, 234, 298, 357
family life 57–8, 63–4, 66, 68, 98, 104,
  106, 122–3, 143–5, 201, 209–10
financial wealth 65, 77, 88, 90, 96, 97,
  110–1, 120, 187, 194, 196, 231, 358
flying 54, 76, 118, 224
forestry degree 58, 72
friendship with John Byrne 55, 83, 89,
  91, 92–3

funeral and memorial service 16–18,
  116–17, 284
Guild Council 55
health 2, 13–14, 65–6, 73, 74, 103,
  200–2, 203–4, 232, 283, 320, 357,
  358
Heytesbury mansion 110
hobbies 71, 77, 112, 146–7, 158, 159,
  164, 187
horses 54, 62, 69, 112–15, 123, 131,
  147, 160, 183, 187, 213, 233, 244–7,
  258
law articles 88
law degree 54, 73, 75, 77
law practice 89, 90–5, 96, 98
Lioncrest Kindergarten 66
marriage 57, 82–5, 248
Massey College 72, 114
and media 13, 76, 132, 136, 138–9,
  140–1, 182, 188, 198, 365
Michaelhouse 66, 68–9, 73
monument 247
and music 175–6
National Union of Australian
  University Students
  (NUAUS) 55
in New Zealand 58, 71, 72
property investment 88, 89, 96, 112,
  144, 160, 230
relationships 76, 95, 98, 101–4,
  216–17, 219, 262
Darrel Jarvis 279–84
Janet 15, 18, 19, 27, 51, 53, 55–7,
  65–6, 79, 80–3, 90, 99, 102–3, 104,
  111, 116–17, 118, 123, 125–6, 142,
  143, 147–8, 160, 163, 168, 175–6,
  185–6, 188–9, 200, 201–2, 209–10,
  218, 220, 224, 228, 229, 230, 233,
  248, 250, 316–17, 320–1, 350,
  355–9, 363–4
mother 72, 116
Simon (brother) 70, 106
restaurant 58, 74
sharetrading 6, 97, 107, 110–11,
  113–14, 121, 178, 180, 187, 194,
  211–12, 241
smoking 199–200
in South Africa 54, 58, 66–71, 72,
  73–5

and takeovers 11–12, 95, 106–7,
110–11, 118–19, 126–42, 178,
180–3, 184, 187, 198, 212–13,
233, 261, 265, 357–8
and theatre 269–70
and trade unions 110, 188–9
at university 54–5, 58, 72, 73, 75
and value of money 66, 76, 111, 134,
158, 160
on wealth and happiness 111
will 232, 235–6, 239, 350, 358
see also Robert Holmes à Court Art
Foundation; Robert Holmes à Court
Collection; Robert Holmes à Court
Foundation
Holmes à Court, Simon (brother) 58,
62, 63, 66, 69, 70, 73, 106
Holmes à Court, Simon (son) 13, 17,
123, 143, 144, 145–6, 148, 169–72,
237, 239, 346, 347, 349, 351, 353
Holmes à Court, Will 123, 124, 125,
237, 239, 242, 289
hospice care 164–5
Howard, John 323, 324, 325
Hughes, Rex 200–1
Humes Industries Barhad 258
Hunt, Hilde 68
Hunter, Dale 35, 37, 84, 100

industrial disputes and relations 108–9,
188–9
International Railway Systems
(Electronics) Pty Ltd (IRSE) 257
ITC Entertainment Pty Ltd 4

Jabiru Prospect 183
Jaguar 213
Jarvis, Darrel 18–19, 163, 250, 255, 259,
269, 270, 275, 276–300, 302–3, 304–6,
310, 311–12, 314, 316, 318, 321–2,
325, 328, 329–30, 333–4, 342, 344,
347, 348–9, 351–3, 359, 362
Jet Save 131
Jewell, Jane Eliza 28
Jewell, Richard Roach 29
John Fairfax and Sons 141, 142, 241
John Forrest National Park 24
John Holland Construction 110, 246,
252–60, 288, 292, 294, 296, 297, 301,

302, 306, 307, 308, 309–10, 325–8,
330–1, 344, 353–4, 361, 362
Johnston, Richard 268, 269–70, 271,
272, 273, 293, 307
Johnston, Steve 186, 211, 212, 255
Jolly, Alec 40
Jones, Ethnée Celia *see* Holmes à
Court, Ethnée Celia
Jones, Tony 149–50, 155, 247
Joondalup Development Corporation
135, 213–15
Jurien Bay 89

Karpin, David 333, 352
Keall, Stables & Brinsden 88
Keating, Paul 192, 224, 308, 315, 323–4,
364
Keatsmanor Pty Ltd 254
Kelly, Rod 167, 228, 338–42
Kessell, Dale *see* Hunter, Dale
Key Transport 296, 300, 309, 332, 361
Keysbrook Stud 112, 245, 246
King Edward Memorial Hospital for
Women 166
Kngwarreye, Emily Kane 160–1, 230

Lamb, Larry 139
Lee, George 26, 28
Lee, John Bartlett 26
Lee, Judith 22, 30
Lee, Reenie 22, 30
Lee, Violet 22, 25, 26, 27, 28, 29, 30, 41
'Lift Off' 223, 224–5, 230, 233
Lloyd Webber, Andrew 261, 262, 265–7
Long, Dorman 60
Loreto Convent site 240–1
Loton, Brian 190, 193, 195, 198
Louise, Madam Myra 23

McAlpine, Alistair 206
McCrann, Terry 140, 141, 233
McCullock, James 325
McFadgen, Paddy 90
McIlwraith, John 135, 137, 140, 205
McKay, Brian 150, 151, 155, 247
McKenzie, Ian 68
Mackintosh, Cameron 261, 262–5, 319
McLean, Adrian 311, 329
Macpherson, Keith 135, 138

McVay, Pete 287
Mahoney, Ken 35, 36, 84
Mairs, Alec 136, 138, 210, 331, 352
Malaysian Airlines 354
Maley, Karen 325, 328
Markland House 209, 210
Maxwell, Robert 213, 267
Mazza, Jim 97
Meadows, Frances 43
media
    and Janet Holmes à Court 15, 104,
        147–8, 253, 237–9, 294, 307,
        312–13, 324, 325–6, 337, 343, 361
    and Robert Holmes à Court 13, 76,
        132, 135–6, 139–40, 141–2, 181,
        188, 199, 204, 230–1, 261, 365
Menzies, Robert 32
Merrill Lynch 196–7
Mills-Edwards, Charles 339–40
MIM Holdings 187
Mincorp Petroleum NL 183
mining boom 90–4
Modern Women's Club 31–2
Morris, Graham 4
Morris, Peter 289
Morrison, Jim 107
Mount Clifford 97
Mount Lawley 26
MRH Holmes à Court and Co 89, 90–5
Mundaring 28
Murdoch, John 107, 108, 110, 204
Murdoch, Rupert 118, 119–20, 127–8,
    139, 141, 142
Murphy, Mrs 72
Murray, Sandra 168

National Business Review 142
National Companies and Securities
    Commission (NCSC) 208–9
National Union of Australian University
    Students (NUAUS) 55
Newby, Liz 105
Newman, Alan 161, 173, 203, 211
Newman, Shirley 37
News Group 141
newspaper industry 135–42, 300
nickel boom 90–1, 93, 95, 96
Noble, Shane 276
Nordlinger, Angela 15

Nordlinger, Bob 256, 257
Norfolk Island 85, 93–4
Northern Songs 128, 161

Oates, Florence 58
Oates, Paul 73
Oates, Reverend William 58
O'Connor, John 197
Osborne, Sue 43
O'Duill, Olaf 289, 294, 296
Ono, Yoko 161
Otto, Clive 250
Owen, Michael 322

Packer, Kerry 142
Pakula, Alan 132
Parfitt, Robert 221
Parker, David 219–20
Patterson, Grant 48
Pearce, Greg 225, 229, 230
Pennant Holdings 252, 253, 255, 306
Perth Institute of Contemporary Art
    (PICA) 150, 151
Petroleum Distributors 127
Phillips, June and Harvey 100
Pioneer Concrete 204
Pitman, Val 4, 13, 89–90, 102–3, 144,
    283
Poolman, Bob 149
Poser, Nick 245
Powell, Greg 247
Prescott, John 195, 198
Prichard, Katharine Susannah 32, 33, 78
PRT Video 131
Pullan, Bob 84

Quarry Industries 121
Queensland Press Ltd 141
Quinn, Bill 114

Ranford, Benjamin Bristow 28
Ranford, Bern (nee Lee)
    and Aboriginal people 33–4, 336
    activist 27, 34
    and Australian Women's Army Service
        29
    character 23, 25, 26, 27, 31
    education 27–8
    family history 25–6